Fiat 500 & Panda
Owners Workshop Manual

Martynn Randall

Models covered

500 & Panda Hatchbacks

Petrol: 1.1 litre (1108cc) & 1.2 litre (1242cc)
Turbo-diesel: 1.3 litre (1248cc) 'MultiJet'

Also covers most mechanical features of Convertible
Does NOT cover models with 0.9 litre 2-cylinder 'TwinAir' or 1.4 litre petrol engines, semi-automatic transmission, Abarth or 4x4

(5558 - 8AV1 - 320)

© Haynes Publishing 2016

ABCDE
FGHIJ
KLMNO

A book in the **Haynes Owners Workshop Manual Series**

ISBN **978 0 85733 873 0**

British Library Cataloguing in Publication Data
A catalogue record for this book is available from the British Library.

Printed in Malaysia

Haynes Publishing
Sparkford, Yeovil, Somerset BA22 7JJ, England

Haynes North America, Inc
859 Lawrence Drive, Newbury Park, California 91320, USA

Printed using NORBRITE BOOK 48.8gsm (CODE: 40N6533) from NORPAC; procurement system certified under Sustainable Forestry Initiative standard. Paper produced is certified to the SFI Certified Fiber Sourcing Standard (CERT - 0094271)

Contents

LIVING WITH YOUR FIAT 500/PANDA

Roadside repairs

Weekly checks

Lubricants and fluids

Tyre pressures

MAINTENANCE

Routine maintenance and servicing

Contents

REPAIRS AND OVERHAUL

Engine and associated systems

Transmission

Brakes and suspension

Body equipment

Wiring diagrams

REFERENCE

Index

The Fiat Panda was introduced in the UK in January 2004, whilst the 500 was introduced in January 2008. Both models were intended to replace earlier models renowned for their economy and sense of fun. The Panda was only available as a 5-door hatchback, and the 500 as a 3-door hatchback. The Panda was launched with a choice of 1.1 and 1.2 litre petrol, and 1.3 litre diesel engines, whereas the 500 was fitted with the 1.2 litre petrol or 1.3 litre diesel engines. Although other engines were available, they are not covered in this manual.

The petrol engines are of the four-cylinder single overhead camshaft (SOHC) 8-valve configuration, in-line type, whereas the diesel engine is four-cylinder double-overhead camshaft (DOHC) 16-valve design with direct, common rail fuel injection and a turbocharger.

The engines all have sophisticated emission control systems, including catalytic converters, particulate filter, EVAP, EGR, etc.

All models covered by this manual are equipped with a 5-speed manual gearbox. Although a semi-automatic 'Duo-logic' and four-wheel (4x4) drive transmissions were available, they are not covered.

All models have front-wheel-drive with fully-independent front suspension, and semi-independent rear suspension with a torsion beam and trailing arms.

A wide range of standard and optional equipment is available within the Panda/500 range to suit most tastes, including electric power steering, air conditioning, remote central locking, electric windows, electric sunroof, anti-lock braking system, electronic alarm system and supplemental restraint systems.

For the home mechanic, the Panda/500 is a relatively straightforward vehicle to maintain, and most of the items requiring frequent attention are easily accessible.

Your Fiat Panda/500 manual

The aim of this manual is to help you get the best value from your vehicle. It can do so in several ways. It can help you decide what work must be done (even should you choose to get it done by a garage), provide information on routine maintenance and servicing, and give a logical course of action and diagnosis when random faults occur. However, it is hoped that you will use the manual by tackling the work yourself. On simpler jobs, it may even be quicker than booking the car into a garage and going there twice, to leave and collect it. Perhaps most important, a lot of money can be saved by avoiding the costs a garage must charge to cover its labour and overheads.

The manual has drawings and descriptions to show the function of the various components, so that their layout can be understood. Then the tasks are described and photographed in a clear step-by-step sequence.

References to the 'left' or 'right' are in the sense of a person in the driver's seat, facing forward.

Project vehicles

The main vehicle used in the preparation of this manual, and which appears in many of the photographic sequences, was a Fiat 500 hatchback with a 1.3 litre diesel engine. Additional work was carried out on Pandas with 1.1 and 1.2 litre petrol, and 1.3 litre diesel engines, and a 500 with a 1.2 litre petrol engine.

Acknowledgements

Thanks are due to Draper Tools Limited and Auto Service Tools Limited (asttools.co.uk), who provided some of the workshop tools, and to all those people at Sparkford who helped in the production of this manual.

We take great pride in the accuracy of information given in this manual, but vehicle manufacturers make alterations and design changes during the production run of a particular vehicle of which they do not inform us. No liability can be accepted by the authors or publishers for loss, damage or injury caused by any errors in, or omissions from, the information given.

Working on your car can be dangerous. This page shows just some of the potential risks and hazards, with the aim of creating a safety-conscious attitude.

General hazards

Scalding

• Don't remove the radiator or expansion tank cap while the engine is hot.
• Engine oil, transmission fluid or power steering fluid may also be dangerously hot if the engine has recently been running.

Burning

• Beware of burns from the exhaust system and from any part of the engine. Brake discs and drums can also be extremely hot immediately after use.

Crushing

• When working under or near a raised vehicle, always supplement the jack with axle stands, or use drive-on ramps. *Never venture under a car which is only supported by a jack*.
• Take care if loosening or tightening high-torque nuts when the vehicle is on stands. Initial loosening and final tightening should be done with the wheels on the ground.

Fire

• Fuel is highly flammable; fuel vapour is explosive.
• Don't let fuel spill onto a hot engine.
• Do not smoke or allow naked lights (including pilot lights) anywhere near a vehicle being worked on. Also beware of creating sparks (electrically or by use of tools).
• Fuel vapour is heavier than air, so don't work on the fuel system with the vehicle over an inspection pit.
• Another cause of fire is an electrical overload or short-circuit. Take care when repairing or modifying the vehicle wiring.
• Keep a fire extinguisher handy, of a type suitable for use on fuel and electrical fires.

Electric shock

• Ignition HT and Xenon headlight voltages can be dangerous, especially to people with heart problems or a pacemaker. Don't work on or near these systems with the engine running or the ignition switched on.

• Mains voltage is also dangerous. Make sure that any mains-operated equipment is correctly earthed. Mains power points should be protected by a residual current device (RCD) circuit breaker.

Fume or gas intoxication

• Exhaust fumes are poisonous; they can contain carbon monoxide, which is rapidly fatal if inhaled. Never run the engine in a confined space such as a garage with the doors shut.
• Fuel vapour is also poisonous, as are the vapours from some cleaning solvents and paint thinners.

Poisonous or irritant substances

• Avoid skin contact with battery acid and with any fuel, fluid or lubricant, especially antifreeze, brake hydraulic fluid and Diesel fuel. Don't syphon them by mouth. If such a substance is swallowed or gets into the eyes, seek medical advice.
• Prolonged contact with used engine oil can cause skin cancer. Wear gloves or use a barrier cream if necessary. Change out of oil-soaked clothes and do not keep oily rags in your pocket.
• Air conditioning refrigerant forms a poisonous gas if exposed to a naked flame (including a cigarette). It can also cause skin burns on contact.

Asbestos

• Asbestos dust can cause cancer if inhaled or swallowed. Asbestos may be found in gaskets and in brake and clutch linings. When dealing with such components it is safest to assume that they contain asbestos.

Special hazards

Hydrofluoric acid

• This extremely corrosive acid is formed when certain types of synthetic rubber, found in some O-rings, oil seals, fuel hoses etc, are exposed to temperatures above 4000C. The rubber changes into a charred or sticky substance containing the acid. *Once formed, the acid remains dangerous for years. If it gets onto the skin, it may be necessary to amputate the limb concerned*.
• When dealing with a vehicle which has suffered a fire, or with components salvaged from such a vehicle, wear protective gloves and discard them after use.

The battery

• Batteries contain sulphuric acid, which attacks clothing, eyes and skin. Take care when topping-up or carrying the battery.
• The hydrogen gas given off by the battery is highly explosive. Never cause a spark or allow a naked light nearby. Be careful when connecting and disconnecting battery chargers or jump leads.

Air bags

• Air bags can cause injury if they go off accidentally. Take care when removing the steering wheel and trim panels. Special storage instructions may apply.

Diesel injection equipment

• Diesel injection pumps supply fuel at very high pressure. Take care when working on the fuel injectors and fuel pipes.

⚠️ *Warning: Never expose the hands, face or any other part of the body to injector spray; the fuel can penetrate the skin with potentially fatal results*.

Remember...

DO

• Do use eye protection when using power tools, and when working under the vehicle.

• Do wear gloves or use barrier cream to protect your hands when necessary.

• Do get someone to check periodically that all is well when working alone on the vehicle.

• Do keep loose clothing and long hair well out of the way of moving mechanical parts.

• Do remove rings, wristwatch etc, before working on the vehicle – especially the electrical system.

• Do ensure that any lifting or jacking equipment has a safe working load rating adequate for the job.

DON'T

• Don't attempt to lift a heavy component which may be beyond your capability – get assistance.

• Don't rush to finish a job, or take unverified short cuts.

• Don't use ill-fitting tools which may slip and cause injury.

• Don't leave tools or parts lying around where someone can trip over them. Mop up oil and fuel spills at once.

• Don't allow children or pets to play in or near a vehicle being worked on.

The following pages are intended to help in dealing with common roadside emergencies and breakdowns. You will find more detailed fault finding information at the back of the manual, and repair information in the main chapters.

If your car won't start and the starter motor doesn't turn

☐ Open the bonnet and make sure that the battery terminals are clean and tight (pull up the positive terminal cover for access).

☐ Switch on the headlights and try to start the engine. If the headlights go very dim when you're trying to start, the battery is probably flat. Get out of trouble by jump starting (see next page) using a friend's car.

If your car won't start even though the starter motor turns as normal

☐ Is there fuel in the tank?

☐ Has the engine immobiliser been deactivated? This should happen automatically, on inserting the ignition key. However, if a replacement key has been obtained (other than from a Fiat dealer), it may not contain the transponder chip necessary to deactivate the system. Even 'proper' replacement keys have to be coded to work properly – a procedure for this is outlined in the vehicle handbook.

☐ Is there moisture on electrical components under the bonnet? Switch off the ignition, then wipe off any obvious dampness with a dry cloth. Spray a water-repellent aerosol product (WD-40 or equivalent) on ignition and fuel system electrical connectors like those shown in the photos. Pay special attention to the ignition coil wiring connector and HT leads (where applicable).

A Check the security and condition of the battery connections – pull up the positive terminal cover for access.

B Check the wiring plug and HT lead connections to the ignition coil and spark plug (petrol models – air filter removed).

C Check the ECU wiring plugs.

Check that all electrical connections are secure (with the ignition switched off). Spray the connector plugs with a water-dispersant spray like WD-40 if you suspect a problem due to damp. Diesel models do not usually suffer from damp starting problems, but check all visible connector plugs just in case.

D Check that none of the engine compartment fuses have blown.

E Check the throttle body connection.

Jump starting

Jump starting will get you out of trouble, but you must correct whatever made the battery go flat in the first place. There are three possibilities:

1 *The battery has been drained by repeated attempts to start, or by leaving the lights on.*

2 *The charging system is not working properly (alternator drivebelt slack or broken, alternator wiring fault or alternator itself faulty).*

3 *The battery itself is at fault (electrolyte low, or battery worn out).*

When jump-starting a car, observe the following precautions:

✓ Before connecting the booster battery, make sure that the ignition is switched off.

Caution: Remove the key in case the central locking engages when the jump leads are connected

✓ Ensure that all electrical equipment (lights, heater, wipers, etc) is switched off.

✓ Take note of any special precautions printed on the battery case.

✓ Make sure that the booster battery is the same voltage as the discharged one in the vehicle.

✓ If the battery is being jump-started from the battery in another vehicle, the two vehicles MUST NOT TOUCH each other.

✓ Make sure that the transmission is in neutral (or PARK, in the case of automatic transmission).

Budget jump leads can be a false economy, as they often do not pass enough current to start large capacity or diesel engines. They can also get hot.

1 Connect one end of the red jump lead to the positive (+) terminal of the flat battery

2 Connect the other end of the red lead to the positive (+) terminal of the booster battery.

3 Connect one end of the black jump lead to the negative (-) terminal of the booster battery

4 Connect the other end of the black jump lead to a bolt or bracket on the engine block, well away from the battery, on the vehicle to be started.

5 Make sure that the jump leads will not come into contact with the fan, drive-belts or other moving parts of the engine.

6 Start the engine using the booster battery and run it at idle speed. Switch on the lights, rear window demister and heater blower motor, then disconnect the jump leads in the reverse order of connection. Turn off the lights etc.

Wheel changing

Note: *The models covered by this manual are equipped with either a spare wheel or an 'Automatic Fix & Go' tyre repair kit. Follow the relevant procedure.*

⚠️ *Warning: Do not change a wheel in a situation where you risk being hit by other traffic. On busy roads, try to stop in a lay-by or a gateway. Be wary of passing traffic while changing the wheel – it is easy to become distracted by the job in hand.*

Preparation

☐ When a puncture occurs, stop as soon as it is safe to do so.

☐ Park on firm level ground, if possible, and well out of the way of other traffic.
☐ Use hazard warning lights if necessary.
☐ If you have one, use a warning triangle to alert other drivers of your presence.
☐ Apply the handbrake and engage first or reverse gear.
☐ Chock the wheels opposite the one being removed – a couple of large stones will do for this. Some models are supplied with a wheel chock in the car's tool kit – pull and twist the two halves of the chock to form the triangular shape.
☐ If the ground is soft, use a flat piece of wood to spread the load under the foot of the jack.

Changing the wheel

1 The spare wheel and tools are stored in the luggage compartment. Fold back the floor covering and lift up the cover panel.

2 Unscrew the retaining bolt, and lift out the tool container, followed by the spare wheel.

3 Where applicable, using the screwdriver provided, prise off the wheel trim or centre cover for access to the wheel bolts. Models with alloy wheels may have special locking bolts – these are removed with a special tool, which should be provided with the wheel brace (or it may be in the glovebox).

4 Slacken each wheel bolt by a half turn, using the wheel brace. If the bolt are too tight, DON'T stand on the wheel brace to undo them – call for assistance from one of the motoring organisations.

5 Two jacking points are provided on each side – use the one nearest the punctured wheel. Locate the jack head at the point in the lower sill flange indicated by the indentation in the metal sill (don't jack the vehicle at any other point of the sill, nor on a plastic panel). Turn the jack handle clockwise until the wheel is raised clear of the ground.

6 Unscrew the wheel bolts, and remove the wheel.

7 Fit the spare wheel, and screw in the bolts. Lightly tighten the bolts with the wheel brace, then lower the vehicle to the ground. Securely tighten the wheel bolts, then refit the wheel trim or centre cover, as applicable. Note that the wheel bolts should be slackened and retightened to the specified torque at the earliest possible opportunity.

Finally . . .

- ☐ Remove the wheel chocks.
- ☐ Stow the punctured wheel and tools back in the luggage compartment, and secure them in position.
- ☐ Check the tyre pressure on the tyre just fitted. If it is low, or if you don't have a pressure gauge with you, drive slowly to the next garage and inflate the tyre to the correct pressure. In the case of the narrow 'space-saver' spare wheel this pressure is much higher than for a normal tyre.

- ☐ The special lightweight 'space-saver' spare wheel, is narrower than standard. The 'space-saver' spare wheel is intended only for temporary use, and **must** be replaced with a standard wheel as soon as possible. Drive with particular care with this wheel fitted, especially through corners and when braking; do not exceed 50 mph.
- ☐ Have the punctured wheel repaired as soon as possible, or another puncture will leave you stranded.

Automatic Fix & Go tyre repair kit

⚠️ *Warning: Do not repair a tyre in a situation where you risk being hit by other traffic. On busy roads, try to stop in a lay-by or a gateway. Be wary of passing traffic while repairing the tyre – it is easy to become distracted by the job in hand.*

Preparation

- ☐ When a puncture occurs, stop as soon as it is safe to do so.

- ☐ Park on firm level ground, if possible, and well out of the way of other traffic.
- ☐ Use hazard warning lights if necessary.
- ☐ If you have one, use a warning triangle to alert other drivers of your presence.
- ☐ Before attempting to repair the puncture, note the following:
  - *The kit can be used to repair tyres with damage to the tread or shoulder up to a maximum diameter of 4 mm. Damage to the tyre sidewall cannot be repaired.*

- *Do not operate the compressor for more than 20 consecutive minutes or it may overheat.*
- *This repair is designed for temporary use only. Have the damaged tyre replaced at the earliest opportunity.*
- *Put on gloves (supplied in the kit) before commencing the repair. The sealant can be harmful if it comes into contact with skin, eyes, etc.*

1 The tyre repair kit is stored in the luggage compartment. Fold back the floor covering and lift up the cover panel.

2 The tool kit is located under the driver's seat.

3 Remove the valve cap from the relevant tyre.

4 Attach the flexible filler tube to the tyre valve and tighten the retaining ring nut.

5 Start the engine, then switch on the compressor and inflate the tyre to the pressure specified at the end of this Chapter. If after 5 minutes it's still impossible to achieve a pressure of at least 1.5 bar, disconnect the filler tube and roll the car fowards/backwards approximately 10 metres to redistribute the sealant within the tyre, then repeat the inflation procedure. If it's still not possible to achieve 1.5 bar, the tyre is too badly damaged, and having the vehicle recovered is the only option.

6 With the tyre correctly inflated, disconnect the filler tube, and refit the valve cap. Check the pressure again after 10 minutes of driving.

Towing

When all else fails, you may find yourself having to get a tow home – or of course you may be helping somebody else. Long-distance recovery should only be done by a garage or breakdown service. For shorter distances, DIY towing using another car is easy enough, but observe the following points:

- ☐ Use a proper tow-rope – they are not expensive. The vehicle being towed must display an ON TOW sign in its rear window.
- ☐ Always turn the ignition key to the 'on' position when the vehicle is being towed, so that the steering lock is released, and that the direction indicator and brake lights will work.
- ☐ The towing eye is of the screw-in type, and is found in the spare wheel well. The towing eye screws into a threaded hole, accessible

after prising out a cover on the right-hand side of the bumpers **(see illustration)**.
- ☐ Before being towed, release the handbrake and make sure the transmission is in neutral.
- ☐ Note that greater-than-usual pedal pressure will be required to operate the brakes, since the vacuum servo unit is only operational with the engine running.
- ☐ The driver of the car being towed must keep the tow-rope taut at all times to avoid snatching.
- ☐ Make sure that both drivers know the route before setting off.
- ☐ Only drive at moderate speeds, and keep the distance towed to a minimum. Drive smoothly, and allow plenty of time for slowing down at junctions.

Identifying leaks

Puddles on the garage floor or drive, or obvious wetness under the bonnet or underneath the car, suggest a leak that needs investigating. It can sometimes be difficult to decide where the leak is coming from, especially if an engine undershield is fitted. Leaking oil or fluid can also be blown rearwards by the passage of air under the car, giving a false impression of where the problem lies.

 Warning: Most automotive oils and fluids are poisonous. Wash them off skin, and change out of contaminated clothing, without delay.

 The smell of a fluid leaking from the car may provide a clue to what's leaking. Some fluids are distinctively coloured. It may help to remove the engine undershield, clean the car carefully and to park it over some clean paper overnight as an aid to locating the source of the leak.
Remember that some leaks may only occur while the engine is running.

Sump oil

Engine oil may leak from the drain plug...

Oil from filter

...or from the base of the oil filter.

Gearbox oil

Gearbox oil can leak from the seals at the inboard ends of the driveshafts.

Antifreeze

Leaking antifreeze often leaves a crystalline deposit like this.

Brake fluid

A leak occurring at a wheel is almost certainly brake fluid.

Power steering fluid

Power steering fluid may leak from the pipe connectors on the steering rack.

Introduction

There are some very simple checks which need only take a few minutes to carry out, but which could save you a lot of inconvenience and expense.

These *Weekly checks* require no great skill or special tools, and the small amount of time they take to perform could prove to be very well spent, for example:

☐ Keeping an eye on tyre condition and pressures, will not only help to stop them wearing out prematurely, but could also save your life.

☐ Many breakdowns are caused by electrical problems. Battery-related faults are particularly common, and a quick check on a regular basis will often prevent the majority of these.

☐ If your car develops a brake fluid leak, the first time you might know about it is when your brakes don't work properly. Checking the level regularly will give advance warning of this kind of problem.

☐ If the oil or coolant levels run low, the cost of repairing any engine damage will be far greater than fixing the leak, for example.

Underbonnet check points

◀ Panda petrol engine (1.2 litre shown)

A *Engine oil level dipstick*
B *Engine oil filler cap*
C *Coolant expansion tank*
D *Brake fluid reservoir*
E *Screen washer fluid reservoir*
F *Battery*
G *Clutch fluid reservoir*

◀ 500 diesel engine

A *Engine oil level dipstick*
B *Engine oil filler cap*
C *Coolant expansion tank*
D *Brake and clutch fluid reservoir*
E *Screen washer fluid reservoir*
F *Battery*

Engine oil level

Before you start

✔ Make sure that your car is on level ground.

✔ Check the oil level before the car is driven, or at least 5 minutes after the engine has been switched off.

 HAYNES HiNT *If the oil is checked immediately after driving the vehicle, some of the oil will remain in the upper engine components, resulting in an inaccurate reading on the dipstick.*

The correct oil

Modern engines place great demands on their oil. It is very important that the correct oil for your car is used (see *Lubricants and fluids*).

Car care

● If you have to add oil frequently, you should check whether you have any oil leaks. Place some clean paper under the car overnight, and check for stains in the morning. If there are no leaks, the engine may be burning oil, or the oil may only be leaking when the engine is running.

● Always maintain the level between the upper and lower dipstick marks (see photo 3). If the level is too low severe engine damage may occur. Oil seal failure may result if the engine is overfilled by adding too much oil.

1 The dipstick is located on the right-hand side of the engine (see *Underbonnet check points* for exact location). Withdraw the dipstick. Using a clean rag or paper towel, remove all oil from the dipstick.

2 Insert the clean dipstick into the tube as far as it will go, then withdraw it again. Note the oil level on the end of the dipstick, which should be between the MAX and MIN marks. If the oil level is only just above, or below, the MIN mark, topping-up is required.

3 Oil is added through the filler cap. Unscrew the cap . . .

4 . . . and top-up the level; a funnel may be useful in reducing spillage. Add the oil slowly, checking the level on the dipstick often, and allowing time for the oil to fall to the sump. Add oil until the level is just up to the MAX mark on the dipstick – don't overfill (see *Car care*)

Coolant level

⚠ *Warning: DO NOT attempt to remove the expansion tank pressure cap when the engine is hot, as there is a very great risk of scalding. Do not leave open containers of coolant about, as it is poisonous.*

Car care

● With a sealed-type cooling system, adding coolant should not be necessary on a regular basis. If frequent topping-up is required, it is likely there is a leak. Check the radiator, all hoses and joint faces for signs of staining or wetness, and rectify as necessary.

● It is important that antifreeze is used in the cooling system all year round, not just during the winter months. Don't top-up with water alone, as the antifreeze will become too diluted.

1 The coolant level varies with the temperature of the engine, and is visible through the expansion tank. When the engine is cold, the coolant level should be between the MAX and MIN marks on the side of the reservoir. When the engine is hot, the level may rise slightly above the MAX mark.

2 If topping-up is necessary, wait until the engine is cold. Slowly unscrew the expansion tank cap, to release any pressure present in the cooling system, and remove it.

3 Add a mixture of water and antifreeze to the expansion tank until the coolant level is halfway between the level marks. Use only the specified antifreeze – if using Fiat antifreeze, make sure it is the same type and colour as that already in the system. Refit the cap and tighten it securely.

Brake and clutch fluid level

All models have a hydraulically-operated clutch which on some models uses the same fluid as the braking system, whereas on others the fluid is stored in a separate reservoir.

⚠️ **Warning:**
● *Brake fluid can harm your eyes and damage painted surfaces, so use extreme caution when handling and pouring it.*
● *Do not use fluid that has been standing open for some time, as it absorbs moisture from the air, which can cause a dangerous loss of braking effectiveness.*

HAYNES HiNT
● *Make sure that your car is on level ground.*
● *The fluid level in the reservoir will drop slightly as the brake pads wear down, but the fluid level must never be allowed to drop below the MIN mark.*

Safety first!
● If the reservoir requires repeated topping-up this is an indication of a fluid leak somewhere in the system, which should be investigated immediately.
● If a leak is suspected, the car should not be driven until the braking system has been checked. Never take any risks where brakes are concerned.

1 The brake fluid reservoir is located on the left-hand side of the engine compartment.

2 On models with a separate clutch fluid reservoir, it's located on the right, or left-hand side of the engine compartment.

3 The MAX and MIN marks are indicated on the side of the reservoir. The fluid level must be kept between the marks at all times. Clutch fluid reservoir . . .

4 . . . and brake fluid reservoir.

5 If topping-up is necessary, first wipe clean the area around the filler cap to prevent dirt entering the hydraulic system. Unscrew the reservoir cap and carefully lift it out of position. Inspect the reservoir; if the fluid is dirty, the hydraulic system should be drained and refilled (see the relevant part of Chapter 1).

6 Carefully add fluid, taking care not to spill it onto the surrounding components. Use only the specified fluid; mixing different types can cause damage to the system. After topping-up to the correct level, securely refit the cap and wipe off any spilt fluid.

Tyre condition and pressure

It is very important that tyres are in good condition, and at the correct pressure - having a tyre failure at any speed is highly dangerous. Tyre wear is influenced by driving style - harsh braking and acceleration, or fast cornering, will all produce more rapid tyre wear. As a general rule, the front tyres wear out faster than the rears. Interchanging the tyres from front to rear ("rotating" the tyres) may result in more even wear. However, if this is completely effective, you may have the expense of replacing all four tyres at once! Remove any nails or stones embedded in the tread before they penetrate the tyre to cause deflation. If removal of a nail does reveal that the tyre has been punctured, refit the nail so that its point of penetration is marked. Then immediately change the wheel, and have the tyre repaired by a tyre dealer.

Regularly check the tyres for damage in the form of cuts or bulges, especially in the sidewalls. Periodically remove the wheels, and clean any dirt or mud from the inside and outside surfaces. Examine the wheel rims for signs of rusting, corrosion or other damage. Light alloy wheels are easily damaged by "kerbing" whilst parking; steel wheels may also become dented or buckled. A new wheel is very often the only way to overcome severe damage.

New tyres should be balanced when they are fitted, but it may become necessary to re-balance them as they wear, or if the balance weights fitted to the wheel rim should fall off. Unbalanced tyres will wear more quickly, as will the steering and suspension components. Wheel imbalance is normally signified by vibration, particularly at a certain speed (typically around 50 mph). If this vibration is felt only through the steering, then it is likely that just the front wheels need balancing. If, however, the vibration is felt through the whole car, the rear wheels could be out of balance. Wheel balancing should be carried out by a tyre dealer or garage.

1 *Tread Depth - visual check*
The original tyres have tread wear safety bands (B), which will appear when the tread depth reaches approximately 1.6 mm. The band positions are indicated by a triangular mark on the tyre sidewall (A).

2 *Tread Depth - manual check*
Alternatively, tread wear can be monitored with a simple, inexpensive device known as a tread depth indicator gauge.

3 *Tyre Pressure Check*
Check the tyre pressures regularly with the tyres cold. Do not adjust the tyre pressures immediately after the vehicle has been used, or an inaccurate setting will result.

Tyre tread wear patterns

Shoulder Wear

Underinflation (wear on both sides)
Under-inflation will cause overheating of the tyre, because the tyre will flex too much, and the tread will not sit correctly on the road surface. This will cause a loss of grip and excessive wear, not to mention the danger of sudden tyre failure due to heat build-up.
Check and adjust pressures
Incorrect wheel camber (wear on one side)
Repair or renew suspension parts
Hard cornering
Reduce speed!

Centre Wear

Overinflation
Over-inflation will cause rapid wear of the centre part of the tyre tread, coupled with reduced grip, harsher ride, and the danger of shock damage occurring in the tyre casing.
Check and adjust pressures

If you sometimes have to inflate your car's tyres to the higher pressures specified for maximum load or sustained high speed, don't forget to reduce the pressures to normal afterwards.

Uneven Wear

Front tyres may wear unevenly as a result of wheel misalignment. Most tyre dealers and garages can check and adjust the wheel alignment (or "tracking") for a modest charge.
Incorrect camber or castor
Repair or renew suspension parts
Malfunctioning suspension
Repair or renew suspension parts
Unbalanced wheel
Balance tyres
Incorrect toe setting
Adjust front wheel alignment
Note: *The feathered edge of the tread which typifies toe wear is best checked by feel.*

Wiper blades

✔ Only fit good-quality blades.

✔ When removing an old wiper blade, note how it is fitted. Fitting new blades can be a tricky exercise, and noting how the old blade came off can save time.

✔ While the wiper blade is removed, take care not to knock the wiper arm from its locked position, or it could strike the glass.

✔ Offer the new blade into position the same way round as the old one. Ensure that it clicks home securely, otherwise it may come off in use, damaging the glass.

Note: *Fitting details for wiper blades vary according to model, and according to whether genuine Fiat wiper blades have been fitted. Use the procedures and illustrations shown as a guide for your car.*

 HAYNES HiNT *If smearing is still a problem despite fitting new wiper blades, try cleaning the glass with neat screenwash additive or methylated spirit.*

1 Check the condition of the wiper blades; if they are cracked or show any signs of deterioration, or if the glass swept area is smeared, renew them. Wiper blades should be renewed annually, regardless of their apparent condition.

2 To remove a windscreen wiper blade on Panda models, pull the arm fully away from the glass until it locks. Swivel the blade through 90°, press the locking tab with your fingers and slide the blade out of the arm's hooked end.

3 To remove a windscreen wiper blade on 500 models, pull the arm fully away from the glass until it locks. Press the release button with your fingers and slide the blade out of the arm's hooked end.

4 Don't forget to check the tailgate wiper blade as well (where applicable). Remove the blade by prising apart the blade casing.

Washer fluid level

● The windscreen washer reservoir also supplies the tailgate washer jet, where applicable. On models so equipped, the same reservoir also serves the headlight washers.

● Screenwash additives not only keep the windscreen clean during foul weather, they also prevent the washer system freezing in cold weather – which is when you are likely to need it most. Don't top-up using plain water as the screenwash will become too diluted, and will freeze during cold weather.

 Caution: On no account use coolant antifreeze in the washer system – this could discolour or damage paintwork.

1 The washer fluid reservoir filler neck is located on the right-hand side of the engine compartment. The washer level cannot easily be seen. Remove the filler cap, and look down the filler neck – if fluid is not visible, topping-up may be required.

2 When topping-up the reservoir, add a screenwash additive in the quantities recommended on the additive bottle.

Battery

Caution: Before carrying out any work on the vehicle battery, read the precautions given in 'Safety first!' at the start of this manual.

✔ Make sure that the battery tray is in good condition, and that the clamp is tight. Any 'white' corrosion on the terminals or surrounding area can be removed with a solution of water and baking soda; thoroughly rinse all cleaned areas with water. Any metal parts damaged by corrosion should be covered with a zinc-based primer, then painted.

✔ Periodically check the charge condition of the battery. On the original-equipment battery, the state of charge may be shown by an indicator 'eye' in the top of the battery, which should be green – if the indicator is clear, or red, the battery may need charging or even renewal (see Chapter 5A).

✔ If the battery is flat, and you need to jump start your vehicle, see *Roadside repairs*.

HAYNES HINT

Battery corrosion can be kept to a minimum by applying a layer of petroleum jelly to the clamps and terminals after they are reconnected.

1 The battery is located in the left-hand front corner of the engine compartment – prise up the plastic cover over the positive terminal. The exterior of the battery should be inspected periodically for damage such as a cracked case or cover.

2 Check the tightness of battery clamps to ensure good electrical connections. You should not be able to move them. Also check each cable for cracks and frayed conductors.

3 If corrosion (white, fluffy deposits) is evident, remove the cables from the battery terminals, clean them with a small wire brush, then refit them. Automotive stores sell a tool for cleaning the battery post . . .

4 . . . as well as the battery cable clamps

Electrical systems

✔ Check all external lights and the horn. Refer to the appropriate Sections of Chapter 12 for details if any of the circuits are found to be inoperative.

✔ Visually check all accessible wiring connectors, harnesses and retaining clips for security, and for signs of chafing or damage.

 HAYNES HiNT *If you need to check your brake lights and indicators unaided, back up to a wall or garage door and operate the lights. The reflected light should show if they are working properly.*

1 If a single indicator light, brake light or headlight has failed, it is likely that a bulb has blown and will need to be renewed. Refer to Chapter 12 for details. If both brake lights have failed, it is possible that the switch has failed (see Chapter 9).

2 If more than one indicator light or tail light has failed, it is likely that either a fuse has blown or that there is a fault in the circuit (see Chapter 12). The main fusebox is located below the facia panel, and is accessed by unclipping a panel in the passenger's side oddments tray (500 models) . . .

3 . . . or undoing 2 fasteners at the lower edge of the driver's side panel (Panda models). The auxiliary fusebox is located next to the battery – unclip and remove the cover for access.

4 To renew a blown fuse, simply pull it out and fit a new fuse of the correct rating (see Chapter 12). Spare fuses, and a fuse removal tool, are provided in the auxiliary fusebox. If the fuse blows again, it is important that you find out why – a complete checking procedure is given in Chapter 12.

Lubricants and fluids

Engine

Petrol . . . . Multigrade engine oil, fully-synthetic, viscosity SAE 5W/40 or 10W/40 to ACEA A3 and API SL or better
Fiat classification 9.5535-S2

Diesel . . . . Multigrade engine oil, fully-synthetic, viscosity SAE 5W/30 or 5W/40 to ACEA B4 and API CF or better*
Fiat classification 9.5535-S1

Manual transmission . . . . Fiat gear oil

Cooling system . . . . Paraflu UP

Brake/clutch fluid reservoir . . . . Hydraulic fluid to DOT 4

* On engines with a particulate filter, use low-ash oil; consult a dealer for a suitable type.

Tyre pressures (cold)

Note: *Pressures apply to original-equipment tyres, and may vary if any other make or type of tyre is fitted; check with the tyre manufacturer or supplier for correct pressures if necessary.*

Normal load (up to 3 passengers)	Front	Rear
Petrol engine models		
155/80 R 13, 165/65 R 14 and 175/65 R14	2.0 bar (29 psi)	1.8 bar (26 psi)
All other sizes	2.2 bar (32 psi)	2.1 bar (30 psi)
Diesel engine models		
Panda models	2.2 bar (32 psi)	1.8 bar (26 psi)
500 models	2.2 bar (32 psi)	2.1 bar (30 psi)
Fully laden		
Panda models:		
Petrol models	2.2 bar (32 psi)	2.2 bar (32 psi)
Diesel models	2.3 bar (33 psi	2.2 bar 32 psi)
500 models:		
165/65 R 14	2.2 bar (32 psi)	2.2 bar (32 psi)
175/65 R14:		
Petrol models	2.2 bar (32 psi)	2.2 bar (32 psi)
Diesel models	2.3 bar (33 psi)	2.2 bar (32 psi)
185/55 R15	2.3 bar (33 psi)	2.3 bar (33 psi)
195/45 R 16	2.4 bar (35 psi)	2.3 bar (33 psi)
Space-saver temporary spare tyre		
All models	2.8 bar (41 psi)	2.8 bar (41 psi)

Chapter 1 Part A:
Routine maintenance and servicing - petrol models

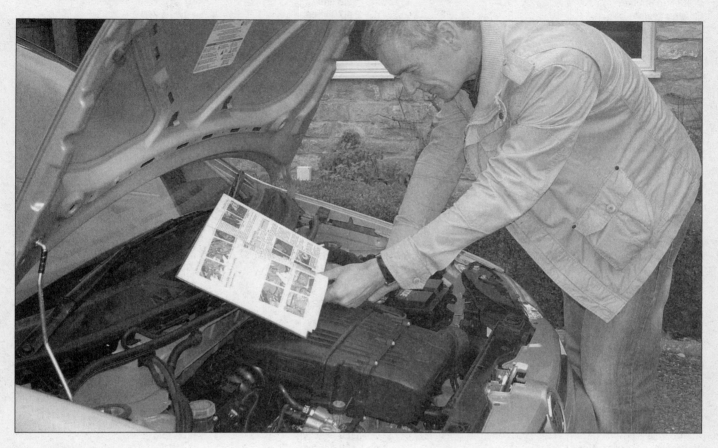

Contents

Degrees of difficulty

| **Easy,** suitable for novice with little experience | | **Fairly easy,** suitable for beginner with some experience | | **Fairly difficult,** suitable for competent DIY mechanic | | **Difficult,** suitable for experienced DIY mechanic | | **Very difficult,** suitable for expert DIY or professional | |

Lubricants and fluids

Refer to end of *Weekly checks* on page 0•18

Capacities

Engine oil (including filter):
  1.1 litre engines . . . . 3.5 litres
  1.2 litre engines . . . . 2.8 litres
Cooling system. . . . . 4.70 litres
Manual transmission . . . . 1.65 litres
Fuel tank . . . . 35.0 litres

Engine

Auxiliary drivebelt tension:
  Models without air conditioning . . . . 5.0 mm deflection midway between pulleys
  Models with air conditioning . . . . Controlled by automatic tensioner
Valve clearances (cold):
  Intake . . . . 0.35 ± 0.05 mm
  Exhaust. . . . . 0.45 ± 0.05 mm
  Cam follower (tappet) shim sizes . . . . 3.20 to 4.70 mm in increments of 0.05 mm

Cooling system

Antifreeze mixture (50% antifreeze) . . . . Protection down to –35ºC
Note: *Refer to antifreeze manufacturer for latest recommendations.*

Ignition system

Ignition timing. . . . . Refer to Chapter 5B

Spark plugs:

	Type	Electrode gap
Panda engines	NGK DCPR7E-N10	Pre-set
500 engines	NGK ZKR7A-10	Pre-set

Remote control

Battery type CR2032

Brakes

Brake pad lining minimum thickness . . . . 1.5 mm
Brake shoe friction material minimum thickness . . . . 2.0 mm

Torque wrench settings

	Nm	lbf ft
Roadwheel bolts:		
Steel wheel	85	63
Aluminium wheel	98	72
Spark plugs	25	18
Sump drain plug	20	15
Transmission oil filler plug	20	15

The maintenance intervals in this manual are provided with the assumption that you, not the dealer, will be carrying out the work. These are the minimum maintenance intervals recommended by us for vehicles driven daily. If you wish to keep your vehicle in peak condition at all times, you may wish to perform some of these procedures more often. We encourage frequent maintenance, because it enhances the efficiency, performance and resale value of your vehicle.

When the vehicle is new, it should be serviced by a dealer service department (or other workshop recognised by the vehicle manufacturer as providing the same standard of service) in order to preserve the warranty. The vehicle manufacturer may reject warranty claims if you are unable to prove that servicing has been carried out as and when specified, using only original equipment parts or parts certified to be of equivalent quality.

Every 250 miles or weekly
☐ Refer to *Weekly checks*

Every 6000 miles or 6 months – whichever comes first
☐ Reset the service interval indicator (Section 2)
☐ Renew the engine oil and filter (Section 3)
Note: *Frequent oil and filter changes are good for the engine and we recommend that the oil and filter are renewed more frequently than Fiat recommend, especially if the vehicle is used on a lot of short journeys*

Every 12 000 miles or 12 months – whichever comes first
In addition to the items listed above, carry out the following:
☐ Check the condition and tension of the auxiliary drivebelt (Section 4)
☐ Hose and fluid leak check (Section 5)
☐ Check the front brake pads for wear (Section 6)
☐ Check the condition of the driveshaft gaiters (Section 7)
☐ Check the steering and suspension components for condition and security (Section 8)
☐ Check the underbody and sealant for damage (Section 9)
☐ Check the condition of the exhaust system and its mountings (Section 10)
☐ Check and if necessary adjust the handbrake (Section 11)
☐ Renew the pollen filter (Section 12)
☐ Lubricate all hinges and locks (Section 13)
☐ Carry out a road test (Section 14)

Every 24 000 miles or 2 years – whichever comes first
In addition to the items listed above, carry out the following:
☐ Check and if necessary adjust the valve clearances (Section 15)
☐ Renew the spark plugs (Section 16)
☐ Check the condition of the spark plug HT leads (Section 17)
☐ Check the engine management system (Section 18)
☐ Renew the brake fluid (Section 19)
☐ Renew the engine coolant (Section 20)

Every 36 000 miles or 3 years – whichever comes first
In addition to the items listed above, carry out the following:
☐ Renew the air filter element (Section 21)
☐ Check the condition of the timing belt (Section 22)
☐ Check and if necessary top-up the manual transmission oil level (Section 23)
☐ Check the rear brake shoes for wear (Section 24)

Every 48 000 miles or 4 years – whichever comes first
In addition to the items listed above, carry out the following:
☐ Renew the timing belt (Section 25)*
☐ Check the operation of the evaporative loss system (Section 26)
☐ Check the condition and operation of the crankcase emission control system (Section 27)
☐ Renew the remote control battery (Section 28)
* Note: *Although the normal interval for timing belt renewal is 72 000 miles, it is strongly recommended that the belt is renewed at 48 000 miles on vehicles which are subjected to intensive use, ie, mainly short journeys or a lot of stop-start driving. The actual belt renewal interval is therefore very much up to the individual owner, but bear in mind that severe engine damage will result if the belt breaks.*

Every 72 000 miles
☐ Renew the auxiliary drivebelt (Section 4)

Underbonnet view – 1.2 litre Euro 5 Panda model shown (others similar)

1 Oil filler cap
2 Air filter housing
3 Battery
4 Engine management ECU
5 Engine oil level dipstick
6 Clutch fluid reservoir
7 Brake fluid reservoir
8 Coolant expansion tank cap
9 Fuel pressure release valve
10 Engine compartment fuse/relay box

Underbonnet view of a 500 model

1 Oil filler cap
2 Air filter housing
3 Battery
4 Engine management ECU
5 Engine oil level dipstick
6 Clutch fluid reservoir
7 Brake fluid reservoir
8 Coolant expansion tank cap
9 Fuel pressure release valve
10 Engine compartment fuse/relay box

Front underbody view

1 Engine oil drain plug
2 Front subframe
3 Lower arm
4 Steering track rod end
5 Anti-roll bar
6 Transmission drain plug
7 Catalytic converter
8 Engine oil filter
9 Driveshaft
10 Brake caliper
11 Rear engine mounting link

Rear underbody view

1 Fuel tank
2 Handbrake cable
3 Rear silencer
4 Coil spring
5 Rear axle
6 Fuel filler pipe
7 Shock absorber
8 Brake pipe

1 Introduction

1 This Chapter is designed to help the home mechanic maintain his/her vehicle for safety, economy, long life and peak performance.

2 The Chapter contains a master maintenance schedule, and Sections dealing specifically with each task in the schedule. Visual checks, adjustments, component renewal and other helpful items are included. Refer to the accompanying illustrations of the engine compartment and the underside of the vehicle for the locations of the various components.

3 Servicing your vehicle in accordance with the mileage/time maintenance schedule and the following Sections will provide a planned maintenance programme, which should result in a long and reliable service life. This is a comprehensive plan, so maintaining some items but not others at the specified service intervals will not produce the same results.

4 As you service your vehicle, you will discover that many of the procedures can, and should, be grouped together, because of the particular procedure being performed, or because of the proximity of two otherwise unrelated components to one another. For example, if the vehicle is raised for any reason, the exhaust can be inspected at the same time

as the suspension and steering components.

5 The first step in this maintenance programme is to prepare yourself before the actual work begins. Read through all the Sections relevant to the work to be carried out, then make a list and gather all the parts and tools required. If a problem is encountered, seek advice from a parts specialist, or a dealer service department.

Regular maintenance

6 If, from the time the vehicle is new, the routine maintenance schedule is followed closely, and frequent checks are made of fluid levels and high-wear items, as suggested throughout this manual, the engine will be kept in relatively good running condition, and the need for additional work will be minimised.

7 It is possible that there will be times when the engine is running poorly due to the lack of regular maintenance. This is even more likely if a used vehicle, which has not received regular and frequent maintenance checks, is purchased. In such cases, additional work may need to be carried out, outside of the regular maintenance intervals.

8 If engine wear is suspected, a compression test (refer to Chapter 2A) will provide valuable information regarding the overall performance of the main internal components. Such a test can be used as a basis to decide on the extent of the work to be carried out. If, for example, a compression test indicates serious internal

engine wear, conventional maintenance as described in this Chapter will not greatly improve the performance of the engine, and may prove a waste of time and money, unless extensive overhaul work is carried out first.

9 The following series of operations are those usually required to improve the performance of a generally poor-running engine:

Primary operations

a) Clean, inspect and test the battery (See 'Weekly checks').

b) Check all the engine-related fluids (See 'Weekly checks').

c) Check the condition and tension of the auxiliary drivebelt(s) (Section 4).

d) Check the condition of all hoses, and check for fluid leaks (Section 5).

e) Renew the spark plugs (Section 16).

f) Inspect the ignition HT leads (Section 17).

g) Check the condition of the air filter, and renew if necessary (Section 21).

10 If the above operations do not prove fully effective, carry out the following secondary operations:

Secondary operations

11 All items listed under *Primary operations*, plus the following:

a) Check the charging system (Chapter 5A).

b) Check the ignition system (Chapter 5B).

c) Check the fuel system (Chapter 4A).

d) Renew the ignition HT leads (Section 17).

Every 6000 miles or 6 months

2 Service interval indicator reset

1 It would appear that the service interval indicator can only be reset using Fiat diagnostic equipment, or generic EOBD compatible equivalent. Entrust this task to a Fiat dealer or suitably-equipped repairer.

3 Engine oil and filter renewal

1 Frequent oil and filter changes are the most important preventative maintenance which can be undertaken by the DIY owner. As engine oil ages, it becomes diluted and contaminated, which leads to premature engine wear.

2 Before starting this procedure, gather all the necessary tools and materials. Also make sure that you have plenty of clean rags and newspapers handy to mop-up any spills. Ideally, the engine oil should be warm, as it will drain better, and any impurities suspended in the oil will be removed with it. Take care, however, not to touch the exhaust or any other hot parts of the engine when working

under the vehicle. To avoid any possibility of scalding, and to protect yourself from possible skin irritants and other harmful contaminants in used engine oils, it is advisable to wear gloves when carrying out this work. Access to the underside of the vehicle will be greatly improved if it can be raised on a lift, driven onto ramps, or jacked up and supported on axle stands (see *Jacking and vehicle support*). Whichever method is chosen, make sure that the vehicle remains level, or if it is at an angle, that the drain plug is at the lowest point.

3 Slacken the drain plug about half a turn using a 12 mm Allen key/bit **(see illustration)**. Position the draining container under the drain

3.3 Engine oil drain plug location (arrowed)

plug, then remove the plug completely **(see Haynes Hint)**.

4 Allow some time for the old oil to drain, noting that it may be necessary to reposition the container as the oil flow slows to a trickle.

5 After all the oil has drained, wipe off the drain plug with a clean rag, then clean the area around the drain plug opening and refit the plug. Tighten the plug to the specified torque.

HAYNES HiNT

Keep the drain plug pressed into the sump while unscrewing it by hand the last couple of turns. As the plug releases, move it away sharply so that the stream of oil issuing from the sump runs into the container, not up your sleeve.

6 Move the container into position under the oil filter, which is located on the front right-hand side of the engine.

7 Using an oil filter removal tool if necessary, slacken the filter initially, then unscrew it by hand the rest of the way **(see illustration)**. Empty the oil in the old filter into the container.

8 Use a clean rag to remove all oil, dirt and sludge from the filter sealing area on the engine. Check the old filter to make sure that the rubber sealing ring has not stuck to the engine. If it has, carefully remove it.

9 Apply a light coating of clean engine oil to the sealing ring on the new filter, then screw it into position on the engine **(see illustration)**. Tighten the filter firmly by hand only – **do not** use any tools.

10 Remove the old oil and all tools from under the car then lower it to the ground (if applicable).

11 Withdraw the dipstick, and remove the oil filler cap from the cylinder head cover. Fill the engine, using the correct grade and type of oil (see *Lubricants and fluids*). An oil can spout or funnel may help to reduce spillage. Pour in half the specified quantity of oil first, then wait

3.7 Using an oil filter removal tool to initially slacken the oil filter

a few minutes for the oil to run to the sump. Continue adding oil a small quantity at a time until the level is up to the MAX mark on the dipstick. Refit the filler cap.

12 Start the engine and run it for a few minutes; check for leaks around the oil filter seal and the sump drain plug. Note that there may be a delay of a few seconds before the oil pressure warning light goes out when the engine is first started, as the oil circulates through the engine oil galleries and the new oil filter before the pressure builds-up.

3.9 Apply a light coating of clean engine oil to the sealing ring on the new filter

13 Switch off the engine, and wait a few minutes for the oil to settle in the sump once more. With the new oil circulated and the filter completely full, recheck the level on the dipstick, and add more oil as necessary.

14 Dispose of the used engine oil and filter safely, referring to *General repair procedures* in the Reference Chapter. Do not discard the old filter with domestic household waste. The facility for waste oil disposal provided by many local council refuse tips generally has a filter receptacle alongside.

Every 12 000 miles or 12 months

4 Auxiliary drivebelt check and renewal

Note: *On models with a manually-adjusted drivebelt, Fiat specify the use of a special tool to correctly set the drivebelt tension. If access to this equipment cannot be obtained, an approximate setting can be achieved using the method described below. If the method described is used, the tension should be checked using the special tool at the earliest possible opportunity.*

1 A single, multi-ribbed auxiliary drivebelt is used on all models. The belt drives the alternator, or alternator and air conditioning compressor according to equipment fitted. On models without air conditioning, the belt is adjusted manually, whereas on models with air conditioning adjustment is by means of an automatic spring-loaded tensioning mechanism.

Checking

2 Firmly apply the handbrake, then jack up the front of the car and support it securely on axle stands (see *Jacking and vehicle*

support). Remove the right-hand front wheel roadwheel.

3 Working under the right-hand wheel arch, undo the retaining screws and remove the wheel arch liner front and centre panels for access to the crankshaft pulley **(see illustration)**. On 500 models, undo the retaining bolts and remove the support bracket between the front subframe and vehicle body prior to removing the wheel arch liner panel **(see illustration)**.

4 Using a socket on the crankshaft pulley bolt, rotate the crankshaft so that the full length of the drivebelt can be examined.

4.3a Undo the screws, pull back the front section of the wheel arch liner (arrowed), then remove the centre panel (arrowed)

4.3b On 500 models, undo the bolts (arrowed) and remove the bracket

4.7a Alternator lower pivot bolt (arrowed) . . .

4.7b . . . and upper adjustment bolts (arrowed)

Look for cracks, splitting and fraying on the surface of the belt; check also for signs of glazing (shiny patches) and separation of the belt plies. If damage or wear is visible, the belt should be renewed. Note that Fiat recommend changing the belt at 72 000 miles regardless of condition.

5 If the condition of the belt is satisfactory, where applicable check the drivebelt tension as described below.

Renewal

Models without air conditioning

6 If not already done, proceed as described in paragraphs 2 and 3.

7 Slacken the alternator lower pivot bolt and the upper adjustment bolts **(see illustrations)**. Swivel the alternator towards the engine and slip the drivebelt off the alternator pulley.

8 Unbolt and remove the crankshaft TDC sensor from the front of the engine (refer to Chapter 4A, Section 9).

9 Remove the drivebelt from the crankshaft pulley.

10 When renewing a drivebelt, ensure that the correct type is used. Fit the belt around the two pulleys then swivel the alternator outwards to take up any slack in the belt.

11 Refit the crankshaft TDC sensor, then adjust the drivebelt tension correctly as described below.

Models with air conditioning

12 If not already done, proceed as described in paragraphs 2 and 3.

13 Undo the two bolts and remove the drivebelt guard **(see illustration)**.

14 Using a socket or spanner on the drivebelt tensioner pulley retaining bolt, rotate the tensioner clockwise against the spring pressure to release the tension from the belt **(see illustration)**. Hold the tensioner in this position and slip the drivebelt off the alternator and air conditioning compressor pulleys. Allow the tensioner to return to the released position.

15 Unbolt and remove the crankshaft TDC sensor from the front of the engine (refer to Chapter 4A, Section 9).

16 Remove the drivebelt from the crankshaft pulley.

17 When renewing a drivebelt, ensure that the correct type is used.

18 Fit the belt around the pulleys, then rotate the tensioner until the belt can be slipped into place over the tensioner pulley.

19 Release the tensioner to allow the spring-loaded arm to automatically tension the belt.

20 Refit the crankshaft TDC sensor, then locate the drivebelt guard in position and secure with the two retaining bolts.

21 Refit the wheel arch liner panels and roadwheel, then lower the car to the ground.

Tensioning

22 Correct tensioning of the belt will ensure that it has a long life. A belt which is too slack will slip and perhaps squeal. Beware, however, of overtightening, as this can cause wear in the alternator bearings. On models equipped with air conditioning the correct belt tension is maintained automatically by means of the

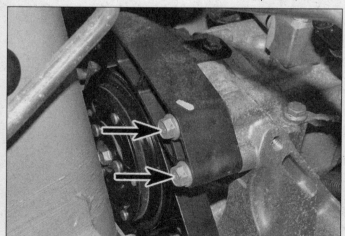

4.13 Undo the bolts (arrowed) and remove the belt guard

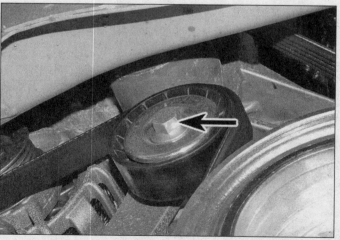

4.14 Rotate the tensioner (arrowed) clockwise against the spring pressure

A leak in the cooling system will usually show up as white or antifreeze-coloured deposits on the area adjoining the leak.

6.2 Measure the thickness of the friction material (arrowed)

7.1 Check the condition of the driveshaft gaiters

spring-loaded tensioning mechanism. On models without air conditioning, the tension must be adjusted manually as follows.

23 The belt should be tensioned so that, under firm thumb pressure, there is approximately 5.0 mm of free movement at the mid-point between the pulleys. To adjust the drivebelt, slacken the alternator pivot and adjustment bolts (if not already done) then swivel the alternator outwards until the belt tension is correct. Hold the alternator in this position and fully-tighten the adjustment bolts followed by the pivot bolt.

24 Refit the wheel arch liner panels and roadwheel, then lower the car to the ground.

5 Hose and fluid leak check

1 Visually inspect the engine joint faces, gaskets and seals for any signs of water or oil leaks. Pay particular attention to the areas around the camshaft cover, cylinder head, oil filter and sump joint faces. Bear in mind that, over a period of time, some very slight seepage from these areas is to be expected – what you are really looking for is any indication of a serious leak. Should a leak be found, renew the offending gasket or oil seal by referring to the appropriate Chapters in this manual.

2 Also check the security and condition of all the engine-related pipes and hoses. Ensure that all cable-ties or securing clips are in place and in good condition. Clips which are broken or missing can lead to chafing of the hoses, pipes or wiring, which could cause more serious problems in the future.

3 Carefully check the radiator hoses and heater hoses along their entire length. Renew any hose which is cracked, swollen or deteriorated. Cracks will show up better if the hose is squeezed. Pay close attention to the hose clips that secure the hoses to the cooling system components. Hose clips can pinch and puncture hoses, resulting in cooling system leaks.

4 Inspect all the cooling system components (hoses, joint faces etc.) for leaks **(see Haynes Hint)**. Where any problems of this nature are found on system components, renew the component or gasket with reference to Chapter 3.

5 Where applicable, inspect the automatic transmission fluid cooler hoses for leaks or deterioration.

6 With the vehicle raised, inspect the fuel tank and filler neck for punctures, cracks and other damage. The connection between the filler neck and tank is especially critical. Sometimes a rubber filler neck or connecting hose will leak due to loose retaining clamps or deteriorated rubber.

7 Carefully check all rubber hoses and metal fuel lines leading away from the fuel tank. Check for loose connections, deteriorated hoses, crimped lines, and other damage. Pay particular attention to the vent pipes and hoses, which often loop up around the filler neck and can become blocked or crimped. Follow the lines to the front of the vehicle, carefully inspecting them all the way. Renew damaged sections as necessary.

8 From within the engine compartment, check the security of all fuel hose attachments and pipe unions, and inspect the fuel hoses and vacuum hoses for kinks, chafing and deterioration.

6 Front brake pad check

1 Firmly apply the handbrake, then jack up the front of the car and support it securely on axle stands (see *Jacking and vehicle support*). Remove the front roadwheels.

2 Using a steel rule, measure the thickness of the friction material of the brake pads on both front brakes. This must not be less than 1.5 mm **(see illustration)**.

3 For a comprehensive check, the brake pads should be removed and cleaned. The operation of the caliper can then also be checked, and the condition of the brake disc itself can be fully examined on both sides. Refer to Chapter 9 for further information.

4 If any pad's friction material is worn to the

specified thickness or less, *all four pads must be renewed as a set.* Refer to Chapter 9.

5 On completion refit the roadwheels and lower the car to the ground.

7 Driveshaft gaiter check

1 With the car raised and securely supported on stands (see *Jacking and vehicle support*), turn the steering onto full lock, then slowly rotate the roadwheel. Inspect the condition of the outer constant velocity (CV) joint rubber gaiters, squeezing the gaiters to open out the folds. Check for signs of cracking, splits or deterioration of the rubber, which may allow the grease to escape, and lead to water and grit entry into the joint. Also check the security and condition of the retaining clips. Repeat these checks on the inner CV joints **(see illustration)**. If any damage or deterioration is found, the gaiters should be renewed (see Chapter 8).

2 At the same time, check the general condition of the CV joints themselves by first holding the driveshaft and attempting to rotate the wheel. Repeat this check by holding the inner joint and attempting to rotate the driveshaft. Any appreciable movement indicates wear in the joints, wear in the driveshaft splines, or a loose driveshaft retaining nut.

8 Steering and suspension check

Front suspension and steering

1 Firmly apply the handbrake, then jack up the front of the car and support it securely on axle stands (see *Jacking and vehicle support*).

2 Inspect the balljoint dust covers and the steering rack and pinion gaiters for splits, chafing or deterioration. Any wear of these will cause loss of lubricant, together with dirt and water entry, resulting in rapid deterioration of the balljoints or steering gear.

3 Grasp the roadwheel at the 12 o'clock and 6 o'clock positions, and try to rock it **(see**

illustration). Very slight free play may be felt, but if the movement is appreciable, further investigation is necessary to determine the source. Continue rocking the wheel while an assistant depresses the footbrake. If the movement is now eliminated or significantly reduced, it is likely that the hub bearings are at fault. If the free play is still evident with the footbrake depressed, then there is wear in the suspension joints or mountings.

4 Now grasp the wheel at the 9 o'clock and 3 o'clock positions, and try to rock it as before. Any movement felt now may again be caused by wear in the hub bearings or the steering track rod balljoints. If the inner or outer balljoint is worn, the visual movement will be obvious.

5 Using a large screwdriver or flat bar, check for wear in the suspension mounting bushes by levering between the relevant suspension component and its attachment point. Some movement is to be expected as the mountings are made of rubber, but excessive wear should be obvious. Also check the condition of any visible rubber bushes, looking for splits, cracks or contamination of the rubber.

6 With the car standing on its wheels, have an assistant turn the steering wheel back-and-forth about an eighth of a turn each way. There should be very little, if any, lost movement between the steering wheel and roadwheels. If this is not the case, closely observe the joints and mountings previously described, but in addition check the steering column universal joints for wear, and the rack and pinion steering gear itself.

Strut/shock absorber check

7 Check for any signs of fluid leakage around the suspension strut/shock absorber body, or from the rubber gaiter around the piston rod. Should any fluid be noticed, the suspension strut/shock absorber is defective internally, and should be renewed. **Note:** *Suspension struts/shock absorbers should always be renewed in pairs on the same axle.*

8 The efficiency of the suspension strut/shock absorber may be checked by bouncing the vehicle at each corner. Generally speaking, the body will return to its normal position and stop after being depressed. If it rises and returns on a rebound, the suspension strut/shock

8.3 Grasp the roadwheel at the 12 and 6 o'clock positions, and try to rock it

absorber is probably suspect. Examine also the suspension strut/shock absorber upper and lower mountings for any signs of wear.

9 Underbody sealant check

1 Jack up the front and rear of the car and support it securely on axle stands (see *Jacking and vehicle support*). Alternatively position the car over an inspection pit.

2 Check the underbody, wheel housings and side sills for rust and/or damage to the underbody sealant. If evident, repair as necessary.

10 Exhaust system check

1 With the engine cold (at least an hour after the vehicle has been driven), check the complete exhaust system from the engine to the end of the tailpipe. The exhaust system is most easily checked with the car raised on a hoist, or suitably supported on axle stands (see *Jacking and vehicle support*), so that the exhaust components are readily visible and accessible.

2 Check the exhaust pipes and connections for evidence of leaks, severe corrosion and damage. Make sure that all brackets and mountings are in good condition, and that all relevant nuts and bolts are tight **(see illustration)**. Leakage at any of the joints or in other parts of the system will usually show up

10.2 Check the condition of the rubber exhaust mountings (arrowed)

as a black sooty stain in the vicinity of the leak.

3 Rattles and other noises can often be traced to the exhaust system, especially the brackets and mountings. Try to move the pipes and silencers. If the components are able to come into contact with the body or suspension parts, secure the system with new mountings. Otherwise separate the joints (if possible) and twist the pipes as necessary to provide additional clearance.

11 Handbrake check and adjustment

Apply the handbrake by pulling it through a maximum of five clicks of the ratchet mechanism and check that this locks the rear wheels, holding the vehicle stationary on an incline. In this position, there should be sufficient reserve travel in the handbrake lever to allow for brake shoe wear and cable stretching. If not, the handbrake mechanism should be adjusted as described in Chapter 9.

12 Pollen filter renewal

1 The pollen filter is located under the facia on the driver's side, adjacent to the heater blower motor.

2 Undo the retaining screw(s) remove the footwell kickpanel adjacent to the heater air distribution housing **(see illustrations)**.

12.2a Undo the screws (arrowed) . . .

12.2b . . . and remove the driver's side footwell kick panel – Panda models . . .

12.2c . . . and 500 models (arrowed)

3 Unclip the cover, and withdraw the filter from its housing (see illustrations).
4 Wipe clean the filter housing then fit the new filter. Refit the cover and footwell panel.

13 Hinge and lock lubrication

1 Lubricate the hinges of the bonnet, doors and tailgate with a light general-purpose oil. Similarly, lubricate all latches, locks and lock strikers. At the same time, check the security and operation of all the locks, adjusting them if necessary (see Chapter 11).
2 Lightly lubricate the bonnet release mechanism and cable with a suitable grease.

14 Road test

Instruments and electrical equipment

1 Check the operation of all instruments and electrical equipment.
2 Make sure that all instruments read correctly, and switch on all electrical equipment in turn, to check that it functions properly.

Steering and suspension

3 Check for any abnormalities in the steering, suspension, handling or road feel.
4 Drive the vehicle, and check that there are no unusual vibrations or noises.
5 Check that the steering feels positive, with no excessive sloppiness, or roughness,

12.3a Unclip the cover (arrowed) . . .

and check for any suspension noises when cornering and driving over bumps.

Drivetrain

6 Check the performance of the engine, clutch, transmission and driveshafts.
7 Listen for any unusual noises from the engine, clutch and gearbox/transmission.
8 Make sure that the engine runs smoothly when idling, and that there is no hesitation when accelerating.
9 Check that the clutch action is smooth and progressive, that the drive is taken up smoothly, and that the pedal travel is not excessive. Also listen for any noises when the clutch pedal is depressed.
10 Check that all gears can be engaged smoothly without noise, and that the gear lever action is smooth and not abnormally vague or notchy.
11 Listen for a metallic clicking sound from the front of the vehicle, as the vehicle is driven slowly in a circle with the steering on full lock. Carry out this check in both directions. If a clicking noise is heard, this indicates wear in a driveshaft joint, in which case renew the joint if necessary.

12.3b . . . and withdraw the filter element

Braking system

12 Make sure that the vehicle does not pull to one side when braking, and that the wheels do not lock when braking hard. Note: Under heavy braking, vibration may be felt through the brake pedal. This is a normal feature of ABS operation, and does not constitute a fault.
13 Check that there is no vibration through the steering when braking.
14 Check that the handbrake operates correctly without excessive movement of the lever, and that it holds the vehicle stationary on a slope.
15 Test the operation of the brake servo unit as follows. With the engine off, depress the footbrake four or five times to exhaust the vacuum. Hold the brake pedal depressed, then start the engine. As the engine starts, there should be a noticeable give in the brake pedal as vacuum builds-up. Allow the engine to run for at least two minutes, and then switch it off. If the brake pedal is depressed now, it should be possible to detect a hiss from the servo as the pedal is depressed. After about four or five applications, no further hissing should be heard, and the pedal should feel considerably harder.

Every 24 000 miles or 2 years

15 Valve clearance check and adjustment

1 The importance of having the valve clearances correctly adjusted cannot be overstressed, as they vitally affect the performance of the engine. Adjustment should only be necessary when the valve gear has become noisy, after engine overhaul, or when trying to trace the cause of power loss. The clearances are checked as follows. The engine must be cold for the check to be accurate.
2 Apply the handbrake then jack up the right-hand front of the car and support on an axle stand (see Jacking and vehicle support). Engage 4th gear. The engine can now be rotated by turning the right-hand front roadwheel.
3 Remove all spark plugs as described in Section 16.

4 Remove the camshaft cover as described in Chapter 2A.
5 Each valve clearance must be checked when the high point of the cam lobe is pointing directly upward away from the cam follower.
6 Check the clearances in the firing order 1–3–4–2, No 1 cylinder being at the timing belt end of the engine. This will minimise the amount of crankshaft rotation required.
7 Insert the appropriate feeler blade between the heel of the cam and the cam follower shim of the first valve (see illustration). If necessary alter the thickness of the feeler blade until it is a stiff, sliding fit. Record the thickness, which will represent the valve clearance for this particular valve.
8 Turn the engine, check the second valve clearance and record it.
9 Repeat the operations on all the remaining valves, recording their respective clearances.
10 Remember that the clearance for intake and exhaust valves differs – see Specifications.

Counting from the timing belt end of the engine, the valve sequence is:

Intake	2–4–5–7
Exhaust	1–3–6–8

11 Where clearances are incorrect, the particular shim will have to be changed. To

15.7 Check the valve clearance with feeler gauge

15.11 Using a modified C-spanner and a screwdriver to remove a shim

15.13 Shim thickness is marked on the lower face

remove the shim, turn the crankshaft until the high point of the cam is pointing directly upward. The cam follower will now have to be depressed so that the shim can be extracted. Special tools are commercially available to do the job, otherwise you will have to make up a forked lever to locate on the rim of the cam follower. This must allow room for the shim to be prised out by means of the cut-outs provided in the cam follower rim **(see illustration)**.

12 Once the shim is extracted, establish its thickness and change it for a thicker or thinner one to bring the previously recorded clearance within specification. For example, if the measured valve clearance was 1.27 mm too great, a shim *thicker* by this amount will be required. Conversely, if the clearance was 1.27 mm too small, a shim *thinner* by this amount will be required.

13 Shims have their thickness (mm) engraved on them; although the engraved side should be fitted so as not to be visible, wear still occurs and often obliterates the number. In this case, measuring their thickness with a metric micrometer is the only method to establish their thickness **(see illustration)**.

14 In practice, if several shims have to be changed, they can often be interchanged, between valves so avoiding the necessity of having to buy more new shims than is necessary, but do not turn the engine with any shims missing.

15 If more than two or three valve clearances are found to be incorrect, it may be more convenient to remove the camshaft for easier removal of the shims.

16 Where no clearance can be measured, even with the thinnest available shim in position, the valve will have to be removed and the end of its stem ground off squarely. This will reduce its overall length by the minimum amount to provide a clearance. This job should be entrusted to an engine reconditioning specialist as it is important to keep the end of the valve stem square.

17 On completion, refit the camshaft cover as described in Chapter 2A, and the spark plugs as described in Section 16.

18 Lower the car to the ground.

16 Spark plug renewal

1 The correct functioning of the spark plugs is vital for the correct running and efficiency of the engine. It is essential that the plugs fitted are appropriate for the engine (a suitable type is specified at the beginning of this Chapter). If this type is used and the engine is in good condition, the spark plugs should not need attention between scheduled renewal intervals. Spark plug cleaning is rarely necessary, and should not be attempted unless specialised equipment is available, as damage can easily be caused to the firing ends.

2 To remove the plugs first remove the air cleaner assembly with reference to Chapter 4A. If the marks on the original-equipment spark plug (HT) leads cannot be seen, mark the leads 1 to 4, to correspond to the cylinder the lead serves (No 1 cylinder is at the timing belt end of the engine). Pull the leads from the plugs by gripping the end fitting, not the lead, otherwise the lead connection may be fractured **(see illustration)**.

3 It is advisable to remove the dirt from the spark plug recesses using a clean brush, vacuum cleaner or compressed air before removing the plugs, to prevent dirt dropping into the cylinders.

4 Unscrew the plugs using a spark plug box spanner or a deep socket and extension bar **(see illustration)**. Keep the socket aligned with the spark plug – if it is forcibly moved to one side, the ceramic insulator may be broken off. As each plug is removed, examine it as follows.

5 Examination of the spark plugs will give a good indication of the condition of the engine. If the insulator nose of the spark plug is clean and white, with no deposits, this is indicative of a weak mixture or too hot a plug (a hot plug transfers heat away from the electrode slowly, a cold plug transfers heat away quickly).

6 If the tip and insulator nose are covered with hard black-looking deposits, this indicates that the mixture is too rich. If the plug is black and oily, then it is likely that the engine is fairly worn, as well as the mixture being too rich.

7 If the insulator nose is covered with light tan to greyish-brown deposits, then the mixture is correct and it is likely that the engine is in good condition.

8 The spark plug electrode gap is of considerable importance, as if it is too large or too small, the size of the spark and its efficiency will be seriously impaired. The gap should be set to the value given in the *Specifications* at the beginning of this Chapter. Note that if the recommended spark plugs are fitted, the electrode gap is pre-set by the manufacturer and should not require adjustment.

9 To set the gap, measure it with a feeler blade and then bend open, or closed, the outer plug electrode until the correct gap is achieved. The centre electrode should never be bent, as this may crack the insulator and cause plug failure, if nothing worse. If using feeler blades, the gap is correct when the appropriate-size blade is a firm sliding fit **(see illustration)**.

10 Special spark plug electrode gap adjusting tools are available from most motor accessory shops, or from some spark plug manufacturers.

16.2 Pull the spark plug lead end fitting from the plug

16.4 Use a spark plug socket to unscrew the plug

16.9 Adjusting a spark plug electrode gap

It is often difficult to insert spark plugs into their holes without cross-threading them. To avoid this possibility, fit a short length of rubber or plastic hose over the end of the spark plug. The flexible hose acts as a universal joint, to help align the plug with the plug hole. Should the plug begin to cross-thread, the hose will slip on the spark plug, preventing thread damage to the cylinder head.

11 Before fitting the spark plugs, check that the threaded connector sleeves are tight, and that the plug exterior surfaces and threads are clean **(see Haynes Hint)**.
12 Remove the rubber hose (if used), and tighten the plug to the specified torque using the spark plug socket and a torque wrench. Refit the remaining spark plugs in the same manner.
13 Connect the HT leads in their correct order, and refit the air cleaner assembly.

17 Ignition system check

⚠️ *Warning: Due to the high voltages produced by the electronic ignition system, extreme care must be taken when working on the system with the ignition switched on. Persons with surgically-implanted cardiac pacemaker devices should keep well clear of the ignition circuits, components and test equipment.*

1 The spark plug (HT) leads should be checked whenever new spark plugs are fitted.
2 Remove the air cleaner assembly as described in Chapter 4A.
3 Pull the leads from the plugs by gripping the end fitting, not the lead, otherwise the lead connection may be fractured.
4 Check inside the end fitting for signs of corrosion, which will look like a white crusty powder. Push the end fitting back onto the spark plug, ensuring that it is a tight fit on the plug. If not, remove the lead again and use pliers to carefully crimp the metal connector inside the end fitting until it fits securely on the end of the spark plug.
5 Using a clean rag, wipe the entire length of the lead to remove any built-up dirt and grease. Once the lead is clean, check for burns, cracks and other damage. Do not bend the lead

excessively, nor pull the lead lengthways – the conductor inside might break.
6 Disconnect the other end of the lead from the ignition coil. Again, pull only on the end fitting. Check for corrosion and a tight fit in the same manner as the spark plug end. Refit the lead securely on completion.
7 Check the remaining leads one at a time, in the same way.
8 If new spark plug (HT) leads are required, purchase a set for your specific car and engine.
9 Refit the air cleaner assembly on completion of the checks.
10 Even with the ignition system in first-class condition, some engines may still occasionally experience poor starting attributable to damp ignition components. To disperse moisture, a water-dispersant aerosol should be liberally applied.

18 Engine management system check

1 This check is part of the manufacturer's maintenance schedule, and involves testing the engine management system using special dedicated test equipment. Such testing will allow the test equipment to read any fault codes stored in the electronic control unit memory.
2 Unless a fault is suspected, this test is not essential, although it should be noted that it is recommended by the manufacturers.
3 If access to suitable test equipment is not possible, make a thorough check of all ignition, fuel and emission control system components, hoses, and wiring, for security and obvious signs of damage. Further details of the fuel system, emission control system and ignition system can be found in the relevant parts of Chapters 4 and 5.

19 Brake fluid renewal

⚠️ *Warning: Brake hydraulic fluid can harm your eyes and damage painted surfaces, so use extreme caution when handling and pouring it. Do not use fluid that has been standing open for some time, as it absorbs moisture from the air. Excess moisture can cause a dangerous loss of braking effectiveness.*

1 The procedure is similar to that for the bleeding of the hydraulic system as described in Chapter 9, except that the brake fluid reservoir should be emptied by siphoning, using a clean poultry baster or similar before starting, and allowance should be made for the old fluid to be expelled when bleeding a section of the circuit.
2 Working as described in Chapter 9, open the first bleed screw in the sequence, and pump the brake pedal gently until nearly all the old fluid has been emptied from the master cylinder reservoir.

3 Top-up to the MAX level with new fluid, and continue pumping until only the new fluid remains in the reservoir, and new fluid can be seen emerging from the bleed screw. Tighten the screw, and top the reservoir level up to the MAX level line.
4 Work through all the remaining bleed screws in the sequence until new fluid can be seen at all of them. Be careful to keep the master cylinder reservoir topped-up to above the MIN level at all times, or air may enter the system and greatly increase the length of the task.
5 When the operation is complete, check that all bleed screws are securely tightened, and that their dust caps are refitted. Wash off all traces of spilt fluid, and recheck the master cylinder reservoir fluid level.
6 Check the operation of the brakes before taking the car on the road.

20 Coolant renewal

⚠️ *Warning: Wait until the engine is cold before starting this procedure. Do not allow antifreeze to come in contact with your skin, or with the painted surfaces of the vehicle. Rinse off spills immediately with plenty of water. Never leave antifreeze lying around in an open container, or in a puddle in the driveway or on the garage floor. Children and pets are attracted by its sweet smell, but antifreeze can be fatal if ingested.*

Cooling system draining

1 With the engine completely cold, cover the expansion tank cap with a wad of rag, and slowly turn the cap anti-clockwise to relieve the pressure in the cooling system (a hissing sound will normally be heard). Wait until any pressure remaining in the system is released, then continue to turn the cap until it can be removed.

Panda models

2 Position a suitable container beneath the radiator bottom hose connection, then release the retaining clip and ease the hose from the radiator stub **(see illustration)**. If the hose

20.2 Squeeze together the release clip each side (arrowed) and disconnect the radiator lower hose – Panda models

20.3 Slacken the radiator drain plug (arrowed) – 500 models

20.4a Radiator bleed screw (arrowed – viewed from beneath)

joint has not been disturbed for some time, it will be necessary to gently manipulate the hose to break the joint. Do not use excessive force, or the radiator stub could be damaged. Allow the coolant to drain into the container.

500 models

3 A radiator drain plug is located at the lower left-hand end of the radiator. Position a suitable container beneath, then undo the drain plug and allow the coolant to escape **(see illustration)**.

All models

4 The cooling system bleed screws should be opened to aid the draining process and help prevent airlocks. These are located on the top right-hand edge of the radiator, and on the heater inlet hose **(see illustrations)**. If the coolant has been drained for a reason other than renewal, then provided it is clean and less than two years old, it can be re-used, though this is not recommended.

5 Once all the coolant has drained, reconnect the hose to the radiator and secure it in position with the retaining clip, or tighten the drain plug as applicable.

Radiator flushing

6 Refer to Chapter 3.

Cooling system filling

7 Before attempting to fill the cooling system, make sure that all hoses and clips are in good condition, and that the clips are tight. Note that an antifreeze mixture must be used all year round, to prevent corrosion of the engine components (see below).

8 Remove the expansion tank filler cap, and fill the system by slowly pouring the coolant into the expansion tank to prevent airlocks from forming. Ensure that all bleed screws are open.

9 If the coolant is being renewed, begin by pouring in a couple of litres of water, followed by the correct quantity of antifreeze, then

top-up with more water. Periodically squeeze the radiator top and bottom hoses to help expel any trapped air in the system.

10 Continue adding coolant until it is seen to emerge from the bleed screws. Close each bleed screw in turn as the coolant emerges.

11 Top-up the coolant level to the MAX mark and refit the expansion tank cap. Ensure that all bleed screws are closed.

12 Start the engine and run it at idling speed for two to three minutes. Allow the engine to continue running until the electric cooling fan operates, periodically increasing the engine speed gradually to 2000 to 3000 rpm.

13 Stop the engine and allow it to cool down completely.

14 Check for leaks, particularly around disturbed components. Check the coolant level in the expansion tank, and top-up if necessary. Note that the system must be cold before an accurate level is indicated in the expansion tank.

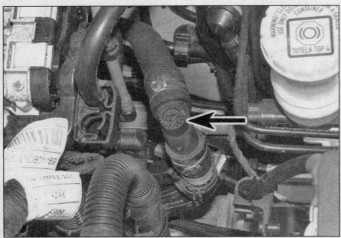

20.4b The heater hose bleed screw (arrowed) is located at the left-hand end of the cylinder head . . .

20.4c . . . or at the engine compartment bulkhead (arrowed)

Antifreeze mixture

15 The antifreeze should always be renewed at the specified intervals. This is necessary not only to maintain the antifreeze properties, but also to prevent corrosion which would otherwise occur as the corrosion inhibitors become progressively less effective.

16 Always use a monoethylene-glycol based antifreeze of the specified type (see *Lubricants and fluids*). The quantity of antifreeze and levels of protection are indicated in the *Specifications*.

17 Before adding antifreeze, the cooling system should be completely drained, preferably flushed, and all hoses checked for condition and security.

18 After filling with antifreeze, a label should be attached to the expansion tank, stating the type and concentration of antifreeze used, and the date installed. Any subsequent topping-up should be made with the same type and concentration of antifreeze.

Caution: Do not use engine antifreeze in the windscreen/tailgate washer system, as it will cause damage to the vehicle paintwork. A screenwash additive should be added to the washer system in the quantities stated on the bottle.

Every 36 000 miles or 3 years

21 Air filter renewal

1.1 litre engines

1 Release the retaining clips, lift off the air cleaner cover and take out the filter element **(see illustrations)**.

2 Remove any debris that may have collected inside the air cleaner and wipe the inner surfaces clean.

3 Fit a new air filter element in position, ensuring that the edges are securely seated. Refit the air cleaner cover and secure with the retaining clips.

1.2 litre engines

Up to Euro 5 emissions level

4 Refer to paragraphs 1 to 3.

Euro 5 emissions level

5 Undo the bolts securing the air cleaner housing to the cylinder head cover, then pull the assembly upwards from the mountings without disconnecting the breather or vacuum hoses **(see illustration)**.

6 Undo the upper and lower retaining bolts and separate the halves of the air cleaner assembly. Take out the filter element **(see illustrations)**.

7 Remove any debris that may have collected inside the air cleaner and wipe the inner surfaces clean.

8 Fit a new air filter element in position, ensuring that the edges are securely seated.

9 Refitting is a reversal of removal.

22 Timing belt inspection

1 The function of the timing belt is to drive the camshaft and coolant pump. Should the belt slip or break in service, the valve timing will be disturbed and piston-to-valve contact will occur, resulting in serious engine damage. It is

21.1a Release the clip each side . . .

21.1b . . . the clip underneath . . .

21.1c . . . then remove the cover and element

21.5 Undo the bolt each side (arrowed) and lift the air cleaner housing upwards a little

21.6a Undo the bolts (arrowed) and separate the halves of the air cleaner assembly . . .

21.6b . . . then lift out the air filter element

23.2 Transmission oil filler/level plug (arrowed)

24.2 Pull the rubber grommet from the brake shoe inspection hole (arrowed)

therefore vitally important that the condition of the belt and surrounding components should be checked very carefully.

2 To gain access to the belt, remove the timing belt covers as described in Chapter 2A.

3 With the covers removed, inspect the timing belt for any signs of uneven wear, splitting, or oil contamination. Pay particular attention to the roots of the teeth. To enable the full length of the belt to be examined, turn the crankshaft using a spanner or socket on the crankshaft sprocket centre bolt.

4 Check for any signs of coolant leakage from the coolant pump or oil leakage from the crankshaft right-hand oil seal. If there is any doubt about the condition of the belt, it should be renewed as described in Chapter 2A. If any coolant or oil leakage is evident, trace the source of the leak and rectify it before fitting the new timing belt.

5 On completion of the inspection, refit the timing belt covers as described in Chapter 2A.

23 Manual transmission oil level check

1 Park the car on a level surface, if possible over an inspection pit or on a ramp as the filler/level plug is best reached from under the engine compartment. The oil level must be checked before the car is driven, or at least 5 minutes after the engine has been switched off. If the oil is checked immediately after driving the car, some of the oil will remain distributed around the transmission components, resulting in an inaccurate level reading.

2 Wipe clean the area around the filler/level plug, which is situated on the front of the transmission (see illustration). Using an Allen key, unscrew the plug and clean it.

3 The oil level should reach the lower edge of the filler/level hole. A certain amount of oil will have gathered behind the filler/level plug, and will trickle out when it is removed; this does **not** necessarily indicate that the level is correct. To ensure that a true level is established, wait until the initial trickle has stopped, then add oil as necessary until a trickle of new oil can be seen emerging. The level will be correct when the flow ceases; use only good-quality oil of the specified type. Make sure that the vehicle is completely level when checking the level and do not overfill.

4 When the level is correct refit and tighten the plug and wipe away any spilt oil.

24 Rear brake shoe check

1 Chock the front wheels then jack up the rear of the car and support it on axle stands (see *Jacking and vehicle support*). Remove the rear roadwheels.

2 Using the inspection hole at the edge of the brake drum, check that the linings are not worn below the minimum thickness given in the *Specifications* (see illustration). If necessary use an electric torch.

3 If the friction material on any shoe is worn down to the specified minimum thickness or less, all four shoes must be renewed as a set.

4 At the same time check for signs of brake fluid leakage.

5 For a comprehensive check, the brake drum should be removed and cleaned. This will allow the wheel cylinders to be checked, and the condition of the brake drum itself to be fully examined (see Chapter 9).

6 On completion of the check, lower the car to the ground.

Every 48 000 miles or 4 years

25 Timing belt renewal

Refer to Chapter 2A.

26 Evaporative loss system check

1 Refer to Chapter 4B, Section 2, and check that all wiring and hoses are correctly connected to the evaporative loss system components.

27 Emission control system check

1 Refer to Chapter 4B. A full check of the emissions control system must be made by a Fiat dealer.

28 Remote control battery renewal

Panda models

1 Using a small flat-bladed screwdriver,

28.1a Carefully prise apart . . .

prise apart the halves of the key casing (see illustrations).

2 Note the orientation of the battery, and remove it from the casing.

3 Insert the new battery into place, with the positive (+) side upwards (see illustration). Avoid touching the battery or the terminals with bare fingers.

28.1b . . . the halves of the casing

28.3 Fit the new battery, positive (+) side up

28.6a Rotate the screw to the 'unlock' position . . .

28.6b . . . and remove the battery case

28.8 The positive (+) mark on the battery must be on the same side as the mark on the casing (arrowed)

4 Snap the 2 halves of the control together, and check for correct operation.

500 models

5 Press the button to release the key blade.

6 Rotate the screw to the 'unlock' position and remove the battery case from the side of the fob **(see illustrations)**.

7 Note the orientation of the battery, and remove it from the casing.

8 Insert the new battery into place, with the positive (+) side of the battery on the same side as the positive mark on the casing **(see illustration)**. Avoid touching the battery or the terminals with bare fingers.

9 Refit the battery case and rotate the screw to the 'locked' position.

Chapter 1 Part B:
Routine maintenance and servicing – diesel models

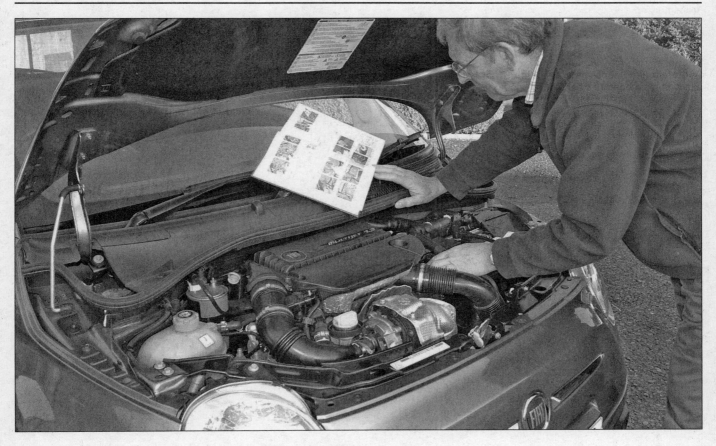

Contents

Degrees of difficulty

Easy, suitable for novice with little experience	**Fairly easy,** suitable for beginner with some experience	**Fairly difficult,** suitable for competent DIY mechanic	**Difficult,** suitable for experienced DIY mechanic	**Very difficult,** suitable for expert DIY or professional

Lubricants and fluids .... Refer to *Weekly checks* on page 0•18

Capacities

Engine

Engine oil (including oil filter) .... 2.8 litres
Difference between MIN and MAX dipstick marks .... 1.0 litre
Cooling system .... 4.6 litres

Transmission

Manual transmission .... 1.65 litre
Fuel tank .... 35 litres

Cooling system

Antifreeze mixture (50% antifreeze) .... Protection down to -40°C
Note: *Refer to antifreeze manufacturer for latest recommendations.*

Brakes

Brake pad lining minimum thickness .... 1.5 mm
Brake shoe friction material minimum thickness .... 2.0 mm

Torque wrench settings

	Nm	lbf ft
Engine oil filter housing cover	25	18
Fuel filter retaining collar (pre-Euro 5 models)	30	22
Roadwheel bolts:		
Steel wheel	85	63
Aluminium wheel	98	72
Sump drain plug	20	15

Every 250 miles or weekly

☐ Refer to *Weekly checks*

Every 10 000 miles or 6 months – whichever comes first

☐ Reset the service interval indicator (Section 2)
☐ Renew the engine oil and filter (Section 3)

Note: *Fiat recommend that the engine oil and filter are changed every 20 000 miles or 12 months if the vehicle is being operated under the standard service schedule. However, oil and filter changes are good for the engine and we recommend that the oil and filter are renewed more frequently, especially if the vehicle is used on a lot of short journeys.*

Every 20 000 miles or 12 months – whichever comes first

In addition to the items listed above, carry out the following:
☐ Check all underbonnet and underbody components, pipes and hoses for leaks (Section 4)
☐ Drain the water from the fuel filter (Section 5)
☐ Check the condition of the front brake pads, calipers and discs (Section 6)
☐ Check the condition of the rear brake shoes (Section 7)
☐ Check the condition of all brake fluid pipes and hoses (Section 8)
☐ Check the condition of the front suspension and steering components, particularly the rubber gaiters and seals (Section 9)
☐ Check the condition of the driveshaft joint gaiters, and the driveshaft joints (Section 10)
☐ Check the condition of the exhaust system components (Section 11)
☐ Check the condition of the rear suspension components (Section 12)
☐ Check the bodywork and underbody for damage and corrosion, and check the condition of the underbody corrosion protection (Section 13)
☐ Lubricate all door, bonnet and tailgate hinges and locks (Section 14)
☐ Check the operation of the horn, all lights, and the wipers and washers (Section 15)
☐ Renew the pollen filter (Section 16)
☐ Carry out a road test (Section 17)

The maintenance intervals in this manual are provided with the assumption that you, not the dealer, will be carrying out the work. These are the minimum maintenance intervals based on the standard service schedule recommended by the manufacturer for vehicles driven daily. If you wish to keep your vehicle in peak condition at all times, you may wish to perform some of these procedures more often. We encourage frequent maintenance, because it enhances the efficiency, performance and resale value of your vehicle.

If the vehicle is driven in dusty areas, used to tow a trailer, or driven frequently at slow speeds (idling in traffic) or on short journeys, more frequent maintenance intervals are recommended.

When the vehicle is new, it should be serviced by a dealer service department (or other workshop recognised by the vehicle manufacturer as providing the same standard of service) in order to preserve the warranty. The vehicle manufacturer may reject warranty claims if you are unable to prove that servicing has been carried out as and when specified, using only original equipment parts or parts certified to be of equivalent quality.

Every 40 000 miles or 2 years – whichever comes first

In addition to the items listed above, carry out the following:
☐ Renew the air cleaner filter element (Section 18)
☐ Auxiliary drivebelt check and renewal (Section 19)
☐ Check the operation of the handbrake and adjust if necessary (Section 20)

Every 2 years, regardless of mileage

☐ Renew the battery for the remote control handset (Section 21)
☐ Renew the brake and clutch fluid (Section 22)
☐ Renew the coolant (Section 23)*
☐ Exhaust emission test (Section 24)

* Note: *Vehicles using Fiat silicate-free 'red' coolant do not need the coolant renewed on a regular basis.*

Every 3 years, regardless of mileage

☐ Renew the fuel filter (Section 25)

Every 48 000 miles

☐ Check the manual transmission oil level (Section 26)

Every 100 000 miles or 10 years – whichever comes first

☐ Renew the auxiliary drivebelt (Section 19)

Underbonnet view – Panda models

1 Engine oil level dipstick
2 Engine oil filler cap
3 Engine oil filter
4 Fuel filter
5 Coolant expansion tank
6 Air filter cover
7 Fuse/relay box
8 Clutch fluid reservoir
9 Brake fluid reservoir
10 Engine management ECU
11 Screenwash fluid reservoir

Underbonnet view – 500 models

1 Engine oil level dipstick
2 Engine oil filler cap
3 Fuel filter
4 Coolant expansion tank
5 Clutch/brake fluid reservoir
6 Air filter housing
7 Battery
8 Engine compartment fuse/relay box
9 Engine management ECU
10 Airflow meter
11 Screenwash fluid reservoir

Front underbody view

1 Engine oil drain plug
2 Air conditioning compressor
3 Lower suspension arm
4 Steering track rod end
5 Brake caliper
6 Anti-roll bar
7 Catalytic converter/particulate filter
8 Right-hand driveshaft
9 Rear engine mounting link rod
10 Radiator lower hose

Rear underbody view

1 Fuel tank
2 Rear exhaust silencer
3 Handbrake cable
4 Shock absorber
5 Coil spring
6 Brake pipe
7 Rear axle
8 Fuel filler pipe

1 General information

1 This Chapter is designed to help the home mechanic maintain his/her vehicle for safety, economy, long life and peak performance.

2 The Chapter contains a master maintenance schedule, followed by Sections dealing specifically with each task in the schedule. Visual checks, adjustments, component renewal and other helpful items are included. Refer to the accompanying illustrations of the engine compartment and the underside of the vehicle for the locations of the various components.

3 Servicing your vehicle in accordance with the mileage/time maintenance schedule and the following Sections will provide a planned maintenance programme, which should result in a long and reliable service life. This is a comprehensive plan, so maintaining some items but not others at the specified service intervals will not produce the same results.

4 As you service your vehicle, you will discover that many of the procedures can – and should – be grouped together, because of the particular procedure being performed, or because of the proximity of two otherwise-unrelated components to one another. For example, if the vehicle is raised for any reason, the exhaust can be inspected at the same time as the suspension and steering components.

5 The first step in this maintenance programme is to prepare yourself before the actual work begins. Read through all the Sections relevant to the work to be carried out, then make a list and gather all the parts and tools required. If a problem is encountered, seek advice from a parts specialist, or a dealer service department.

Regular maintenance

6 If, from the time the vehicle is new, the routine maintenance schedule is followed closely, and frequent checks are made of fluid levels and high-wear items, as suggested throughout this manual, the engine will be kept in relatively good running condition, and the need for additional work will be minimised.

7 It is possible that there will be times when the engine is running poorly due to the lack of regular maintenance. This is even more likely if a used vehicle, which has not received regular and frequent maintenance checks, is purchased. In such cases, additional work may need to be carried out, outside of the regular maintenance intervals.

8 If engine wear is suspected, a compression test or leakdown test (refer to Chapter 2B) will provide valuable information regarding the overall performance of the main internal components. Such a test can be used as a basis to decide on the extent of the work to be carried out. If, for example, the test indicates serious internal engine wear, conventional maintenance as described in this Chapter will not greatly improve the performance of the engine, and may prove a waste of time and money, unless extensive overhaul work is carried out first.

9 The following series of operations are those most often required to improve the performance of a generally poor-running engine:

Primary operations

a) Clean, inspect and test the battery (refer to 'Weekly checks').
b) Check all the engine-related fluids (refer to 'Weekly checks').
c) Check the condition and tension of the auxiliary drivebelt (Section 19).
d) Check the condition of the air cleaner element, and renew if necessary (Section 18).
e) Renew the fuel filter (Section 25).
f) Check the condition of all hoses, and check for fluid leaks (Section 4).

10 If the above operations do not prove fully effective, carry out the following secondary operations:

Secondary operations

11 All items listed under *Primary operations*, plus the following:

a) Check the charging system (refer to Chapter 5A).
b) Check the pre/post-heating system (refer to Chapter 5A).
c) Check the fuel, exhaust and emission control systems (refer to the appropriate Parts of Chapter 4).

Every 10 000 miles or 6 months

2 Service interval indicator reset

1 It would appear that the service interval indicator can only be reset using Fiat diagnostic equipment, or generic EOBD compatible equivalent. Entrust this task to a Fiat dealer or suitably-equipped repairer.

3 Engine oil and filter renewal

1 Before starting this procedure, gather together all the necessary tools and materials. Also make sure that you have plenty of clean rags and newspapers handy, to mop-up any spills. Ideally, the engine oil should be warm, as it will drain more easily, and more built-up sludge will be removed with it. Take care not to touch the exhaust or any other hot parts of the engine when working under the vehicle. To avoid any possibility of scalding, and to protect yourself from possible skin irritants and other harmful contaminants in used engine oils, it is advisable to wear gloves when carrying out this work.

2 Access to the underside of the vehicle will be greatly improved if it can be raised on a lift, driven onto ramps, or jacked up and supported on axle stands (see *Jacking and vehicle support*). Whichever method is chosen, make sure that the vehicle remains level, or if it is at an angle, that the drain plug is at the lowest point. Where fitted, remove the screws and clips and remove the engine undertray for access.

3 Remove the oil filler cap from the filler tube at the front of the engine **(see illustration)**.

4 Using a spanner, or preferably a suitable socket and bar, slacken the drain plug about half a turn **(see illustration)**. Position the

3.3 Unscrew the oil filler cap

3.4 Slacken the sump drain plug (arrowed)

As the drain plug threads release, move it sharply away so the stream of oil issuing from the sump runs into the container, not up your sleeve.

3.6a Slacken the hose clamp (arrowed) . . .

3.6b . . . prise out the yellow locking catch (arrowed) and disconnect the wiring plug . . .

draining container under the drain plug, then remove the plug completely (see Haynes Hint).

5 Allow some time for the oil to drain, noting that it may be necessary to reposition the container as the oil flow slows to a trickle.

6 Position another container under the oil filter located at the front of the engine. **Note:** *On 95 bhp 500 models, access to the oil filter cap is restricted. To improve access, slacken the clamp securing the air intake hose to the turbocharger, disconnect the mass airflow meter wiring plug, undo the cold air intake duct retaining bolt, and pull the air cleaner upwards from its mountings. Move the air cleaner housing to one side (see illustrations).*

7 Undo the nut/bolts and remove the metal heat shield (where fitted) located over the filter housing (see illustration).

8 Using a large socket, unscrew the cover and remove it from the top of the oil filter housing (see illustrations). Lift out the old filter element.

9 Wipe clean the oil filter cover and the filter housing.

10 Lubricate the sealing rings of the new filter with clean engine oil, then, on Euro 5 emissions engines, insert the filter into the

3.6c . . . then remove the air intake duct retaining bolt (arrowed) . . .

3.6d . . . pull up the air cleaner housing and move it to one side

3.7 Undo the nut/bolts (arrowed) and remove the metal shield

3.8a Engine oil filter cap (arrowed) – pre-Euro 5 engines . . .

3.8b . . . and Euro 5 95 bhp engines (arrowed)

3.10a Lubricate the sealing rings (arrowed) . . .

3.10b . . . and fit the filter into the cover – Euro 5 engines

3.10c Lubricate the sealing rings (arrowed) . . .

3.10d . . . then insert the filter into the housing

3.11 Lubricate the new sealing ring

cover. On pre-Euro 5 emissions engines, fit the filter into the housing (see illustrations).

11 Renew the sealing ring on the oil filter cover, and lubricate the new sealing ring with clean engine oil (see illustration). Refit the oil filter cover and tighten it to the specified torque. Refit the heat shield (where applicable) over the filter housing.

12 After all the oil has drained, wipe the drain plug and the sealing washer/O-ring with a clean rag. Examine the condition of the sealing washer/O-ring, and renew it if it shows signs of damage which may prevent an oil-tight seal. Clean the area around the drain plug opening, and refit the plug complete with the washer/O-ring. Tighten the plug to the specified torque, using a torque wrench.

13 Remove the old oil and all tools from under the vehicle then refit the undertray (where applicable) and lower the vehicle to the ground.

14 Fill the engine through the filler tube using the correct grade and type of oil (refer to *Weekly checks* for details of topping-up). Pour in half the specified quantity of oil first, then wait a few minutes for the oil to drain into the sump. Continue to add oil, a small quantity at a time, until the level is up to the lower mark on the dipstick. Adding approximately a further 1.0 litre will bring the level up to the upper mark on the dipstick.

15 Start the engine and run it until it reaches normal operating temperature. While the engine is warming-up, check for leaks around the oil filter and the sump drain plug.

16 Stop the engine, and wait at least five minutes for the oil to settle in the sump once more. With the new oil circulated and the filter now completely full, recheck the level on the dipstick, and add more oil as necessary.

17 Dispose of the used engine oil and filter safely, with reference to *General repair procedures* in the Reference Chapter of this manual. Do not discard the old filter with domestic household waste. The facility for waste oil disposal provided by many local council refuse tips and/or recycling centres generally has a filter receptacle alongside.

Every 20 000 miles or 12 months

4 Hose and fluid leak check

Note: *Also refer to Section 8.*

1 Visually inspect the engine joint faces, gaskets and seals for any signs of water or oil leaks. Pay particular attention to the areas around the camshaft cover, cylinder head, oil filter and sump joint faces. Similarly, check the transmission and (where applicable) the air conditioning compressor for oil leakage. Bear in mind that, over a period of time, some very slight seepage from these areas is to be expected; what you are really looking for is any indication of a serious leak. Should a leak be found, renew the offending gasket or oil seal by referring to the appropriate Chapters in this manual.

2 Also check the security and condition of all the engine-related pipes and hoses. Ensure that all cable-ties or securing clips are in place, and in good condition. Clips which are broken or missing can lead to chafing of the hoses pipes or wiring, which could cause more serious problems in the future.

3 Carefully check the radiator hoses and heater hoses along their entire length. Renew any hose which is cracked, swollen or deteriorated. Cracks will show up better if the hose is squeezed. Pay close attention to the hose clips that secure the hoses to the cooling system components. Hose clips can pinch and puncture hoses, resulting in cooling system leaks. If wire-type hose clips are used, it may be a good idea to update them with screw-type clips.

4 Inspect all the cooling system components (hoses, joint faces, etc) for leaks. Where any problems of this nature are found on system components, renew the component or gasket with reference to Chapter 3 (see Haynes Hint).

A leak in the cooling system will usually show up as white- or antifreeze-coloured deposits on the area adjoining the leak.

5.3a Fuel filter drain screw (arrowed) – pre-Euro 5 engines

5.3b Fuel filter drain/bleed screw (arrowed) – Euro 5 engines

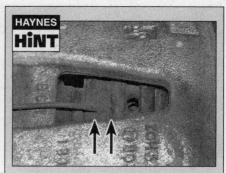

For a quick check, the thickness of the friction material remaining on the inner brake pad can be measured through the aperture in the caliper body.

5 With the vehicle raised, inspect the fuel tank and filler neck for punctures, cracks and other damage. The connection between the filler neck and tank is especially critical. Sometimes, a rubber filler neck or connecting hose will leak due to loose retaining clamps or deteriorated rubber.

6 Carefully check all rubber hoses and metal or plastic fuel lines leading away from the fuel tank. Check for loose connections, deteriorated hoses, crimped lines and other damage. Pay particular attention to the vent pipes and hoses, which often loop up around the filler neck and can become blocked or crimped. Follow the lines to the front of the vehicle, carefully inspecting them all the way. Renew damaged sections as necessary. Similarly, whilst the vehicle is raised, take the opportunity to inspect all underbody brake fluid pipes and hoses.

7 From within the engine compartment, check the security of all fuel hose attachments and pipe unions, and inspect the fuel hoses and vacuum hoses for kinks, chafing and deterioration.

5 Fuel filter water draining

Caution: Before starting any work on the fuel filter, wipe clean the filter assembly and the area around it; it is essential that no dirt or other foreign matter is allowed into the system. Obtain a suitable container into which the filter can be drained and place rags or similar material under the filter assembly to catch any spillages. Do not allow diesel fuel to contaminate components such as the alternator and starter motor, the coolant hoses and engine mountings, and any wiring.

1 The fuel filter is located at the rear of the engine compartment, on the left-hand side.
2 Attach a suitable length of plastic or rubber tube to the drain tube on the base or top of the fuel filter (as applicable), ensuring that the tube is a secure fit. Place the other end of the tube in a suitable container.
3 Unscrew the drain screw approximately two turns **(see illustrations)**.

4 Switch on the ignition for approximately 20 seconds. The in-tank fuel pump will pressurise the system and force water out of the drain screw outlet.
5 On completion, switch off the ignition and tighten the drain screw. Remove the drain tube and dispose of the drained water/fuel safely.

6 Front brake pad and disc check

1 Firmly apply the handbrake, then jack up the front of the vehicle and support it securely on axle stands (see *Jacking and vehicle support*). Remove the front roadwheels.
2 For a quick check, the pad thickness can be carried out via the inspection hole on the caliper **(see Haynes Hint)**. Using a steel rule, measure the thickness of the pad friction linings. This must not be less than that indicated in the *Specifications*.
3 The view through the caliper inspection hole gives a rough indication of the state of the brake pads. For a comprehensive check, the brake pads should be removed and cleaned. The operation of the caliper can then also be checked, and the condition of the brake disc itself can be fully examined on both sides. Chapter 9 contains a detailed description of how the brake disc should be checked for wear and/or damage.
4 If any pad's friction material is worn to the specified thickness or less, *all four pads must be renewed as a set*. Refer to Chapter 9 for details.
5 On completion, refit the roadwheels and lower the vehicle to the ground.

7 Rear brake shoe check

1 Chock the front wheels then jack up the rear of the car and support it on axle stands (see *Jacking and vehicle support*). Remove the rear roadwheels.
2 Using the inspection hole at the edge of the brake drum, check that the linings are not worn below the minimum thickness given

in the *Specifications* **(see illustration)**. If necessary use an electric torch.
3 If the friction material on any shoe is worn down to the specified minimum thickness or less, all four shoes must be renewed as a set.
4 At the same time check for signs of brake fluid leakage.
5 For a comprehensive check, the brake drum should be removed and cleaned. This will allow the wheel cylinders to be checked, and the condition of the brake drum itself to be fully examined (see Chapter 9).
6 On completion of the check, lower the car to the ground.

8 Brake fluid pipe and hose check

1 The brake hydraulic system includes a number of metal pipes, which run from the master cylinder to the hydraulic modulator of the anti-lock braking system (ABS) and then to the front and rear brake assemblies. Flexible hoses are fitted between the pipes and the front and rear brake assemblies, to allow for steering and suspension movement.
2 When checking the system, first look for signs of leakage at the pipe or hose unions, then examine the flexible hoses for signs of cracking, chafing or deterioration of the

7.2 Prise out the grommet and check the brake shoes linings through the inspection hole (arrowed)

9.4 Grasp the roadwheel and try to rock it

10.2 Check the condition of the CV joint gaiters

11.3 Check the condition of the exhaust rubber mountings (arrowed)

rubber. Bend the hoses sharply between the fingers (but do not actually bend them double, or the casing may be damaged) and check that this does not reveal previously-hidden cracks, cuts or splits. Check that the pipes and hoses are securely fastened in their clips.

3 Carefully working along the length of the metal pipes, look for dents, kinks, damage of any sort, or corrosion. Light corrosion can be polished off, but if the depth of pitting is significant, the pipe must be renewed.

9 Front suspension and steering check

1 Apply the handbrake, then raise the front of the vehicle and securely support it on axle stands (see *Jacking and vehicle support*).

2 Inspect the balljoint dust covers and the steering gear gaiters for splits, chafing or deterioration.

3 Any wear of these components will cause loss of lubricant, and may allow water to enter the components, resulting in rapid deterioration of the balljoints or steering gear.

4 Grasp each roadwheel at the 12 o'clock and 6 o'clock positions, and try to rock it **(see illustration)**. Very slight free play may be felt, but if the movement is appreciable, further investigation is necessary to determine the source. Continue rocking the wheel while an assistant depresses the footbrake. If the movement is now eliminated or significantly reduced, it is likely that the hub bearings are at fault. If the free play is still evident with the footbrake depressed, then there is wear in the suspension joints or mountings.

5 Now grasp each wheel at the 9 o'clock and 3 o'clock positions, and try to rock it as before. Any movement felt now may again be caused by wear in the hub bearings or the steering track rod end balljoints. If the track rod end balljoint is worn, the visual movement will be obvious.

6 Using a large screwdriver or flat bar, check for wear in the suspension mounting bushes by levering between the relevant suspension component and its attachment point. Some movement is to be expected, as the mountings are made of rubber, but excessive wear

should be obvious. Also check the condition of any visible rubber bushes, looking for splits, cracks or contamination of the rubber.

7 Check for any signs of fluid leakage around the suspension struts, or from the rubber gaiters around the piston rods. Should any fluid be noticed, the suspension strut is defective internally, and should be renewed. **Note:** *Suspension struts should always be renewed in pairs on the same axle.*

8 With the vehicle standing on its wheels, have an assistant turn the steering wheel back-and-forth about an eighth of a turn each way. There should be very little, if any, lost movement between the steering wheel and roadwheels. If this is not the case, closely observe the joints and mountings previously described. In addition, check the steering column universal joints for wear, and also check the rack-and-pinion steering gear itself.

9 The efficiency of each suspension strut may be checked by bouncing the vehicle at each front corner. Generally speaking, the body will return to its normal position and stop after being depressed. If it rises and returns on a rebound, the suspension strut is probably suspect. Also examine the suspension strut upper mountings for any signs of wear.

10 Driveshaft check

1 Firmly apply the handbrake, then jack up the front of the car and support it securely on axle stands (see *Jacking and vehicle support*).

2 Turn the steering onto full lock then slowly rotate the roadwheel. Inspect the condition of the outer constant velocity (CV) joint rubber gaiters while squeezing the gaiters to open out the folds **(see illustration)**. Check for signs of cracking, splits or deterioration of the rubber which may allow the grease to escape and lead to water and grit entry into the joint. Also check the security and condition of the retaining clips. Repeat these checks on the inner CV joints. If any damage or deterioration is found, the gaiters should be renewed as described in Chapter 8.

3 At the same time, check the general condition of the CV joints themselves by

first holding the driveshaft and attempting to rotate the wheel. Repeat this check by holding the inner joint and attempting to rotate the driveshaft. Any appreciable movement indicates wear in the joints, wear in the driveshaft splines or a loose driveshaft retaining nut.

11 Exhaust system check

1 With the engine cold (at least an hour after the vehicle has been driven), check the complete exhaust system from the engine to the end of the tailpipe. The exhaust system is most easily checked with the vehicle raised on a hoist, or suitably-supported on axle stands, so that the exhaust components are readily visible and accessible (see *Jacking and vehicle support*).

2 Check the exhaust pipes and connections for evidence of leaks, severe corrosion and damage. Make sure that all brackets and mountings are in good condition, and that all relevant nuts and bolts are tight. Leakage at any of the joints or in other parts of the system will usually show up as a black sooty stain in the vicinity of the leak.

3 Rattles and other noises can often be traced to the exhaust system, especially the brackets and mountings **(see illustration)**. Try to move the pipes and silencers. If the components are able to come into contact with the body or suspension parts, secure the system with new mountings. Otherwise separate the joints (if possible) and twist the pipes as necessary to provide additional clearance.

12 Rear suspension check

1 Chock the front wheels, then jack up the rear of the vehicle and support securely on axle stands (see *Jacking and vehicle support*).

2 Inspect the rear suspension components for any signs of obvious wear or damage. Pay particular attention to the rubber mounting bushes, and renew if necessary (see Chapter 10).

3 Grasp each roadwheel at the 12 o'clock and 6 o'clock positions **(see illustration 9.4)**, and try to rock it. Any excess movement indicates wear in the wheel bearings. Wear may also be accompanied by a rumbling sound when the wheel is spun, or a noticeable roughness if the wheel is turned slowly. The wheel bearing can be renewed as described in Chapter 10.

4 Check for any signs of fluid leakage around the shock absorber bodies. Should any fluid be noticed, the shock absorber is defective internally, and should be renewed. **Note:** *Shock absorbers should always be renewed in pairs on the same axle.*

5 With the vehicle standing on its wheels, the efficiency of each shock absorber may be checked by bouncing the vehicle at each rear corner. Generally speaking, the body will return to its normal position and stop after being depressed. If it rises and returns on a rebound, the shock absorber is probably suspect.

13 Bodywork and underbody condition check

1 Jack up the front and rear of the car and support it securely on axle stands (see *Jacking and vehicle support*). Alternatively position the car over an inspection pit.

2 Check the underbody, wheel housings and side sills for rust and/or damage to the underbody sealant. If evident, repair as necessary.

14 Hinge and lock lubrication

1 Work around the vehicle and lubricate the hinges of the bonnet, doors and tailgate with a light machine oil.

2 Lightly lubricate the bonnet release mechanism and exposed section of inner cable with a smear of grease.

3 Check the security and operation of all hinges, latches and locks, adjusting them where required. Check the operation of the central locking system.

4 Check the condition and operation of the

16.2c Footwell kick panel screws (arrowed) – 500 models

bonnet and tailgate support struts, renewing them both if either is leaking or no longer able to support the bonnet/tailgate securely when raised.

15 Electrical systems check

1 Check the operation of all the electrical equipment, ie, lights, direction indicators, horn, etc. Refer to the appropriate sections of Chapter 12 for details if any of the circuits are found to be inoperative.

2 Note that the brake light switch is described in Chapter 9.

3 Check all accessible wiring connectors, harnesses and retaining clips for security, and for signs of chafing or damage. Rectify any faults found.

16 Pollen filter renewal

1 The pollen filter is located under the facia on the driver's side, adjacent to the heater blower motor.

2 Undo the retaining screw(s) remove the footwell kick panel adjacent to the heater air distribution housing **(see illustrations)**.

3 Unclip the cover, and withdraw the filter from its housing **(see illustrations)**.

4 Wipe clean the filter housing then fit the new filter. Refit the cover and footwell panel.

16.2a Undo the screws (arrowed) . . .

16.3a Unclip the cover (arrowed) . . .

17 Road test

Instruments and electrical equipment

1 Check the operation of all instruments, warning lights and electrical equipment.

2 Make sure that all instruments read correctly, and switch on all electrical equipment in turn, to check that it functions properly.

Steering and suspension

3 Check for any abnormalities in the steering, suspension, handling or road 'feel'.

4 Drive the vehicle, and check that there are no unusual vibrations or noises.

5 Check that the steering feels positive, with no excessive 'sloppiness', or roughness, and check for any suspension noises when cornering and driving over bumps.

Drivetrain

6 Check the performance of the engine, clutch, transmission and driveshafts.

7 Listen for any unusual noises from the engine, clutch and transmission.

8 Make sure that the engine runs smoothly when idling, and that there is no hesitation when accelerating.

9 Check that the clutch action is smooth and progressive, that the drive is taken up smoothly, and that the pedal travel is not

16.2b . . . and remove the footwell kick panel – Panda models

16.3b . . . and pull out the pollen filter element

excessive. Also listen for any noises when the clutch pedal is depressed.

10 Check that all gears can be engaged smoothly without noise, and that the gear lever action is smooth and not abnormally vague or 'notchy'.

11 Listen for a metallic clicking sound from the front of the vehicle, as the vehicle is driven slowly in a circle with the steering on full lock. Carry out this check in both directions. If a clicking noise is heard, this indicates wear in a driveshaft joint (see Chapter 8).

Braking system

12 Make sure that the vehicle does not pull to one side when braking.

13 Check that there is no vibration through the steering when braking. **Note:** *Under heavy braking, vibration may be felt through the brake pedal. This is a normal feature of ABS operation, and does not constitute a fault*

14 Check that the handbrake operates correctly, without excessive movement of the lever, and that it holds the vehicle stationary on a slope.

15 Test the operation of the brake servo unit as follows. Depress the footbrake four or five times to exhaust the vacuum, then start the engine. As the engine starts, there should be a noticeable 'give' in the brake pedal as vacuum builds-up. Allow the engine to run for at least two minutes, and then switch it off. If the brake pedal is now depressed again, it should be possible to detect a hiss from the servo as the pedal is depressed. After about four or five applications, no further hissing should be heard, and the pedal should feel considerably harder.

Every 40 000 miles or 2 years

18 Air cleaner element renewal

1 The air cleaner is located above the engine.
2 Undo the screws and remove the air filter cover (see illustrations).

Pre-Euro 5 emissions level

3 Lift out the seal, and remove the filter element (see illustration).

Euro 5 emissions level

4 Lift out the filter element (see illustration).

All models

5 Wipe out the casing and the cover.
6 Fit the new filter, noting that the rubber locating flange should be uppermost, and secure the cover with the screws.
7 Refit the upper air intake hose and reconnect the airflow meter wiring connector.

19 Auxiliary drivebelt check and renewal

Note: *The manufacturers recommend that the tensioner roller is checked and if necessary renewed at the same time as the drivebelt.*

Check

1 Due to their function and material make-up, drivebelts are prone to failure after a long period of time and should therefore be inspected regularly.

2 Apply the handbrake, then jack up the front of the vehicle and support it on axle stands (see *Jacking and vehicle support*). Remove the right-hand front roadwheel and the wheel arch liner covers for access to the right-hand side of the engine. On 500 models, undo the 2 bolts and remove the support bracket between the front subframe and the vehicle body, prior to removing the wheel arch liner panel (see illustrations).

3 With the engine stopped, inspect the full length of the drivebelt for cracks and separation of the belt plies. It will be necessary to turn the engine (using a spanner or socket and bar on the crankshaft pulley bolt) so that the belt can be inspected thoroughly. Twist the belt between the pulleys so that both sides can be viewed. Also check for fraying, and glazing which gives the belt a shiny

18.2a Air filter cover screws (arrowed) – pre-Euro 5 models . . .

18.2b . . . and Euro 5 models (arrowed)

18.3 Air filter element – pre-Euro 5 models

18.4 Air filter element – Euro 5 models

19.2a Remove the front section and centre section of the wheel arch liner (arrowed)

19.2b On 500 models, undo the bolts (arrowed) and remove the support bracket

19.6 Rotate the tensioner clockwise to relieve the tension

appearance. Check the pulleys for nicks, cracks, distortion and corrosion. If the belt shows signs of wear or damage, it should be renewed as a precaution against breakage in service.

Renewal

4 If not already done, apply the handbrake, then jack up the front of the vehicle and support it on axle stands (see *Jacking and vehicle support*). Remove the right-hand front roadwheel and the wheel arch liner cover for access to the right-hand side of the engine. On 500 models, undo the 2 bolts and remove the support bracket between the front subframe and the vehicle body, prior to removing the wheel arch liner panel **(see illustrations 21.2a and 21.2b)**.

5 If the drivebelt is to be re-used, mark it to indicate its normal running direction.

6 Using a spanner on the pulley centre bolt, turn the tensioner clockwise, against the spring tension **(see illustration)**.

7 Slip the drivebelt from the pulleys.

8 Locate the new drivebelt on the pulleys in the correct routing. If the drivebelt is being re-used, make sure it is fitted the correct way around.

9 Turn back the tensioner, then release it, making sure that the drivebelt ribs locate correctly on each of the pulley grooves.

10 The remainder of refitting is a reversal of removal.

20 Handbrake operation and adjustment check

Apply the handbrake by pulling it through a maximum of five clicks of the ratchet mechanism and check that this locks the rear wheels, holding the vehicle stationary on an incline. In this position, there should be sufficient reserve travel in the handbrake lever to allow for brake shoe wear and cable stretching. If not, the handbrake mechanism should be adjusted as described in Chapter 9.

Every 2 years

21 Remote control battery renewal

Panda models

1 Using a small flat-bladed screwdriver, prise apart the halves of the key casing **(see illustrations)**.

2 Note the orientation of the battery, and remove it from the casing.

3 Insert the new battery into place, with the positive (+) side upwards **(see illustration)**. Avoid touching the battery or the terminals with bare fingers.

4 Snap the 2 halves of the control together, and check for correct operation.

500 models

5 Press the button to release the key blade.

6 Rotate the screw to the 'unlock' position

and remove the battery case from the side of the fob **(see illustrations)**.

7 Note the orientation of the battery, and remove it from the casing.

8 Insert the new battery into place, with the positive (+) side of the battery on the same side as the positive mark on the casing **(see illustration)**. Avoid touching the battery or the terminals with bare fingers.

9 Refit the battery case and rotate the screw to the 'locked' position.

21.1a Carefully prise apart . . .

21.1b . . . the halves of the casing

21.3 Fit the new battery, positive (+) side up

21.6a Rotate the screw to the 'unlock' position . . .

21.6b . . . and remove the battery case

21.8 The positive (+) mark on the battery must be on the same side as the mark on the casing (arrowed)

22 Hydraulic fluid renewal

⚠ *Warning: Hydraulic fluid can harm your eyes and damage painted surfaces, so use extreme caution when handling and pouring it. Do not use fluid that has been standing open for some time, as it absorbs moisture from the air. Excess moisture can cause a dangerous loss of braking effectiveness.*

1 The procedure is similar to that for the bleeding of the hydraulic system as described in Chapter 9, except that the brake fluid reservoir should be emptied by siphoning, using a clean poultry baster or similar before starting, and allowance should be made for the old fluid to be expelled when bleeding a section of the circuit.

2 Working as described in Chapter 9, open the first bleed screw in the sequence, and pump the brake pedal gently until nearly all the old fluid has been emptied from the master cylinder reservoir.

3 Top-up to the MAX level with new fluid, and continue pumping until only the new fluid remains in the reservoir, and new fluid can be seen emerging from the bleed screw. Tighten the screw, and top the reservoir level up to the MAX level line.

4 Work through all the remaining bleed screws in the sequence until new fluid can be seen at all of them. Be careful to keep the master cylinder reservoir topped-up to above the MIN level at all times, or air may enter the system and greatly increase the length of the task.

5 When the operation is complete, check that all bleed screws are securely tightened, and that their dust caps are refitted. Wash off all traces of spilt fluid, and recheck the master cylinder reservoir fluid level.

6 Check the operation of the brakes before taking the car on the road.

23 Coolant renewal

Note: *Fiat do not specify renewal intervals for the antifreeze mixture, as the mixture used to fill the system when the vehicle is new is designed to last the lifetime of the vehicle. However, it is strongly recommended that the coolant is renewed at the intervals specified in the Maintenance schedule as a precaution against possible engine corrosion problems. This is particularly advisable if the coolant has been renewed using an antifreeze other than that specified by Fiat. With many antifreeze types, the corrosion inhibitors become progressively less effective with age. It is up to the individual owner whether or not to follow this advice.*

⚠ *Warning: Wait until the engine is cold before starting this procedure. Do not allow antifreeze*

23.2 Radiator lower hose release clip (arrowed) – shown with the bumper removed for clarity

to come in contact with your skin, or with the painted surfaces of the vehicle. Rinse off spills immediately with plenty of water. Never leave antifreeze lying around in an open container, or in a puddle in the driveway or on the garage floor. Children and pets are attracted by its sweet smell, but antifreeze can be fatal if ingested.

Cooling system draining

1 With the engine completely cold, cover the expansion tank cap with a wad of rag, and slowly turn the cap anti-clockwise to relieve the pressure in the cooling system (a hissing sound will normally be heard). Wait until any pressure remaining in the system is released, then continue to turn the cap until it can be removed.

Panda models

2 Position a suitable container beneath the radiator bottom hose connection, then release the retaining clip and ease the hose from the radiator stub **(see illustration)**. If the hose joint has not been disturbed for some time, it will be necessary to gently manipulate the hose to break the joint. Do not use excessive force, or the radiator stub could be damaged. Allow the coolant to drain into the container.

500 models

3 A drain plug is located at the lower left-hand end of the radiator. Position a suitable container beneath, then undo the drain plug and allow the coolant to escape **(see illustration)**.

23.4 Radiator bleed screw (arrowed) – radiator removed for clarity

23.3 The drain plug (arrowed) is at the left-hand end of the radiator

All models

4 The cooling system bleed screws should be opened to aid the draining process and help prevent airlocks. These are located on the top right-hand edge of the radiator (all models), and on the heater inlet hose (not 95 bhp models) **(see illustration)**. If the coolant has been drained for a reason other than renewal, then provided it is clean and less than two years old, it can be re-used, though this is not recommended.

5 Once all the coolant has drained, reconnect the hose to the radiator and secure it in position with the retaining clip, or tighten the drain plug as applicable.

Radiator flushing

6 Refer to Chapter 3.

Cooling system filling

7 Before attempting to fill the cooling system, make sure that all hoses and clips are in good condition, and that the clips are tight. Note that an antifreeze mixture must be used all year round, to prevent corrosion of the engine components (see below).

8 Remove the expansion tank filler cap, and fill the system by slowly pouring the coolant into the expansion tank to prevent airlocks from forming. Ensure that all bleed screws are open.

9 If the coolant is being renewed, begin by pouring in a couple of litres of water, followed by the correct quantity of antifreeze, then top-up with more water. Periodically squeeze the radiator top and bottom hoses to help expel any trapped air in the system.

10 Continue adding coolant until it is seen to emerge from the bleed screws. Close each bleed screw in turn as the coolant emerges.

11 Top-up the coolant level to the MAX mark and refit the expansion tank cap. Ensure that all bleed screws are closed.

12 Start the engine and run it at idling speed for two to three minutes. Allow the engine to continue running until the electric cooling fan operates, periodically increasing the engine speed gradually to 2000 to 3000 rpm.

13 Stop the engine and allow it to cool down completely.

14 Check for leaks, particularly around disturbed components. Check the coolant level in the expansion tank, and top-up if necessary. Note that the system must be cold before an accurate level is indicated in the expansion tank.

Antifreeze mixture

15 The antifreeze should always be renewed at the specified intervals. This is necessary not only to maintain the antifreeze properties, but also to prevent corrosion which would otherwise occur as the corrosion inhibitors become progressively less effective.

16 Always use a monoethylene-glycol based antifreeze of the specified type (see *Lubricants*

and fluids). The quantity of antifreeze and level of protection are indicated in the *Specifications*.

17 Before adding antifreeze, the cooling system should be completely drained, preferably flushed, and all hoses checked for condition and security.

18 After filling with antifreeze, a label should be attached to the expansion tank, stating the type and concentration of antifreeze used, and the date installed. Any subsequent topping-up should be made with the same type and concentration of antifreeze.

Caution: Do not use engine antifreeze in the windscreen/tailgate washer system, as it will cause damage to the vehicle paintwork. A screenwash additive should be added to the washer system in the quantities stated on the bottle.

24 Exhaust emission check

1 The exhaust emission check is carried out initially after 3 years, then every 2 years, however, on vehicles which are subject to intensive use (eg, taxis/hire cars/ambulances) it must be carried out annually. The check involves checking the engine management system operation by plugging an electronic tester into the system diagnostic socket to check the electronic control unit (ECU) memory for faults (see Chapter 4B).

2 In reality, if the vehicle is running correctly and the engine management warning light in the instrument panel is functioning normally, then this check need not be carried out.

Every 3 years

25 Fuel filter renewal

Caution: Before starting any work on the fuel filter, wipe clean the filter assembly and the area around it; it is essential that no dirt or other foreign matter is allowed into the system. Obtain a suitable container into which the filter can be drained and place rags or similar material under the filter assembly to catch any spillages.

Do not allow diesel fuel to contaminate components such as the starter motor, the coolant hoses and engine mountings, and any wiring.

1 The fuel filter is located at the rear of the engine compartment, on the right-hand side.

Pre-Euro 5 emissions level

2 Disconnect the wiring plug from the preheating device on the top of the filter assembly (see illustration).

3 Note their fitted positions, and disconnect the fuel pipe from the top of the filter cover at the quick-release connector (see illustration).

Suitably cover or plug the open hose connections to prevent dirt entry.

4 Undo the collar at the top of the filter, using a suitable tool, then lift the filter element and cover assembly from place (see illustrations).

5 Rotate the filter element clockwise approximately 50°, and pull it from the cover (see illustration).

6 The new filter element is supplied in a protective casing. Remove the upper part of the casing, align the arrows on the top of the element with the arrows on the underside of

25.2 Slide out the locking peg and disconnect the wiring plug

25.3 Pull back the collar and disconnect the fuel pipe

25.4a Using a suitable tool, slacken . . .

25.4b . . . and remove the collar . . .

25.4c . . . followed by the cover and filter element

25.5 Rotate the filter element 50° <u>clockwise</u> and detach it from the cover

25.6a Open the top part of the filter protective casing . . .

25.6b . . . and align the arrows

25.8 Renew the sealing ring

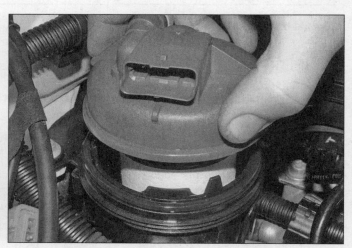

25.9 The cover will only fit in one position

25.11 Pull back the yellow catch (1), then depress the release buttons (2) and disconnect the hoses

25.12 Undo the clamp bolt (arrowed)

25.13 Disconnect the wiring plug from the base of the filter

the cover, and press the element into place **(see illustrations)**. Try not to touch the filter element with bare fingers.

7 Remove the lower part of the element protective casing.
8 Renew the sealing ring at the top of the filter housing **(see illustration)**.
9 Lower the filter/cover into the housing, noting that it will only fit correctly in one position **(see illustration)**. Refit the collar and tighten it to the specified torque. If a suitable tool is not available, tighten the collar securely.
10 Reconnect the fuel pipe, and preheater wiring plug.

Euro 5 emissions level

11 Release the connectors and disconnect the hoses from the top of the filter **(see illustration)**. Suitably cover or plug the open hose connections to prevent dirt entry.

12 Undo the retaining bolt and open the filter clamp **(see illustration)**. Take care not to drop the clamp.
13 Slide the filter upwards and disconnect the wiring plug from the base **(see illustration)**.
14 Reconnect the wiring plug, and lower the filter into position.
15 Close the retaining clamp, and tighten the retaining bolt securely.
16 Reconnect the fuel hoses.

All models

17 Bleed the fuel system as described in Chapter 4B and check all disturbed components to ensure that there are no leaks (of air or fuel) when the engine is restarted.
18 On completion, safely dispose of the drained fuel.

Every 48 000 miles

26 Manual transmission oil level check

1 Park the car on a level surface, if possible over an inspection pit or on a ramp as the filler/level plug is best reached from under the engine compartment. The oil level must be checked before the car is driven, or at least 5 minutes after the engine has been switched off. If the oil is checked immediately after driving the car, some of the oil will remain distributed around the transmission components, resulting in an inaccurate level reading.
2 Wipe clean the area around the filler/level plug, which is situated on the front of the

transmission **(see illustration)**. Using an Allen key, unscrew the plug and clean it.
3 The oil level should reach the lower edge of the filler/level hole. A certain amount of oil will have gathered behind the filler/level plug, and will trickle out when it is removed; this does **not** necessarily indicate that the level is correct. To ensure that a true level is established, wait until the initial trickle has stopped, then add oil as necessary until a trickle of new oil can be seen emerging. The level will be correct when the flow ceases; use only good-quality oil of the specified type. Make sure that the vehicle is completely level when checking the level and do not overfill.
4 When the level is correct refit and tighten the plug and wipe away any spilt oil.

26.2 The filler/level plug (arrowed) is located on the front of the transmission

Chapter 2 Part A:
Petrol engine in-car repair procedures

Contents

Degrees of difficulty

Easy, suitable for novice with little experience	**Fairly easy,** suitable for beginner with some experience	**Fairly difficult,** suitable for competent DIY mechanic	**Difficult,** suitable for experienced DIY mechanic	**Very difficult,** suitable for expert DIY or professional

Specifications

General

Engine code:*	
1108 cc engine	187.A1.000
1242 cc engine:	
Euro 4	188.A4.000
Euro 5	169.A4.000
Bore:	
1108 cc engine	70.0 mm
1242 cc engine	70.8 mm
Stroke:	
1108 cc engine	72.0 mm
1242 cc engine	78.86 mm
Compression ratio:	
1108 cc engine	9.6:1
1242 cc engine:	
Euro 4	9.8:1
Euro 5	11.1:1
Engine output:	
Power:	
1108 cc engine	54 bhp (40 kW) @ 5000 rpm
1242 cc engine:	
Euro 4	60 bhp (44 kW) @ 5000 rpm
Euro 5	70 bhp (51 kW) @ 5500 rpm
Torque:	
1108 cc engine	88 Nm @ 2750 rpm
1242 cc engine:	
Euro 4	102 Nm @ 2500 rpm
Euro 5	102 Nm @ 3000 rpm
Firing order	1-3-4-2
No 1 cylinder location	Timing belt (right-hand) end of engine
Timing belt tension	see Text

* **Note:** *See 'Vehicle identification' for the location of code marking on the engine.*

Lubrication system

Oil pump type	By-rotor driven from front of crankshaft
Outer rotor-to-housing clearance	0.080 to 0.186 mm
Axial clearance	0.025 to 0.056 mm

Torque wrench settings

	Nm	lbf ft
Big-end bearing cap bolts:*		
Stage 1	20	15
Stage 2	Angle-tighten a further 40°	
Camshaft bearing cap bolts:		
M6	10	7
M8	20	15
Camshaft cover bolts	8	6
Camshaft sprocket bolt	70	52
Crankshaft oil seal housing bolts	10	7
Crankshaft pulley bolts	25	18
Crankshaft sprocket centre bolt:		
Stage 1	20	15
Stage 2	Angle-tighten a further 90°	
Cylinder head bolts:*		
Stage 1	30	22
Stage 2	Angle-tighten a further 90°	
Stage 3	Angle-tighten a further 90°	
Engine/transmission attachment bolts	80	59
Engine/transmission mountings:		
Left hand mounting-to-body nuts	50	37
Left-hand mounting bracket-to-transmission bolts	50	37
Left-hand mounting centre bolt:		
Panda models	80	59
500 models	130	96
Rear mounting-to-subframe bolt	80	59
Rear mounting-to-transmission bolt/nut	80	59
Right-hand mounting lower bracket-to-cylinder head bolts:		
Panda models	50	37
500 models	60	44
Right-hand mounting upper bracket-to-lower bracket nuts:		
Panda models	50	37
500 models	60	44
Right-hand mounting-to-body nuts:		
Panda models	50	37
500 models	60	44
Flywheel bolts:*		
Stage 1	15	11
Stage 2	Angle-tighten a further 40°	
Main bearing cap bolts:		
Stage 1	20	15
Stage 2	Angle-tighten a further 90°	
Oil pressure warning light switch	30	22
Oil pump retaining bolts	10	7
Subframe to body support bracket (500 models)	50	37
Sump nuts/bolts:		
M6	10	7
M8	25	18
Timing belt tensioner nut	28	21

* Do not re-use.

1 General information

Using this Chapter

This Part of Chapter 2 is devoted to in-car repair procedures for the petrol engine. Similar information covering the diesel engines will be found in Part B of this Chapter. Part C covers the removal of the engine/transmission as a unit, and describes the engine dismantling and overhaul procedures.

In Parts A and B, the assumption is made that the engine is installed in the car, with all ancillaries connected. If the engine has been removed for overhaul, the preliminary dismantling information which precedes each operation may be ignored.

Engine description

The engine covered in this Part of Chapter 2 is a water-cooled, single overhead camshaft (SOHC), in-line four-cylinder unit, with cast iron cylinder block and aluminium-alloy cylinder head. The engine is mounted transversely at the front of the car, with the transmission bolted to the left-hand end.

The cylinder head carries the camshaft which is driven by a toothed timing belt and runs in three bearings. It also houses the intake and exhaust valves, which are closed by single coil springs, and which run in guides pressed into the cylinder head. The camshaft actuates the valves directly via cam followers mounted in the cylinder head. Adjustment of the valve clearances is by means of shims located on top of the followers. The cylinder head contains integral oilways which supply and lubricate the followers (tappets).

The crankshaft is supported by five main bearings, and endfloat is controlled by a thrust bearing fitted to the upper section of the centre main bearing.

Engine coolant is circulated by a pump, driven by the timing belt. For details of the cooling system, refer to Chapter 3.

Lubricant is circulated under pressure by a pump, driven from the front of the crankshaft. Oil is drawn from the sump through a strainer, and then forced through an externally-mounted, renewable screw-on filter. From there, it is distributed to the cylinder head, where it lubricates the camshaft journals and tappets, and also to the crankcase, where it lubricates the main bearings, connecting rod big- and small-ends, gudgeon pins and cylinder bores.

Operations with engine in car

The following work can be carried out with the engine in the vehicle:
a) Compression pressure – testing.
b) Valve clearances – checking and adjustment (see Chapter 1A).
c) Camshaft cover – removal and refitting.
d) Timing belt covers – removal and refitting.
e) Timing belt – removal, refitting and adjustment.
f) Timing belt tensioner and sprockets – removal and refitting.
g) Camshaft and cam followers – removal and refitting.
h) Cylinder head – removal and refitting.
i) Camshaft oil seal – renewal.
j) Crankshaft oil seals – renewal.
k) Flywheel – removal, inspection and refitting.
l) Engine mountings – inspection and renewal.
m) Sump – removal and refitting.
n) Oil pump and pick-up tube assembly – removal, inspection and refitting.

2 Top dead centre (TDC) for No 1 piston – locating

General information

1 The camshaft is driven by the crankshaft, by means of a timing belt and sprockets. Both sprockets rotate in phase with each other and this provides the correct valve timing as the engine rotates. When the timing belt is removed during servicing or repair, it is possible for the camshaft and crankshaft to rotate independently of each other and the correct valve timing is then lost.
2 The design of the engine is such that potentially damaging piston-to-valve contact may occur if the camshaft is rotated when any of the pistons are stationary at, or near, the top of their stroke.
3 For this reason it is important that the correct phasing between the camshaft and crankshaft is preserved whilst the timing belt is off the engine. This is achieved by setting the engine in a reference position (known as Top Dead Centre or TDC) before the timing belt is removed and then preventing the camshaft and crankshaft from rotating until the belt is refitted. Similarly, if the engine has been dismantled for overhaul, the engine can be set to the correct position during reassembly to ensure that the correct shaft phasing is restored.
4 TDC is the highest point in the cylinder that each piston reaches as the crankshaft turns. Each piston reaches TDC at the end of the compression stroke and again at the end of the exhaust stroke. However, for the purpose of timing the engine, TDC refers to the position of No 1 piston at the end of its compression stroke. On all engines in this manual, No 1 piston (and cylinder) is at the timing belt end of the engine.
5 On 500 models, only the post-modification 1.2 litre engine (EV02 or Euro 5) is fitted. On Panda models 2 types of engine are fitted (see illustrations):

Pre-modification engines

Square, press-fit oil filler caps, and camshaft covers retained by 4 bolts.

2.5a Pre-modification engine. Note the square oil filler cap (arrowed)

2.5b EV02 engine. Note the round oil filler cap, and the camshaft position sensor (arrowed)

2.5c Euro 5 emissions level engines still have a round oil filler cap . . .

2.5d . . . but the engine management ECU is bolted to the left-hand end of the cylinder head cover

2.13a Camshaft sprocket and cylinder head TDC timing marks aligned (arrowed)

2.13b Crankshaft sprocket and oil pump casing TDC marks aligned (arrowed)

Post-modification EV02 engines

Round oil filler caps, camshaft covers retained by 8 bolts, camshaft position sensor at the timing belt end of the camshaft cover, and a conventional throttle cable.

Euro 5 emissions level engines

Round oil filler caps, camshaft covers retained by 8 bolts, no throttle cable fitted, and the engine management ECU bolted to the left-hand end of the camshaft cover.

6 Pre-modification engines are further split into two types, depending on engine numbers. Consequently there are three different procedures for locating the correct position for the piston in cylinder No 1. On pre-modification engines it will be necessary to refer to the engine number to determine which procedure is to be followed. The engine number is stamped on the cylinder block, just below the cylinder head joint at the timing belt end.

7 With the engine identified, refer to procedure A, B or C as follows:

Engine number up to 2533527 (pre-modification) – refer to Procedure A.
Engine number from 2533528 (pre-modification) – refer to Procedure B.
Post-modification engines (EV02/Euro 5 emissions level) – refer to Procedure C.

Procedure A

8 The camshaft sprocket is equipped with a marking which, when aligned with a reference notch on the cylinder head, indicates that the camshaft is correctly positioned with

the piston of cylinder No 1 at TDC on its compression stroke.

9 The crankshaft sprocket is also equipped with a timing mark – when this is aligned with a reference marking on the oil pump cover, the engine is set with the pistons of cylinders No 1 and 4 at TDC. Note that it is the camshaft positioning that determines whether a piston is on its compression or exhaust stroke.

10 Remove the timing belt upper and lower covers as described in Section 4.

11 Remove the spark plugs as described in Chapter 1A.

12 Turn the engine in its normal direction of rotation (using a socket or spanner on the crankshaft sprocket centre bolt) until pressure can be felt at No 1 cylinder spark plug hole.

13 Continue turning the engine until the camshaft sprocket TDC timing mark is aligned with the notch on the cylinder head and the crankshaft sprocket timing mark is aligned with the mark on the oil pump casing **(see illustrations)**.

14 The engine is now set at TDC for No 1 cylinder on compression.

Procedure B

Note: *Fiat special tools 1.860.895.000, 1.871.008.400 and 2.000.004.000 will be required for this procedure. Note that these tools may be readily available from automotive tools specialists.*

15 The engines in the range covered by this procedure are not equipped with conventional timing marks and it is therefore necessary to

use special tools to determine TDC for No 1 piston, and the correct corresponding position for the camshaft.

16 Remove the timing belt upper and lower covers as described in Section 4.

17 Remove the spark plugs as described in Chapter 1A.

18 Identify the spark plug HT leads at their ignition coil connections, then disconnect the leads from the two coils. Also disconnect the LT wiring connector from each coil.

19 Undo the retaining bolt, and the upper and lower retaining nuts, and remove the ignition coils, complete with mounting bracket, from the end of the cylinder head **(see illustrations)**.

20 Turn the engine in its normal direction of rotation (using a socket or spanner on the crankshaft sprocket centre bolt) until pressure can be felt at No 1 cylinder spark plug hole.

21 It is now necessary to set up a dial test indicator so that the TDC position of No 1 piston can be determined. If Fiat special tool 1.860.895.000 (comprising an adapter for the dial test indicator) is available, screw it into No 1 spark plug hole and mount the gauge on the adapter. If the Fiat tool is not available, an alternative method is as follows.

22 Mount a conventional dial test indicator in a suitable position (using a piece of scrap metal as a mounting bracket, if necessary) so that the gauge probe is directly above No 1 spark plug location. Obtain a length of dowel rod to act as an extension to the gauge probe, and round off one end of the rod with a file.

23 To make a guide for the dowel rod, break off the ceramic upper section of an old spark plug and remove the centre electrode and earth tip. The easiest way to do this is to mount the spark plug in a vice (after removing the ceramic upper section) and drill a hole down through the centre of the plug. The diameter of the drill bit should be the same as the diameter of the dowel rod to be used.

24 Screw the spark plug guide into No 1 spark plug hole, then insert the dowel rod (round end first) through the plug into No 1 cylinder so that it contacts the piston. Move the dial test indicator into position with its probe contacting the dowel rod **(see illustration)**.

25 Turn the engine by means of the crankshaft

2.19a Undo the retaining bolt and the upper/lower retaining nuts . . .

2.19b . . . then remove the ignition coil, complete with mounting bracket

2.24 Dial test indicator and probe set up for checking TDC on No 1 piston

2.26 The locking tool (1) fits into the slot (2) in the end of the camshaft

2.34a Note that the slot in the camshaft (arrowed) is _not_ horizontal

2.34b The locking tool (arrowed) fits into the slot and is secured to the upper surface of the cylinder head

sprocket until the highest reading is shown on the gauge, indicating that No 1 piston is at TDC. Take care when doing this as it is very easy for the dowel rod to jam in its guide.

26 At the other end of the engine, observe the position of the slot in the end of the camshaft, visible through the opening normally covered by the ignition coil mounting bracket. Fit the special tool (No 2.000.004.000) into the slot in the camshaft, and secure it to the cylinder head and cover **(see illustration)**. The engine is now correctly set at TDC for No 1 cylinder on compression.

27 If the tool will not align with the camshaft slot and the studs, remove the dowel rod (to avoid jamming) then turn the crankshaft through one complete revolution, returning No 1 piston to the TDC position as described above.

Procedure C

Note: *Fiat special tools 2.000.004.400 and 2.000.004.500 (or alternatives) will be required for this procedure.*

28 The engines in the range covered by this procedure are not equipped with conventional timing marks and it is therefore necessary to use special tools to determine the correct position for No 1 piston, and the correct corresponding position for the camshaft.

29 Remove the camshaft cover as described in Section 7.

30 Remove the timing belt upper and lower covers as described in Section 4.

31 Remove the spark plugs as described in Chapter 1A.

Panda models

32 Identify the spark plug HT leads at their ignition coil connections, then disconnect the leads from the coils. Also disconnect the LT wiring connector from the coils.

33 Undo the retaining fasteners, and remove the ignition coils as described in Chapter 5B.

All models

34 Turn the engine by means of the crankshaft sprocket until the Fiat tool No 2.000.004.400 locates correctly in the slot at the left-hand end of the camshaft, and with the upper mating surface of the cylinder head. Secure the tool to the cylinder head using the bolt(s) provided. Note that aftermarket equivalents of these tools may be available **(see illustrations)**.

35 With the camshaft locked in place it must be possible to locate the crankshaft locking

tool (No 2.000.004.500) over the end of the crankshaft, and secure it to the engine block as shown **(see illustration)**.

3 Compression test – description and interpretation

1 When engine performance is down, or if misfiring occurs which cannot be attributed to the ignition or fuel systems, a compression test can provide diagnostic clues as to the engine's condition. If the test is performed regularly, it can give warning of trouble before any other symptoms become apparent.

2 The engine must be fully warmed-up to normal operating temperature, the battery must be fully-charged, and all the spark plugs must be removed (see Chapter 1A). The aid of an assistant will also be required.

3 Disable the ignition and fuel injection systems by disconnecting the wiring multiplug connectors at the engine management ECU, referring to Chapter 4A for further information.

4 Fit a compression tester to the No 1 cylinder spark plug hole – the type of tester which screws into the plug thread is to be preferred.

5 Have the assistant hold the throttle wide open, and crank the engine on the starter motor; after one or two revolutions, the compression pressure should build-up to a

2.34c Suitable tools like these from Auto Service Tools Limited are needed

2.35 Lock the crankshaft with the special tool as shown (arrowed)

4.4 Pull back the yellow locking catch, and disconnect the camshaft position sensor wiring plug (arrowed)

4.6 Undo the nuts (arrowed) and remove the right-hand engine mounting and bracket

maximum figure, and then stabilise. Record the highest reading obtained.

6 Repeat the test on the remaining cylinders, recording the pressure in each.

7 All cylinders should produce very similar pressures; a difference of more than 2 bars between any two cylinders indicates a fault. Note that the compression should build-up quickly in a healthy engine; low compression on the first stroke, followed by gradually-increasing pressure on successive strokes, indicates worn piston rings. A low compression reading on the first stroke, which does not build-up during successive strokes, indicates leaking valves or a blown head gasket (a cracked head could also be the cause). Deposits on the undersides of the valve heads can also cause low compression.

8 Although Fiat do not specify exact compression pressures, as a guide, any cylinder pressure of below 10 bars can be considered as less than healthy. Refer to a Fiat dealer or other specialist if in doubt as to whether a particular pressure reading is acceptable.

9 If the pressure in any cylinder is low, carry out the following test to isolate the cause. Introduce a teaspoonful of clean oil into that cylinder through its spark plug hole, and repeat the test.

10 If the addition of oil temporarily improves the compression pressure, this indicates that bore or piston wear is responsible for the pressure loss. No improvement suggests that leaking or burnt valves, or a blown head gasket, may be to blame.

11 A low reading from two adjacent cylinders is almost certainly due to the head gasket having blown between them; the presence of coolant in the engine oil will confirm this.

12 If the compression reading is unusually high, the combustion chambers are probably coated with carbon deposits. If this is the case, the cylinder head should be removed and decarbonised.

13 On completion of the test, refit the spark plugs and reconnect the engine management ECU wiring connectors.

4 Timing belt covers – removal and refitting

Removal

Upper cover

1 Disconnect the battery negative terminal as described in Chapter 5A.

2 Although not strictly necessary, to improve access, remove the air cleaner assembly as described in Chapter 4A.

3 If both the upper and lower timing belt covers are to be removed, firmly apply the handbrake, then jack up the front of the car and support it securely on axle stands (see *Jacking and vehicle support*). Remove the right-hand front roadwheel, then undo the fasteners and remove the engine undertray (where fitted).

4 On all except Euro 5 emissions engines, disconnect the wiring connector from the camshaft position sensor, then undo the

bolt and pull the sensor from place **(see illustration)**.

5 Place a trolley jack beneath the right-hand side of the engine, with a block of wood on the jack head. Raise the jack until it is supporting the weight of the engine.

6 Undo the nuts securing the right-hand engine mounting to the body and the nuts securing the mounting upper bracket to the lower bracket on the engine. Lift the mounting and upper bracket assembly off the studs and remove it from the car **(see illustration)**.

7 Undo the bolts and remove the right-hand mounting lower bracket from the cylinder head **(see illustration)**. If necessary, raise the engine a little to facilitate removal of the bracket.

8 Release the wiring harness from the clip on the side of the cover.

9 Undo the upper cover retaining bolts **(see illustration)**.

10 Lift the cover upwards, slip the TDC sensor and oil pressure switch wiring out of the groove, and remove the upper cover from the engine.

Lower cover

11 Remove the upper cover as described previously.

12 On 500 models, undo the bolts and

4.7 Remove the engine mounting bracket (arrowed) from the end of the cylinder head

4.9 Timing belt covers retaining bolt locations (arrowed)

4.12 Remove the subframe support bracket (arrowed) – 500 models

4.14 Crankshaft position sensor retaining bolt (arrowed) – viewed from underneath

4.16 Crankshaft pulley retaining bolts (arrowed). Note the locating pin (arrowed)

remove the subframe-to-body support bracket **(see illustration)**.

13 Working under the right-hand wheel arch, undo the retaining screws and remove the wheel arch liner centre panel for access to the crankshaft pulley.

14 Undo the retaining bolt and pull the crankshaft TDC sensor from the mounting bracket **(see illustration)**.

15 Remove the auxiliary drivebelt as described in Chapter 1A.

16 Undo the bolts and remove the crankshaft pulley from the sprocket **(see illustration)**.

17 Undo the retaining bolt and remove the lower timing cover **(see illustration 4.9)**.

Refitting

18 Refitting is the reverse sequence to removal, bearing in mind the following points:

a) *Tighten the engine mounting and crankshaft pulley retaining nuts/bolts to the specified torque.*

b) *Refit and adjust the auxiliary drivebelt as described in Chapter 1A.*

c) *Refit the air cleaner assembly as described in Chapter 4A.*

---

5 Timing belt – removal and refitting

Note: *Up to engine No 2533527, Fiat specify the use of special timing belt tension setting tools to correctly adjust the timing belt tension. As it is unlikely that this equipment will be available to the home mechanic, an approximate setting can be achieved using the method described below. If the method described is used, the tension must be checked using the special tools at the earliest possible opportunity. Do not drive the vehicle over large distances, or use high engine speeds, until the belt tension is known to be correct. Refer to a Fiat dealer or approved repairer for advice.*

General information

1 The function of the timing belt is to drive the camshaft and coolant pump. Should the belt slip or break in service, the valve timing will

be disturbed and piston-to-valve contact will occur, resulting in serious engine damage.

2 The timing belt should be renewed at the specified intervals (see Chapter 1A) or earlier if it is contaminated with oil, or if it is at all noisy in operation (a scraping noise due to uneven wear).

3 If the timing belt is being removed, it is a wise precaution to check the condition of the coolant pump at the same time (check for signs of coolant leakage). This may avoid the need to remove the timing belt again at a later stage, should the coolant pump fail.

Removal

4 Set the engine at the correct piston position as described in Section 2.

5 Release the nut on the timing belt tensioner, move the tensioner pulley away from the belt and retighten the nut to hold the pulley in the retracted position **(see illustration)**.

6 If the timing belt is to be re-used, use white paint or chalk to mark the direction of rotation on the belt (if markings do not already exist), then slip the belt off the sprockets. Note that the crankshaft and camshaft must not be rotated whilst the belt is removed.

7 Check the timing belt carefully for any signs of uneven wear, splitting, or oil contamination. Pay particular attention to the roots of the teeth. Renew it if there is the slightest doubt about its condition. If the engine is undergoing an overhaul, renew the belt as a matter of course, regardless of its apparent condition. The cost of a new belt is nothing compared with the

cost of repairs should the belt break in service. If signs of oil contamination are found, trace the source of the oil leak and rectify it. Wash down the engine timing belt area and all related components, to remove all traces of oil.

Refitting

8 Before refitting, thoroughly clean the timing belt sprockets. Check that the tensioner pulley rotates freely, without any sign of roughness. If necessary, renew the tensioner pulley as described in Section 6.

9 Referring to Section 2, make sure that the crankshaft and camshaft are still set at their correct positions and, where applicable, the camshaft and crankshaft are locked in the correct positions using the special tools.

10 From engine No 2533528 and post-modification engines (see Section 2), slacken the camshaft sprocket retaining bolt, while holding the sprocket stationary using a suitable tool **(see Tool Tip)**. Note that on

5.5 Undo the nut (arrowed) and move the timing belt tensioner pulley away from the belt

TOOL TiP

To make a camshaft sprocket holding tool, obtain two lengths of steel strip about 6 mm thick by 30 mm wide or similar, one 600 mm long, the other 200 mm long (all dimensions are approximate). Bolt the two strips together to form a forked end, leaving the bolt slack so that the shorter strip can pivot freely. At the end of the each 'prong' of the fork, secure a bolt with a nut and a lock nut, to act as the fulcrums; these will engage with the cut-outs in the sprocket and should protrude by about 30 mm.

5.10 Unscrew the bolt cap (arrowed) on Euro 5 emissions models

5.12 Use right-angled circlip pliers to turn the tensioner pulley and fully-tension the timing belt

5.16 Rotate the tensioner until it's in the maximum tension position – pointer (1) as shown (arrowed)

Euro 5 models, the sprocket bolt cap must first be removed **(see illustration)**.

11 On all engines, with the arrows on the timing belt pointing in the direction of engine rotation, engage the timing belt with the crankshaft sprocket first, then place it around the coolant pump sprocket and the camshaft sprocket. Finally slip the belt around the tensioner pulley.

Up to engine number 2533527

12 Release the tensioner nut and insert the jaws of a pair of right-angled circlip pliers (or similar) into the two holes on the front face of the tensioner pulley. Rotate the pulley anti-clockwise against the belt until the belt is quite taut **(see illustration)**. Check that the crankshaft and camshaft are still at their TDC positions and that, where applicable, the sprocket timing marks are still aligned.

13 Maintain the effort applied to the tensioner pulley, then tighten the retaining nut to the specified torque.

14 Turn the crankshaft through two complete turns in the normal direction of rotation and check that when the centre of the longest run of the belt is gripped between finger and thumb it can only just be twisted through 90°.

15 If the belt appears to be too slack or too tight, set the engine at the TDC position as described previously and repeat the complete tensioning procedure.

Caution: The above procedure serves only as a rough guide to setting the belt tension.

The tension must be checked accurately by a Fiat dealer or suitably-equipped repairer, using the specialised checking equipment at the earliest opportunity.

From engine number 2533528

16 Release the tensioner nut and insert the jaws of a pair of right-angled circlip pliers (or similar) into the two holes on the front face of the tensioner pulley. Rotate the pulley to the position of maximum tension, until the moving reference is positioned as shown **(see illustration)**.

17 Maintain the effort applied to the tensioner pulley, then tighten the retaining nut to the specified torque.

18 Tighten the camshaft sprocket retaining bolt to the specified torque, while holding the sprocket stationary using the method described previously. Remove the dial test indicator and the camshaft locking tool.

19 Turn the engine clockwise through two complete revolutions, then hold the tensioner pulley stationary, slacken the tensioner nut, and rotate the pulley until the moving reference aligns with the fixed reference **(see illustration)**. Tighten the tensioner nut to the specified torque.

Post-modification engines

20 Release the tensioner nut and insert the jaws of a pair of right-angled circlip pliers (or similar) into the two holes on the front face of the tensioner pulley. Rotate the pulley anti-

clockwise to the stop – the pulley is now in the maximum tension position **(see illustration)**.

21 Tighten the camshaft sprocket retaining bolt to the specified torque, while holding the sprocket stationary using the method described previously, and refit the bolt cap (where applicable). Remove the camshaft and crankshaft locking tools.

22 Turn the engine clockwise through two complete revolutions, then hold the tensioner pulley stationary, slacken the tensioner nut, and rotate the pulley until the tensioner front fork is aligned with the rear fork **(see illustration)**. Tighten the tensioner nut to the specified torque.

23 With the engine positioned again as described in Section 2, check that the camshaft and crankshaft locking tools can be fitted. If not, repeat the complete tensioning procedure.

All engines

24 Where applicable, refit the ignition coil mounting bracket to the cylinder head and secure with the bolt and nuts tightened securely. Reconnect the HT leads and the LT wiring connectors.

25 Refit the timing belt covers, the crankshaft pulley, auxiliary drivebelt, spark plugs and the air cleaner assembly, with reference to Chapter 1A.

26 Refit the front wheel and lower the car to the ground.

5.19 Rotate the tensioner so the pointers (arrowed) align with each other

5.20 Rotate the tensioner anti-clockwise until the pointer (1) is in the maximum tension position (2)

5.22 Align the front fork with the rear fork (arrowed) – viewed with a mirror

6 Timing belt tensioner and sprockets – removal, inspection and refitting

Timing belt tensioner

Removal

1 Set the engine as described in Section 2.
2 Loosen the nut on the timing belt tensioner and move the tensioner pulley away from the belt. Keep the belt engaged with the sprockets using a cable-tie or string.
3 Completely unscrew the nut and slide the tensioner off the mounting stud.

Inspection

4 Wipe the tensioner clean but do not use solvents that may contaminate the bearings. Spin the tensioner pulley on its hub by hand. Stiff movement or excessive free play is an indication of severe wear; the tensioner is not a serviceable component, and should be renewed.

Refitting

5 Slide the tensioner pulley over the mounting stud and fit the retaining nut.
6 Check and adjust the tension of the timing belt as described in Section 5.
7 Where applicable, refit the ignition coil mounting bracket to the cylinder head and secure with the bolt and nuts tightened securely. Reconnect the HT leads and the LT wiring connectors.
8 Refit the timing belt covers, the crankshaft pulley, auxiliary drivebelt, spark plugs and the air cleaner assembly. Adjust the tension of the auxiliary drivebelt as described in Chapter 1A.
9 Refit the front wheel and lower the car to the ground.

Camshaft sprocket

Removal

10 Remove the timing belt as described in Section 5.
11 Slacken the camshaft sprocket retaining bolt while holding the sprocket stationary with a suitable tool (see Tool Tip in Section 5). Where applicable (Euro 5 engines with variable valve timing), unscrew the cap to access the camshaft bolt (see illustration 5.10).
12 Unscrew and remove the retaining bolt and washer, then slide the sprocket from the end of the camshaft.

Inspection

13 With the sprocket removed, examine the camshaft oil seal for signs of leaking. If necessary, refer to Section 8 and renew it.
14 Check the sprocket teeth for damage.
15 Wipe clean the sprocket and camshaft mating surfaces.

Refitting

16 Locate the sprocket on the end of the camshaft, then refit the bolt and washer. Up to engine No 2533527 (see Section 2), tighten

the bolt to the specified torque while holding the camshaft stationary using the method described previously. On all other engines, the retaining bolt is tightened during the timing belt refitting procedure.
17 Refit the timing belt as described in Section 5.

Crankshaft sprocket

Removal

18 Remove the timing belt as described in Section 5.
19 To prevent crankshaft rotation whilst the sprocket retaining bolt is being slackened, the flywheel ring gear must be locked using a suitable tool made from steel angle (see Tool Tip). Remove the cover plate from the base of the transmission bellhousing and bolt the tool to the lower bolt hole in the bellhousing flange so it engages with the ring gear teeth.
20 Using a suitable socket and extension bar, unscrew the crankshaft sprocket retaining bolt and slide the sprocket off the end of the crankshaft.

Inspection

21 With the sprocket removed, examine the crankshaft oil seal for signs of leaking. If necessary, refer to Section 9 and renew it.
22 Check the sprocket teeth for damage.
23 Wipe clean the sprocket and crankshaft mating surfaces.

Refitting

24 Slide the sprocket onto the crankshaft making sure the integral key engages with the slot on the end of the crankshaft. Refit the retaining bolt and tighten it to the specified torque. Hold the crankshaft stationary while the bolt is tightened using the method described in paragraph 19.
25 Refit the timing belt as described in Section 5.

7 Camshaft cover – removal and refitting

Note: Refer to Section 2 for information about engine identification.

Removal

All except Euro 5 emissions engines

1 Remove the air cleaner assembly as described in Chapter 4A.
2 Disconnect the wiring connector from the camshaft position sensor located at the timing belt end of the camshaft cover, then undo the retaining bolt and remove the sensor (see illustration 4.4).
3 Disconnect the accelerator cable inner end from the throttle cam and withdraw the outer cable from the grommet on the mounting bracket.
4 Disconnect the crankcase emission system hose from the outlet stub on the camshaft cover.

A flywheel ring gear locking tool can be made from a short strip of steel bent to form a right-angle. Cut a slot in the upper part and bend this part up to engage with the ring gear teeth. File the edges to form a tooth profile. Drill a hole in the lower part to enable the tool to be bolted to the bellhousing flange.

5 Release the clips and disconnect the fuel injector wiring duct from the slots on the camshaft cover.
6 Undo the timing belt upper cover retaining bolt at the rear of the camshaft cover, and the upper retaining bolt at the front.
7 Progressively unscrew the mounting bolts from the top of the camshaft cover and lift off the cover – note the location of any supports on the bolts. If it sticks, do not attempt to lever it off – instead free it by working around the cover and tapping it lightly with a soft-faced mallet.
8 Recover the camshaft cover gasket. Inspect the gasket carefully, and renew it if damage or deterioration is evident.
9 Clean the mating surfaces of the cylinder head and camshaft cover thoroughly, removing all traces of oil and old gasket – take care to avoid damaging the surfaces as you do this.

Euro 5 emissions engines

10 Remove the air cleaner assembly as described in Chapter 4A.
11 Remove the battery and support tray as described in Chapter 5A.
12 Remove the engine management ECU as described in Chapter 4A.
13 Undo the screws and remove the wiring loom bracket (see illustration).

7.13 Wiring loom support bracket screws (arrowed)

7.14 Undo the bolts and remove the ECU support bracket

7.15 Disconnect the breather hose from the camshaft cover

7.16 Camshaft position sensor retaining bolt (arrowed)

7.17 Variable valve timing solenoid wiring plug (arrowed)

7.20 Disconnect the earth lead (arrowed)

7.21 Undo the bolts (arrowed) and remove the bracket

14 Disconnect the camshaft position sensor wiring plug, then undo the bolts/nut and remove the ECU support bracket **(see illustration)**.

15 Release the clamp and disconnect the engine breather hose from the camshaft cover **(see illustration)**.

16 Undo the retaining bolt and pull the camshaft position sensor from place **(see illustration)**.

17 Disconnect the variable valve timing solenoid (where fitted) wiring plug **(see illustration)**.

18 Undo the bolts securing the upper timing belt cover **(see illustration 4.9)**.

19 Remove the ignition coils as described in Chapter 5B.

20 Disconnect the earth lead from the camshaft cover **(see illustration)**.

21 Undo the bolts and move the oxygen sensor connector mounting bracket **(see illustration)**.

22 Progressively unscrew the mounting bolts from the top of the camshaft cover and lift off the cover – note the location of any supports on the bolts. If it sticks, do not attempt to lever it off – instead free it by working around the cover and tapping it lightly with a soft-faced mallet.

23 Recover the camshaft cover gasket.

Inspect the gasket carefully, and renew it if damage or deterioration is evident.

24 Clean the mating surfaces of the cylinder head and camshaft cover thoroughly, removing all traces of oil and old gasket – take care to avoid damaging the surfaces as you do this. On models with variable valve timing, check, and if necessary renew the O-rings on the underside of the camshaft cover **(see illustration)**.

Refitting

25 Locate a new gasket on the camshaft cover and make sure it is correctly seated **(see illustration)**.

7.24 Note the O-ring seals (arrowed) on the underside of the cover on models with variable valve timing

7.25 Fit the gasket into the groove

7.26 A special tool (arrowed) is available to ensure the camshaft cover is flush with the cylinder head

26 Lower the cover onto the cylinder head, making sure the gasket is not displaced. On post-modification engines, ensure the cover is flush with the cylinder head at the left-hand end **(see illustration)**.

27 Insert the cover retaining bolts and tighten them progressively to the specified torque.

28 The remainder of refitting is the reverse sequence to removal.

8 Camshaft oil seal – renewal

1 Remove the timing belt and camshaft sprocket as described in Sections 5 and 6.
2 On post-modification engines (see Section 2), undo the bolts and remove the camshaft bearing cap **(see illustration)**.
3 On all engines, punch or drill a small hole in the oil seal. Screw a self-tapping screw into the hole, and pull on the screw with pliers to extract the seal.
4 Clean the seal housing, and polish off any burrs or raised edges which may have caused the seal to fail in the first place.
5 Lubricate the lips of the new seal with clean engine oil, and drive it into position until it seats on its locating shoulder. Use a suitable tubular drift, such as a socket, which bears only on the hard outer edge of the seal. Take care not to damage the seal lips during fitting. Note that the seal lips should face inwards.

9.2 Carefully prise the crankshaft right-hand oil seal from the oil pump housing

8.2 Undo the bolts (arrowed) and remove the bearing cap

6 Refit the camshaft bearing cap, and tighten the bolts to the specified torque.
7 Refit the camshaft sprocket and timing belt as described in Sections 6 and 5.

9 Crankshaft oil seals – renewal

Right-hand side oil seal

1 The front oil seal is located in the oil pump casing on the front of the crankshaft. Remove the timing belt as described in Section 5 and the crankshaft sprocket as described in Section 6.
2 Using a small screwdriver, carefully prise the oil seal from the oil pump casing, taking care not to damage the surface of the crankshaft **(see illustration)**.
3 Clean the seating in the housing and the surface of the crankshaft. To prevent damage to the new oil seal as it is being fitted, wrap some adhesive tape around the end of the crankshaft and lightly oil it.
4 Lubricate the oil seal lip with clean engine oil then offer it up to the oil pump casing. Ensure that the sealing lip is facing inwards **(see illustration)**.
5 Using a suitable tubular drift, drive the oil seal squarely into the casing **(see illustration)**. Remove the adhesive tape.

9.4 Locate the new oil seal on the oil pump housing with the sealing lips facing inwards

6 Refit the crankshaft sprocket and timing belt as described in Sections 6 and 5.

Left-hand side oil seal

7 Remove the flywheel as described in Section 12.
8 Using a suitable hooked instrument, remove the oil seal from the oil seal housing, taking care not to damage the surface of the crankshaft.
9 Clean the seating in the housing and the surface of the crankshaft. Check the crankshaft for burrs which may damage the sealing lip of the new seal, and if necessary use a fine file to remove them.
10 Dip the new seal in clean engine oil and carefully locate it over the crankshaft flange, making sure that it is the correct way around.
11 Progressively tap the oil seal into the housing keeping it square to prevent distortion. A block of wood is useful for this purpose.
12 Refit the flywheel with reference to Section 12.

10 Camshaft and followers – removal, inspection and refitting

Removal

1 Remove the timing belt and camshaft sprocket as described in Sections 5 and 6.
2 Remove the camshaft cover as described in Section 7.
3 If not already done as part of the timing belt removal procedure, identify the spark plug HT leads at their ignition coil connections, then disconnect the leads from the two coils. Also disconnect the LT wiring connector from each coil.
4 Undo the retaining bolt, and the upper and lower retaining nuts, and remove the ignition coils, complete with mounting bracket, from the end of the cylinder head.
5 Mark the positions of the camshaft bearing caps, numbering them from the timing belt end. Where applicable, remove the camshaft locking tool from the left-hand end of the camshaft.
6 Unbolt and remove the lubrication pipe

9.5 Use a suitable tubular drift to the drive the oil seal squarely in to the housing

10.6a Prise out the feed stub of the camshaft lubrication pipe . . .

10.6b . . . and remove the lubrication pipe from the bearing caps

10.6c When removing the camshaft bearing caps, note the position of the long and short locating dowels

(prise the oil feed stub out with a screwdriver) – where fitted. Unscrew the remaining bolts and take off the bearing caps (see illustrations). Note that the pipe is not fitted to post-modification engines.

7 Lift the camshaft carefully from the cylinder head, checking that the valve clearance shims and cam followers are not withdrawn by the adhesion of the oil. Recover the oil seal from the end of the camshaft.

8 Remove the shims and cam followers, but keep them in their originally fitted order.

Inspection

9 Inspect the camshaft for wear on the surfaces of the lobes and journals. Normally their surfaces should be smooth and have a dull shine; look for scoring and pitting. Accelerated wear will occur once the hardened exterior of the camshaft has been damaged.

10 Examine the bearing cap and journal surfaces for signs of wear.

11 To measure the camshaft endfloat, temporarily refit the camshaft then push the camshaft to one end of the cylinder head as far as it will travel. Attach a dial test indicator to the cylinder head and zero it, then push the camshaft as far as it will go to the other end of the cylinder head and record the gauge reading. Verify the reading by pushing the camshaft back to its original position and checking that the gauge indicates zero again.

12 Where the camshaft and bearings are worn excessively, consider renewing the complete cylinder head, together with camshaft and cam followers. A reconditioned head may be available from engine overhaul specialists.

Refitting

13 Lubricate the cam followers and locate them in their correct positions in the cylinder head. Locate the shims in the cam followers making sure they are in their original positions.

14 Lubricate the journals then locate the camshaft in the cylinder head with the cam lobes of No 1 cylinder facing upwards (ie, No 1 piston at TDC).

15 Refit the bearing caps in their correct positions then locate the lubrication pipe (where fitted) over the bearing caps. Press

in the oil feed stub then refit the bearing cap retaining bolts. Progressively tighten the bolts to the specified torque.

16 Lubricate the lips of the new seal with clean engine oil, and drive it into position until it seats on its locating shoulder. Use a suitable tubular drift, such as a socket, which bears only on the hard outer edge of the seal. Take care not to damage the seal lips during fitting. Note that the seal lips should face inwards. Where applicable, refit the oil retaining cap at the right-hand end of the camshaft (see illustration 8.2).

17 Check the condition of the sealing O-ring on the ignition coil mounting bracket and renew the seal if necessary.

18 Unless the ignition coil mounting bracket was removed as part of the timing belt removal procedure, it can be refitted at this stage. Locate the bracket on the cylinder head and secure with the bolt and nuts tightened securely. Reconnect the HT leads and the LT wiring connectors.

19 Refit the camshaft sprocket and timing belt as described in Sections 6 and 5.

20 Check and if necessary adjust the valve clearances as described in Chapter 1A, then refit the camshaft cover as described in Section 7.

11 Cylinder head – removal and refitting

Removal

1 Disconnect the battery, and battery tray as described in Chapter 5A.

2 Drain the cooling system as described in Chapter 1A.

3 Remove the intake and exhaust manifolds as described in Chapter 4A.

4 Remove the timing belt as described in Section 5.

5 Remove the camshaft cover as described in Section 7.

6 Disconnect the radiator hose from the thermostat housing on the left-hand end of the cylinder head.

7 If not already done, disconnect the LT wiring connectors at the ignition coils.

8 Unscrew the cylinder head bolts half a turn at a time in the reverse order to that specified for tightening (see illustration 11.21). When the bolts are free, remove them with their washers.

9 Lift the cylinder head from the block. If it is stuck tight, insert pieces of wood into the exhaust or intake ports, and use them as levers to rock the head off the block. On no account drive levers into the gasket joint, or attempt to tap the head sideways, as it is located on positioning dowels.

10 Remove and discard the cylinder head gasket.

11 The cylinder head can be dismantled as described in Chapter 2C after removing the camshaft and cam followers as described in Section 10.

Preparation for refitting

12 The mating faces of the cylinder head and cylinder block must be perfectly clean before refitting the head. Use a hard plastic or wooden scraper to remove all traces of gasket and carbon; also clean the piston crowns. Take particular care when cleaning the piston crowns as the soft aluminium alloy is easily damaged. Make sure that the carbon is not allowed to enter the oil and water passages – this is particularly important for the lubrication system, as carbon could block the oil supply to the engine's components. Using adhesive tape and paper, seal the water, oil and bolt holes in the cylinder block. To prevent carbon entering the gap between the pistons and bores, smear a little grease in the gap. After cleaning each piston, use a small brush to remove all traces of grease and carbon from the gap, then wipe away the remainder with a clean rag. Clean all the pistons in the same way.

13 Check the mating surfaces of the cylinder block and the cylinder head for nicks, deep scratches and other damage. If slight, they may be removed carefully with a file, but if excessive, machining may be the only alternative to renewal. If warpage of the cylinder head gasket surface is suspected, use a straight-edge to check it for distortion.

Refer to Part C of this Chapter if necessary.

14 Check the condition of the cylinder head bolts, and particularly their threads, whenever they are removed. Wash the bolts in a suitable solvent, and wipe them dry. Check each bolt for any sign of visible wear or damage, renewing them if necessary. Although Fiat do not specify that the bolts must be renewed, it is strongly recommended that the bolts should be renewed as a complete set whenever they are disturbed.

15 Refit the camshaft and followers as described in Section 10, then adjust the valve clearances as described in Chapter 1A before refitting the cylinder head to the block.

Refitting

16 Before refitting the assembled cylinder head, make sure that the head and block mating surfaces are perfectly clean, and that the bolt holes in the cylinder block have been mopped out to clear any oil.

17 Referring to Section 2, make sure that the crankshaft and camshaft are still set at their correct TDC positions and, where applicable, the camshaft is locked in the correct position using the special tool.

18 The new gasket should not be removed from its nylon cover until required for use. Fit the gasket dry, and make sure that the mating surfaces on the head and block are perfectly clean.

19 Place the gasket on the cylinder block so that the word ALTO can be read from above **(see illustration)**.

20 Lower the cylinder head onto the block so that it locates on the positioning dowels.

21 The cylinder head bolt threads must be clean and lightly lubricated. Screw the bolts in finger-tight then working progressively and in the sequence shown, tighten all the cylinder head bolts to the Stage 1 torque setting given in the *Specifications*, using a torque wrench and a suitable socket **(see illustration)**. With all the bolts tightened to their Stage 1 setting, working again in the specified sequence, first angle-tighten the bolts through the specified Stage 2 angle, then again through the Stage 3 angle, using a socket and extension

bar. It is recommended that an angle-measuring gauge is used during this stage of tightening, to ensure accuracy.

22 Refit the intake and exhaust manifolds as described in Chapter 4A.

23 Refit the camshaft cover as described in Section 7.

24 Refit the timing belt as described in Section 5.

25 Reconnect the LT wiring connectors at the ignition coils (where applicable).

26 Reconnect the battery then fill and bleed the cooling system as described in Chapter 1A.

12 Flywheel – removal, inspection and refitting

Removal

1 Remove the transmission as described in Chapter 7A, then remove the clutch assembly as described in Chapter 6.

2 The flywheel must now be held stationary while the bolts are loosened. A home-made locking tool may be fabricated from a piece of scrap metal and used to lock the ring gear **(see Tool Tip in Section 6)**. Bolt the tool to one of the transmission bellhousing mounting bolt holes on the cylinder block.

3 Mark the position of the flywheel with respect to the crankshaft using a dab of paint. Unscrew and remove the mounting bolts, together with the spacer plate, then lift off the flywheel. Discard the flywheel bolts; new ones must be used on refitting.

Inspection

4 If the flywheel's clutch mating surface is deeply scored, cracked or otherwise damaged, the flywheel must be renewed. However, it may be possible to have it surface-ground; seek the advice of a Fiat dealer or engine reconditioning specialist.

5 If the ring gear is badly worn or has missing teeth, the flywheel must be renewed.

Refitting

6 Clean the mating surfaces of the flywheel and crankshaft. Remove any remaining locking compound from the threads of the crankshaft holes, using the correct-size tap, if available.

7 If the new retaining bolts are not supplied with their threads already precoated, apply a suitable thread-locking compound to the threads of each bolt.

8 Offer up the flywheel to the crankshaft, using the alignment marks made during removal, and fit the new retaining bolts together with the spacer plate.

9 Lock the flywheel using the method employed on removal, and tighten the retaining bolts to the specified torque.

10 Refit the clutch as described in Chapter 6, and the transmission as described in Chapter 7A.

13 Engine mountings – inspection and renewal

Inspection

1 Firmly apply the handbrake, then jack up the front of the car and support it securely on axle stands (see *Jacking and vehicle support*).

2 Check the mounting rubbers to see if they are cracked, hardened or separated from the metal at any point; renew the mounting if any such damage or deterioration is evident.

3 Check that all the mounting's fasteners are securely tightened; use a torque wrench to check if possible.

4 Using a large screwdriver or a crowbar, check for wear in the mounting by carefully levering against it to check for free play. Where this is not possible, enlist the aid of an assistant to move the engine/transmission back-and-forth, or from side-to-side, while you watch the mounting. While some free play is to be expected, even from new components, excessive wear should be obvious. If excessive free play is found, check first that the fasteners are correctly secured, then renew any worn components as described below.

11.19 Place the cylinder head gasket on the block so that the word ALTO can be read from above

11.21 Cylinder head bolt tightening sequence

H14336

13.14 Left-hand mounting nuts and central bolt (arrowed)

13.21 Rear mounting bolts (arrowed)

Renewal

Right-hand mounting

5 Place a trolley jack beneath the right-hand side of the engine, with a block of wood on the jack head. Raise the jack until it is supporting the weight of the engine.

6 On some Panda models, undo the retaining bolt and move the coolant expansion tank to one side to access the mounting.

7 Undo the nuts securing the engine mounting to the body and the nuts securing the mounting upper bracket to the lower bracket on the engine (see illustration 4.6). Lift the mounting and upper bracket assembly off the studs and remove it from the car.

8 Undo the nut, withdraw the through-bolt and separate the mounting from the upper engine bracket.

9 Attach the new mounting to the upper engine bracket and secure with the nut and through-bolt. Do not fully-tighten the nut at this stage.

10 Locate the mounting assembly on the body and lower engine bracket, refit the nuts and tighten them to the specified torque.

11 Securely tighten the through-bolt and nut securing the mounting to the upper engine bracket, then remove the trolley jack.

Left-hand mounting

12 Remove the battery and battery tray as described in Chapter 5A.

13 Place a trolley jack beneath the transmission, with a block of wood on the jack head. Raise the jack until it is supporting the weight of the engine/transmission.

14 Unscrew the nuts securing the left-hand mounting to the body (see illustration).

15 Unscrew the bolt securing the mounting to the transmission bracket and lift the mounting off the transmission bracket stud.

16 Locate the new mounting in the transmission bracket, refit the bolt and tighten it to the specified torque.

17 Refit the mounting-to-body nuts and tighten them to the specified torque.

18 Remove the trolley jack, then refit the battery tray and battery as described in Chapter 5A.

Rear mounting

19 Firmly apply the handbrake, then jack up

the front of the car and support it securely on axle stands (see *Jacking and vehicle support*).

20 Temporarily support the weight of the engine/transmission using a trolley jack.

21 Working beneath the vehicle, unscrew the bolt securing the rear mounting assembly to the subframe (see illustration).

22 Unbolt the rear mounting assembly from the transmission and withdraw from under the vehicle.

23 Fitting the new mounting is a reversal of the removal procedure, ensuring that all mounting bolts are tightened to the specified torque.

14 Sump – removal and refitting

Removal

1 Firmly apply the handbrake, then jack up the front of the car and support it securely on axle stands (see *Jacking and vehicle support*). Drain the engine oil as described in Chapter 1A.

2 On 1.2 litre models, undo the bolts and remove the bracket joining the transmission to the cylinder block (see illustration).

3 Undo the bolts and remove the exhaust pipe support bracket (see illustration).

4 Unbolt and remove the cover plate from the base of the transmission bellhousing.

5 Unscrew the sump securing bolts and nuts then cut through as much of the joint

14.2 Transmission-to-cylinder block bracket bolts (arrowed)

sealant as possible using a sharp knife. Pull the sump downwards to release it from the remaining sealant and remove it from under the car.

6 Thoroughly clean the sump and the cylinder block mating surfaces ensuring that all traces of old sealant are removed.

Refitting

7 Apply a 3.0 mm bead of RTV silicone sealant to the sump flange, then locate the sump in position. Refit the retaining bolts and nuts and tighten to the specified torque.

8 The remainder of refitting is a reversal of removal.

9 Lower the car to the ground and wait at least 1 hour before filling the engine with oil as described in Chapter 1A.

15 Oil pump and pick-up tube – removal, inspection and refitting

Removal

1 Remove the timing belt and crankshaft sprocket as described in Sections 5 and 6.

2 Drain the engine oil and remove the oil filter as described in Chapter 1A.

3 Remove the sump as described in Section 14.

4 Remove the coolant pump as described in Chapter 3.

5 Disconnect the wiring connector from the oil pressure switch on the side of the pump casing.

6 Undo the oil pump retaining bolts, noting the location of the longer bolt, and withdraw the pump assembly from the front of the engine. Recover the gasket.

Inspection

7 With the pump on the bench, undo the two bolts and remove the pick-up tube. Using a small screwdriver or similar tool, hook out the pick-up tube sealing O-ring from the pump body.

8 The pressure relief valve components can be removed for examination by depressing

14.3 Exhaust pipe support bracket (arrowed)

15.8a Remove the oil pump pressure relief valve keeper plate

15.8b Oil pump pressure relief valve components

15.9 Use an impact driver to remove the oil pump rear cover plate screws

the spring and pulling out the keeper plate **(see illustrations)**.

9 If pump wear is suspected, check the rotors in the following way. Extract the fixing screws and remove the rear cover plate. The screws are very tight, and will probably require the use of an impact screwdriver **(see illustration)**.

10 Inspect the pump rotors, pump casing and cover for any signs of wear or damage. If satisfactory, refit the rotors to the pump casing ensuring that the orientation marks are facing upwards.

11 Check the clearance between the outer rotor and the pump casing using feeler blades. Check the rotor endfloat by placing a straight-edge across the pump casing, and checking the gap between the straight-edge and rotor face **(see illustrations)**. If the clearances are outside the specified tolerance, renew the oil pump complete.

12 If the pump is unworn, lubricate the rotors with clean engine oil then place the cover plate in position. Apply thread-locking compound to the retaining screws and tighten the screws securely.

13 Locate a new O-ring in the pump casing then refit the pick-up tube. Secure the tube with the two bolts tightened securely.

14 Lubricate the pressure relief valve components then refit the valve, spring and end cap, securing the assembly with the keeper plate.

15 Lever out the crankshaft oil seal and drive a new one squarely into the oil pump casing **(see illustrations)**. Lubricate the oil seal lips with clean engine oil.

15.11a Measure the oil pump outer rotor-to-pump casing clearance

16 Prior to refitting, prime the pump by pouring clean engine oil into its inlet duct, while at the same time turning the oil pump inner rotor.

Refitting

17 Ensure that the oil pump and cylinder block mating faces are clean, then place a new gasket on the pump casing. Retain the gasket in position by inserting two of the pump retaining bolts.

18 Locate the pump on the cylinder block, insert the retaining bolts and tighten them progressively to the specified torque.

19 Refit the coolant pump as described in Chapter 3.

20 Refit the sump as described in Section 14.

21 Refit the crankshaft sprocket and timing belt as described in Sections 6 and 5.

15.11b Measure the oil pump rotor clearance

22 Reconnect the oil pressure switch wiring connector.

23 Fit a new oil filter then fill the engine with oil and coolant as described in Chapter 1A.

16 Oil pressure warning light switch – removal and refitting

1 Firmly apply the handbrake, then jack up the front of the car and support it securely on axle stands (see *Jacking and vehicle support*).

2 Disconnect the wiring plug from the switch, then unscrew it from the oil filter housing **(see illustration)**. Be prepared for oil spillage.

3 Screw the switch into the housing, and tighten it to the specified torque.

4 Reconnect the wiring plug and lower the vehicle to the ground. Check the engine oil level as described in *Weekly checks*.

15.15a Prise out the oil pump seal

15.15b Use a suitable socket to fit the new oil seal

16.2 The oil pressure switch (arrowed) is located on the oil filter housing

Notes

Chapter 2 Part B:
Diesel engine in-car repair procedures

Contents

Degrees of difficulty

Easy, suitable for novice with little experience	**Fairly easy,** suitable for beginner with some experience	**Fairly difficult,** suitable for competent DIY mechanic	**Difficult,** suitable for experienced DIY mechanic	**Very difficult,** suitable for expert DIY or professional

Specifications

General

Engine type	Four-cylinder, in-line, water-cooled. Chain-driven double overhead camshafts, 16 valves
Manufacturer's engine codes:*	
70 bhp (51 kW)	188A8000
75 bhp (55 kW)	169A1000
95 bhp (70 kW)	169B1000
Bore	69.6 mm
Stroke	82.0 mm
Capacity	1248 cc
Firing order	1-3-4-2 (No 1 cylinder at timing chain end)
Direction of crankshaft rotation	Clockwise (viewed from timing chain end of engine)
Compression ratio:	
70 bhp (51 kW)	18.1:1
75 bhp (55 kW)	17.6:1
95 bhp (70 kW)	16.8:1
Torque output:	
70 bhp (51 kW)	145 Nm @ 1500 rpm
75 bhp (55 kW)	145 Nm @ 1500 rpm
95 bhp (70 kW)	200 Nm @ 1500 rpm

* For details of engine code location, see 'Vehicle identification' in the Reference Chapter.

Compression pressures

Maximum difference between any two cylinders . . . . 1.5 bar

Lubrication system

Oil pump type	Gear-type, driven directly from crankshaft
Oil pressure at 80ºC (approximate)	1.4 bars at idle speed
Oil pump clearances:	
Outer rotor-to-body clearance	0.10 to 0.23 mm
Rotor endfloat	0.050 to 0.075 mm

Torque wrench settings

	Nm	lbf ft
Auxiliary drivebelt tensioner to cylinder block	50	37
Big-end bearing cap nuts:*		
Stage 1	20	15
Stage 2	Angle-tighten a further 40°	
Camshaft drivegear bolts	150	111
Camshaft housing closure bolts	15	11
Camshaft housing to cylinder head:		
M8 stud bolts	25	18
M7 bolts	18	13
Camshaft position sensor retaining bolt	7	5
Camshaft sprocket bolt	150	111
Coolant pipe-to-heat exchanger bolts	9	7
Crankshaft pulley hub to crankshaft:†*		
Stage 1	50	37
Stage 2	Angle-tighten a further 90°	
Crankshaft pulley to pulley hub	25	18
Cylinder block baseplate bolts:*		
M10 bolts:		
Stage 1	20	15
Stage 2	Angle-tighten a further 90°	
M8 bolts	30	22
Cylinder head bolts:*		
Stage 1	40	30
Stage 2	Angle-tighten a further 90°	
Stage 3	Angle-tighten a further 90°	
Engine/transmission mountings:		
Left-hand:		
Mounting to body	50	37
Mounting to transmission bracket	130	96
Transmission bracket to transmission	50	37
Rear mounting/torque link:		
Mounting to subframe	80	59
Mounting to transmission bracket	80	59
Transmission bracket to transmission	80	59
Right-hand:		
Engine bracket-to-engine bolts	60	44
Mounting-to-body nuts	60	44
Mounting-to-engine bracket nuts	60	44
Engine-to-transmission bolts	60	44
Engine-to-transmission support bracket bolts	30	22
Flywheel bolts:*		
Stage 1	15	11
Stage 2	Angle-tighten a further 35°	
Fuel rail mounting bracket-to-camshaft housing bolts	25	18
Oil cooler/heat exchanger to oil filter housing	9	7
Oil filter housing cover	25	18
Oil filter housing to cylinder block	9	7
Sump drain plug	20	15
Sump to cylinder block baseplate	9	7
Timing chain guide rail bolts	9	7
Timing chain tensioner bolts	9	7
Timing chain tensioner rail pivot bolt	9	7
Timing cover retaining nuts/bolts	9	7

* *Use new fasteners*
† *Left-hand thread*

1 General information

How to use this Chapter

This Part of Chapter 2 describes the repair procedures which can reasonably be carried out on the engine while it remains in the vehicle. If the engine has been removed from the vehicle and is being dismantled as described in Chapter 2C, any preliminary dismantling procedures can be ignored.

Note that, while it may be possible physically to overhaul items such as the piston/connecting rod assemblies while the engine is in the vehicle, such tasks are not usually carried out as separate operations, and usually require the execution of several additional procedures (not to mention the cleaning of components and of oilways); for this reason, all such tasks are classed as major overhaul procedures, and are described in Chapter 2C.

Chapter 2C describes the removal of the engine/transmission unit from the vehicle, and the full overhaul procedures which can then be carried out.

Engine description

The 1.3 litre common-rail diesel engine is of sixteen-valve, in-line four-cylinder, double overhead camshaft (DOHC) type, mounted transversely at the front of the car with the transmission attached to its left-hand end.

The crankshaft runs in five main bearings. Thrustwashers are fitted to No 3 main bearing shell (upper half) to control crankshaft endfloat.

The cylinder block is made of cast iron and the cylinder bores are an integral part of the block. On this type of engine the cylinder bores are sometimes referred to as having dry liners. An aluminium baseplate is bolted to the cylinder block and forms the lower half of the crankcase.

The connecting rods rotate on horizontally-split bearing shells at their big-ends. The pistons are attached to the connecting rods by gudgeon pins, which are a sliding fit in the connecting rod small-end eyes and retained by circlips. The aluminium-alloy pistons are fitted with three piston rings – two compression rings and an oil control ring.

The camshafts are situated in a separate housing bolted to the top of the cylinder head. The exhaust camshaft is driven by the crankshaft by a hydraulically-tensioned timing chain and drives the intake camshaft via a spur gear. Each cylinder has four valves (two intake and two exhaust), operated via rocker arms which are supported at their pivot ends by hydraulic self-adjusting valve lifters (tappets). One camshaft operates the intake valves, and the other operates the exhaust valves.

The intake and exhaust valves are each closed by a single valve spring, and operate in guides pressed into the cylinder head.

A rotor-type oil pump is located in the timing cover attached to the cylinder block, and is driven directly from the crankshaft. An oil cooler (heat exchanger) is fitted to keep the oil temperature stable under arduous operating conditions.

The coolant pump is located externally on the timing cover, and is driven by the auxiliary drivebelt.

Operations with engine in place

The following operations can be carried out without having to remove the engine from the vehicle.

a) Removal and refitting of the cylinder head.
b) Removal and refitting of the timing cover.
c) Removal and refitting of the timing chain, tensioner, sprockets and guide rails.
d) Removal and refitting of the camshaft housing.
e) Removal and refitting of the hydraulic tappets and rocker arms.
f) Removal and refitting of the camshafts.
g) Removal and refitting of the sump.
h) Removal and refitting of the big-end bearings, connecting rods, and pistons.*
i) Removal and refitting of the oil pump.
j) Removal and refitting of the oil cooler/ heat exchanger.
k) Renewal of the crankshaft oil seals.
l) Renewal of the engine mountings.
m) Removal and refitting of the flywheel.

* Although the operation marked with an asterisk can be carried out with the engine in the vehicle (after removal of the sump), it is preferable for the engine to be removed, in the interests of cleanliness and improved access. For this reason, the procedure is described in Chapter 2C.

2 Compression test – description and interpretation

Compression test

Note: *A compression tester specifically designed for diesel engines must be used for this test.*

1 When engine performance is down, or if misfiring occurs which cannot be attributed to the fuel system, a compression test can provide diagnostic clues as to the engine's condition. If the test is performed regularly, it can give warning of trouble before any other symptoms become apparent.

2 A compression tester specifically intended for diesel engines must be used, because of the higher pressures involved. The tester is connected to an adapter which normally screws into the glow plug or injector hole. However, on these models, an adapter suitable for use in the injector holes will be required. It is unlikely to be worthwhile buying such a tester for occasional use, but it may be possible to borrow or hire one – if not, have the test performed by a garage.

3 Unless specific instructions to the contrary are supplied with the tester, observe the following points:

a) *The battery must be in a good state of charge, the air filter must be clean, and the engine should be at normal operating temperature.*
b) *All the fuel injectors must be removed before starting the test (see Chapter 4B).*
c) *Open the cover on the engine compartment fuse/relay box and remove the fuel pump fuse.*

4 Screw the compression tester and adapter in to the fuel injector hole of No 1 cylinder.

5 With the help of an assistant, crank the engine on the starter motor; after one or two revolutions, the compression pressure should build-up to a maximum figure, and then stabilise. Record the highest reading obtained.

6 Repeat the test on the remaining cylinders, recording the pressure in each.

7 All cylinders should produce very similar pressures; any difference greater than that specified indicates the existence of a fault. Note that the compression should build-up quickly in a healthy engine; low compression on the first stroke, followed by gradually-increasing pressure on successive strokes, indicates worn piston rings. A low compression reading on the first stroke, which does not build-up during successive strokes, indicates leaking valves or a blown head gasket (a cracked head could also be the cause). **Note:** *The cause of poor compression is less easy to establish on a diesel engine than on a petrol one. The effect of introducing oil into the cylinders ('wet' testing) is not conclusive, because there is a risk that the oil will sit in the recess on the piston crown instead of passing to the rings.*

8 On completion of the test, refit the fuel pump relay, then refit the fuel injectors as described in Chapter 4B.

Leakdown test

9 A leakdown test measures the rate at which compressed air fed into the cylinder is lost. It is an alternative to a compression test, and in many ways it is better, since the escaping air provides easy identification of where pressure loss is occurring (piston rings, valves or head gasket).

10 The equipment needed for leakdown testing is unlikely to be available to the home mechanic. If poor compression is suspected, have the test performed by a dealership.

3 Engine assembly/valve timing holes – general information and usage

Note: *Do not attempt to rotate the engine whilst the camshafts are locked in position. If the engine is to be left in this state for a long period of time, it is a good idea to place suitable warning notices inside the car, and in the engine compartment. This will reduce the*

3.2 Camshaft timing slot (arrowed) for use with the camshaft locking tools

3.3a Insert an 8.0 mm diameter drill bit/rod (arrowed) through the hole in the transmission bellhousing into the corresponding hole in the flywheel

3.3b Use a drill bit (arrowed) to lock the crankshaft through the additional timing hole provided in the flywheel

possibility of the engine being accidentally cranked on the starter motor, which is likely to cause damage with the locking tools in place.

1 To accurately set the valve timing for all operations requiring removal and refitting of the timing chain, timing slots are machined in the camshafts and corresponding holes are drilled in the camshaft housing. Timing holes are also drilled in the flywheel, and transmission bellhousing. The holes are used in conjunction with camshaft and crankshaft locking tools to lock the camshafts and crankshaft when all the pistons are positioned at the mid-point of their stroke. This arrangement prevents the possibility of the valves contacting the pistons when refitting the cylinder head or timing chain, and also ensures that the correct valve timing can be obtained. The design of the engine is such that there are no conventional timing marks on the crankshaft or camshaft sprockets to indicate the normal TDC position. Therefore, for any work on the timing chain, camshafts or cylinder head, the locking tools must be used.

2 The Fiat special tool for locking the camshafts comprises a spring-loaded plunger free to slide in the bore of the tool body. The tool body is screwed into the camshaft housing timing hole (after removal of a closure plug) so that the sliding plunger contacts the exhaust camshaft. The plunger is retained in contact with the camshaft by the spring. The crankshaft is then rotated by means of the

crankshaft pulley bolt until a machined slot in the camshaft aligns with the tool plunger (see illustration). The spring then forces the plunger into engagement with the slot, locking the camshaft in the timing position. To accurately check the valve timing, or for any work that entails removal of the camshafts or their drivegears, two of these tools will be required, one for each camshaft.

3 The Fiat special tool for locking the crankshaft is simply an 8 mm diameter pin which is inserted through a hole in the bellhousing to engage with a corresponding hole in the rim of the flywheel. An additional hole is provided in the inner face of the flywheel with a corresponding hole in the cylinder block, for use when the transmission has been removed (see illustrations).

4 The Fiat tool number for the camshaft locking tools is 1.871.000.900.

5 Although the Fiat camshaft locking tools (or aftermarket equivalents) are relatively inexpensive and should be readily available, it is possible to fabricate suitable alternatives, with the help of a local machine shop, as described below. Once the tools have been made up, their usage is described in the relevant Sections of this Chapter where the tools are required.

Camshaft locking tool

6 Remove the air cleaner housing as described in Chapter 4B. Note that for access

to the front hole on 95 bhp Euro 5 engines, the turbocharger must be removed as described in Chapter 4B, and for access to the rear hole the fuel common rail must be removed (Chapter 4B), followed by the mounting plate (see illustration).

7 Unscrew the closure bolt from the valve timing checking hole on the front face of the camshaft housing. The bolt is located above, and just between, Nos 2 and 3 glow plugs.

8 Using the closure bolt as a pattern, obtain a length of threaded dowel rod (thread pitch 1.5 mm), or suitable bolt to screw into the closure bolt hole. With the help of a machine shop or engineering works, make up the camshaft locking tool by having the dowel rod or bolt machined (see illustrations). Note that for some of the procedures described in this Chapter, two locking tools will be needed, one for each camshaft.

9 To refit the closure bolt, thoroughly clean the bolt threads and apply suitable thread-locking compound. Screw the bolt into the camshaft housing and tighten to the specified torque.

Crankshaft locking tool

10 An 8.0 mm diameter drill bit or rod can be used to lock the crankshaft

3.6 Remove the mounting plate (arrowed) to access the rear camshaft timing hole

3.8a To make an alternative camshaft locking tool . . .

Suitable roll pin for fitting / removing tool

10
4
13
10
25

All dimensions in mm   H 31234

3.8b . . . have suitable dowel rods or bolts machined to the dimensions shown

4.4 Disconnect the injector wiring then move the wiring harness guide forward

4.5 Unscrew the closure bolt from the valve timing checking hole on each side of the camshaft housing

4.7 If the Fiat camshaft locking tools are being used, screw the tools into the valve timing checking holes. Ensure the mark on the tool plunger (arrowed) is facing upwards

4 Valve timing – checking and adjustment

Note: *Certain special tools will be required for this operation. Read through the entire procedure to familiarise yourself with the work involved, then either obtain the manufacturer's special tools, or use the alternatives described. New gaskets and sealing rings will also be required for all disturbed components.*

Checking

1 Disconnect the battery negative terminal as described in Chapter 5A.
2 Remove the air cleaner assembly as described in Chapter 4B.
3 Move the plastic hose/pipe guide on the top of the engine to one side.
4 Release the locking catches securing the wiring connectors to the four injectors, then disconnect the injector wiring, while at the same time moving the wiring harness guide forward **(see illustration)**.
5 Unscrew the closure bolt from the valve timing checking hole on each side of the camshaft housing **(see illustration)**. Note that

for access to the front hole on 95 bhp Euro 5 engines, the turbocharger must be removed as described in Chapter 4B, and for access to the rear hole the fuel common rail must be removed (Chapter 4B), followed by the mounting plate.
6 The camshafts must now be set to the timing position, to enable a camshaft locking tool to be inserted (see Section 3).
7 If the Fiat camshaft locking tools or similar alternatives are available, screw one of the tools into each of the valve timing checking holes. Ensure that the mark on the tool plunger is facing upwards **(see illustration)**. Using a socket or spanner on the crankshaft pulley hub bolt, turn the crankshaft in the normal direction of rotation (clockwise as viewed from the right-hand side of the car) until the spring-loaded plungers of the locking tools slide into engagement with the slot on each camshaft. There will be an audible click from each tool when this happens and the plungers will be seen to move in, towards the camshafts.
8 If the home-made locking tools described in Section 3 are being used, insert a screwdriver through the valve timing checking hole on the front of the camshaft housing, and into contact with the exhaust camshaft. Using a socket or spanner on the crankshaft pulley hub bolt, turn

the crankshaft in the normal direction of rotation (clockwise as viewed from the right-hand side of the car) until the screwdriver can be felt to engage with the slot in the camshaft. Screw the tool into the camshaft housing until resistance is felt, then turn the crankshaft slightly until the camshaft slot is correctly aligned, and the tool can be screwed fully in **(see illustrations)**. Repeat this procedure for the intake camshaft.
9 Firmly apply the handbrake, then jack up the front of the car and support it securely on axle stands (see *Jacking and vehicle support*).
10 Insert the crankshaft locking tool or suitable alternative (see Section 3) into the timing hole at the side of the transmission bellhousing and into engagement with the flywheel **(see illustration 3.3a)**. It may be necessary to turn the crankshaft very slightly one way or the other (within the limits of any slack afforded by the timing chain/tensioner) to allow the tool to fully engage.
11 If the crankshaft locking tool has engaged fully, then the valve timing is correct. Refit the disturbed components as described in the following paragraphs. If it is not possible to fully insert the crankshaft locking tool, then it will be necessary to adjust the valve timing as described later in this Section.

4.8a Screw one of the tools (arrowed) into each hole in the camshaft housing . . .

4.8b . . . so the end of the tool engages with the slot in the camshaft (camshaft removed for clarity)

TOOL TiP

To make a sprocket holding tool, obtain two lengths of steel strip about 6 mm thick by about 30 mm wide or similar, one 600 mm long and the other 200 mm long (all dimensions are approximate). Bolt the two strips together to form a forked end, leaving the bolt slack to that the sorter strip can pivot freely. At the other end of each 'prong' of the fork, drill a suitable hole and fit a nut and bolt to allow the tool to be bolted to the crankshaft pulley hub.

12 Remove the camshaft locking tools from both sides of the camshaft housing.
13 Thoroughly clean the closure bolt threads and apply suitable thread-locking compound. Screw the bolts into the camshaft housing and tighten to the specified torque.
14 Reconnect the fuel injector wiring connectors and secure with the locking catches.
15 Refit the three bolts securing the plastic wiring harness guide to the top of the camshaft housing.
16 Refit the air cleaner assembly as described in Chapter 4B, then reconnect the battery and lower the car to the ground.

Adjustment

17 Remove the crankshaft pulley as described in Section 5.
18 It will now be necessary to hold the crankshaft pulley hub to enable the retaining bolt to be removed. Fiat special tools No 1.871.000.200 and 1.860.831.000 are available for this purpose, however, a home-made tool can easily be fabricated **(see Tool Tip)**.
19 Using the Fiat tool or the home-made alternative, hold the pulley hub stationary and unscrew the retaining bolt. **Note:** *The pulley hub retaining bolt has a left-hand thread and is unscrewed by turning it clockwise.*
20 Withdraw the pulley hub from the crankshaft and refit the retaining bolt sufficiently tight to allow the crankshaft to be turned.
21 Using a socket or spanner on the crankshaft pulley hub bolt, turn the crankshaft as necessary, until it is possible to fully insert the crankshaft locking tool into engagement with the flywheel.
22 Undo the bolt, refit the crankshaft pulley hub, and refit the bolt.
23 Hold the pulley hub using the holding tool and tighten the bolt to the specified torque.

24 Remove the crankshaft locking tool.
25 Refit the crankshaft pulley as described in Section 5.

5 Crankshaft pulley – removal and refitting

Removal

1 Apply the handbrake, then jack up the front of the vehicle and support it on axle stands (see *Jacking and vehicle support*). Remove the right-hand front roadwheel and the front, and lower sections of the inner wheel arch liner for access to the crankshaft pulley.
2 Remove the auxiliary drivebelt as described in Chapter 1B. Prior to removal, mark the direction of rotation on the belt to ensure the belt is refitted the same way around.
3 Slacken and remove the four retaining bolts securing the pulley to the pulley hub. If necessary, prevent the crankshaft from turning by inserting an 8.0 mm diameter drill bit or rod into the special hole in the transmission bellhousing – see Section 4.

Refitting

4 Refit the crankshaft pulley to the pulley hub. Refit the pulley retaining bolts, tightening them to the specified torque.
5 Refit the auxiliary drivebelt as described in Chapter 1B using the mark made prior to removal to ensure the belt is fitted the correct way around.
6 Refit the wheel arch liner panels and roadwheel, then lower the car to the ground and tighten the wheel bolts to the specified torque.

6 Timing cover – removal and refitting

Note: *The special tools described in Section 3, together with additional tools, will be required for this operation. Read through the entire procedure and also the procedures contained in Section 3 to familiarise yourself with the work involved, then either obtain the manufacturer's special tools, or use the alternatives described. New gaskets and sealing rings will be needed for all disturbed components, together with a tube of suitable gasket sealant.*

Removal

1 On models with air conditioning, have the refrigerant circuit evacuated by a Fiat dealer or suitably-equipped repairer.
2 Disconnect the battery negative terminal as described in Chapter 5A.
3 Referring to the procedures contained in Chapter 1B, drain the engine oil and the cooling system. Refit the drain plug, using a new seal, when the oil has drained. Close the cooling system when the coolant has drained.
4 Remove the crankshaft pulley as described in Section 5.

5 Remove the air cleaner assembly as described in Chapter 4B.
6 Disconnect the wiring connector at the camshaft position sensor on the top of the camshaft housing.
7 Disconnect the wiring connectors at the four glow plugs.
8 Unscrew the three bolts securing the plastic wiring harness guide to the top of the camshaft housing.
9 Release the locking catches securing the wiring connectors to the four injectors, then disconnect the injector wiring, while at the same time moving the wiring harness guide forward **(see illustration 4.4)**.
10 Unscrew the closure bolt from the valve timing checking hole on the exhaust camshaft side of the camshaft housing **(see illustration 4.5)**.
11 If the Fiat camshaft locking tool or similar alternative is available (see Section 3), screw the tool into the valve timing checking hole. Ensure that the mark on the tool plunger is facing upwards. Using a socket or spanner on the crankshaft pulley hub bolt, turn the crankshaft in the normal direction of rotation (clockwise as viewed from the right-hand side of the car) until the spring-loaded plunger of the locking tool slides into engagement with the slot on the camshaft. There will be an audible click from the tool when this happens, and the plunger will be seen to move in, towards the camshaft.
12 If the home-made locking tool described in Section 3 is being used, insert a screwdriver through the valve timing checking hole on the front of the camshaft housing, and into contact with the exhaust camshaft. Using a socket or spanner on the crankshaft pulley hub bolt, turn the crankshaft in the normal direction of rotation (clockwise as viewed from the right-hand side of the car) until the screwdriver can be felt to engage with the slot in the camshaft. Screw the tool into the camshaft housing until resistance is felt, then turn the crankshaft slightly until the camshaft slot is correctly aligned, and the tool can be screwed fully in **(see illustrations 4.8a and 4.8b)**.
13 On models with air conditioning, undo the retaining bolt and detach the refrigerant pipe from the expansion valve to the compressor **(see illustration)**. Plug the openings to prevent contamination.

6.13 Disconnect the refrigerant pipe (arrowed) from the air conditioning compressor

6.16 Remove the hose (arrowed) between the turbocharger and the intercooler – 500 models (front panel removed for clarity)

6.22 Drivebelt tensioner retaining bolt (arrowed)

6.23 Working through the pulley apertures, unscrew and remove the coolant pump retaining nuts

14 Undo the retaining bolt and move the coolant expansion tank to one side.
15 On 500 models, disconnect the fuel pipes, undo the retaining bolts and remove the fuel filter assembly – refer to Chapter 1B if necessary.
16 Slacken the clamps and remove the air supply hose between the turbocharger and the intercooler **(see illustration)**.
17 Position a trolley/workshop jack under the engine, with a block of wood on the jack head to prevent damage.
18 Undo the bolts/nuts securing the right-hand engine mounting assembly, then remove the mounting support bracket from the cylinder head.
19 It will now be necessary to hold the crankshaft pulley hub to enable the retaining bolt to be removed. Fiat special tools No 1.871.000.200 and 1.860.831.000 are available for this purpose, however, a home-made tool can easily be fabricated **(see Tool Tip in Section 4)**.
20 Using the Fiat tool or the home-made alternative, hold the pulley hub stationary and unscrew the retaining bolt. **Note:** *The pulley hub retaining bolt has a left-hand thread and is unscrewed by turning it clockwise.*
21 Withdraw the pulley hub from the crankshaft and refit the retaining bolt sufficiently tight to allow the crankshaft to be turned.
22 Undo the bolt and remove the auxiliary drivebelt tensioner **(see illustration)**.

6.26 Remove the bracket (arrowed) between the engine and transmission

23 Working through the apertures in the pulley, unscrew and remove the four coolant pump retaining nuts **(see illustration)**.
24 Withdraw the coolant pump from the cylinder block studs. **Note:** *Coolant which is trapped in the cylinder block will leak out when the pump is removed.* Recover the pump sealing ring, and discard it; a new one must be used on refitting.
25 Remove the centre exhaust pipe as described in Chapter 4B.
26 Undo the bolts and remove the support bracket underneath between the engine cylinder block and the transmission bellhousing **(see illustration)**.
27 Remove the sump as described in Section 12.
28 Release the wiring harness from the

6.28 Unclip the wiring harnesses/hoses from the timing cover

support clips on the timing cover and move the harness to one side **(see illustration)**.
29 Undo the retaining bolt and detach the crankcase ventilation hose attachment at the timing cover **(see illustration)**.
30 Undo the bolts and nuts securing the timing cover to the cylinder block, cylinder block baseplate, cylinder head and camshaft housing. Using a flat-bladed screwdriver inserted behind the lugs on the edge of the timing cover, carefully prise the cover free and remove it from the engine **(see illustrations)**. Recover the timing cover gasket, a new gasket will be required for refitting.
31 Thoroughly clean the timing cover and remove all traces of gasket and sealant from all the mating surfaces. Similarly clean the cylinder block baseplate, cylinder block,

6.29 Timing cover breather hose retaining bolt (arrowed)

6.30a Use a flat-bladed screwdriver to prise behind the lugs on the edge . . .

6.30b . . . and release the timing cover

6.34 Apply a bead of sealant across the housing joints

cylinder head and camshaft housing mating surfaces. Ensure that all traces of old sealant are removed, particularly from the joint areas between these components.

32 Obtain all new gaskets and components as necessary ready for refitting. In addition, a new crankshaft oil seal will be required together with a tube of Loctite 5900 sealant, or equivalent. Fiat special tool

6.36 Timing cover bolt tightening sequence. Arrows indicate the location the 3 nuts

No 1.879.900.600, or a suitable alternative, will be required to centralise the timing cover during refitting.

Refitting

33 Prior to refitting the timing cover, ensure that the face of the timing chain sprocket on the crankshaft is free from oil or grease.

34 Apply a 2 mm bead of Loctite 5900 across the camshaft housing-to-cylinder head joint, the cylinder head-to-cylinder block joint and the cylinder block-to-baseplate joint **(see illustration)**.

35 Place the new gasket in position on the engine then locate the timing cover over the gasket. Insert the Fiat tool No 1.879.900.600 or a suitable equivalent, over the crankshaft and into engagement with the timing cover.

36 Refit the bolts and nuts securing the timing cover to the engine, and tighten them to the specified torque, in the sequence shown **(see illustration)**.

37 Remove the centering tool and carefully prise out the old crankshaft oil seal with a screwdriver or similar hooked tool. Clean the oil seal seat with a wooden or plastic scraper.

38 Tap a new crankshaft oil seal into position until it is flush with the outer face of the timing cover, using a suitable socket or tube, or a wooden block.

39 The remainder of refitting is a reversal of removal, noting the following points:

a) Tighten all fasteners to their correct torque where given.

b) Refill the engine oil and cooling systems as described in Chapter 1B.

c) Upon completion, start the engine and check for oil leaks before venturing out on the road.

d) Have the air conditioning system recharged by a Fiat dealer or suitably-equipped repairer where applicable.

7 Timing chain, sprockets, tensioner and guide rails – removal and refitting

Removal

1 Lock the camshafts and crankshaft in position as described in Section 3.

2 Remove the timing cover as described in Section 6.

3 With the camshafts and crankshafts locked in place, slacken the camshaft sprocket retaining bolt.

4 Push the timing chain tensioner plunger back into its bore and insert a drill bit or similar tool to retain it in the released position **(see illustration)**.

5 Undo the two retaining bolts and remove the tensioner from the cylinder head **(see illustration)**.

6 Undo the lower pivot bolt and remove the chain tensioner rail **(see illustrations)**.

7 Completely undo the camshaft sprocket

7.4 With the chain tensioner compressed, lock it with a suitable drill bit (arrowed)

7.5 Undo the bolts and remove the tensioner

7.6a Undo the lower pivot bolt . . .

7.6b . . . and remove the chain tensioner rail

TOOL TIP

To make a sprocket holding tool, obtain two lengths of steel strip about 6 mm thick by about 30 mm wide or similar, one 600 mm long, the other 200 mm long (all dimensions are approximate). Bolt the two strips together to form a forked end, leaving the bolt slack so that the shorter strip can pivot freely. At the other end of each 'prong' of the fork, drill a suitable hole and fit a nut/ bolt. The bolts can be engaged with the holes in the sprocket to hold the sprocket stationary.

bolt **(see Tool tip)**, then slide the crankshaft sprocket off the end of the crankshaft, and remove the chain complete with camshaft sprocket **(see illustration)**.

8 Undo the two retaining bolts and remove the timing chain guide rail **(see illustration)**.

9 Inspect the timing chain, sprockets, tensioner rail and guide rail for any sign of wear or deformation, and renew any suspect components as necessary.

10 Push the timing chain tensioner plunger into the tensioner body and remove the locking drill bit. Check that the tensioner plunger is free to move in and out of the tensioner body with no trace of binding. If any binding or sticking of the plunger is felt, renew the tensioner assembly. On completion of the check, or if a new tensioner is being fitted, compress the plunger and refit the locking drill bit.

Refitting

11 Locate the timing chain guide rail in position, refit the two retaining bolts and tighten the bolts to the specified torque.

8.11a Place a new gasket on the cylinder head . . .

7.7 Hold the sprocket stationary and slacken the retaining bolt

12 Fit the sprocket to the camshaft (letters/ numbers facing outwards) and screw in the retaining bolt and tighten it to the specified torque, using a home-made tool to prevent rotation.

13 Thoroughly clean the crankshaft and crankshaft sprocket, ensuring that there is no oil or grease on the contact faces.

14 Place the sprocket in the timing chain, then engage the chain over the camshaft sprocket. Slide the crankshaft sprocket over the end of the crankshaft.

15 Refit the timing chain tensioner rail, screw in the lower pivot bolt and tighten the bolt to the specified torque.

16 Refit the timing chain tensioner and tighten the two retaining bolts to the specified torque. Depress the tensioner plunger, withdraw the locking drill bit and release the plunger.

17 Refit the timing cover as described in Section 6.

8 Camshaft housing – removal and refitting

Removal

1 Refer to the procedures contained in Chapter 4B, and remove the following components:
a) *High-pressure fuel pump.*
b) *Fuel rail.*
c) *Fuel injectors.*
d) *Turbocharger.*
e) *Throttle body (Euro 5 engines only).*

8.11b . . . locate the camshaft housing in position . . .

7.8 Undo the retaining bolts (arrowed) and remove the chain guide rail

2 Disconnect the engine wiring harness at the following connectors, if not already done:
a) *Crankshaft speed/position sensor.*
b) *Manifold pressure sensor.*
c) *EGR valve.*
d) *Starter/alternator.*

3 Move the disconnected wiring harnesses to one side.

4 Remove the timing cover as described in Section 6.

5 Remove the timing chain, sprockets and tensioner as described in Section 7.

6 Undo the bolts and remove the engine lifting bracket and fuel rail mounting bracket from the camshaft housing.

7 Undo the 16 bolts, and 2 stud bolts, securing the camshaft housing to the cylinder head.

8 Lift the camshaft housing off the cylinder head and recover the gasket.

9 Thoroughly clean the mating faces of the cylinder head and camshaft housing and obtain a new gasket for refitting.

Refitting

10 Check that all the hydraulic tappets and rocker arms are correctly positioned in the cylinder head and none have been disturbed.

11 Place a new gasket on the cylinder head, then locate the camshaft housing in position. Refit the two stud bolts to align the assembly but only tighten them finger-tight at this stage **(see illustrations)**.

12 Using a straight-edge, align the front face of the camshaft housing with the front face of the cylinder head. Lightly tighten the two stud

8.11c . . . then refit the two stud bolts to align the assembly

8.15 Camshaft housing retaining bolt tightening sequence

9.9a Unscrew the retaining bolt . . .

drivegears and sprocket should be slackened as follows.

3 It will be necessary to hold the camshaft sprocket to enable the drivegear and sprocket retaining bolts to be slackened. Use a home-made tool **(see Tool Tip in Section 7)**.

4 Working through the vacuum pump aperture, and using the holding tool to prevent rotation of the camshaft, slacken the intake camshaft drivegear retaining bolt. Working through the high-pressure fuel pump aperture, slacken the exhaust camshaft drivegear retaining bolt in the same way.

5 Again, using the holding tool, slacken the camshaft sprocket retaining bolt.

6 Continue with the camshaft housing removal procedure as described in Section 8, paragraphs 7 to 9.

7 With the camshaft housing removed, unscrew the retaining bolt and withdraw the camshaft position sensor from the top of the housing.

8 Turn the housing over and remove the camshaft locking tool.

9 Unscrew the previously-slackened retaining bolt, lift off the drivegear and carefully withdraw the intake camshaft from the camshaft housing **(see illustrations)**. Using quick-drying paint, correction fluid or a label, suitably mark the sprocket and camshaft to identify them as the intake components.

10 At the exhaust camshaft, unscrew the previously-slackened retaining bolt and lift off the camshaft sprocket. Unscrew the retaining bolt, lift off the drivegear and carefully withdraw the exhaust camshaft from the camshaft housing **(see illustrations)**. Using

bolts to retain the housing and maintain the alignment.

13 Refit the camshaft housing retaining bolts, noting that the longer bolt is fitted at the flywheel end of the housing between the high-pressure fuel pump and vacuum pump locations. Progressively screw in the retaining bolts to gradually draw the housing down and into contact with the cylinder head.

14 Using the straight-edge, check the alignment of the camshaft housing and cylinder head once more and correct if necessary.

15 Working in the sequence shown, tighten the camshaft housing retaining bolts to the specified torque **(see illustration)**. Note that the torque setting for the two stud bolts is different from the other bolts.

16 Refit the engine lifting bracket and fuel rail mounting bracket to the camshaft housing. Refit the three retaining bolts and tighten to the specified torque.

17 Refit the timing chain, sprockets and tensioner as described in Section 7.

18 Refit the timing cover as described in Section 6.

19 Reconnect the engine wiring harness to the connectors listed in paragraph 2.

20 Refit the fuel injectors, fuel rail, turbocharger (500 models only) and high-pressure fuel pump as described in Chapter 4B.

9 Camshafts – removal, inspection and refitting

Removal

1 Carry out the operations described in Section 8, paragraphs 1 to 6.

2 Before removing the camshaft housing completely, the retaining bolts for the camshaft

9.9b . . . lift off the drivegear . . .

9.9c . . . and withdraw the intake camshaft from the housing

9.10a Unscrew the bolt and lift off the exhaust side sprocket

9.10b Undo the retaining bolt . . .

9.10c . . . lift off the drivegear . . .

9.10d . . . and withdraw the exhaust side camshaft from the housing

9.18 Insert the tools (arrowed) to lock the camshafts in the timing position

9.23 Hold the sprocket stationary and tighten the retaining bolt

9.24 While still holding the sprocket, tighten the drivegear retaining bolt on each camshaft

quick-drying paint, correction fluid or a label, suitably mark the sprocket and camshaft to identify them as the exhaust components.

Inspection

11 Examine the camshaft bearing surfaces and cam lobes for signs of wear ridges and scoring. Renew the camshaft if any of these conditions are apparent. Examine the condition of the bearing surfaces in the camshaft housing. If the any wear or scoring is evident, the camshaft housing will need to be renewed.

12 If either camshaft is being renewed, it will be necessary to renew all the rocker arms and tappets for that camshaft also (see Section 10).

13 Check the condition of the camshaft drivegears and sprocket for chipped or damaged teeth, wear ridges and scoring. Renew any components as necessary.

Refitting

14 Prior to refitting, thoroughly clean all components and dry with a lint-free cloth. Ensure that all traces of oil and grease are removed from the contact faces of the drivegears, sprocket and camshafts.

15 Lubricate the exhaust camshaft bearing journals in the camshaft housing and carefully insert the exhaust camshaft. Ensuring that the contact faces are clean and dry, refit the drivegear to the camshaft and insert the retaining bolt. Screw in the bolt two or three turns at this stage.

16 Locate the sprocket on the exhaust

camshaft with the writing on the sprocket facing away from the camshaft housing. Insert the retaining bolt and screw in the bolt two or three turns at this stage.

17 Lubricate the intake camshaft bearing journals in the camshaft housing and carefully insert the intake camshaft. Ensuring that the contact faces are clean and dry, refit the drivegear to the camshaft and insert the retaining bolt. Screw in the bolt two or three turns at this stage.

18 Turn each camshaft to align the timing slot with the valve timing checking hole in the camshaft housing. Insert the camshaft locking tools (either the Fiat tool or the home-made equivalent described in Section 3) ensuring that the tools fully engage with the camshaft slots **(see illustration)**.

19 With the camshafts locked in the timing position, tighten the drivegear retaining bolts and the sprocket retaining bolt to 20 Nm (15 lbf ft). Note that this is only an initial setting to retain the components. Final tightening is carried out after the camshaft housing has been refitted to the cylinder head.

20 Refit the camshaft position sensor to the camshaft housing and tighten the retaining bolt securely.

21 Refit the camshaft housing to the cylinder head as described in Section 8, paragraphs 10 to 15.

22 With the camshaft housing installed, final tightening of the drivegear and sprocket retaining bolts can be carried out.

23 Using the method employed on removal to hold the sprocket, tighten the sprocket

retaining bolt to the specified torque **(see illustration)**.

24 While still holding the sprocket with the tool, tighten the exhaust camshaft drivegear retaining bolt to the specified torque followed by the intake camshaft drivegear retaining bolt **(see illustration)**.

25 Remove the locking tool from the intake camshaft, but leave the exhaust camshaft locking tool in place.

26 Continue with the camshaft housing refitting procedure as described in Section 8, paragraphs 16 to 20.

---

10 Hydraulic tappets and rocker arms – removal, inspection and refitting

Removal

1 Remove the camshaft housing as described in Section 8.

2 Obtain sixteen small, oil-tight clean plastic containers, and number them intake 1 to 8 and exhaust 1 to 8; alternatively, divide a larger container into sixteen compartments and number each compartment accordingly.

3 Withdraw each rocker arm and hydraulic tappet in turn, unclip the rocker arm from the tappet, and place them in their respective container **(see illustrations)**. Do not interchange the rocker arms and tappets, or the rate of wear will be much increased. Fill each container with clean engine oil and ensure that the tappet is submerged.

Inspection

4 Examine the rocker arm and hydraulic tappet bearing surfaces for wear ridges and scoring. Renew any rocker arm or tappet on which these conditions are apparent.

5 If any new hydraulic tappets are obtained, they should be immersed in a container of clean engine oil prior to refitting.

Refitting

6 Liberally oil the cylinder head hydraulic tappet bores and the tappets. Working on one assembly at a time, clip the rocker arm back onto the tappet, then refit the tappet to the cylinder head, ensuring that it is refitted to its

10.3a Withdraw each rocker arm and tappet in turn . . .

10.3b . . . then unclip the arm from the tappet

11.2a Prise out the clip a little (arrowed) and pull the heater hoses from the stubs at the engine compartment bulkhead

11.2b On 95 bhp models, disconnect the lower heater hose at the metal pipe (arrowed) on the engine compartment bulkhead

original bore. Position each tappet so the oil channel hole is turned towards the outside of the cylinder head, aligned with the oil gallery. Lay the rocker arm over its respective valve.

7 Refit the remaining tappets and rocker arms in the same way.

8 With all the tappets and rocker arms in place, refit the camshaft housing as described in Section 8.

11 Cylinder head –
removal and refitting

Note: *This is an involved, complex task. On 500 models with the 95 bhp engine, it is recommended that the engine/transmission unit is removed from the vehicle as described in Chapter 2C, due to the limited access available.*

Removal

1 Remove the camshaft housing as described in Section 8, and the hydraulic tappets and rocker arms as described in Section 10. **Note:** *To improve access, remove the bonnet as described in Chapter 11.*

2 Release the clamps, and disconnect the coolant hoses from the heater pipe stubs at the engine compartment bulkhead **(see illustrations)**.

3 Remove the exhaust gas recirculation (EGR) valve and cooler as described in Chapter 4C.

4 Withdraw the engine oil dipstick, then undo the retaining bolt securing the dipstick guide tube to the intake manifold.

5 Using a small screwdriver, lift up the locking catch and disconnect the manifold pressure sensor wiring connector.

6 Undo the two bolts and free the crankcase ventilation system oil separator from the intake manifold **(see illustration)**.

7 Make a final check to ensure all wiring looms/plugs, coolant/vacuum hoses that would prevent the cylinder head from being removed, have been disconnected.

8 Working in the **reverse** of the tightening sequence **(see illustration 11.27b)**, progressively slacken the cylinder head bolts by half a turn at a time, until all bolts can be unscrewed by hand. Note that an M12 RIBE socket bit will be required to unscrew the bolts. Remove the cylinder head bolts and recover the washers. The cylinder head bolts must be discarded and renewed, regardless of their apparent condition

9 Engage the help of an assistant and lift the cylinder head from the cylinder block. Take care as it is a bulky and heavy assembly.

10 Remove the gasket and keep it for identification purposes (see paragraph 16).

11 If the cylinder head is to be dismantled for overhaul, then refer to Part C of this Chapter.

Preparation for refitting

12 The mating faces of the cylinder head and cylinder block/crankcase must be perfectly clean before refitting the head. Use a hard plastic or wood scraper to remove all traces of gasket and carbon; also clean the piston crowns. Take particular care, as the surfaces are damaged easily. Also, make sure that the carbon is not allowed to enter the oil and water passages – this is particularly important for the lubrication system, as carbon could block the oil supply to any of the engine's components. Using adhesive tape and paper, seal the water, oil and bolt holes in the cylinder

block/crankcase. To prevent carbon entering the gap between the pistons and bores, smear a little grease in the gap. After cleaning each piston, use a small brush to remove all traces of grease and carbon from the gap, then wipe away the remainder with a clean rag. Clean all the pistons in the same way.

13 Check the mating surfaces of the cylinder block/crankcase and the cylinder head for nicks, deep scratches and other damage. If slight, they may be removed carefully with a file, but if excessive, machining may be the only alternative to renewal.

14 Ensure that the cylinder head bolt holes in the crankcase are clean and free of oil. Syringe or soak up any oil left in the bolt holes. This is most important in order that the correct bolt tightening torque can be applied and to prevent the possibility of the block being cracked by hydraulic pressure when the bolts are tightened.

15 If warpage of the cylinder head gasket surface is suspected, use a straight-edge to check it for distortion. Refer to Part C of this Chapter if necessary.

16 On this engine, the cylinder head-to-piston clearance is controlled by fitting different thickness head gaskets. The gasket thickness can be determined by looking at the left-hand front corner of the gasket and checking on the number of holes **(see illustration)**.

11.6 Undo the bolts (arrowed) and detach the oil separator from the manifold

11.16 Cylinder head gasket thickness identification hole (arrowed)

11.19 Use a dial test indicator (DTI) to measure the piston protrusion

11.26 Align the end of the cylinder head with the block

Holes in gasket	Gasket thickness
No holes	0.67 to 0.77 mm
One hole	0.77 to 0.87 mm
Two holes	0.87 to 0.97 mm

The correct thickness of gasket required is selected by measuring the piston protrusions as follows.

17 Remove the crankshaft locking tool from the bellhousing and temporarily refit the crankshaft pulley hub retaining bolt to enable the crankshaft to be turned.

18 Mount a dial test indicator securely on the block so that its pointer can be easily pivoted between the piston crown and block mating surface. Turn the crankshaft to bring No 1 piston roughly to the TDC position. Move the dial test indicator probe over and in contact with No 1 piston. Turn the crankshaft back-and-forth slightly until the highest reading is shown on the gauge, indicating that the piston is at TDC.

19 Zero the dial test indicator on the gasket surface of the cylinder block then carefully move the indicator over No 1 piston. Measure its protrusion at the highest point between the valve cut-outs, and then again at its highest point between the valve cut-outs at 90° to the first measurement **(see illustration)**. Repeat this procedure with No 4 piston.

20 Rotate the crankshaft half a turn (180°) to bring No 2 and 3 pistons to TDC. Ensure the crankshaft is accurately positioned then measure the protrusions of No 2 and 3 pistons at the specified points. Once all pistons have

been measured, rotate the crankshaft to position all the pistons at their mid-stroke and refit the crankshaft locking tool. If the tool will not engage the hole in the flywheel, turn the crankshaft one complete turn and try again.

21 Select the correct thickness of head gasket required by determining the largest amount of piston protrusion, and using the following table.

Piston protrusion measurement	Gasket thickness required
0.028 to 0.127 mm	0.67 to 0.77 mm (no holes)
0.128 to 0.227 mm	0.77 to 0.87 mm (one hole)
0.228 to 0.327 mm	0.87 to 0.97 mm (two holes)

Refitting

22 Wipe clean the mating surfaces of the cylinder head and cylinder block/crankcase. Place the new gasket in position with the words ALTO/TOP uppermost.

23 If not already done, rotate the crankshaft to position all the pistons at their mid-stroke and refit the crankshaft locking tool. If the tool will not engage the hole in the flywheel, turn the crankshaft one complete turn and try again. Once the tool is in place, remove the crankshaft pulley hub retaining bolt.

24 With the aid of an assistant, carefully refit the cylinder head assembly to the block, aligning it with the locating dowels.

25 Apply a thin film of engine oil to the bolt threads and the underside of the bolt heads.

Carefully enter each new cylinder head bolt into its relevant hole (*do not drop them in*). Screw all bolts in, by hand only, until finger-tight.

26 Using a straight-edge, align the front face of the cylinder head with the front face of the cylinder block **(see illustration)**. Lightly tighten the cylinder head bolts to retain the head and maintain the alignment.

27 Working progressively in the sequence shown, tighten the cylinder head bolts to their Stage 1 torque setting, using a torque wrench and suitable socket **(see illustrations)**.

28 Once all bolts have been tightened to the Stage 1 torque, working again in the same sequence, go around and tighten all bolts through the specified Stage 2 angle, then through the specified Stage 3 angle using an angle-measuring gauge **(see illustration)**.

29 The remainder of refitting is a reversal of removal.

12 Sump – removal and refitting

Removal

1 Disconnect the battery negative terminal as described in Chapter 5A.

2 Apply the handbrake, then jack up the front of the vehicle and support it on axle stands (see *Jacking and vehicle support*). Remove the right-hand roadwheel and lower panel in the wheel arch liner.

3 Drain the engine oil as described in Chapter 1B, then fit a new sealing ring and refit the drain plug, tightening it to the specified torque. It is also recommended that the oil filter is renewed at the same time.

4 Referring to the relevant procedures contained in Chapter 4B, remove the centre exhaust pipe and rear silencer.

5 Undo the bolts and remove the bracket between the rear/lower engine mounting rod and the transmission housing.

6 Undo the retaining bolts and remove the cylinder block-to-transmission support underneath **(see illustration 6.26)**. Note the locations of the different length bolts to aid refitting.

11.27a Tighten the cylinder head bolts to the Stage 1 setting . . .

11.27b . . . in the sequence shown . . .

11.28 . . . and use an angle-gauge for Stage 2 and 3 settings

12.7 Disconnect the oil level sensor wiring plug

7 Disconnect the oil level sensor wiring connector at the rear of the sump (where fitted) **(see illustration)**.

8 Undo the bolts and nuts securing the sump to the cylinder block baseplate and timing cover. Using a wide-bladed scraper or similar tool inserted between the sump and baseplate, carefully break the joint, then remove the sump from under the car.

Refitting

9 Thoroughly clean the inside and outside of the sump ensuring that all traces of old sealant are removed from the mating face. Also clean the cylinder block baseplate mating face to remove all traces of old sealant.

10 Apply a 2 mm bead of silicone sealant to the sump mating face, ensuring the sealant

12.10 Apply a bead of sealant to the sump mating face, ensuring the sealant runs around the inside of the bolt holes

bead runs around the inside of the bolt holes **(see illustration)**. Position the sump on the cylinder block baseplate, then refit the thirteen bolts and two nuts. Progressively tighten the bolts/nuts to the specified torque. Reconnect the oil level sensor wiring connector.

11 Refit the sump reinforcement bracket to

the cylinder block baseplate and transmission bellhousing and secure with the five bolts, tightened securely.

12 The remainder of refitting is a reversal of removal, noting the following points:
 a) Tighten all fasteners to their specified torque where given.
 b) Fill the engine with fresh oil with reference to Chapter 1B.
 c) Check for oil leaks before taking the vehicle out onto the road.

13 Oil pump – removal, inspection and refitting

Removal

1 Remove the timing cover as described in Section 6.

2 Undo the two retaining bolts and remove the oil pick-up pipe from the oil pump cover on the rear of the timing cover. Remove the rubber seal from the pick-up pipe, noting that a new seal will be required for refitting **(see illustrations)**.

3 Remove the securing screws and withdraw the oil pump cover from the rear of the timing cover **(see illustration)**.

4 Remove the inner and outer rotor from the timing cover and wipe them clean. Also clean the rotor location in the timing cover **(see illustrations)**.

13.2a Remove the oil pick-up pipe from the oil pump cover . . .

13.2b . . . then remove the rubber seal from the pick-up pipe

13.3 Undo the screws and remove the oil pump cover

13.4a Remove the oil pump inner rotor . . .

13.4b . . . and outer rotor from the timing cover

13.5a Unscrew the oil pressure relief valve cap . . .

13.5b . . . then withdraw the spring . . .

13.5c . . . and the plunger

13.7 Check the oil pump rotor endfloat

13.8 Check the outer rotor-to-body clearance

13.13 Align the dot marks (arrowed) on the rotors

5 The oil pressure relief valve components can also be removed from the timing cover by unscrewing the cap. Withdraw the cap, the spring and the plunger (see illustrations).

Inspection

6 Check for any signs of scoring, pitting, scuffing or general wear on the rotors and their location in the timing cover. Renew any components as necessary. If the pump components are satisfactory, check the rotor clearances as follows.
7 Locate the inner and outer rotor back in the timing cover. Check the clearance between the end faces of the gears and the housing (endfloat) using a straight-edge and a feeler gauge (see illustration).
8 Check the outer rotor-to-body clearance using a feeler gauge (see illustration).
9 If the clearances are outside the specified limits, renew the components as necessary.
10 Examine the pressure relief valve spring and plunger, and renew if any sign of damage or wear is evident.
11 Ensure that the rotor location in the interior of the timing cover is scrupulously clean before commencing reassembly.

Refitting

12 Thoroughly clean the pressure relief valve components, and lubricate them with clean engine oil before refitting. Insert the plunger and spring, then apply thread-locking compound to the cap threads and refit the cap. Tighten the cap securely.
13 Ensure that the rotors are clean, then

lubricate them with clean engine oil. Locate the inner and outer rotor back in the timing cover, with the dot marks aligned and facing away from the timing cover (see illustration).
14 Ensure that the mating faces of the rear cover and the pump housing are clean, then refit the rear cover. Refit and tighten the securing screws securely.
15 Fit a new rubber seal to the oil pick-up pipe and locate the pipe on the oil pump cover. Refit the two retaining bolts and tighten securely.
16 Refit the timing cover as described in Section 6.

14 Crankshaft oil seals – renewal

Timing cover oil seal

Note: *The design of the engine is such that once the crankshaft pulley hub bolt is undone the valve timing will be lost unless suitable locking tools are used to retain the camshafts and crankshaft in the timing position. Refer to the information contained in Section 3 for further details and obtain the tools described.*
1 Remove the crankshaft pulley as described in Section 5.
2 Lock the camshafts and crankshaft in position as described in Section 3.
3 It will now be necessary to hold the crankshaft pulley hub to enable the retaining bolt to be removed. Fiat special tools No

1.871.000.200 and 1.860.831.000, however, a home-made tool can easily be fabricated (see **Tool Tip in Section 4**).
4 Using the Fiat tool or the home-made alternative, hold the pulley hub stationary and unscrew the retaining bolt. **Note:** *The pulley hub retaining bolt has a **left-hand thread** and is unscrewed by turning it clockwise.*
5 Withdraw the pulley hub from the crankshaft.
6 Carefully prise out the old crankshaft oil seal with a screwdriver or similar hooked tool. Clean the oil seal seat with a wooden or plastic scraper.
7 Tap the new oil seal into position until it is flush with the outer face of the timing cover, using a suitable socket or tube, or a wooden block.
8 Thoroughly clean the crankshaft pulley hub, ensuring that the timing chain sprocket contact face is free from oil or grease.
9 Refit the pulley hub to the crankshaft, then refit the retaining bolt. Using the method employed on removal to hold the pulley hub stationary, tighten the retaining bolt to the specified torque.
10 The remainder of refitting is a reversal of removal.

Transmission end oil seal

Note: *Fiat special tool 1.870.900.200 or a suitable equivalent oil seal fitting tool will be required for this operation.*
11 Remove the flywheel as described in Section 16.
12 Carefully prise out the old seal from its

14.14 Fit the oil seal to the fitting tool, so that the seal lip is spread open towards the crankshaft side

14.15b ... then tap the seal into position using a wooden block or similar

15.7 Undo the nut/bolts (arrowed) and remove the heat shield

14.15a Position the seal and tool over the end of the crankshaft . . .

14.16 Remove the fitting tool from the seal

location using a screwdriver or similar hooked tool.

13 Clean the oil seal seat with a wooden or plastic scraper.

14 Fit the new seal to the Fiat tool, or equivalent fitting tool, so that the seal lip is spread open toward the crankshaft side **(see illustration)**.

15 Position the seal, together with the fitting tool, over the end of the crankshaft, then tap the seal into position using a suitable socket or tube, or a wooden block, until it is flush with the outer faces of the cylinder block and baseplate **(see illustrations)**.

16 Once the seal is in position, remove the fitting tool **(see illustration)**.

17 Refit the flywheel as described in Section 16.

15 Oil cooler/heat exchanger – removal and refitting

Removal

1 Disconnect the battery negative terminal as described in Chapter 5A.

2 Remove the air cleaner assembly as described in Chapter 4B.

3 Referring to the procedures contained in Chapter 4B, separate the exhaust system front section from the catalytic converter.

4 Drain the cooling system as described in Chapter 1B.

95 bhp 500 models

5 Remove the turbocharger as described in Chapter 4B.

All other models

6 Undo the bolts and remove the catalytic converter heat shield.

All models

7 Undo the nut and bolts then remove the oil filter heat shield (where fitted) **(see illustration)**.

8 Undo the two bolts securing the coolant pipe to the oil filter housing **(see illustration)**. Recover the gasket noting that a new one will be required for refitting.

9 Unscrew the banjo union bolt and release the turbocharger oil supply pipe from the oil filter housing **(see illustration)**. Recover the two copper washers from the banjo union, and suitably cover the end of the pipe to prevent dirt entry. Note that new copper washers will be required for refitting.

10 Slacken the retaining clip and disconnect

15.8 Undo the coolant pipe retaining bolts (arrowed)

15.9 Undo the turbo oil supply pipe banjo bolt (arrowed) from the oil filter housing

the radiator bottom hose from the outlet at the base of the oil filter housing.

11 Undo the three bolts securing the heat shield to the heat exchanger (see illustrations).

12 Undo the remaining bolt and remove the oil filter housing and heat exchanger assembly from the cylinder block. Recover the rubber seal from the rear of the housing. Note that a new seal will be required for refitting.

13 Undo the three retaining bolts and withdraw the heat exchanger from the oil filter housing (see illustration). Recover the four sealing rings, noting that new sealing rings will be required for refitting.

Refitting

14 Thoroughly clean the heat exchanger and oil filter housing, then fit the four new sealing rings to the filter housing.

15 Place the heat exchanger in position and secure with the three retaining bolts, securely tightened.

16 Place a new rubber seal on the oil filter housing, ensuring the seal is fully engaged with the housing grooves (see illustration).

17 Position the oil filter housing on the cylinder block and fit the lower left retaining bolt finger-tight. Place the heat shield support bracket in position and fit the remaining three retaining bolts. Tighten the four bolts to the specified torque.

18 The remainder of refitting is a reversal of removal.

16 Flywheel – removal, inspection and refitting

Note: *New flywheel retaining bolts will be required on refitting.*

Removal

1 Remove the clutch assembly as described in Chapter 6.

2 Prevent the flywheel from turning by inserting one of the bellhousing-to-engine retaining bolts. Rest a large screwdriver

16.3 Flywheel retaining bolts (arrowed)

15.11a Undo the bolts (arrowed) and remove the heat shield – non-95 bhp models . . .

15.13 Oil cooler/heat exchanger retaining bolts (arrowed)

against the bolt with its end in contact with the flywheel ring gear teeth.

3 Slacken and remove the retaining bolts and remove the flywheel (see illustration). Do not drop it, as it is very heavy.

Inspection

4 Examine the flywheel for wear or chipping of the ring gear teeth. Renewal of the ring gear is possible but is not a task for the home mechanic; renewal requires the new ring gear to be heated (up to 180° to 230°C) to allow it to be fitted.

5 Examine the flywheel for scoring of the clutch face. If the clutch face is scored, the flywheel may be surface-ground, but renewal is preferable.

6 If there is any doubt about the condition of the flywheel, seek the advice of a Fiat dealer or engine reconditioning specialist. They will be able to advise if it is possible to recondition it or whether renewal is necessary.

Refitting

7 Clean the mating surfaces of the flywheel and crankshaft.

8 Apply a drop of locking compound to the threads of each of the new flywheel retaining bolts (unless they are precoated) then refit the flywheel and install the new bolts.

9 Lock the flywheel using the method employed on removal then, working in a diagonal sequence, evenly and progressively tighten the retaining bolts to the specified torque setting.

15.11b . . . and 95 bhp models

15.16 Ensure the new seal fully engages with the housing grooves

10 Refit the clutch as described in Chapter 6.

17 Engine/transmission mountings – inspection and renewal

Inspection

1 To improve access, firmly apply the handbrake, then jack up the front of the vehicle and support it on axle stands (see *Jacking and vehicle support*).

2 Check the mounting blocks (rubbers) to see if they are cracked, hardened or separated from the metal at any point. Renew the mounting block if any such damage or deterioration is evident.

3 Check that all the mounting securing nuts and bolts are securely tightened, using a torque wrench to check if possible.

4 Using a large screwdriver, or a similar tool, check for wear in the mounting blocks by carefully levering against them to check for free play. Where this is not possible, enlist the aid of an assistant to move the engine/gearbox unit back-and-forth, and from side-to-side, while you observe the mountings. While some free play is to be expected, even from new components, excessive wear should be obvious. If excessive free play is found, check first to see that the securing nuts and bolts are correctly tightened, then renew any worn components as described in the following paragraphs.

17.10 Undo the nuts (arrowed) and remove the mounting

17.11 Undo the bolts (arrowed) and remove the engine mounting bracket

17.18 Left-hand mounting-to-bracket bolt (arrowed)

Note: *Before slackening any of the engine mounting bolts/nuts, the relative positions of the mountings to their various brackets should be marked to ensure correct alignment upon refitting.*

Right-hand mounting renewal

5 Apply the handbrake, then jack up the front of the vehicle and support it on axle stands (see *Jacking and vehicle support*).
6 Remove the air cleaner assembly as described in Chapter 4B.
7 On models 07/06-on, release the clamps and remove the air intake hose from the turbocharger.
8 On 500 models, undo the retaining bolt and move the coolant expansion tank to one side.
9 Position a workshop/trolley jack beneath the engine with a block of wood on the jack head, and support the weight of the engine.
10 Undo the nuts securing the mounting to the body and cylinder head bracket **(see illustration)**. Remove the mounting.
11 If necessary, undo the bolts securing the engine mounting bracket to the cylinder block and cylinder head, and remove the bracket **(see illustration)**.
12 If removed, refit the engine mounting bracket and tighten the bolts to the specified torque.
13 Place the engine mounting in position and tighten the retaining bolts to the specified torque.

14 The remainder of refitting is a reversal of removal.

Left-hand mounting renewal

15 Apply the handbrake, then jack up the front of the vehicle and support it on axle stands (see *Jacking and vehicle support*).
16 Remove the battery and battery tray as described in Chapter 5A.
17 Position a workshop/trolley jack beneath the transmission with a block of wood on the jack head, and support the weight of the transmission.
18 Undo the bolt securing the mounting bracket to the transmission bracket **(see illustration)**.
19 Undo the two bolts mounting to the body and remove the mounting assembly from the car.
20 Refitting is a reversal of removal. Ensure all bolts are tightened to their specified torques.

Rear mounting/ torque rod renewal

21 Apply the handbrake, then jack up the front of the vehicle and support it on axle stands (see *Jacking and vehicle support*).

95 bhp 500 models

22 Working under the vehicle, undo the bolts securing the torque rod bracket to the transmission **(see illustration)**.
23 Undo the bolt securing the torque rod to the subframe, and remove the rod.

24 Undo the bolt securing the torque rod to the bracket.
25 Refitting is a reversal of removal. Ensure all bolts are tightened to their specified torques.

All other models

26 Referring to the relevant procedures contained in Chapter 4B, remove the centre exhaust pipe and rear silencer.
27 Undo the bolts securing the rod to the subframe and transmission bracket, and remove it **(see illustration)**.
28 Refitting is a reversal of removal. Ensure all bolts are tightened to their specified torques.

18 Oil pressure warning light switch – removal and refitting

Removal

1 The oil pressure warning light switch is screwed into the front left-hand end of the cylinder head **(see illustration)**.
2 Pull back the cover and disconnect the wiring from the switch.
3 Place some cloth rags beneath the switch, then unscrew the switch from the block.

Refitting

4 Refitting is a reversal of removal, and tighten the switch securely.

17.22 Rear mounting/torque rod (arrowed) – 95 bhp models

17.27 Rear mounting/torque rod (arrowed) – all other models

18.1 Oil pressure warning light switch (arrowed)

Chapter 2 Part C:
Engine removal and overhaul procedures

Contents

Degrees of difficulty

Easy, suitable for novice with little experience	**Fairly easy,** suitable for beginner with some experience	**Fairly difficult,** suitable for competent DIY mechanic	**Difficult,** suitable for experienced DIY mechanic	**Very difficult,** suitable for expert DIY or professional

Specifications

Petrol engines

Cylinder head
Maximum gasket face distortion	0.1 mm
Overall height of cylinder head (sealing surface-to-sealing surface) . . .	126.5 ± 0.35 mm

Valves and guides
Valve stem diameter.	6.982 to 7.000 mm
Valve face angle	45° 30' ± 5'
Valve stem-to-guide clearance.	0.022 to 0.058 mm

Cylinder block
Bore diameter:	
Nominal size:	
1.1 litre	70.00 mm
1.2 litre	70.80 mm
Oversizes available.	0.4 mm

Pistons and piston rings
Piston diameter (nominal):	
1.1 litre	69.96 to 69.99 mm
1.2 litre (measured 8.5 mm up from base of skirt)	70.76 to 70.77 mm
Piston-to-bore clearance	0.030 to 0.050 mm
Piston ring-to-groove clearance:	
Top compression ring.	0.040 to 0.080 mm
2nd compression ring.	0.020 to 0.055 mm
Oil scraper ring.	0.020 to 0.055 mm
Piston ring end gap:	
Top compression ring.	0.20 to 0.40 mm
2nd compression ring.	0.25 to 0.45 mm
Oil scraper ring.	0.20 to 0.45 mm

Crankshaft and bearings
Bearing journal diameters (standard):	
Main bearings (nominal)	47.98 mm
Big-end bearings (nominal).	41.98 mm
Endfloat	0.05 to 0.26 mm

Torque wrench settings
Refer to Chapter 2A *Specifications*

Diesel engines

Cylinder head

Maximum permissible distortion of sealing face	0.1 mm
Overall height of cylinder head (sealing surface-to-sealing surface) . . .	105.45 to 105.55 mm
Valve seat width	1.5 to 1.7 mm
Valve seat angle	45°

Valves and guides

Valve stem diameter.	5.90 to 5.94 mm
Valve head diameter.	22.0 mm
Maximum permissible valve stem play in guide.	0.028 to 0.064 mm
Valve clearances.	Automatic adjustment by hydraulic valve lifters

Cylinder block

Cylinder bore diameters.	69.600 to 69.630 mm (nominal)

Pistons and rings

Piston diameter	69.520 to 69.550 mm (nominal)
Ring end gap:	
Top compression ring.	0.20 to 0.30 mm
Second compression ring.	1.00 to 1.50 mm
Oil control ring	0.25 to 0.50 mm

Crankshaft and bearings

Main bearing journal diameter	50.855 to 51.000 mm (nominal)
Big-end bearing journal diameter.	42.455 to 42.600 mm (nominal)
Endfloat	0.055 to 0.265 mm

Torque wrench settings

Refer to Chapter 2B *Specifications*

1 General information

Included in this Part of Chapter 2 are details of removing the engine/transmission from the car and general overhaul procedures for the cylinder head, cylinder block/crankcase and all other engine internal components.

The information given ranges from advice concerning preparation for an overhaul and the purchase of parts, to detailed step-by-step procedures covering removal, inspection, renovation and refitting of engine internal components.

After Section 6, all instructions are based on the assumption that the engine has been removed from the car. For information concerning in-car engine repair, as well as the removal and refitting of those external components necessary for full overhaul, refer to Part A or B of this Chapter (as applicable) and to Section 6. Ignore any preliminary dismantling operations described in Part A or B that are no longer relevant once the engine has been removed from the car.

Apart from torque wrench settings, which are given at the beginning of Part A or B (as applicable), all specifications relating to engine overhaul are at the beginning of this Part of Chapter 2.

2 Engine overhaul – general information

It is not always easy to determine when, or if, an engine should be completely overhauled, as a number of factors must be considered.

High mileage is not necessarily an indication that an overhaul is needed, while low mileage does not preclude the need for an overhaul. Frequency of servicing is probably the most important consideration. An engine which has had regular and frequent oil and filter changes, as well as other required maintenance, should give many thousands of miles of reliable service. Conversely, a neglected engine may require an overhaul very early in its life.

Excessive oil consumption is an indication that piston rings, valve seals and/or valve guides are in need of attention. Make sure that oil leaks are not responsible before deciding that the rings and/or guides are worn. Perform a compression test, as described in Part A (petrol engines) or B (diesel engines) of this Chapter, to determine the likely cause of the problem.

Check the oil pressure with a gauge fitted in place of the oil pressure switch, and compare it with that specified. If it is extremely low, the main and big-end bearings, and/or the oil pump, are probably worn out.

Loss of power, rough running, knocking or metallic engine noises, excessive valve gear noise, and high fuel consumption may also point to the need for an overhaul, especially if they are all present at the same time. If a complete service does not cure the situation, major mechanical work is the only solution.

A full engine overhaul involves restoring all internal parts to the specification of a new engine. During a complete overhaul, the pistons and the piston rings are renewed, and the cylinder bores are reconditioned. New main and big-end bearings are generally fitted; if necessary, the crankshaft may be reground, to compensate for wear in the journals. The valves are also serviced as well, since they are usually in less-than-perfect condition at this point. Always pay careful attention to the condition of the oil pump when overhauling the engine, and renew it if there is any doubt as to its serviceability. The end result should be an as-new engine that will give many trouble-free miles.

Critical cooling system components such as the hoses, thermostat and coolant pump should be renewed when an engine is overhauled. The radiator should also be checked carefully, to ensure that it is not clogged or leaking.

Before beginning the engine overhaul, read through the entire procedure, to familiarise yourself with the scope and requirements of the job. Check on the availability of parts and make sure that any necessary special tools and equipment are obtained in advance. Most work can be done with typical hand tools, although a number of precision measuring tools are required for inspecting parts to determine if they must be renewed.

The services provided by an engineering machine shop or engine reconditioning specialist will almost certainly be required, particularly if major repairs such as crankshaft regrinding or cylinder reboring are necessary. Apart from carrying out machining operations, these establishments will normally handle the inspection of parts, offer advice concerning reconditioning or renewal and supply new components such as pistons, piston rings and bearing shells. It is recommended that the establishment used is a member of the Federation of Engine Re-Manufacturers, or a similar society.

Always wait until the engine has been completely dismantled, and until all components (especially the cylinder block/crankcase and the crankshaft) have been inspected, before deciding what service and repair operations must be performed by an engineering works. The condition of these components will be the major factor to consider when determining whether to overhaul the original engine, or to buy a reconditioned unit. Do not, therefore, purchase parts or have overhaul work done on other components until they have been thoroughly inspected. As a general rule, time is the primary cost of an overhaul, so it does not pay to fit worn or sub-standard parts.

As a final note, to ensure maximum life and minimum trouble from a reconditioned engine, everything must be assembled with care, in a spotlessly-clean environment.

3 Engine removal – methods and precautions

On all Panda/500 models, the engine must be removed complete with the transmission as an assembly. There is insufficient clearance in the engine compartment to remove the engine leaving the transmission in the vehicle. On Panda models, the assembly is removed by raising the front of the vehicle, and lowering the assembly from the engine compartment, whereas on 500 models the front panel is removed and the engine/transmission assembly is lowered slightly, then removed from the front of the vehicle.

If you have decided that the engine must be removed for overhaul or major repair work, several preliminary steps should be taken.

Locating a suitable place to work is extremely important. Adequate work space, along with storage space for the car, will be needed. If a workshop or garage is not available, at the very least, a flat, level, clean work surface is required.

Cleaning the engine compartment and engine/transmission before beginning the removal procedure will help keep tools clean and organised.

An engine hoist will also be necessary. Make sure the equipment is rated in excess of the combined weight of the engine and transmission. Safety is of primary importance, considering the potential hazards involved in removing the engine/transmission from the car.

The help of an assistant is essential. Apart from the safety aspects involved, there are many instances when one person cannot simultaneously perform all of the operations required during engine/transmission removal.

Plan the operation ahead of time. Before starting work, arrange for the hire of or obtain all of the tools and equipment you will need. Some of the equipment necessary to perform engine/transmission removal and installation safely (in addition to an engine hoist) is as follows: a heavy duty trolley jack, complete sets of spanners and sockets as described in the rear of this manual, wooden blocks, and plenty of rags and cleaning solvent for mopping-up spilled oil, coolant and fuel. If the hoist must be hired, make sure that you arrange for it in advance, and perform all of the operations possible without it beforehand. This will save you money and time.

Plan for the car to be out of use for quite a while. An engineering machine shop or engine reconditioning specialist will be required to perform some of the work which cannot be accomplished without special equipment. These places often have a busy schedule, so it would be a good idea to consult them before removing the engine, in order to accurately estimate the amount of time required to rebuild or repair components that may need work.

During the engine/transmission removal procedure, it is advisable to make notes of the locations of all brackets, cable ties, earthing points, etc, as well as how the wiring harnesses, hoses and electrical connections are attached and routed around the engine and engine compartment. An effective way of doing this is to take a series of photographs of the various components before they are disconnected or removed; the resulting photographs will prove invaluable when the engine/transmission is refitted.

Always be extremely careful when removing and refitting the engine/transmission. Serious injury can result from careless actions. Plan ahead and take your time, and a job of this nature, although major, can be accomplished successfully.

4 Petrol engine and transmission unit – removal, separation and refitting

Note: Such is the complexity of the power unit arrangement on these vehicles, and the variations that may be encountered according to model and optional equipment fitted, that the following should be regarded as a guide to the work involved, rather than a step-by-step procedure. Where differences are encountered, or additional component disconnection or removal is necessary, make notes of the work involved as an aid to refitting.

Removal

1 On models with air conditioning, have the refrigerant circuit evacuated by a Fiat dealer or suitably-equipped repairer.
2 Position the steering with the front roadwheels straight-ahead, and lock the steering by removing the ignition key.
3 Apply the handbrake, then jack up the front of the vehicle and support it on axle stands (see *Jacking and vehicle support*). Remove both front roadwheels, and the right-hand inner wheel arch liner for access to the crankshaft pulley. Where necessary, remove the engine compartment undertray and the engine top cover. Note that Panda models must be raised sufficiently high (at least 700 mm) to enable the engine/transmission assembly to be withdrawn from under the front of the vehicle.
4 To improve access, remove the bonnet as described in Chapter 11.
5 Remove the engine management ECU as described in Chapter 4A.
6 Remove the battery and battery tray as described in Chapter 5A.
7 If necessary, drain the engine oil as described in Chapter 1A.
8 Remove the air cleaner assembly as described in Chapter 4A.
9 Drain the cooling system as described in Chapter 1A.
10 On Panda models, note their fitted positions and loom routing, then disconnect the wiring plugs from the various engine components as necessary. Move the wiring loom to one side.
11 On 500 models, disconnect the engine wiring loom wiring plug at the front, left-hand corner of the engine.
12 Disconnect the oxygen sensor(s) wiring plugs.
13 Prise the servo one-way valve from place, and move the vacuum pipe to one side.
14 Release the clamps and disconnect the heater hoses from the engine compartment bulkhead.
15 Depressurise the fuel system as described in Chapter 4A, then disconnect the fuel feed pipe **(see illustration)**. Be prepared for fuel

4.15 Squeeze together the sides (arrowed) and pull out the fuel pipe from the end of the fuel rail

4.24a Upper and lower crossmembers (arrowed)

4.24b Note the spacer (arrowed) fitted between the upper crossmember and the front panel

4.25 Undo the bolts (arrowed) securing the front panel to the wing each side

spillage, and take adequate precautions. Clamp or plug the open unions, to minimise further fuel loss.

16 On models with an accelerator cable, disconnect the accelerator cable from the throttle body, and move the cable to one side. Refer to Chapter 4A if necessary.

17 On models without an accelerator cable, remove the throttle body as described in Chapter 4A.

18 Release the clamp and disconnect the upper radiator coolant hose.

500 models

19 Remove the front bumper as described in Chapter 11.

20 Remove the front light units as described in Chapter 12.

21 Disconnect the wiring plugs from the horn, electric cooling fan, refrigerant pipe pressure sensor (where applicable) and the front impact sensor.

22 Disconnect the cable from the bonnet lock – see Chapter 11.

23 Undo the bolt and detach the refrigerant pipes from the condenser (where applicable). Plug the openings to prevent contamination, and discard the pipe seals – new ones must be fitted.

24 Make alignment marks between the crossmembers, front panel, chassis legs, and retaining bolts each side, then undo the bolts and remove the upper and lower front crossmembers. Note the spacer fitted behind the upper crossmember **(see illustrations)**.

25 Undo the retaining bolts, and with the help

of as assistant, remove the front panel **(see illustration)**.

All models

26 On models with air conditioning, remove the refrigerant pipe from the expansion valve to the compressor, from the expansion valve to the condenser, and the compressor to the condenser (where not already done so). Plug the openings to prevent contamination, and discard the pipe seals – new ones must be fitted.

27 Disconnect the earth lead and reversing light switch wiring plug from the transmission **(see illustration)**.

28 Disconnect the clutch cable (where fitted) from the release lever on the transmission, with reference to Chapter 6.

29 Disconnect the gearchange cables from the levers on the transmission, then undo the bolts and detach the cables support bracket from the transmission. Refer to Chapter 7 if necessary.

30 Remove the centre exhaust pipe and rear silencer as described in Chapter 4A.

31 Undo the bolts and remove the exhaust manifold heat shield.

32 Remove the retaining clips and release the flexible brake pipes from the suspension strut each side.

33 Remove both driveshafts as described in Chapter 8.

34 Remove the lower/rear torque rod from under the engine/transmission as described in Chapter 2A.

35 Undo the retaining nuts and remove the exhaust manifold.

36 Attach a suitable hoist and lifting tackle to the engine lifting brackets on the cylinder head and transmission, and support the weight of the engine/transmission.

37 On Panda models, remove the front subframe as described in Chapter 10. On 500 models, undo the bolts and remove the front section of the subframe each side **(see illustration)**.

38 Unscrew the nuts securing the right-hand engine mounting to the engine lower mounting bracket and vehicle body, and remove the mounting assembly.

39 Slacken the two nuts securing the left-hand engine mounting to the vehicle body, then undo the central bolt securing the mounting to the transmission.

40 Make a final check to ensure that all relevant pipes, hoses, wires, etc, have been disconnected, and that they are positioned clear of the engine and transmission.

41 With the help of an assistant, carefully lower the engine/transmission assembly to the ground. Make sure that the surrounding components in the engine compartment are not damaged. Ideally, the assembly should be lowered onto a trolley jack or low platform with castors, so that it can easily be withdrawn from under the car.

42 Ensure that the assembly is adequately supported, then disconnect the engine hoist and lifting tackle, and withdraw the engine/transmission assembly from under the front of the vehicle.

43 Clean away any external dirt using paraffin or a water-soluble solvent and a stiff brush.

44 With reference to Chapter 7, unbolt the transmission from the engine. Carefully withdraw the transmission from the engine. Ensure that its weight is not allowed to hang on the input shaft while engaged with the clutch friction disc. Note that the transmission locates on dowels positioned in the rear of the cylinder block.

Refitting

45 With reference to Chapter 7, refit the transmission to the engine and tighten the bolts to the specified torque.

46 With the front of the vehicle raised and supported on axle stands, move the engine/

4.27 Disconnect the wiring plug (arrowed) from the reversing light switch

4.37 Undo the bolts (arrowed) and remove the front section of the subframe each side

5.10 Disconnect the wiring as necessary to allow the wiring loom to remain with the engine

5.13a Pull back the collar and disconnect the fuel pipes – pre-Euro 5 engines

5.13b Fuel filter bracket mounting bolts (arrowed) – Euro 5 engines

transmission assembly under the vehicle, ensuring that the assembly is adequately supported.

47 Reconnect the hoist and lifting tackle to the engine lifting brackets, and carefully raise the engine/transmission assembly up into the engine compartment with the help of an assistant.

48 Reconnect the right- and left-hand engine/transmission mountings and tighten the bolt/nuts to the specified torque given in Chapter 2A.

49 The reminder of refitting is a reversal of removal, noting the following points:

a) Tighten all fasteners to their specified torque where given.

b) Fill the engine with fresh oil as described in Chapter 1A.

c) Replenish the coolant as described in Chapter 1A.

d) Check for leaks before venturing out onto the road.

5 Diesel engine and transmission unit – removal, separation and refitting

Note: Such is the complexity of the power unit arrangement on these vehicles, and the variations that may be encountered according to model and optional equipment fitted, that the following should be regarded as a guide to the work involved, rather than a step-by-step procedure. Where differences are encountered, or additional component disconnection or removal is necessary, make notes of the work involved as an aid to refitting.

Removal

1 On models with air conditioning, have the refrigerant circuit evacuated by a Fiat dealer or suitably-equipped repairer.

2 Position the steering with the front roadwheels straight-ahead, and lock the steering by removing the ignition key.

3 Apply the handbrake, then jack up the front of the vehicle and support it on axle stands (see *Jacking and vehicle support*). Remove both front roadwheels, and the right-hand

inner wheel arch liner for access to the crankshaft pulley. Where fitted, remove the engine compartment undertray. Note that Panda models must be raised sufficiently high (at least 700 mm) to enable the engine/transmission assembly to be withdrawn from under the front of the vehicle.

4 To improve access, remove the bonnet as described in Chapter 11.

5 Remove the battery and battery tray as described in Chapter 5A.

6 If necessary, drain the engine oil as described in Chapter 1B.

7 Remove the air cleaner assembly as described in Chapter 4B.

8 Drain the cooling system as described in Chapter 1B.

9 Remove the preheater control unit as described in Chapter 5A.

10 Note their fitted positions, and disconnect the various wiring plugs/connections necessary to allow the engine wiring loom to remain with the engine as it's removed **(see illustration)**.

11 Release the clamps, undo the retaining bolts and remove the air pipe/hose from the intercooler to the turbocharger, and the intercooler to the air cleaner housing.

12 Release the hose clamps, undo the retaining bolt and remove the coolant expansion tank from the inner wing (where applicable).

13 Disconnect the hoses and the wiring plug, then undo the bolts and remove the fuel

filter complete with mounting bracket **(see illustrations)**. Be prepared for fuel spillage, and take adequate precautions. Clamp or plug the open unions, to minimise further fuel loss. Note also that the pipes are of different diameter to avoid confusion when reconnecting.

14 Depress the release button and disconnect the servo hose from the vacuum pump.

15 Remove the throttle housing as described in Chapter 4B for access to the heater hoses on the bulkhead.

16 Prise out the retaining clips and disconnect the heater hoses from the engine compartment bulkhead. Note that on 95 bhp 500 models, disconnect the lower heater hose at the metal pipe on the right-hand side of the bulkhead **(see illustrations)**.

17 Release the clamp and disconnect the upper radiator coolant hose, and (if not already done so) the lower hose.

500 models

18 Remove the front bumper as described in Chapter 11.

19 Remove the front dipped light units as described in Chapter 12.

20 Disconnect the wiring plugs from the horn, electric cooling fan, cooling fan resistor, refrigerant pipe pressure sensor and the front impact sensor (where applicable). Release the wiring looms from and retaining clips on the front panel.

21 Disconnect the cable from the bonnet lock – see Chapter 11.

5.16a Prise out the clip (arrowed) a little and disconnect the heater hoses at the bulkhead

5.16b On 95 bhp models, disconnect the lower hose at the metal pipe (arrowed) on the bulkhead

5.24 Turbocharger vane position vacuum solenoid (arrowed)

22 Undo the bolt and detach the refrigerant pipes from the condenser (where applicable), then release the pipes from the retaining clips – see Chapter 3. Plug the openings to prevent contamination, and discard the pipe seals – new ones must be fitted.

23 Make alignment marks between the crossmembers, front panel, chassis legs and retaining bolts each side, then undo the bolts and remove the upper and lower front crossmembers. Note the spacer fitted behind the upper crossmember **(see illustrations 4.24a and 4.24b)**.

24 On 95 bhp models, undo the bolt and detach the turbocharger vane position vacuum solenoid from the front panel **(see illustration)**.

25 Undo the retaining bolts, and with the help of as assistant, remove the front panel **(see illustration 4.25)**. Support the panel assembly as the bolts are removed.

All models

26 Disconnect the wiring plug, undo the retaining nut and detach the particulate filter pressure sensor from the engine compartment bulkhead (where fitted) **(see illustration)**. Unclip the hoses as the sensor is withdrawn.

27 Undo the retaining bolts and disconnect the refrigerant pipes from the compressor. Plug the openings to prevent contamination. Discard the pipes seals – new ones must be fitted.

28 Disconnect the fuel return hose from the manifold above the cylinder head **(see illustrations)**.

29 Disconnect the earth lead and reversing light switch wiring plug from the transmission **(see illustration 4.27)**.

30 Disconnect the clutch cable (where fitted) from the release lever on the transmission, with reference to Chapter 6.

31 Disconnect the clutch fluid pipe (where fitted) at connection beneath the battery location, with reference to Chapter 6, and unclip the pipe from the bracket.

32 Disconnect the gearchange cables from the levers on the transmission, and the support bracket on the transmission. Refer to Chapter 7 if necessary.

33 Remove the centre exhaust pipe and rear silencer as described in Chapter 4B.

34 Remove the retaining clips and release the flexible brake pipes from the suspension strut each side.

35 Remove both driveshafts as described in Chapter 8.

36 Remove the lower/rear torque rod from under the engine/transmission as described in Chapter 2B.

37 Attach a suitable hoist and lifting tackle to the engine lifting brackets on the cylinder head and transmission, and support the weight of the engine/transmission.

38 On Panda models, remove the front subframe as described in Chapter 10. On 500 models, undo the bolts and remove the front section of the subframe each side **(see illustration 4.37)**.

39 Unscrew the nuts securing the right-hand engine mounting to the engine lower mounting bracket and vehicle body, and remove the mounting assembly.

40 Slacken the two nuts/bolts securing the left-hand engine mounting to the vehicle body, then undo the central bolt securing the mounting to the transmission.

41 Make a final check to ensure that all relevant pipes, hoses, wires, etc, have been disconnected, and that they are positioned clear of the engine and transmission.

42 With the help of an assistant, carefully lower the engine/transmission assembly to the ground. Make sure that the surrounding components in the engine compartment are not damaged. Ideally, the assembly should be lowered onto a trolley jack or low platform with castors, so that it can easily be withdrawn from under the car.

43 Ensure that the assembly is adequately supported, then disconnect the engine hoist and lifting tackle, and withdraw the engine/transmission assembly from under the front of the vehicle.

44 Clean away any external dirt using paraffin or a water-soluble solvent and a stiff brush.

45 With reference to Chapter 7, unbolt the transmission from the engine. Carefully withdraw the transmission from the engine. Ensure that its weight is not allowed to hang on the input shaft while engaged with the clutch friction disc. Note that the transmission locates on dowels positioned in the rear of the cylinder block.

Refitting

46 With reference to Chapter 7, refit the transmission to the engine and tighten the bolts to the specified torque.

47 With the front of the vehicle raised and supported on axle stands, move the engine/transmission assembly under the vehicle, ensuring that the assembly is adequately supported.

48 Reconnect the hoist and lifting tackle to the engine lifting brackets, and carefully raise the engine/transmission assembly up into the engine compartment with the help of an assistant.

49 Reconnect the right- and left-hand engine/transmission mountings and tighten the bolt/nuts to the specified torque given in Chapter 2B.

50 The reminder of refitting is a reversal of removal, noting the following points:

 a) *Tighten all fasteners to their specified torque where given.*

 b) *Fill the engine with fresh oil as described in Chapter 1B.*

 c) *Replenish the coolant as described in Chapter 1B.*

 d) *Check for leaks before venturing out onto the road.*

5.26 Particulate filter pressure sensor (arrowed) on the left-hand side of the engine compartment bulkhead

5.28a Depress the release button (arrowed) and disconnect the return hose – pre-Euro 5 engines . . .

5.28b . . . and Euro 5 engines (arrowed)

6 Engine overhaul – dismantling sequence

1 It is much easier to dismantle and work on the engine if it is mounted on a portable engine stand. These stands can often be hired from a tool hire shop. Before the engine is mounted on a stand, the flywheel should be removed, so that the stand bolts can be tightened into the end of the cylinder block/crankcase.

2 If a stand is not available, it is possible to dismantle the engine with it blocked up on a sturdy workbench, or on the floor. Be extra careful not to tip or drop the engine when working without a stand.

3 If you are going to obtain a reconditioned engine, all the external components must be removed first, to be transferred to the new engine (just as they will if you are doing a complete engine overhaul yourself). These components include the following:

a) Engine wiring harness and supports.
b) Alternator and air conditioning compressor mounting brackets (as applicable).
c) Coolant pump (where applicable) and inlet/outlet housings.
d) Dipstick tube.
e) Fuel system components.
f) All electrical switches and sensors.
g) Intake and exhaust manifolds and, where fitted, the turbocharger.
h) Oil filter and oil cooler/heat exchanger.
i) Flywheel.

Note: When removing the external components from the engine, pay close attention to details that may be helpful or important during refitting. Note the fitted position of gaskets, seals, spacers, pins, washers, bolts, and other small items.

4 If you are obtaining a 'short' engine (which consists of the engine cylinder block/crankcase, crankshaft, pistons and connecting rods all assembled), then the cylinder head, sump, oil pump, and timing chain/belt will have to be removed also.

5 Before beginning the dismantling and overhaul procedures, make sure that you have all of the correct tools necessary. See *Tools and working facilities* for further information.

6 If you are planning a complete overhaul, the engine can be dismantled, and the internal components removed, in the order given below.

Petrol engines

a) Intake and exhaust manifolds (see Chapter 4A).
b) Coolant pump (see Chapter 3).
c) Cylinder head (see Chapter 2A).
d) Flywheel (see Chapter 2A).
e) Sump (see Chapter 2A).
f) Oil pump (see Chapter 2A).
g) Timing belt and sprockets (see Chapter 2A).
h) Pistons/connecting rod assemblies (see Section 10).
i) Crankshaft (see Section 11).

Diesel engines

a) Sump (see Chapter 2B).
b) Coolant pump (see Chapter 3).
c) Timing chain and sprockets (see Chapter 2B).
d) Oil pump (see Chapter 2B).
e) Camshaft housing (see Chapter 2B).
f) Cylinder head (see Chapter 2B).
g) Intake and exhaust manifolds (see Chapter 4B).
h) Flywheel (see Chapter 2B).
i) Pistons/connecting rod assemblies (see Section 10).
j) Crankshaft (see Section 11).

7 Cylinder head – dismantling

Note: New and reconditioned cylinder heads may be available from the manufacturer, and from engine overhaul specialists. Due to the fact that some specialist tools are required for the dismantling and inspection procedures, and new components may not be readily available, it may be more practical and economical for the home mechanic to purchase a reconditioned head rather than to dismantle, inspect and recondition the original head. A valve spring compressor tool will be required for this operation.

1 With the cylinder head removed as described in Chapter 2A or 2B, clean away all external dirt, and remove the following components as applicable, if not already done:

a) Manifolds (see Chapter 4A or 4B).
b) Spark plugs (petrol engines – see Chapter 1A).
c) Glow plugs (diesel engines – see Chapter 5A).
d) Camshafts and followers (petrol engines – see Chapter 2A).
e) Hydraulic tappets and rocker arms (diesel engines – see Chapter 2B).
f) Engine lifting brackets.

2 To remove a valve, fit a valve spring compressor tool. Ensure that the arms of the compressor tool are securely positioned on the head of the valve and the spring cap **(see illustration)**. The valves are deeply-recessed on petrol engines, and a suitable extension piece may be required for the spring compressor.

3 Compress the valve spring to relieve the pressure of the spring cap acting on the collets.

4 Extract the two split collets by hooking them out using a small screwdriver, then slowly release the compressor tool **(see illustration)**.

5 Remove the valve spring cap and the spring, then withdraw the valve through the combustion chamber. Remove the valve stem oil seal (using long-nosed pliers if

7.2 Fit a valve spring compressor tool, ensuring that the arms of the compressor are securely positioned

7.4 Extract the two split collets by hooking them out using a small screwdriver

7.5a **Remove the valve spring cap . . .**

7.5b **. . . and the spring . . .**

7.5c **. . . then withdraw the valve through the combustion chamber**

7.5d **Remove the valve stem oil seal . . .**

7.5e **. . . and the spring seat**

7.6 **Place each valve assembly in a labelled polythene bag or similar container**

necessary), and the spring seat **(see illus-trations)**.

6 Repeat the procedure for the remaining valves, keeping all components in strict order so that they can be refitted in their original positions, unless all the components are to be renewed. If the components are to be kept and used again, place each valve assembly in a labelled polythene bag or a similar small container **(see illustration)**. Note that as with cylinder numbering, the valves are normally numbered from the timing chain/belt end of the engine. Make sure that the valve components are identified as intake and exhaust, as well as numbered.

8 Cylinder head and valve components – cleaning and inspection

1 Thorough cleaning of the cylinder head and valve components, followed by a detailed inspection, will enable a decision to be made on whether further work is necessary before reassembling the components.

Cleaning

2 Scrape away all traces of old gasket material and sealing compound from the cylinder head surfaces. Take care not to damage the cylinder head surfaces, as the head is made of light alloy.

3 Scrape away the carbon from the combustion chambers and ports, then wash the cylinder head thoroughly with paraffin or a suitable solvent.

4 Scrape off any heavy carbon deposits that may have formed on the valves, then use a power-operated wire brush to remove deposits from the valve heads and stems.

Inspection

Note: *Be sure to perform all the following inspection procedures before concluding that the services of a machine shop or engine overhaul specialist are required. Make a list of all items that require attention.*

Cylinder head

5 Inspect the head very carefully for cracks, evidence of coolant leakage, and other damage. If cracks are found, a new cylinder head should be obtained.

6 Use a straight-edge and feeler blade to check that the cylinder head surface is not distorted **(see illustration)**. If the specified distortion limit is exceeded, it may be possible to have the cylinder head resurfaced, provided that the overall height of the head is not reduced to less than the specified minimum.

7 Examine the valve seats in each of the combustion chambers. If the seats are severely pitted, cracked or burned, then they will need to be recut or renewed by an engine overhaul specialist. If only slight pitting is evident, this can be removed by grinding the valve heads and seats together with coarse, then fine, grinding paste, as described later in this Section.

8 If the valve guides are worn, indicated by

a side-to-side motion of the valve, oversize valve guides may be available, and valves with oversize stems can be fitted. This work is best carried out by an engine overhaul specialist. A dial gauge may be used to determine whether the amount of side play of a valve exceeds the specified maximum.

9 Check the tappet bores in the cylinder head for wear. If excessive wear is evident, the cylinder head must be renewed. Also check the tappet oil holes in the cylinder head for obstructions.

Valves

10 Examine the head of each valve for pitting, burning, cracks and general wear, and check the valve stem for scoring and wear ridges. Rotate the valve, and check for any obvious indication that it is bent. Look for pitting and excessive wear on the end of each valve stem. If the valve appears satisfactory at this stage, measure the valve stem diameter at several

8.6 **Check the cylinder head surface for distortion**

8.10 Measure the valve stem diameter using a micrometer

8.12 Grinding-in a valve

8.14 Check each valve spring for squareness

points using a micrometer **(see illustration)**. Any significant difference in the readings obtained indicates wear of the valve stem. Should any of these conditions be apparent, the valve(s) must be renewed. If the valves are in satisfactory condition, they should be ground (lapped) onto their respective seats to ensure a smooth gas-tight seal.

11 Valve grinding is carried out as follows. Place the cylinder head upside-down on a bench, with a block of wood at each end to give clearance for the valve stems.

12 Smear a trace of coarse carborundum paste on the seat face in the cylinder head, and press a suction grinding tool onto the relevant valve head. With a semi-rotary action, grind the valve head to its seat, lifting the valve occasionally to redistribute the grinding paste **(see illustration)**. When a dull, matt, even surface is produced on the faces of both the valve seat and the valve, wipe off the paste and repeat the process with fine carborundum paste. When a smooth unbroken ring of light grey matt finish is produced on both the valve and seat faces, the grinding operation is complete. Carefully clean away every trace of grinding paste, taking great care to leave none in the ports or in the valve guides. Clean the valves and valve seats with a paraffin-soaked rag, then with a clean rag, and finally, if an airline is available, blow the valves, valve guides and cylinder head ports clean.

Valve springs

13 Check that all the valve springs are intact. If any one is broken, all should be renewed.

14 If possible, check the free height of the springs against new ones, then stand each spring on a flat surface and check it for squareness **(see illustration)**. If a spring is found to be too short, or damaged in any way, renew all the springs as a set. Springs suffer from fatigue, and it is a good idea to renew them even if they look serviceable.

Rocker arm components

15 Check the rocker arm thrust faces (the areas that contact the tappets and valve stems) for pits, wear, score-marks or any indication that the surface-hardening has worn through. Check the rocker arm camshaft roller in the same manner. Renew any rocker arms which appear suspect.

Hydraulic tappets

16 Inspect the tappets for obvious signs of wear on the contact faces, and check the oil holes for obstructions, particularly for oil sludge. If excessive wear is evident, or if any tappet has been noisy in operation, all the tappets must be renewed as a set.

9 Cylinder head – reassembly

Note: *New valve stem oil seals should be used on reassembly. A valve spring compressor tool will be required for this operation.*

1 With all the components cleaned, starting at one end of the cylinder head, fit the valve components as follows.

2 Insert the appropriate valve into its guide (if new valves are being fitted, insert each valve into the location to which it has been ground), ensuring that the valve stem is well-lubricated with clean engine oil. If the original components are being refitted, all components must be refitted in their original positions.

3 Fit the spring seat.

4 New valve stem oil seals may be supplied with a fitting sleeve, which fits over the collet groove in the valve stem, to prevent damage to the oil seal as it is slid down the valve stem. If no sleeve is supplied, wind a short length of tape round the top of the valve stem to cover the collet groove.

5 Lubricate the valve stem oil seal with clean engine oil, then push the oil seal down the valve stem using a suitable tube or socket, until the seal is fully engaged with the valve guide **(see illustrations)**. Remove the fitting sleeve or the tape, as applicable, from the valve stem.

6 Fit the valve spring and the spring cap.

7 Fit the spring compressor tool, and compress the valve spring until the spring cap passes beyond the collet groove in the valve stem.

8 Refit the split collets to the groove in the valve stem, with the narrow ends nearest the spring.

9 Slowly release the compressor tool, ensuring that the collets are not dislodged from the groove. When the compressor is fully released, give the top of the valve assembly a tap with a soft-faced mallet to settle the components.

10 Repeat the procedure for the remaining valves, ensuring that if the original components are being used, they are all refitted in their original positions.

11 Refit the components removed in Section 7, paragraph 1.

10 Piston/connecting rod assemblies – removal

Note 1: *On diesel engines, the mating faces of the connecting rods and the big-end bearing caps are 'rough' (not machined), which ensures perfect mating of each individual rod and bearing cap. When the components have been removed from the engine, extreme care*

9.5a Fit the new valve stem oil seal . . .

9.5b . . . and push it down using a suitable tube or socket, until the seal is fully engaged with the spring seat

10.4 Connecting rod and big-end cap identification numbers

10.6 Unscrew the retaining bolts and remove the big-end cap and bearing shell

10.16 Take off the big-end bearing cap and recover the bottom half bearing shell

should be taken not to damage the mating surfaces – eg, do not rest the bearing caps on the mating faces. Ensure that each bearing cap is kept together with its respective rod, to prevent any possibility of the components being refitted incorrectly.

Note 2: *New big-end cap bolts will be required for reassembly.*

Petrol engines

1 Remove the sump and cylinder head as described in Part A of this Chapter.
2 Undo the two bolts and remove the oil pump pick-up tube.
3 If there is a pronounced wear ridge at the top of any bore, it may be necessary to remove it with a scraper or ridge reamer, to avoid piston damage during removal. Such a ridge indicates excess bore wear.
4 Check to see if the big-end caps and connecting rods are numbered **(see illustration)**. If no numbers are visible, use quick-drying paint, or similar, to mark each connecting rod and big-end cap with its respective cylinder number on the flat machined surface provided. Note that No 1 cylinder is at the timing belt end of the engine.
5 Turn the crankshaft to bring pistons 1 and 4 to BDC (bottom dead centre).
6 Unscrew the bolts from No 1 piston big-end bearing cap, and remove the big-end cap and bearing shell **(see illustration)**. If the bearing shells are to be re-used, tape the cap and the shell together.
7 Using a hammer handle, push the piston

up through the bore, and remove it from the top of the cylinder block. Recover the bearing shell, and tape it to the connecting rod for safe-keeping.
8 Loosely refit the big-end cap to the connecting rod, and secure with the bolts – this will help to keep the components in their correct order.
9 Remove No 4 assembly in the same way.
10 Turn the crankshaft through 180° to bring pistons 2 and 3 to BDC (bottom dead centre), and remove them in the same way.

Diesel engines

11 Referring to Chapter 2B, remove the following components:
a) *Timing cover (which includes the sump removal procedure).*
b) *Timing chain, sprockets and tensioner.*
c) *Camshaft housing.*
d) *Cylinder head.*
12 Undo the retaining bolts and remove the oil baffle plate from the cylinder block baseplate.
13 If the connecting rods and big-end caps are not marked to indicate their positions in the cylinder block (ie, marked with cylinder numbers), suitably mark both the rod and cap with quick-drying paint or similar. Note which side of the engine the marks face and accurately record this also. There may not be any other way of identifying which way round the cap fits on the rod when refitting.
14 If there is a pronounced wear ridge at the top of any bore, it may be necessary to remove it with a scraper or ridge reamer, to

avoid piston damage during removal. Such a ridge indicates excessive wear of the cylinder bore.
15 Turn the crankshaft to bring pistons 1 and 4 to BDC (bottom dead centre).
16 Unscrew the bolts from No 1 piston big-end bearing cap. Take off the cap and recover the bottom half bearing shell. If the bearing shells are to be re-used, tape the cap and the shell together **(see illustration)**.
17 Using a hammer handle, push the piston up through the bore, and remove it from the top of the cylinder block. Recover the bearing shell, and tape it to the connecting rod for safe-keeping.
18 Loosely refit the big-end cap to the connecting rod, and secure with the bolts – this will help to keep the components in their correct order.
19 Remove No 4 piston assembly in the same way.
20 Turn the crankshaft through 180° to bring pistons 2 and 3 to BDC (bottom dead centre), and remove them in the same way.

11 Crankshaft – removal

1 Remove the flywheel as described in Chapter 2A or 2B.
2 Remove the pistons and connecting rods, as described in Section 10.
3 Invert the engine so that the crankshaft is uppermost.
4 Before removing the crankshaft, check the endfloat using a dial gauge in contact with the end of the crankshaft. Push the crankshaft fully one way, and then zero the gauge. Push the crankshaft fully the other way, and check the endfloat **(see illustration)**. The result should be compared with the specified limit, and will give an indication as to the size of the main bearing shell thrust journal width which will be required for reassembly.
5 If a dial gauge is not available, a feeler gauge can be used to measure crankshaft endfloat. Push the crankshaft fully towards one end of the crankcase, and insert a feeler gauge between the thrust flange of the main

11.4 Using a dial gauge to check the crankshaft endfloat

11.5 Checking the crankshaft endfloat with a feeler gauge

11.6 Main bearing cap identification markings

11.8 Thrustwashers located on the centre man bearing shell

11.11 Lift the cylinder block baseplate off the cylinder block

bearing shell and the machined surface of the crankshaft web **(see illustration)**. Before measuring, ensure that the crankshaft is fully forced towards one end of the crankcase, to give the widest possible gap at the measuring location. **Note:** *Measure at the bearing with the thrustwasher (see Section 18).*

Petrol engines

6 Note the identification markings on the main bearing caps which should be as follows. One line on the cap nearest the timing belt end, two on the second cap, C on the centre cap, then three and four lines on the remaining caps **(see illustration)**. If no markings are visible, mark them using quick-drying paint.

7 Slacken and remove the main bearing cap retaining bolts, and lift off each bearing cap. Recover the lower bearing shells, and tape them to their respective caps for safe-keeping.

8 Lift the crankshaft from the crankcase and remove the upper bearing shells from the crankcase. Note that the centre main bearing shell incorporates thrustwashers to control crankshaft endfloat **(see illustration)**. If the shells are to be used again, keep them identified for position.

Diesel engines

9 Working in a diagonal sequence, progressively slacken the outer (M8) bolts securing the cylinder block baseplate to the cylinder block.

10 When all the outer bolts have been slackened, repeat the procedure on the inner (M10) retaining bolts.

11 Remove all the bolts and lift the cylinder block baseplate off the cylinder block **(see illustration)**. If the baseplate is initially tight to remove, carefully tap it free using a soft-faced mallet. Alternatively, use a spatula to break the seal between the baseplate and cylinder block.

12 As the baseplate is withdrawn check that the lower main bearing shells come away with the baseplate. If they remain on the crankshaft journals, lift them off and refit them to their respective locations in the baseplate.

13 Lift the crankshaft from the cylinder block and remove the crankshaft oil seal.

14 Extract the upper bearing shells, and identify them for position if they are to be re-used.

12 Cylinder block – cleaning and inspection

Cleaning

1 For complete cleaning, remove all external components (senders, sensors, brackets, oil pipes, coolant pipes, etc) from the cylinder block.

2 Scrape all traces of gasket and/or sealant from the cylinder block and cylinder block baseplate, taking particular care not to damage the cylinder head and sump mating faces.

3 Remove all oil gallery plugs, where fitted. The plugs are usually very tight – they may have to be drilled out and the holes retapped. Use new plugs when the engine is reassembled. On diesel engines, undo the retaining bolts and remove the piston oil spray nozzles from inside the cylinder block **(see illustration)**. Also remove the timing chain oil spray pipe from the front face of the cylinder block.

4 If the block and baseplate (where applicable) are extremely dirty, they should be steam-cleaned.

5 If the components have been steam-cleaned, clean all oil holes and oil galleries one more time on completion. Flush all internal

12.3 Undo the retaining bolts and remove the piston oil spray nozzles – diesel engines only

passages with warm water until the water runs clear. Dry the block and, where necessary, the baseplate thoroughly and wipe all machined surfaces with a light oil. If you have access to compressed air, use it to speed-up the drying process, and to blow out all the oil holes and galleries.

 Warning: Wear eye protection when using compressed air.

6 If the block and baseplate are relatively clean, an adequate cleaning job can be achieved with hot soapy water and a stiff brush. Take plenty of time, and do a thorough job. Regardless of the cleaning method used, be sure to clean all oil holes and galleries very thoroughly, dry everything completely, and coat all cast-iron machined surfaces with light oil.

7 The threaded holes in the cylinder block and baseplate must be clean, to ensure accurate torque readings when tightening fixings during reassembly. Run the correct-size tap (which can be determined from the size of the relevant bolt) into each of the holes to remove rust, corrosion, thread sealant or other contamination, and to restore damaged threads. If possible, use compressed air to clear the holes of debris produced by this operation. Do not forget to clean the threads of all bolts and nuts which are to be re-used, as well.

8 Where applicable, apply suitable sealant to the new oil gallery plugs, and insert them into the relevant holes in the cylinder block. Tighten the plugs securely. On diesel engines, refit the oil spray nozzles into the block and secure with the retaining bolts tightened securely. Refit the timing chain oil spray pipe to the front face of the cylinder block and tighten the two bolts securely.

9 If the engine is to be left dismantled for some time, cover the cylinder block with a large plastic bag to keep it clean and prevent corrosion. Where applicable, refit the baseplate and tighten the bolts finger-tight.

Inspection

10 Visually check the block for cracks, rust and corrosion. Look for stripped threads in the threaded holes. It's also a good idea to have the block checked for hidden cracks by an engine reconditioning specialist that has the equipment to do this type of work, especially if the vehicle had a history of overheating or using coolant. If defects are found, have the block repaired, if possible, or renewed.

11 If in any doubt as to the condition of the cylinder block, have it inspected and measured by an engine reconditioning specialist. If the bores are worn or damaged, they will be able to carry out any necessary reboring (where possible), and supply appropriate oversized pistons, etc.

13 Piston/connecting rod assemblies – inspection

1 Before the inspection process can begin, the piston/connecting rod assemblies must be cleaned, and the original piston rings removed from the pistons. **Note:** *Always use new piston rings when the engine is reassembled.*

2 Carefully expand the old rings over the top of the pistons. The use of two or three old feeler gauges will be helpful in preventing the rings dropping into empty grooves **(see illustration)**. Take care, however, as piston rings are sharp.

3 Scrape away all traces of carbon from the top of the piston. A hand-held wire brush, or a piece of fine emery cloth, can be used once the majority of the deposits have been scraped away.

4 Remove the carbon from the ring grooves in the piston, using an old ring. Break the ring in half to do this (be careful not to cut your fingers – piston rings are sharp). Be very careful to remove only the carbon deposits – do not remove any metal, and do not nick or scratch the sides of the ring grooves.

5 Once the deposits have been removed, clean the piston/connecting rod assembly with paraffin or a suitable solvent, and dry thoroughly. Make sure that the oil return holes in the ring grooves are clear.

6 If the pistons and cylinder bores are not damaged or worn excessively, and if the cylinder block does not need to be rebored, the original pistons can be refitted. Normal piston wear shows up as even vertical wear on the piston thrust surfaces, and slight looseness of the top ring in its groove. New piston rings should always be used when the engine is reassembled.

7 Carefully inspect each piston for cracks around the skirt, at the gudgeon pin bosses, and at the piston ring lands (between the ring grooves).

8 Look for scoring and scuffing on the thrust faces of the piston skirt, holes in the piston crown, and burned areas at the edge of the crown. If the skirt is scored or scuffed, the engine may have been suffering from overheating, and/or abnormal combustion ('pinking') which caused excessively-high operating temperatures. The cooling and lubrication systems should be checked

13.2 Use a feeler gauge to aid removal of a piston ring

thoroughly. A hole in the piston crown, or burned areas at the edge of the piston crown indicates that abnormal combustion (pre-ignition, 'pinking', knocking or detonation) has been occurring. If any of the above problems exist, the causes must be investigated and corrected, or the damage will occur again.

9 Corrosion of the piston, in the form of pitting, indicates that coolant has been leaking into the combustion chamber and/or the crankcase. Again, the cause must be corrected, or the problem may persist in the rebuilt engine.

10 If in any doubt as to the condition of the pistons and connecting rods, have them inspected and measured by an engine reconditioning specialist. If new parts are required, they will be able to supply and fit appropriate-sized pistons/rings, and rebore (where possible) or hone the cylinder block.

14 Crankshaft – inspection

1 Clean the crankshaft using paraffin or a suitable solvent, and dry it, preferably with compressed air if available. Be sure to clean the oil holes with a pipe cleaner or similar probe, to ensure that they are not obstructed.

 Warning: Wear eye protection when using compressed air.

2 Check the main and big-end bearing journals for uneven wear, scoring, pitting and cracking.

3 Big-end bearing wear is accompanied by distinct metallic knocking when the engine is running (particularly noticeable when the engine is pulling from low revs), and some loss of oil pressure.

4 Main bearing wear is accompanied by severe engine vibration and rumble – getting progressively worse as engine revs increase – and again by loss of oil pressure.

5 Check the bearing journal for roughness by running a finger lightly over the bearing surface. Any roughness (which will be accompanied by obvious bearing wear) indicates that the crankshaft requires regrinding.

6 If the crankshaft has been reground, check

15.2 Typical bearing failures

for burrs around the crankshaft oil holes (the holes are usually chamfered, so burrs should not be a problem unless regrinding has been carried out carelessly). Remove any burrs with a fine file or scraper, and thoroughly clean the oil holes as described previously.

7 Have the crankshaft journals measured by an engine reconditioning specialist. If the crankshaft is worn or damaged, they may be able to regrind the journals and supply suitable undersize bearing shells. If no undersize shells are available and the crankshaft has worn beyond the specified limits, it will have to be renewed. Consult your Fiat dealer or engine reconditioning specialist for further information on parts availability.

15 Main and big-end bearings – inspection

1 Even though the main and big-end bearings should be renewed during the engine overhaul, the old bearings should be retained for close examination, as they may reveal valuable information about the condition of the engine.

2 Bearing failure occurs because of lack of lubrication, the presence of dirt or other foreign particles, overloading the engine, or corrosion **(see illustration)**. If a bearing fails, the cause must be found and eliminated before the engine is reassembled, to prevent the failure from happening again.

3 To examine the bearing shells, remove them from the cylinder block, the cylinder block baseplate, the connecting rods and the big-end bearing caps, and lay them out on a clean surface in the same order as they were fitted to the engine. This will enable any bearing problems to be matched with the corresponding crankshaft journal.

4 Dirt and other foreign particles can enter the engine in a variety of ways. Contamination may be left in the engine during assembly, or it may pass through filters or the crankcase ventilation system. Normal engine wear produces small particles of metal, which can eventually cause problems. If particles find their way into the lubrication system, it is likely that they will eventually be carried to the bearings. Whatever the source, these foreign particles often end up embedded in the soft bearing material, and are easily recognised. Large particles will not embed in the bearing, and will score or gouge the bearing and journal. To prevent possible contamination, clean all parts thoroughly, and keep everything spotlessly-clean during engine assembly. Once the engine has been installed in the vehicle, ensure that engine oil and filter changes are carried out at the recommended intervals.

5 Lack of lubrication (or lubrication breakdown) has a number of interrelated causes. Excessive heat (which thins the oil), overloading (which squeezes the oil from the bearing face), and oil leakage (from excessive bearing clearances, worn oil pump or high engine speeds) all contribute to lubrication breakdown. Blocked oil passages, which may be the result of misaligned oil holes in a bearing shell, will also starve a bearing of oil and destroy it. When lack of lubrication is the cause of bearing failure, the bearing material is wiped or extruded from the steel backing of the bearing. Temperatures may increase to the point where the steel backing turns blue from overheating.

6 Driving habits can have a definite effect on bearing life. Full-throttle, low-speed operation (labouring the engine) puts very high loads on bearings, which tends to squeeze out the oil film. These loads cause the bearings to flex, which produces fine cracks in the bearing face (fatigue failure). Eventually the bearing material will loosen in places, and tear away from the steel backing. Regular short journeys can lead to corrosion of bearings, because insufficient engine heat is produced to drive off the condensed water and corrosive gases which form inside the engine. These products collect in the engine oil, forming acid and sludge. As the oil is carried to the bearings, the acid attacks and corrodes the bearing material.

7 Incorrect bearing installation during engine assembly will also lead to bearing failure. Tight-fitting bearings leave insufficient bearing lubrication clearance, and will result in oil starvation. Dirt or foreign particles trapped behind a bearing shell results in high spots on the bearing which can lead to failure.

8 *Do not* touch any shell's bearing surface with your fingers during reassembly; there is a risk of scratching the delicate surface, or of depositing particles of dirt on it.

9 As mentioned at the beginning of this Section, the bearing shells should be renewed as a matter of course during engine overhaul; to do otherwise is false economy.

16 Engine overhaul – reassembly sequence

1 Before reassembly begins, ensure that all necessary new parts have been obtained (particularly gaskets, and various bolts which must be renewed), and that all the tools required are available. Read through the entire procedure to familiarise yourself with the work involved, and to ensure that all items necessary for reassembly of the engine are to hand. In addition to all normal tools and materials, a thread-locking compound will be required. A tube of suitable sealant will be required to seal certain joint faces which are not fitted with gaskets.

2 At this stage, all engine components should be absolutely clean and dry, with all faults repaired. The components should be laid out (or in individual containers) on a completely clean work surface.

3 In order to save time and avoid problems, engine reassembly can be carried out in the following order:

Petrol engines

a) *Piston rings (see Section 17).*
b) *Crankshaft (see Section 18).*
c) *Piston/connecting rod assemblies (see Section 19).*
d) *Timing belt and sprockets (see Chapter 2A).*
e) *Oil pump (see Chapter 2A).*
f) *Sump (see Chapter 2A).*
g) *Flywheel (see Chapter 2A).*
h) *Cylinder head (see Chapter 2A).*
i) *Coolant pump (see Chapter 3).*

j) *Intake and exhaust manifolds (see Chapter 4A).*

Diesel engines

a) *Piston rings (see Section 17).*
b) *Crankshaft (see Section 18).*
c) *Pistons/connecting rod assemblies (see Section 19).*
d) *Flywheel (see Chapter 2B).*
e) *Intake and exhaust manifolds (see Chapter 4B).*
f) *Cylinder head (see Chapter 2B).*
g) *Camshaft housing (see Chapter 2B).*
h) *Oil pump (see Chapter 2B).*
i) *Timing chain and sprockets (see Chapter 2B).*
j) *Coolant pump (see Chapter 3).*
k) *Sump (see Chapter 2B).*

17 Piston rings – refitting

1 Before refitting the new piston rings, the ring end gaps must be checked as follows.

2 Lay out the piston/connecting rod assemblies and the new piston ring sets, so that the ring sets will be matched with the same piston and cylinder during the end gap measurement and subsequent engine reassembly.

3 Insert the top ring into the first cylinder, and push it down the bore slightly using the top of the piston. This will ensure that the ring remains square with the cylinder walls.

4 Measure the end gap using feeler gauges, and compare the measurements with the figures given in the *Specifications* **(see illustration)**.

5 If the gap is too small (unlikely if genuine Fiat parts are used), it must be enlarged or the ring ends may contact each other during engine operation, causing serious damage. Ideally, new piston rings providing the correct end gap should be fitted, but as a last resort, the end gap can be increased by filing the ring ends very carefully with a fine file. Mount the file in a vice equipped with soft jaws, slip the ring over the file with the ends contacting the file face, and slowly move the ring to remove material from the ends – take care, as piston rings are sharp, and are easily broken.

6 With new piston rings, it is unlikely that the end gap will be too large. If they are too large, check that you have the correct rings for your engine and for the particular cylinder bore size.

7 Repeat the checking procedure for each ring in the first cylinder, and then for the rings in the remaining cylinders. Remember to keep rings, pistons and cylinders matched up.

8 Once the ring end gaps have been checked and if necessary corrected, the rings can be fitted to the pistons.

9 The oil control ring (lowest one on the piston) is composed of three sections on diesels (one-piece on petrols), and should be installed first. Fit the lower steel ring, then the spreader ring, followed by the upper steel ring **(see illustration)**.

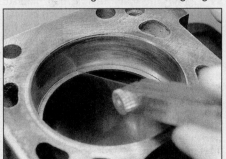

17.4 Measure the piston ring end gap using a feeler gauge

17.9 Fit the oil control spreader ring

17.11 Sectional view showing correct orientation of piston rings

18.5a Main bearing shell (A) and central main bearing shell (B) with thrust flange – petrol engines shown

18.5b Fit the main bearing shell to the cylinder block

10 With the oil control ring components installed, the second (middle) ring can be fitted. It is usually stamped with a mark (TOP) which must face up, towards the top of the piston. **Note:** *Always follow the instructions supplied with the new piston ring sets – different manufacturers may specify different procedures. Do not mix up the top and middle rings, as they have different cross-sections.* Using two or three old feeler blades, as for removal of the old rings, carefully slip the ring into place in the middle groove.

11 Fit the top ring in the same manner, ensuring that, where applicable, the mark on the ring is facing up. If a stepped ring is being fitted, fit the ring with the smaller diameter of the step uppermost **(see illustration)**.

12 Repeat the procedure for the remaining pistons and rings.

18 Crankshaft – refitting

1 Refitting the crankshaft is the first step in the engine reassembly procedure. It is assumed at this point that the cylinder block, baseplate and crankshaft have been cleaned, inspected and repaired or reconditioned as necessary.

2 Position the cylinder block with the baseplate mating face uppermost.

3 Clean the bearing shells and the bearing recesses in both the cylinder block and the baseplate. If new shells are being fitted, ensure that all traces of the protective grease are cleaned off using paraffin. Wipe the shells dry with a clean lint-free cloth.

4 Note that the crankshaft endfloat is controlled by thrustwashers located on the centre main bearing shells. The thrustwashers are incorporated into, or attached to, the bearing shells themselves.

5 If the original bearing shells are being re-used, they must be refitted to their original locations in the block and baseplate **(see illustrations)**.

6 Fit the upper main bearing shells in place in the cylinder block.

Petrol engines

7 Liberally lubricate each bearing shell in the cylinder block, and lower the crankshaft into position **(see illustration)**.

8 If necessary, seat the crankshaft using light taps from a soft-faced mallet on the crankshaft balance webs.

9 Lubricate the lower bearing shells in the main bearing caps with clean engine oil.

10 Fit the main bearing caps to their correct locations, ensuring that they are fitted the correct way round (the bearing shell tab recesses in the block and caps must be on the same side). Insert the bolts loosely.

11 Tighten the main bearing cap bolts to the specified Stage 1 torque wrench setting. Once all the bolts have been tightened to the Stage 1 setting, angle-tighten the bolts through the specified Stage 2 angle, using a socket and extension bar. It is recommended that an angle-measuring gauge is used during this stage of the tightening, to ensure accuracy.

12 Check that the crankshaft rotates freely.

13 Prise out the crankshaft oil seal and fit a new seal to the housing **(see illustrations)**.

14 Lubricate the oil seal lips then carefully locate the oil seal housing into position, using a new gasket. If the oil seal housing was originally fitted without a gasket, apply

18.7 Liberally lubricate each bearing shell in the cylinder block then lower the crankshaft into position

18.13a Use a screwdriver to prise out the oil seal . . .

18.13b . . . locate the new oil seal in the housing . . .

18.13c . . . and used a block of wood to drive it in

18.14 Application area for silicone sealant on the crankshaft oil seal housing

18.16a Liberally lubricate each bearing shell in the cylinder block . . .

18.16b . . . and lower the crankshaft into position

a 3.0 mm bead of RTV silicone sealant to the housing flange **(see illustration)**. Refit the retaining bolts and tighten them securely.
15 Continue with engine reassembly in the sequence given in Section 16.

Diesel engines

16 Liberally lubricate each bearing shell in

the cylinder block, and lower the crankshaft into position **(see illustrations)**.
17 If necessary, seat the crankshaft using light taps from a soft-faced mallet on the crankshaft balance webs.
18 Fit the bearing shells in the baseplate **(see illustration)**.
19 Lubricate the crankshaft journals, and

the bearing shells in the baseplate **(see illustration)**.
20 Ensure that the cylinder block and baseplate mating surfaces are clean and dry, then apply a 2.5 mm diameter bead of sealant to the cylinder block face **(see illustrations)**.
21 Locate the baseplate over the crankshaft and onto the cylinder block.

18.18 Fit the bearing shells in the baseplate . . .

18.19 . . . then lubricate the crankshaft journals, and the bearing shells

18.20a Apply a bead of sealant to the cylinder block mating face . . .

18.20b . . . ensuring the sealant is applied around the inside of the bolt holes as shown

18.22a Tightening sequence for cylinder block baseplate inner (M10) bolts . . .

18.22b . . . and outer (M8) bolts

18.22c Tighten the M10 bolts to the specified torque . . .

18.22d . . . then through the specified angle . . .

18.22e . . . and tighten the outer M8 bolts to the specified torque

22 Fit the new baseplate retaining bolts, then working progressively and in the sequence shown, tighten the inner (M10) bolts to the specified torque, then through the specified angle, in the two stages given in the *Specifications*. Now similarly tighten the outer (M8) retaining bolts to the specified torque in the sequence shown **(see illustrations)**.

All engines

23 Now rotate the crankshaft, and check that

19.2 Press the bearing shells into the connecting rods and caps in their correct positions

it turns freely, with no signs of binding or tight spots.
24 Check the crankshaft endfloat with reference to Section 11.
25 On diesel engines, fit a new crankshaft transmission end oil seal as described in Chapter 2B.
26 Refit the pistons and connecting rods as described in Section 19.
27 Refit the flywheel as described in Chapter 2A or 2B.

19 Pistons/connecting rods – refitting

1 Clean the backs of the big-end bearing shells and the recesses in the connecting rods and big-end caps. If new shells are being fitted, ensure that all traces of the protective grease are cleaned off using paraffin. Wipe the shells, caps and connecting rods dry with a lint-free cloth.
2 Press the bearing shells into the connecting rods and caps in their correct positions **(see illustration)**. **Note:** *When finally refitting the piston/connecting rod assemblies, new*

big-end bearing cap bolts must be used. Ensure that the mating faces of the connecting rods and big-end bearing caps are clean before refitting (refer to Section 10).
3 Lubricate No 1 piston and piston rings, and check that the ring gaps are correctly positioned. Where applicable, the gaps in the upper and lower steel rings of the oil control ring should be offset by 25 to 50 mm to the right and left of the spreader ring gap. The two upper compression ring gaps should be offset by 180° to each other.
4 Liberally lubricate the cylinder bore with clean engine oil.
5 Fit a ring compressor to No 1 piston, then insert the piston and connecting rod into the cylinder bore so that the base of the compressor stands on the block. With the crankshaft big-end bearing journal positioned at its lowest point, tap the piston carefully into the cylinder bore with the wooden handle of a hammer, and at the same time guide the connecting rod onto the bearing journal. Note that the arrow or notch (as applicable) on the piston crown must point towards the timing chain/belt end of the engine **(see illustrations)**.
6 Fit the bearing shells to the bearing caps.

7 Liberally lubricate the bearing journals and bearing shells, and fit the bearing cap in its original location. Tighten the new bearing cap bolts to the Stage 1 torque setting, then tighten all bolts through the specified angles **(see illustrations)**.
8 After refitting each piston/connecting rod assembly, rotate the crankshaft, and check that it turns freely, with no signs of binding or tight spots.
9 Refit the following components.

Petrol engines
a) Refit the oil baffle plate and tighten the retaining bolts securely.
b) Refit the cylinder head as described in Chapter 2A.
c) Refit the timing belt, sprockets and tensioner as described in Chapter 2A.
d) Refit the timing cover as described in Chapter 2A.
e) Refit the sump and oil pick-up pipe as described in Chapter 2A.

Diesel engines
a) Refit the oil baffle plate and tighten the retaining bolts securely.
b) Refit the cylinder head as described in Chapter 2B.
c) Refit the camshaft housing as described in Chapter 2B.
d) Refit the timing chain, sprockets and tensioner as described in Chapter 2B.
e) Refit the timing cover (which includes the sump refitting procedure) as described in Chapter 2B.

20 Engine – initial start-up after overhaul

1 With the engine refitted in the vehicle, double-check the engine oil and coolant levels. Make a final check that everything has been reconnected, and that there are no tools or rags left in the engine compartment.

19.5a Position the piston with the arrow or notch (as applicable) pointing towards the timing chain/belt end of the engine . . .

19.5b . . . then tap the piston carefully into the cylinder bore

19.7a Tighten the big-end bearing cap bolts to the specified torque . . .

19.7b . . . then through the specified angle

2 On diesel engines, prime and bleed the fuel system as described in Chapter 4B.
3 Start the engine, noting that this may take a little longer than usual. Make sure that the oil pressure warning light goes out.
4 While the engine is idling, check for fuel, water and oil leaks. Don't be alarmed if there are some odd smells and smoke from parts getting hot and burning off oil deposits.
5 Assuming all is well, keep the engine idling until hot water is felt circulating through the top hose, then switch off the engine.
6 After a few minutes, recheck the oil and coolant levels as described in *Weekly checks*, and top-up as necessary.
7 Note that there is no need to retighten the cylinder head bolts once the engine has first run after reassembly.
8 If new pistons, rings or crankshaft bearings have been fitted, the engine must be treated as new, and run-in for the first 600 miles. Do not operate the engine at full-throttle, or allow it to labour at low engine speeds in any gear. It is recommended that the oil and filter be changed at the end of this period.

Notes

Chapter 3
Cooling, heating and ventilation systems

Contents

Degrees of difficulty

Easy, suitable for novice with little experience	**Fairly easy,** suitable for beginner with some experience	**Fairly difficult,** suitable for competent DIY mechanic	**Difficult,** suitable for experienced DIY mechanic	**Very difficult,** suitable for expert DIY or professional

Specifications

General
Expansion tank relief valve opening pressure . . . . 0.99 bar

Thermostat
Opening temperature:
   Petrol engines. . . . . 87 ± 2°C
   Diesel engines . . . . 88 ± 2°C

Air conditioning
Lubricant capacity:
   Receiver/drier. . . . . 15 cc
   Pipes . . . . 5 cc
   Evaporator . . . . 40 cc
   Condenser . . . . 40 cc
   Compressor . . . . 80 cc
Lubricant type . . . . Synthetic PAG fluid
Refrigerant capacity . . . . 500 ± 40g

Torque wrench settings

	Nm	lbf ft
Air conditioning compressor mounting bolts	25	18
Coolant pump bolts/nuts:		
Petrol engines	8	6
Diesel engines	9	7
Steering column lower pinch-bolt*	50	37
Thermostat housing bolts:		
Petrol engines	10	7
Diesel engines	25	18

* Do not re-use

1 General information and precautions

The cooling system is of pressurised type, comprising a pump driven by the auxiliary drivebelt (diesel engines) or timing belt (petrol engines), an aluminium crossflow radiator, electric cooling fan, and a thermostat. The system functions as follows. Cold coolant from the radiator passes through the hose to the coolant pump, where it is pumped around the cylinder block and head passages. After cooling the cylinder bores, combustion surfaces and valve seats, the coolant reaches the underside of the thermostat, which is initially closed. The coolant passes through the heater, and is returned to the coolant pump.

When the engine is cold, the coolant circulates only through the cylinder block, cylinder head, expansion tank and heater. When the coolant reaches a predetermined temperature, the thermostat opens and the coolant passes through to the radiator. As the coolant circulates through the radiator, it is cooled by the inrush of air when the car is in forward motion. Airflow is supplemented by the action of the electric cooling fan when necessary. Once the coolant has passed through the radiator, and has cooled, the cycle is repeated.

The electric cooling fan, mounted on the rear of the radiator, is controlled by a thermostatic switch/sensor. At a predetermined coolant temperature, the fan is actuated.

An expansion tank is fitted into the engine compartment to accommodate expansion of the coolant when it gets hot. The expansion tank is connected to the top of the radiator by a small bore rubber hose.

⚠️ *Warning: Do not attempt to remove the expansion tank filler cap, or disturb any part of the cooling system, while the engine is hot; there is a high risk of scalding. If the expansion tank filler cap must be removed before the engine and radiator have fully cooled (even though this is not recommended) the pressure in the cooling system must first be relieved. Cover the* cap with a thick layer of cloth, to avoid scalding, and slowly unscrew the filler cap until a hissing sound can be heard. When the hissing has stopped, indicating that the pressure has reduced, slowly unscrew the filler cap until it can be removed; if more hissing sounds are heard, wait until they have stopped before unscrewing the cap completely. At all times, keep well away from the filler cap opening.*

• *Do not allow antifreeze to come into contact with skin, or with the painted surfaces of the vehicle. Rinse off spills immediately, with plenty of water. Never leave antifreeze lying around in an open container, or in a puddle on the driveway or garage floor. Children and pets are attracted by its sweet smell, but antifreeze can be fatal if ingested.*

• *If the engine is hot, the electric cooling fan may start rotating even if the engine is not running; be careful to keep hands, hair and loose clothing well clear when working in the engine compartment.*

• *Refer to Section 10 for precautions to be observed when working on models equipped with air conditioning.*

2 Cooling system hoses – disconnection and renewal

Note: *Refer to the warnings given in Section 1 of this Chapter before proceeding. Do not attempt to disconnect any hose while the system is still hot.*

1 If the checks described in Chapter 1A or 1B reveal a faulty hose, it must be renewed as follows.

2 First drain the cooling system (see Chapter 1A or 1B). If the coolant is not due for renewal, it may be re-used if it is collected in a clean container.

3 Before disconnecting a hose, first note its routing in the engine compartment, and whether it is secured by any additional retaining clips or cable-ties. Use a pair of pliers to release the clamp-type clips, or a screwdriver to slacken the screw-type clips, then move the clips along the hose, clear of the relevant inlet/outlet union. Carefully work the hose free.

4 Depending on engine, some of the hose attachments may be of the quick-release type. Where this type of hose is encountered, lift the wire retaining clip, then withdraw the hose from the inlet/outlet union **(see illustration)**.

5 Note that the radiator inlet and outlet unions are fragile; do not use excessive force when attempting to remove the hoses. If a hose proves to be difficult to remove, try to release it by rotating the hose ends before attempting to free it.

6 When fitting a hose, first slide the clips onto the hose, then work the hose into position. If clamp-type clips were originally fitted, it is a good idea to use screw-type clips when refitting the hose. If the hose is stiff, use a little soapy water (washing-up liquid is ideal) as a lubricant, or soften the hose by soaking it in hot water.

7 Work the hose into position, checking that it is correctly routed and secured. Slide each clip along the hose until it passes over the flared end of the relevant inlet/outlet union, before tightening the clips securely.

8 Refill the cooling system with reference to Chapter 1A or 1B.

9 Check thoroughly for leaks as soon as possible after disturbing any part of the cooling system.

3 Radiator – removal, inspection and refitting

Removal

Panda models

1 Drain the cooling system as described in Chapter 1A or 1B.

2 Remove the air cleaner assembly as described in Chapter 4A or 4B.

3 Remove the engine cooling fan and shroud as described in Section 5.

4 Remove the radiator grille and front bumper as described in Chapter 11.

5 Release the retaining clips and disconnect the upper and lower radiator coolant hoses **(see illustrations)**.

6 Undo the condenser retaining bolts (where fitted).

2.4 Lift the clip (arrowed) and pull the hose from the union

3.5a Disconnect the radiator lower hose (arrowed) . . .

3.5b . . . and upper hose (arrowed)

3.7 Remove the front panel support bracket (arrowed)

3.8a Lift the radiator retaining clip (arrowed) each side

3.8b Lift the radiator to release the lower mountings (arrowed)

7 Undo the nut/bolts, remove the front panel support bracket **(see illustration)**.

8 Release the clips and slide the radiator upwards at the same time as tilting the top edge rearwards a little to free the lower mountings, then move the lower edge of the radiator rearwards and lower it from place **(see illustrations)**. Carefully pull the condenser forwards a little as the radiator is removed.

500 models

9 Drain the cooling system as described in Chapter 1A or 1B.
10 On diesel models, remove the air cleaner housing as described in Chapter 4B.
11 On diesel models, release the clamps and remove the intercooler upper air hose.
12 Undo the bolts securing the support bracket between the subframe and the body in the right-hand side wheel arch **(see illustration)**.
13 Undo the fasteners and remove the front/centre section of the wheel arch liner.
14 Remove the front bumper as described in Chapter 11.
15 Undo the retaining bolts and remove the upper front crossmember **(see illustration)**.
16 On models with air conditioning, remove the condenser mounting bolts, and move it to one side **(see illustrations 11.7a and 11.7b)**.
17 Slacken the retaining clips, and disconnect the coolant top and bottom hoses from the radiator. If necessary, prise up the clip and disconnect the lower coolant pipe as the radiator is pulled forwards **(see illustration)**.

18 Disconnect the electric cooling fan and resistor wiring plugs.
19 Undo the radiator lower mounting bolt each side, and manoeuvre the radiator and fan assembly from place **(see illustration)**.
20 If required, undo the bolts and separate the cooling fan and shroud from the radiator.

Inspection

21 Clean dirt and debris from the radiator fins, using an airline (in which case, wear eye protection) or a soft brush.
Caution: Be careful, as the fins are easily damaged, and are sharp.
22 If necessary, a radiator specialist can perform a 'flow test' on the radiator, to establish whether an internal blockage exists.
23 A leaking radiator must be referred to a specialist for permanent repair. Do not attempt DIY repairs to a leaking radiator, as damage may result.
24 In an emergency, minor leaks from the radiator can be cured by using a suitable radiator sealant (in accordance with its manufacturer's instructions) with the radiator *in situ*.

Flushing

25 Disconnect the top and bottom hoses and any other relevant hoses from the radiator.
26 Insert a garden hose into the radiator top inlet. Direct a flow of clean water through the radiator, and continue flushing until clean water emerges from the radiator bottom outlet.

3.12 Remove the bracket between the subframe and body (arrowed)

27 If after a reasonable period, the water still does not run clear, the radiator can be flushed with a good proprietary cleaning agent. It is important that their manufacturer's instructions are followed carefully. If the contamination is particularly bad, insert the hose in the radiator bottom outlet, and reverse-flush the radiator.

Refitting

28 Refitting is a reversal of removal, bearing in mind the following points:
 a) *Ensure that all hoses are correctly reconnected, and their retaining clips securely tightened.*
 b) *On completion, refill the cooling system as described in Chapter 1A or 1B.*

3.15 Undo the retaining bolts each side (arrowed) and remove the upper crossmember

3.17 Prise up the clip (arrowed) and disconnect the lower coolant hose as the radiator is pulled forwards

3.19 Undo the radiator mounting bolt (arrowed) each side

4.3 Disconnect the coolant hoses and wiring plug (arrowed) from the thermostat housing – petrol models

4.9 Disconnect the coolant hoses (arrowed) from the thermostat housing – diesel models

4 Thermostat – removal, testing and refitting

Removal

Petrol engines

1 Remove the battery and battery tray as described in Chapter 5A.
2 Drain the cooling system (see Chapter 1A).
3 Slacken the retaining clips, disconnect the coolant hoses and wiring plug from the thermostat housing located at the left-hand end of the cylinder head **(see illustration)**.
4 Slacken and remove the 2 retaining bolts, and remove the thermostat housing.
5 Note that the thermostat is an integral part of the housing, and cannot be renewed separately.
6 Remove the sealing ring from the housing and discard it; a new one should be used on refitting.

Diesel engines

7 Remove the battery and battery tray as described in Chapter 5A.
8 Drain the cooling system (see Chapter 1B).
9 Note their fitted positions, then release the clamps and disconnect the various coolant hoses from the thermostat housing **(see illustration)**.
10 Disconnect the wiring plug from the engine coolant temperature sensor fitted to the thermostat housing.
11 Slacken and remove the retaining bolts, and remove the thermostat housing **(see illustration)**.
12 Note that the thermostat is an integral part of the housing, and cannot be renewed separately.
13 Remove the sealing ring from the housing and discard it; a new one should be used on refitting **(see illustration)**.

Testing

14 If there is any question about the operation of the thermostat, it's best to renew it – they are not usually expensive items. Testing involves heating in, or over, an open pan of boiling water, which carries with it the risk of scalding. A thermostat which has seen more than five years' service may well be past its best already.
15 The opening temperature is marked on the thermostat. If a thermometer is available, the precise opening temperature of the thermostat may be determined, and compared with the value mark on the thermostat.
16 A thermostat which fails to close as the water cools must also be renewed.

Refitting

17 Refitting is a reversal of removal, bearing in mind the following points:
a) Fit the new sealing rings to all applicable mating faces.
b) Tighten the thermostat housing/cover bolts to the specified torque.
c) On completion, refill the cooling system as described in Chapter 1A or 1B.

5 Electric cooling fan – removal and refitting

⚠️ **Warning: If the engine is hot, the cooling fan may start up at any time. Take extra precautions when working in the vicinity of the fan.**

1 Disconnect the battery negative terminal as described in Chapter 5A.
2 Firmly apply the handbrake, then jack up the front of the car and support it securely on axle stands (see *Jacking and vehicle support*).

Removal – Panda models

3 Remove the air cleaner assembly as described in Chapter 4A or 4B.
4 Disconnect the fan wiring plug, and unclip the loom from the shroud **(see illustration)**.
5 Undo the retaining bolts and lift the

4.11 Thermostat housing retaining bolts (arrowed)

4.13 Renew the thermostat housing sealing ring

5.4 Disconnect the cooling fan motor and resistor wiring plugs (arrowed)

5.5a Remove the cooling fan shroud retaining bolts on the left-hand side (arrowed) . . .

5.5b . . . and the right-hand side (arrowed)

5.7 Remove the manifold heat shield (arrowed)

5.12 Cooling fan shroud retaining bolts (arrowed)

5.14 Undo the bolts on the right-hand side, then detach the cooling fan shroud from the lugs on the left-hand side (arrowed)

a) Ensure that the shroud is correctly located on the radiator.
b) Use new cable-ties to secure all disturbed wiring harnesses.
c) On completion, start the engine and run it until it reaches normal operating temperature; continue to run the engine, and check that the cooling fan cuts in and functions correctly.

6 Coolant temperature sensor – testing, removal and refitting

fan and shroud upwards from place (**see illustrations**).

Removal – 500 models

6 Remove the air cleaner assembly as described in Chapter 4A or 4B.

Petrol models

7 Remove the pre-cat oxygen sensor from the exhaust manifold with reference to Chapter 4A, then undo the bolts/nuts and remove the manifold heat shield (**see illustration**).
8 Disconnect the cooling fan wiring plug. Undo the retaining bolts and lower the fan and shroud from place (**see illustration 5.12**).

Diesel models except 95 bhp

9 Release the clamps and remove the upper and lower air hoses from the intercooler.

10 Undo the bolts and remove the rigid air outlet pipe from the turbocharger, and the rigid inlet pipe from the intake manifold.
11 Disconnect the cooling fan resistor wiring plug. Disconnect the cooling fan wiring plug.
12 Undo the retaining bolts, and lower the fan and shroud from place (**see illustration**).

95 bhp diesel models

13 Remove the radiator as described in Section 3.
14 Undo the retaining bolts and detach the cooling fan and shroud from the radiator (**see illustration**).

Refitting

15 Refitting is a reversal of removal, bearing in mind the following points:

Testing

1 Testing of the coolant temperature sensor circuit is best entrusted to a Fiat dealer, who will have the necessary specialist diagnostic equipment.

Removal – petrol engines

2 Drain the cooling system as described in Chapter 1A, to below the level of the sensor.

Models with throttle cable

3 Remove the air cleaner assembly as described in Chapter 4A.
4 Undo the retaining nut/bolt and remove the bracket above the sensor, located at the left-hand rear of the cylinder head. Unclip the wiring loom, HT leads and pipes as the bracket is removed (**see illustration**).
5 Disconnect the sensor wiring plug, then release the clip and disconnect the coolant hose from the sensor (**see illustration**). Plug the openings to prevent contamination.
6 Undo the retaining nuts and remove the sensor assembly.

Models without throttle cable

7 Remove the battery and battery tray as described in Chapter 5A.
8 The sensor is fitted to the thermostat housing at the left-hand end of the cylinder

6.4 Undo the nut/bolt (arrowed) and remove the bracket above the sensor

6.5 Release the clip (arrowed), disconnect the coolant hose, and the wiring plug (arrowed)

6.8 Coolant temperature sensor (arrowed)

6.13 Disconnect the hose, undo the bolt (arrowed) and move the rigid pipe to one side

6.14 Coolant temperature sensor (arrowed)

6.16a Disconnect the wiring plug (arrowed) . . .

6.16b . . . the prise out the clip (arrowed) and remove the temperature sensor

head. Disconnect the sensor wiring plug (see illustration).

9 Unscrew the sensor from place. Be prepared for coolant spillage. Plug the openings to prevent contamination.

Removal – diesel engines

10 The coolant temperature sensor is located on the thermostat housing on the left-hand end of the cylinder head.

11 Drain the cooling system (see Chapter 1B).

12 Remove the battery and battery tray as described in Chapter 5A.

Models up to 06/06

13 Release the clamp, disconnect the hose from the rigid pipe adjacent to the thermostat housing, then undo the support bracket bolt and move the rigid pipe to one side (see illustration).

14 Disconnect the sensor wiring plug, and unscrew the sensor (see illustration).

Be prepared for coolant spillage. Plug the openings to prevent contamination.

Models 07/06-on

15 Remove the battery and battery tray as described in Chapter 5A.

16 Disconnect the sensor wiring plug, then prise out the retaining clip and remove the sensor (see illustrations). Be prepared for coolant spillage. Plug the openings to prevent contamination.

Refitting

17 Refitting is a reversal of removal, bearing in mind the following points:

a) Where applicable fit a new sealing O-ring to the sensor. Where the sensor is fitted without an O-ring, ensure the sensor threads are clean, and apply a smear of suitable sealant to them.

b) On completion, top-up/refill the cooling system as described in Chapter 1A or 1B.

7 Coolant pump – removal and refitting

Removal – petrol engines

1 Disconnect the battery negative terminal as described in Chapter 5A.

2 Drain the cooling system and remove the auxiliary drivebelt as described in Chapter 1A.

3 Remove the timing belt as described in Chapter 2A.

4 Unscrew the retaining nut and the three bolts and withdraw the coolant pump (see illustration). If the pump is stuck, tap it gently using a soft-faced mallet – do not lever between the pump and cylinder block mating faces.

Removal – diesel engines

5 Drain the cooling system with reference to Chapter 1B.

6 Remove the auxiliary drivebelt as described in Chapter 1B.

500 models

7 Release the clamps and remove the lower air hose from the intercooler.

8 Release the clamp and disconnect the upper coolant hose from the radiator.

9 Release the exhaust pipe from the rubber mountings, and allow it to hang down. Take care not to damage the flexible section of the pipe.

10 Undo the retaining bolt and move the coolant expansion tank to one side.

11 Position a trolley/workshop jack under the engine and take the weight. Use a piece of wood on the jack head to prevent damage.

12 Undo the nuts and remove the right-hand engine mounting from the vehicle body and engine support bracket. Gently lower the engine a little to access the coolant pump. Take care not to strain the refrigerant hoses on air conditioned models.

All models

13 Working through the apertures in the pulley, unscrew and remove the coolant pump retaining nuts (see illustration).

14 Withdraw the coolant pump from the cylinder block studs. Note: Coolant which is

7.4 Coolant pump retaining nut (A) and bolts (B)

7.13 Undo the coolant pump retaining nuts – diesel engines

7.15 Remove the coolant pump sealing ring – diesel engines

7.19 Apply a bead of RTV sealant to the coolant pump flange

trapped in the cylinder block will leak out when the pump is removed.

15 Recover the pump sealing ring, and discard it; a new one must be used on refitting **(see illustration)**.

16 Note that it is not possible to overhaul the pump. If it is faulty, the unit must be renewed complete.

Inspection

17 Check the pump body and impeller for signs of excessive corrosion or evidence of coolant leakage. Turn the impeller, and check for stiffness due to corrosion, or roughness due to excessive end play. If any of these conditions are apparent, the pump must be renewed as a complete assembly.

Refitting

Petrol engines

18 Commence refitting by thoroughly cleaning all traces of sealant from the mating faces of the pump and cylinder block.

19 Apply a continuous bead of RTV sealant to the cylinder block mating face of the pump, taking care not to apply excessive sealant, which may enter the pump itself **(see illustration)**.

20 Place the pump in position in the cylinder block, then refit and tighten the nut and bolts to the specified torque.

21 Refit the timing belt as described in Chapter 2A.

22 Refit the auxiliary drivebelt and refill the cooling system as described in Chapter 1A.

23 Reconnect the battery negative terminal as described in Chapter 5A.

Diesel engines

24 Ensure that the pump and cylinder block mating surfaces are clean and dry.

25 Fit a new sealing ring to the pump, and install the pump in the cylinder block.

26 Refit the pump retaining nuts, tightening them to the specified torque setting.

27 The remainder of refitting is a reversal of removal.

28 Upon completion, reconnect the battery then refill the cooling system as described in Chapter 1B.

---

8 Heater/ventilation system – general information

The heater/ventilation system consists of a three-speed (Panda models) or four-speed (500 models) blower, face-level vents in the centre and at each end of the facia, and air ducts to the front footwells and windscreen.

The controls operate flap valves to deflect and mix the air flowing through the various parts of the heater/ventilation system. The flap valves are contained in the air distribution housing, which acts as a central distribution unit, passing air to the various ducts and vents.

Cold air enters the system through the grille at the rear of the engine compartment. A pollen filter is fitted to the ventilation intake, to filter out dust, soot, pollen and spores from the air entering the vehicle.

The air (boosted by the blower fan if required) then flows through the various ducts, according to the settings of the controls. Stale air is expelled through ducts behind the doors. If warm air is required, the cold air is passed through the heater matrix, which is heated by the engine coolant.

A recirculation lever enables the outside air supply to be closed off, while the air inside the vehicle is recirculated. This can be useful to prevent unpleasant odours entering from outside the vehicle, but should only be used briefly, as the recirculated air inside the vehicle will soon deteriorate.

---

9 Heater/ventilation system components – removal and refitting

Heater controls

Facia controls – Panda models

1 Disconnect the battery negative terminal as described in Chapter 5A.

2 Gently pull the control knobs from place **(see illustration)**.

3 Carefully prise the control trims from the facia **(see illustration)**.

9.2 Pull the heater control knobs from place

9.3 Prise the trims from the facia

9.6a Carefully prise the control panel from the facia

9.6b Undo the screws (arrowed) and detach the switch from the control panel

4 If required, the illumination bulbs simply pull from place (see illustration).

5 Refitting is a reversal of removal.

Facia controls – 500 models

6 Carefully prise up the heater/air conditioning control panel. Undo the screws and remove the switch unit from the panel to enable plug disconnection (see illustrations).

7 If required, the illumination bulbs simply pull from the bulbholders (see illustration).

8 Refitting is a reversal of removal.

Controls assembly – all models

9 Remove the complete facia as described in Chapter 11. Release the retaining clips and manoeuvre the heater controls from place.

10 Note their fitted positions and disconnect the control cables and wiring plugs from the rear of the panel (see illustration).

11 Refitting is a reversal of removal. Ensure that the wiring connectors and control cables are correctly routed and reconnected to the control assembly, as noted before removal. Clip the outer cable(s) in position, and check the operation of each knob/lever before refitting the components removed for access.

Heater control assembly cables

12 Remove the complete facia as described in Chapter 11. Mark the position of the heater control cables in their respective retaining clips on the air distribution housing, then prise out the outer cable retaining clips and disconnect the inner cables from their attachments (see illustration 9.10).

13 Disconnect the wiring connectors from the panel, and pull out the illumination bulbholders (see illustration).

14 Note the orientation of the control cables, then release the outer cable retaining clips

and disconnect the inner cable ends from the control levers (see illustrations). Remove the control assembly from the facia. Alternatively, the control cables can be left attached to be removed complete with the control assembly.

15 Refitting is a reversal of removal. Ensure that the wiring connectors and control cables are correctly routed and reconnected to the control assembly, as noted before removal. Clip the outer cable(s) in position, and check the operation of each knob/lever before refitting the components removed for access.

Heater matrix

Panda models

16 Drain the coolant and described in Chapter 1A or 1B.

17 Remove the facia lower centre panel as described in Chapter 11.

9.7 The illumination bulbs (arrowed) simply pull from the bulbholders

9.10 Prise out the clips (arrowed) securing the outer cables

9.13 Pull the bulbholders from the heater control panel

9.14a Disconnect the cables from the distribution flap lever . . .

9.14b . . . the recirculation flap lever . . .

9.14c . . . and the temperature control lever

9.19 Disconnect the heater hoses (arrowed) at the engine compartment bulkhead

9.21 Heater matrix cover screws (arrowed) and pipe securing screw (arrowed)

18 Remove the air cleaner assembly as described in Chapter 4A or 4B.
19 Release the clamps and disconnect the heater matrix hoses at the engine compartment bulkhead **(see illustration)**.
20 Unclip the wiring loom from the matrix cover (where applicable).
21 Undo the 2 screws and remove the matrix cover from the heater housing **(see illustration)**.
22 Undo the screw securing the pipes to the matrix, and slide it from the housing.

500 models

23 Remove the facia lower centre panel as described in Chapter 11.
24 Release the clamps and disconnect the heater matrix hoses at the engine compartment bulkhead **(see illustration)**. Note that on diesel models, to improve access, remove the throttle body as described in Chapter 4B.
25 Undo the screws and remove the matrix/pipes cover from the air distribution housing **(see illustration)**.
26 Undo the screw securing the pipes to the matrix, push the pipes forwards slightly and slide the matrix from the housing **(see illustration)**.

All models

27 Refitting is a reversal of the removal procedure. On completion, top-up/refill the cooling system as described in Chapter 1A or 1B.

Heater blower motor

28 Disconnect the battery negative terminal as described in Chapter 5A.
29 Remove the passenger's side glovebox/oddments tray as described in Chapter 11.
30 Reach under the passenger's side of the

facia, and disconnect the blower motor wiring plug **(see illustration)**.
31 Undo the retaining bolt, rotate the blower motor clockwise, and remove it from the air distribution housing **(see illustration)**.
32 Refitting is a reversal of the removal procedure.

Heater blower motor resistor

33 Set the wheels in the 'straight-ahead' position, engage the steering lock, then disconnect the battery negative terminal as described in Chapter 5A.

9.24 Disconnect the heater hoses (arrowed) at the engine compartment bulkhead

9.25 Heater matrix/pipe cover screws (arrowed)

9.26 Undo the screw (arrowed) and push the matrix pipes forwards a little

9.30 Heater blower motor wiring plug and retaining bolt (arrowed)

9.31 Rotate the heater blower motor *clockwise* and withdraw it from the housing

9.34 Undo the steering column lower pinch-bolt (arrowed)

9.35 Heater blower motor resistor wiring plug and retaining screw (arrowed)

34 Remove the steering column lower pinch-bolt, and pull the column up from the steering rack pinion (see illustration). Discard the bolt – a new one must be fitted. The lower column joint is 'master-splined' to the steering rack pinion, and will only fit in one position.

35 Reach up under the facia and disconnect the wiring connector from the blower motor resistor (see illustration). Note that access is severely limited.

36 Undo the retaining screw and unclip the resistor from the blower motor housing.

37 Refitting is the reverse of removal.

Air distribution housing

Note: *On models with air conditioning, it is not possible to remove the air distribution housing without opening the refrigerant circuit*

(see Sections 10 and 11). Have the refrigerant discharged at a dealer service department or an automotive air conditioning repair facility before proceeding.

38 Remove the complete facia assembly and both front doors as described in Chapter 11.

39 On 500 models, remove the steering column as described in Chapter 10.

40 Drain the cooling system as described in Chapter 1A or 1B.

41 Remove the battery and battery tray as described in Chapter 5A.

42 Working in the engine compartment, release the retaining clips, and disconnect both hoses from the heater matrix unions (see illustration 9.19 and 9.24).

43 On models with air conditioning, undo the retaining nuts and disconnect the refrigerant pipes from the engine compartment bulkhead

(see illustrations). Plug the openings to prevent contamination.

Panda models

44 Undo the retaining bolt securing the fusebox to the passenger compartment facia crossmember. Position the fusebox to one side.

45 Note their fitted positions, then disconnect the wiring plugs from the SRS control unit under the front of the heater housing.

500 models

46 Drill out/remove the shear bolts, remove the anti-tamper shield, and disconnect the accessible wiring plugs from the fusebox/module. Depress the two retaining clips each side, and push the fusebox/module forwards away from the crossmember bracket (see illustrations).

47 On models with the 'stop/start' system, undo the nut securing the voltage stabiliser to the crossmember (see illustration). Slide out the locking catch and disconnect the wiring plug as the module is withdrawn.

All models

48 On manual heating/air conditioning models, prise out the metal clips, disconnect the control cables and wiring plugs, then pull out the illumination bulbholders from the control panel (see illustrations 9.13).

49 On automatic air conditioning models, disconnect the wiring plugs from the control panel.

50 Remove the gearchange lever assembly

9.43a Undo the nuts (arrowed) and pull the refrigerant pipes from the expansion valve on the engine compartment bulkhead

9.43b Renew the refrigerant pipe seals (arrowed)

9.46a Undo the shear bolts (arrowed) at the top (we used a self-grip wrench) . . .

9.46b . . . and remove the metal shield

9.46c Disconnect the wiring plugs from the fusebox/module and release the clips each side (arrowed)

9.47 Voltage stabiliser wiring plug and retaining nut (arrowed)

9.50 Crossmember-to-floor bracket retaining bolts (arrowed)

9.53 Disconnect the evaporator drain tube (arrowed)

9.54a The crossmember is secured by 2 bolts (arrowed) at each end adjacent to the door hinges . . .

9.54b . . . and one each side at the upper edge (arrowed)

9.55a The housing is secured to the crossmember by a nut at the top each side (arrowed) . . .

9.55b . . . and a nut at the lower, rear each side (arrowed)

as described in Chapter 7, then undo the bolts and remove the crossmember-to-floor bracket at the rear of the heater housing **(see illustration)**. Release the wiring loom from the bracket as it's withdrawn.

51 Note their fitted positions, then trace the crossmember wiring loom back to its connectors. Disconnect the plugs/connections, so the wiring loom can be removed along with the crossmember.

52 Cover the carpet directly underneath the air distribution housing, to catch any coolant which may be spilt from the matrix as the housing assembly is removed.

53 Disconnect the evaporator drain tube from the base of the housing on models with air conditioning **(see illustration)**.

54 The facia crossmember is secured by 2 bolts at each end, and 2 bolts in the central, upper area **(see illustrations)**. Undo the bolts, and with the help of an assistant, manoeuvre the crossmember/hear distribution housing form the passenger's compartment. Mop-up any spilt coolant immediately, and wipe the affected area with a damp cloth to prevent staining.

55 Undo the nuts/bolts, and separate the heater distribution housing from the facia crossmember. On 500 models, remove the floor air vent each side. Release any wiring looms as necessary **(see illustrations)**.

56 Refitting is the reverse of removal. On completion, refill the cooling system as described in Chapter 1A or 1B. On models with

air conditioning, have the system evacuated, charged and leak-tested by the specialist who discharged it.

10 Air conditioning system – general information and precautions

General information

1 Air conditioning is available on certain models. It enables the temperature of incoming air to be lowered, and also dehumidifies the air, which makes for rapid demisting and increased comfort.

2 The cooling side of the system works in the same way as a domestic refrigerator. Refrigerant gas is drawn into a belt-driven compressor, and passes into a condenser mounted in front of the radiator, where it loses heat and becomes liquid. The liquid passes through an expansion valve to an evaporator, where it changes from liquid under high pressure to gas under low pressure. This change is accompanied by a drop in temperature, which cools the evaporator. The refrigerant returns to the compressor, and the cycle begins again.

3 Air blown through the evaporator passes to the air distribution unit, where it is mixed with hot air blown through the heater matrix, to achieve the desired temperature in the passenger compartment.

4 The heating side of the system works in the same way as on models without air conditioning (see Section 8).

5 The operation of the system is controlled electronically. Any problems with the system should be referred to a Fiat dealer.

Air conditioning service ports

Panda models

6 The low-pressure and high-pressure service ports are located on the right-hand side of the engine compartment **(see illustration)**.

500 models

7 On petrol models, the low-pressure and high-pressure service ports are located above the air conditioning compressor.

10.6 Refrigerant circuit service ports (arrowed) – Panda petrol models

10.8 Refrigerant circuit service ports (arrowed) – 500 diesel models

8 On diesel models, the low-pressure and high-pressure service ports are located behind the right-hand side headlight (see illustration).

Precautions

9 It is necessary to observe special precautions whenever dealing with any part of the system, its associated components, and any items which necessitate disconnection of the system.

> **Warning:** *The refrigeration circuit contains a liquid refrigerant. This refrigerant is potentially dangerous, and should only be handled by qualified persons. If it is splashed onto the skin, it can cause frostbite. It is not itself poisonous, but in the presence of a naked flame it forms a poisonous gas; inhalation of the vapour through a lighted cigarette could prove fatal. Uncontrolled discharging of the refrigerant is dangerous, and potentially damaging to the environment. It is therefore dangerous to disconnect any part of the system without specialised knowledge and equipment. If for any reason the system must be disconnected, entrust this task to your Fiat dealer or air conditioning specialist.*
> **Caution:** *Do not operate the air conditioning system if it is known to be short of refrigerant, as this may damage the compressor.*

11 Air conditioning system components – removal and refitting

> **Warning:** *The air conditioning system is under high pressure. Do not loosen any fittings or remove any components until after the system has been discharged. Air conditioning refrigerant should be properly discharged into an approved type of container at a dealer service department or an automotive air conditioning repair facility capable of handling R134a refrigerant. Cap or plug the pipe lines as soon as they are disconnected, to prevent the entry of moisture. Always wear eye protection when disconnecting air conditioning system fittings.*

Note: *This Section refers to the components of the air conditioning system itself – refer to Section 9 for details of components common to the heating/ventilation system.*

Condenser

1 Have the refrigerant discharged at a dealer service department or suitably-equipped repairer.
2 Firmly apply the handbrake, then jack up the front of the car and support it securely on axle stands (see *Jacking and vehicle support*).

Panda models

3 Remove the front grille and bumper as described in Chapter 11.
4 With the system discharged, undo the retaining nuts and disconnect the refrigerant pipe connector blocks (see illustration). Discard the O-ring seals – new ones must be used when refitting. Suitably cap the open fittings immediately to keep moisture and contamination out of the system.
5 Undo the nut/bolt and remove the support bracket between the crossmember and the bonnet slam panel.
6 Disconnect the pressure switch wiring plug.
7 Undo the mounting bolts and lift the condenser out from under the vehicle and store it upright, to prevent fluid loss (see illustration). Take care not to damage the condenser fins. Note that the receiver/drier is integral with the condenser.

500 models

8 Remove the front bumper as described in Chapter 11.
9 Undo the bolt securing the refrigerant pipe connector to the right-hand side of the condenser (see illustrations). Discard the pipe seals – new ones must be used when refitting. Suitably cap the open fittings immediately to keep moisture and contamination out of the system.
10 Undo the retaining bolts and manoeuvre the condenser from position. Note that the receiver/drier is integral with the condenser.

All models

11 Refitting is the reverse of removal. Renew the O-rings and lubricate with refrigerant oil.
12 Have the system evacuated, charged and leak-tested by the specialist who discharged it.

Evaporator

13 Have the refrigerant discharged at a dealer service department or a suitably-equipped repairer.

11.4 Undo the nuts (arrowed) and disconnect the refrigerant pipes

11.7a The condenser is secured by a bolt on the right-hand side (arrowed) . . .

11.7b . . . and a bolt (arrowed) on the left-hand side

11.9a Undo the bolt (arrowed) and detach the refrigerant pipe connector

11.9b Renew the pipe seals (arrowed)

11.16a Undo the screws around the edge (arrowed) . . .

11.16b . . . and remove the lower half of the evaporator housing (arrowed)

11.18 Undo enough screws so the housing can be pulled apart slightly, and withdraw the evaporator

14 Remove the air distribution housing as described in Section 9.

15 Unclip the cover and remove the pollen filter from the right-hand side of the housing – refer to Chapter 1A or 1B if necessary.

16 Disconnect the wiring plug, undo the screws and remove the lower half of the evaporator housing **(see illustrations)**. Unclip the temperature probe as the housing is removed.

17 Undo the bolt, release the clip and remove the blower motor **(see illustration 9.30)**.

18 The air distribution housing must now be split vertically. Undo sufficient screws to be able to pull the halves apart in the area of the evaporator, then manoeuvre the evaporator from the housing **(see illustration)**. Using this method allows the various distribution flaps to remain in place.

19 Refitting is the reverse of removal. Renew the O-rings and lubricate with refrigerant oil.

Expansion valve

20 Have the refrigerant discharged at a dealer service department or a suitably-equipped repairer.

21 With the system discharged, undo the retaining nuts and disconnect the refrigerant pipe connector blocks **(see illustration 9.43a)**. Discard the O-ring seals – new ones must be used when refitting. Suitably cap the open fittings immediately to keep moisture and contamination out of the system.

22 Release the refrigerant pipes from the retaining clips on the engine compartment

bulkhead, and pull the pipes away from the expansion valve.

23 Undo the screws and pull the expansion valve from the evaporator pipes **(see illustration)**. Renew the valve O-ring seals.

24 Refitting is the reverse of removal ensuring that all disturbed seals are renewed.

Compressor

25 Have the refrigerant discharged at a dealer service department or a suitably-equipped repairer.

26 Disconnect the battery negative terminal as described in Chapter 5A.

Panda models

27 On petrol models, remove the air cleaner assembly as described in Chapter 4A.

28 Firmly apply the handbrake, then jack up the front of the car and support it securely on axle stands (see *Jacking and vehicle support*). Remove the right-hand front wheel.

29 Release the auxiliary drivebelt from the pulleys as described in Chapter 1A or 1B.

30 With the system discharged, undo the retaining bolt and disconnect the refrigerant pipes from the compressor. Discard the O-ring seals – new ones must be used when refitting. Suitably cap the open fittings immediately to keep moisture and contamination out of the system.

31 Disconnect the compressor wiring connector.

32 On petrol models, undo the bolts and remove the auxiliary belt guard **(see illustration)**.

33 Unbolt the compressor from the

cylinder block/crankcase, then withdraw the compressor from place.

500 models

34 Firmly apply the handbrake, then jack up the front of the car and support it securely on axle stands (see *Jacking and vehicle support*). Remove the right-hand front wheel.

35 On petrol models, remove the air cleaner assembly as described in Chapter 4A.

36 Release the auxiliary drivebelt from the pulleys as described in Chapter 1A or 1B.

37 On diesel models, release the clamps and remove the air hose between the turbocharger and the intercooler.

38 With the system discharged, undo the retaining bolt and disconnect the refrigerant pipes from the compressor **(see illustration)**. Discard the O-ring seals – new ones must be used when refitting. Suitably cap the open fittings immediately to keep moisture and contamination out of the system.

39 Disconnect the compressor wiring connector.

40 Unbolt the compressor from the cylinder block/crankcase, then withdraw the compressor from place.

All models

41 Refit the compressor in the reverse order of removal; renew all seals disturbed.

42 If you are installing a new compressor, refer to the compressor manufacturer's instructions for adding refrigerant oil to the system.

43 Have the system evacuated, charged and leak-tested by the specialist that discharged it.

11.23 Expansion valve retaining screws (arrowed)

11.32 Auxiliary belt guard retaining bolts (arrowed)

11.38 Undo the bolts (arrowed) and disconnect the refrigerant pipes

Chapter 4 Part A:
Fuel and exhaust systems – petrol engines

Contents

Degrees of difficulty

Easy, suitable for novice with little experience	Fairly easy, suitable for beginner with some experience	Fairly difficult, suitable for competent DIY mechanic	Difficult, suitable for experienced DIY mechanic	Very difficult, suitable for expert DIY or professional

Specifications

System type
All models.. Magneti-Marelli IAW sequential fuel injection/ignition system

Fuel system data
Engine idle speed*...................................... 900 ± 50 rpm
Fuel pump type .... Electric, immersed in fuel tank
Fuel pump delivery rate .... 110 litres/hour
Regulated fuel pressure .... 3.5 bars
Crankshaft TDC sensor resistance at 20°C .... 1134 to 1386 ohms
Injector electrical resistance........................... 13.8 to 15.2 ohms
Fuel level sensor:
  Panda models:
    Full .... 6 ± 3 ohms
    Empty.. 310 ± 10 ohms
  500 models:
    Full .... 33 ± 3 ohms
    Empty .... 299 ± 3 ohms
* Not adjustable – controlled by ECU

Recommended fuel
Minimum octane rating.................................. 95 RON unleaded

Torque wrench settings

	Nm	lbf ft
Camshaft position sensor	8	6
Exhaust manifold downpipe support bracket bolt	25	18
Exhaust manifold to cylinder head:		
Panda models	25	18
500 models:		
Stage 1	10	7
Stage 2	Angle-tighten a further 60°	
Exhaust system flange joint	25	18
Exhaust system mounting bracket bolts	30	22
Intake manifold to cylinder head	27	20
Oxygen sensor	40	30

1 General information and precautions

The fuel supply system consists of a fuel tank (which is mounted under the centre of the car, with an electric fuel pump immersed in it) and fuel feed line. The fuel pump supplies fuel to the fuel rail, which acts as a reservoir for the four fuel injectors which inject fuel into the intake tracts.

Note that the engines are built to two different emissions levels:

Euro 4 – models up to 07/06.
Euro 5 – models 07/06-on.

The easiest method of identification is by throttle operation:

Euro 4 models have a throttle cable.
Euro 5 models are equipped with a 'motorised throttle unit', and no cable.

The fuel injection and ignition functions are combined into a single engine management system. The system incorporates a closed-loop catalytic converter and an evaporative emission control system, and complies with the latest emission control standards. Refer to Chapter 5B for information on the ignition side of each system; the fuel side of the system operates as follows.

The fuel pump supplies fuel from the tank to the fuel rail (mounted directly above the fuel injectors) by means of a 'returnless' system. With this arrangement, the fuel filter and fuel pressure regulator are an integral part of the fuel pump assembly located in the fuel tank. The regulator maintains a constant fuel pressure in the supply line to the fuel rail and allows excess fuel to recirculate in the fuel tank, by means of a bypass channel, if the regulated fuel pressure is exceeded. As the fuel filter is an integral part of the pump assembly, fuel filter renewal is no longer necessary as part of the maintenance and servicing schedule.

The fuel injectors are electromagnetic pintle valves which spray atomised fuel into the combustion chambers under the control of the ECU. There are four injectors, one per cylinder, mounted in the intake manifold close to the cylinder head. Each injector is mounted at an angle that allows it to spray fuel directly onto the back of the intake valve(s). The ECU controls the volume of fuel injected by varying the length of time for which each injector is held open. The fuel injection systems are of the sequential type, whereby each injector operates individually in cylinder sequence.

The electrical control system consists of the ECU, along with the following sensors:

a) *Throttle potentiometer – informs the ECU of the throttle valve position, and the rate of throttle opening/closing – models with a throttle cable.*
b) *Engine coolant temperature sensor – informs the ECU of engine temperature (refer to Chapter 3).*
c) *Intake air temperature/pressure sensor – informs the ECU of intake air temperature and load on the engine (expressed in terms of intake manifold vacuum).*
d) *Lambda sensors – inform the ECU of the oxygen content of the exhaust gases.*
e) *Crankshaft TDC sensor – informs the ECU of engine speed and crankshaft angular position.*
f) *Vehicle speed sensor – informs the ECU of the vehicle speed.*
g) *Knock sensor – informs the ECU of pre-ignition (detonation) within the cylinders (refer to Chapter 5B).*
h) *Camshaft position sensor – informs the ECU of which cylinder is on the firing stroke.*
i) *Accelerator pedal potentiometer – informs the ECU of accelerator pedal position and rate of change – Euro 5 emissions level only.*

Signals from each of the sensors are compared by the ECU and, based on this information, the ECU selects the response appropriate to those values, and controls the fuel injectors (varying the pulse width – the length of time the injectors are held open – to provide a richer or weaker air/fuel mixture, as appropriate). The air/fuel mixture is constantly varied by the ECU, to provide the best settings for cranking, starting (with either a hot or cold engine) and engine warm-up, idle, cruising and acceleration.

The ECU also has full control over the engine idle speed, via a stepper motor or throttle valve actuator fitted to the throttle body. On Euro 5 emissions level models, the accelerator pedal potentiometer informs the ECU of accelerator pedal position and from this data, the ECU controls the throttle valve actuator so that a corresponding throttle opening can be obtained. This arrangement is often termed 'drive-by-wire' as there is no direct accelerator cable connection between the accelerator pedal and throttle valve.

The evaporative loss emission control systems are described in more detail in Chapter 4C.

If there is any abnormality in any of the readings obtained from the main engine sensors, the ECU enters its 'back-up' mode. If this happens, the erroneous sensor signal is overridden, and the ECU assumes a pre-programmed 'back-up' value, which will allow the engine to continue running, albeit at reduced efficiency. If the ECU enters this mode, the warning lamp on the instrument panel will be illuminated, and the relevant fault code will be stored in the ECU memory.

If the warning light illuminates, the vehicle should be taken to a Fiat dealer at the earliest opportunity. Once there, a complete test of the engine management system can be carried out, using a special electronic diagnostic test unit which is plugged into the system's diagnostic connector – see Section 8.

 Warning: Many of the procedures in this Chapter require the removal of fuel lines and connections, which may result in some fuel spillage. Before carrying out any operation on the fuel system, refer to the precautions given in 'Safety first!' at the beginning of this manual, and follow them implicitly. Petrol is a highly dangerous and volatile liquid, and the precautions necessary when handling it cannot be overstressed. Note that residual pressure will remain in the fuel lines long after the vehicle was last used. When disconnecting any fuel line, first depressurise the fuel system as described in Section 5.

2 Air cleaner assembly – removal and refitting

Panda models – removal
Pre-Euro 5 models
1 Disconnect the air intake duct from the front panel (see illustration).

2.1 Unclip the intake pipe from the front panel

2.2 Release the clip at the front of the air cleaner housing

2.3 Air cleaner housing retaining bolts (arrowed)

2.4a Disconnect the ventilation hose

2.4b Unclip the throttle cable from the housing

2.6 Disconnect the air intake hose

2.7 Air cleaner housing retaining bolts (arrowed)

2.8a Disconnect the breather hose from the air cleaner housing (arrowed) . . .

2.8b . . . and from the cylinder head cover

2 Release the retaining clip at the front of the air cleaner casing (see illustration).
3 Undo the two retaining bolts, one located on each side of the air cleaner casing (see illustration).
4 Lift the air cleaner casing off the throttle body and disconnect the crankcase ventilation hose from the air cleaner base. Disengage the throttle cable as the casing is withdrawn (see illustrations).
5 Recover the sealing ring between the casing and throttle body. Check the ring for condition and renew it if necessary.

Euro 5 models

6 Pull the air intake hose from the front panel, and disconnect it from the air cleaner housing (see illustration).
7 Undo the two retaining bolts, and pull the air

cleaner assembly upwards from the mounting (see illustration).
8 Release the clamp and disconnect the breather hoses (see illustrations).

500 models – removal

9 Undo the retaining bolt and disconnect the air intake hose from the front panel (see illustration).
10 Undo the two retaining bolts, and pull the air cleaner assembly upwards from the mounting (see illustration 2.7).
11 Release the clamp and disconnect the breather hose.

Refitting – all models

12 Refitting is a reversal of removal but renew the air cleaner filter element, as described in Chapter 1A, if necessary.

3 Accelerator cable – removal, refitting and adjustment

Note: An accelerator cable is only used on 1.1 litre engines. On 1.2 litre engines, a 'drive-by-wire' system is employed, whereby the throttle valve is operated by a throttle valve actuator incorporated in the throttle body. The system is controlled by the engine management ECU using signal inputs from the accelerator pedal potentiometer.

Removal

1 Remove the air cleaner assembly as described in Section 2.
2 Disengage the inner cable from the throttle cam, and withdraw the outer cable from the rubber grommet on the mounting bracket (see illustrations).

2.9 Undo the intake hose retaining bolt (arrowed)

3.2a Disengage the inner cable from the throttle cam (arrowed) . . .

3.2b . . . then pull the outer cable (arrowed) from the grommet

3.9 Pull the clip (arrowed) from the groove in the outer cable

4.3 Accelerator pedal assembly retaining nuts (arrowed) – facia removed for clarity

3 Working back along the length of the cable, free it from any retaining clips or ties, noting its correct routing.

4 From under the facia, inside the car, unhook the cable from the fork at the top of the pedal arm.

5 Release the bulkhead grommet and withdraw the accelerator cable from inside the engine compartment.

Refitting

6 Feed the accelerator cable through the bulkhead grommet, then return to the car and locate the inner cable end fitting in the pedal arm.

7 From within the engine compartment, work along the cable, securing it in position with the retaining clips and ties, and ensuring that the cable is correctly routed.

8 Pass the outer cable through its throttle body mounting bracket grommet, and reconnect the inner cable to the throttle cam. Adjust the cable as described below.

Adjustment

9 Extract the retaining clip from its groove in the outer cable (see illustration).

10 Ensuring that the throttle cam is fully against its stop, gently pull the cable out of its

grommet until all free play is removed from the inner cable.

11 With the cable held in this position, refit the retaining clip to the last exposed outer cable groove in front of the rubber grommet. When the clip is refitted and the outer cable is released, there should be only a small amount of free play in the inner cable.

12 Have an assistant depress the accelerator pedal, and check that the throttle cam opens fully and returns smoothly to its stop.

13 On completion, refit the air cleaner assembly as described in Section 2.

4 Accelerator pedal – removal and refitting

Removal

Models with a throttle cable

1 From under the facia inside the car, unhook the accelerator cable from the fork at the top of the pedal arm.

2 Undo the retaining nuts and lift the pedal off the mounting bracket.

Models without a throttle cable

3 From under the facia inside the car, undo

the nuts securing the pedal and potentiometer assembly to the mounting bracket (see illustration).

4 Withdraw the pedal from its location, disconnect the potentiometer wiring connector, and remove the assembly from the car.

Refitting

5 Refitting is a reversal of removal. Where applicable, check, and if necessary adjust, the accelerator cable as described in Section 3.

5 Fuel system – depressurisation

⚠️ **Warning: The following procedure will merely relieve the pressure in the fuel system – remember that fuel will still be present in the system components and take precautions accordingly before disconnecting any of them.**

Note: Refer to the warning given in Section 1 before proceeding.

1 The fuel system referred to in this Section is defined as the tank-mounted fuel pump, the fuel rail, the fuel injectors, and the metal pipes and flexible hoses of the fuel lines between these components. All these contain fuel which will be under pressure while the engine is running and/or while the ignition is switched on. The pressure will remain for some time after the ignition has been switched off, and must be relieved before any of these components are disturbed for servicing work.

2 Disconnect the battery negative terminal as described in Chapter 5A.

3 Remove the air cleaner assembly as described in Section 2.

4 Locate the Schrader valve situated at the right-hand end of the fuel rail (see illustrations). The Schrader valve works like a tyre valve whereby on depressing the central

5.4a Fuel pressure relief valve (arrowed) – pre-Euro 5 engines ...

5.4b ... and Euro 5 engines (arrowed)

plunger, the system fuel pressure will be released.

5 Unscrew the protective plastic cap from the top of the valve.

6 Place an absorbent rag around the valve then, using a small screwdriver, slowly depress the central plunger to allow the pressure to be released. Ensure that the rag completely covers the valve to catch the fuel spray which will be expelled.

7 On completion of the operations for which system depressurisation was necessary, refit the Schrader valve cap and reconnect the battery negative terminal. Refit the air cleaner assembly as described in Section 2.

6 Fuel pump and fuel gauge sender unit – removal and refitting

Note 1: *Refer to the warning given in Section 1 before proceeding.*
Note 2: *A new sealing O-ring will be required for refitting.*

Removal

1 Disconnect the battery negative terminal as described in Chapter 5A.

2 Depressurise the fuel system as described in Section 5.

3 Remove the rear seat cushion as described in Chapter 11, then lift the floor covering for access to the fuel pump cover.

4 Remove the cover from the aperture in the floor panel **(see illustrations)**. On Panda models, the cover prises from place, whilst on the 500 models, the cover is retained by screws.

5 Release the locking catch and disconnect the wiring connector from the top of the fuel pump **(see illustration)**.

6 Bearing in mind the warning given in Section 1, disconnect the fuel supply line quick-release fitting from the pump unit by pressing the tabs **(see illustration)**. Plug the end of the supply line or cover it with adhesive tape.

7 Unscrew the large locking ring and remove it from the tank. Engage the tool with the ribs of the locking ring, and turn the ring anti-clockwise until it can be unscrewed by hand **(see illustrations)**.

6.4a On Panda models, the access cover prises up . . .

6.4b . . . on 500 models, the cover is retained by screws (arrowed)

6.5 Slide out the locking catch and disconnect the wiring plug

6.6 Press in the locking tab and disconnect the fuel hose

6.7a Engage the tool with the ribs on the locking ring . . .

6.7b . . . then unscrew and remove it

8 Lift the fuel pump and sender unit assembly out of the fuel tank, taking great care not to damage the float arm. Recover the sealing O-ring and discard it – a new one must be used on refitting **(see illustrations)**. Refit the locking ring to the tank after removing the pump/sender unit.

9 Note that the fuel pump and sender unit

6.8a Lift the fuel pump and sender unit from the tank . . .

6.8b . . . taking care not to damage the float arm

6.8c Renew the sealing O-ring

6.9 Check the resistance of the sender unit with the float at full, and zero deflection

6.10 Align the arrow on the cover with the mark on the tank (arrowed)

is only available as a complete assembly – no components are available separately. However, the resistance of the fuel level sender unit can be checked by connecting a multimeter across the sender unit terminals at the plug socket **(see illustration)**. At full deflection (full tank) the resistance should be approximately 34 ohms, and zero deflection (empty tank) should be approximately 298 ohms. If the readings are significantly different than these, the unit may be faulty.

Refitting

10 Refitting is a reversal of the removal procedure using a new sealing ring, and aligning the arrow on the cover with the arrow on the tank **(see illustration)**. Prior to refitting the access cover, reconnect the battery, then start the engine and check the fuel line for signs of leakage.

7 Fuel tank – removal and refitting

Note: *Refer to the warning given in Section 1 before proceeding.*

Removal

1 Before removing the fuel tank, all fuel must be drained from the tank. Since a fuel tank drain plug is not provided, it is therefore preferable to carry out the removal operation when the tank is nearly empty. Before proceeding, disconnect the battery negative terminal as described in Chapter 5A.
2 Working as described in Section 6, disconnect the fuel pump wiring connector and the fuel supply line from the top of the pump.
3 Chock the front wheels, then jack up the rear of the car and securely support it on axle stands (see *Jacking and vehicle support*). Remove the right-hand rear roadwheel.

Panda models

4 Release the rubber mountings and move the exhaust system to one side, for access to the fuel tank heat shield.
5 Undo the retaining nuts, extract the spring clip and remove the heat shield from under the fuel tank.
6 Loosen the clips and disconnect the filler pipe and vent pipe from the right-hand side of the fuel tank. Disconnect the roll-over valve hoses at the quick-release fittings adjacent to the filler pipe **(see illustration)**.
7 Place a trolley jack with an interposed block of wood beneath the tank, then raise the jack until it is supporting the weight of the tank.
8 Undo the fuel tank mounting bolts, then carefully lower the tank from its location. Move the exhaust system as far as possible to one side to provide the necessary clearance for removal.

500 models

9 Remove the exhaust system as described in Section 12.
10 Loosen the clips and disconnect the filler pipe, vent pipe and roll-over valve hoses from fuel tank **(see illustration 7.6)**.
11 Place a trolley jack with an interposed block of wood beneath the tank, then raise

7.6 Disconnect the filler pipe, vent pipe, and the quick-release fittings (arrowed)

the jack until it is supporting the weight of the tank.
12 Undo the fuel tank mounting bolts, then carefully lower the tank from its location, unclipping any hoses from the top of the tank as it's lowered.

All models

13 If the tank is contaminated with sediment or water, remove the fuel pump/fuel gauge sender unit as described in Section 6, and swill the tank out with clean fuel. The tank is injection-moulded from a synthetic material – if seriously damaged, it should be renewed. However, in certain cases, it may be possible to have small leaks or minor damage repaired. Seek the advice of a specialist before attempting to repair the fuel tank.

Refitting

14 Refitting is a reversal of the removal procedure, ensuring that all pipes/hoses are correctly routed and securely reconnected.

8 Engine management system – testing and adjustment

Testing

1 If a fault appears in the engine management system, first ensure that all the system wiring connectors are securely connected and free of corrosion. Ensure that the fault is not due to poor maintenance; ie, check that the air cleaner filter element is clean, the spark plugs are in good condition and correctly gapped, the valve clearances are correctly adjusted (where applicable), the cylinder compression pressures are correct, and that the engine breather hoses are clear and undamaged, referring to the relevant Parts of Chapters 1A and 2A for further information.
2 If these checks fail to reveal the cause of the problem, the vehicle should be taken to a Fiat dealer or suitably-equipped repairer for

testing. A diagnostic socket is located on the right-hand side of the facia **(see illustrations)**, into which a fault code reader or other suitable test equipment can be connected. By using the code reader or test equipment, the engine management ECU (and the various other vehicle system ECUs) can be interrogated, and any stored fault codes can be retrieved. This will allow the fault to be quickly and simply traced, alleviating the need to test all the system components individually, which is a time-consuming operation that carries a risk of damaging the ECU.

Adjustment

3 Experienced home mechanics with a considerable amount of skill and equipment (including a tachometer and an accurately calibrated exhaust gas analyser) may be able to check the exhaust CO level and the idle speed. However, if these are found to be outside the specified tolerance, the car must be taken to a suitably-equipped garage for further testing. Neither the mixture adjustment (exhaust gas CO level) nor the idle speed are adjustable, and should either be incorrect, a fault may be present in the engine management system.

9 Engine management components – removal and refitting

Note: *Refer to the warning given in Section 1 before proceeding.*

Throttle body assembly

1 Disconnect the battery negative terminal as described in Chapter 5A.
2 Remove the air cleaner assembly as described in Section 2.

Models with a throttle cable

3 Disengage the accelerator inner cable from the throttle cam, and withdraw the outer cable from the rubber grommet on the mounting bracket – see Section 3.
4 Disconnect the wiring connectors from idle control stepper motor and throttle potentiometer **(see illustration)**.
5 Slacken and remove the 3 bolts securing the throttle body assembly to the intake manifold, then remove the assembly and collect the sealing O-ring **(see illustration)**.

Models without a throttle cable

6 Disconnect the wiring plug from the throttle body, and unclip the wiring loom from the retaining clips **(see illustration)**.
7 Release the fuel supply, and vacuum/breather hoses from the clips on the throttle body.
8 Undo the retaining bolts, then remove the support bracket and throttle body from the manifold **(see illustration)**.

All models

9 Refitting is a reversal of the removal

8.2a Undo the screws (arrowed) and remove the panel . . .

8.2b . . . to access the diagnostic socket (arrowed) – Panda models

8.2c On 500 models, starting at the lower edge, pull away the trim panel . . .

8.2d . . . to access the diagnostic plug (arrowed)

9.4 Disconnect the wiring plugs (arrowed) from the side of the throttle body

9.5 Throttle body retaining bolts (arrowed)

9.6 Slide out the yellow locking catch (arrowed) and disconnect the wiring plug

9.8 Throttle body retaining bolts (arrowed)

9.13 Prise out the wire retaining clip (arrowed) a little, and disconnect the wiring plug from each injector

9.14 Disconnect the injector loom wiring plug (arrowed)

procedure, bearing in mind the following points:

a) *Ensure the throttle body and intake manifold mating surfaces are clean and dry, then fit the throttle body with a new O-ring, and securely tighten the retaining bolts.*

b) *Adjust the accelerator cable (where applicable) as described in Section 3.*

Fuel rail and injectors

10 Disconnect the battery negative terminal as described in Chapter 5A.

11 Remove the air cleaner assembly as described in Section 2.

12 Depressurise the fuel system as described in Section 5.

13 On models with a throttle cable, disconnect the wiring connectors at the fuel injectors **(see illustration)**.

14 On models without a throttle cable, disconnect the injector wiring plug **(see illustration)**. Release the wiring loom retaining clips.

15 On all engines, disconnect the fuel supply pipe at the quick-release connector on the end of the fuel rail **(see illustration)**.

16 Unscrew the two bolts securing the fuel rail assembly to the intake manifold, then carefully pull the injectors from their manifold

locations **(see illustration)**. Remove the assembly from the engine and remove the injector lower O-ring seals.

17 The injectors can be removed individually from the fuel rail by extracting the relevant metal clip and easing the injector out of the rail. Remove the injector upper O-ring seals.

18 Check the electrical resistance of the injector using a multimeter and compare it with the *Specifications*. **Note:** *If a faulty injector is suspected, before condemning the injector it is worth trying the effect of one of the proprietary injector-cleaning treatments.*

19 Refitting is a reversal of the removal procedure, bearing in mind the following points:

a) *Renew the injector O-ring seals, and smear them with a little petroleum jelly before assembling. Take care when fitting the injectors to the fuel rail and do not press them in further than required to fit the retaining clip otherwise the O-ring seal may be damaged.*

b) *Ensure that the injector retaining clips are securely seated.*

c) *On completion check the fuel rail and injectors for fuel leaks.*

Idle control stepper motor

20 The idle control stepper motor is an integral part of the throttle body and cannot be individually renewed.

Throttle potentiometer

21 The idle control stepper motor is an integral part of the throttle body and cannot be individually renewed.

Intake air temperature/pressure sensor

22 Disconnect the battery negative terminal as described in Chapter 5A.

23 Remove the air cleaner assembly as described in Section 2.

24 Disconnect the wiring connector, undo the screw and remove the sensor from the end of the intake manifold **(see illustrations)**.

9.15 Squeeze together the clips (arrowed) and disconnect the fuel supply pipe

9.16 Fuel rail mounting bolts (arrowed)

9.24a Intake air temperature/pressure sensor wiring plug (arrowed) – pre-Euro 5 engines . . .

9.24b . . . and Euro 5 engines (arrowed)

9.30 Front and rear oxygen sensors (arrowed)

9.31 Front oxygen sensor and wiring plug (arrowed)

9.35 Rear oxygen sensor and wiring plug (arrowed)

25 Refitting is a reversal of the removal procedure.

Coolant temperature sensor

26 Refer to Chapter 3.

Front oxygen sensor

27 Disconnect the battery negative terminal as described in Chapter 5A.
28 Remove the air cleaner assembly as described in Section 2.

Models up to 06/06

29 Undo the bolts/nuts and remove the heat shield from the exhaust manifold (see illustration 11.5a). If necessary, soak the fasteners in releasing agent before attempting to undo them.
30 Disconnect the wiring plug, then unscrew the sensor from the catalytic converter (see illustration).

Models 07/06-on

31 Disconnect the oxygen sensor wiring plug, then unscrew the sensor from the top of the exhaust manifold (see illustration).

All models

32 Refitting is a reversal of removal.

Rear oxygen sensor

33 Disconnect the battery negative terminal as described in Chapter 5A.
34 Raise the rear of the vehicle and support it securely on axle stands (see Jacking and vehicle support).

35 The rear sensor is located after the catalytic converter. Trace the wiring back from the sensor to the connector, and unplug it. Unscrew the sensor from the exhaust pipe (see illustration).
36 Refitting is a reversal of removal.

Crankshaft TDC sensor

37 The crankshaft TDC sensor is located adjacent to the front facing side of the crankshaft pulley (see illustration).
38 Disconnect the battery negative terminal as described in Chapter 5A.
39 Raise the front of the vehicle and support it securely on axle stands (see Jacking and vehicle support).
40 Undo the bolt securing the sensor to the oil pump casing and remove the sensor from its location.
41 Locate the sensor in position and secure with the retaining bolt.
42 The remainder of refitting is a reversal of removal. If a new TDC sensor has been fitted, the following 'learning' procedure must be carried out if the MIL (engine management warning light) flashes after renewal:
  a) Run the engine until it reaches normal operating temperature.
  b) Press the accelerator pedal at least 3 times, revving the engine to at least 6000 rpm each time, allowing the engine to return to idle speed between each press.
  c) If the MIL is still flashing, the procedure must be repeated.

  d) Once the MIL has stopped flashing, turn off the ignition and wait at least 1 minute to allow the ECU to permanently store the data.

Knock sensor

43 Refer to Chapter 5B.

Camshaft position sensor

44 Disconnect the battery negative terminal as described in Chapter 5A.

Pre-Euro 5 models

45 Disconnect the wiring connector from the camshaft position sensor located at the timing belt end of the camshaft cover (see illustration).
46 Undo the retaining bolt and withdraw the sensor from the camshaft cover.

Euro 5 models

47 Remove the battery and battery tray as described in Chapter 5A.
48 Move the engine wiring loom to one side, then disconnect the wiring plug, undo the retaining bolt and pull sensor from place (see illustration).

All models

49 Refitting is a reversal of the removal procedure.

Electronic control unit (ECU)

50 Disconnect the battery negative terminal as described in Chapter 5A.

9.37 Crankshaft TDC sensor (arrowed)

9.45 Camshaft position sensor (arrowed) – pre-Euro 5 emissions engines

9.48 On Euro 5 emissions engines, the camshaft position sensor (arrowed) is located at the left-hand end of the cylinder head

9.51 Slide out the locking catches and disconnect the wiring plugs from the top of the ECU

9.52 Undo the nut (arrowed) and disconnect the earth lead

9.53a Undo the retaining nuts (arrowed) . . .

9.53b . . . then remove the retaining bracket and withdraw the ECU

9.54 Release the clip (arrowed), pivot up the locking catch and disconnect the ECU wiring plugs

9.55 ECU mounting nuts (arrowed)

Pre-Euro 5 models

51 Disconnect the two wiring connectors from the top of the ECU **(see illustration)**.
52 Undo the bolt/nut securing the earth lead (where fitted) to the ECU **(see illustration)**.
53 Undo the two mounting bolts or nuts (as applicable) and remove the ECU **(see illustrations)**.

Euro 5 models

54 Disconnect the two wiring connectors from the top of the ECU **(see illustration)**.
55 Undo the mounting nuts and remove the ECU **(see illustration)**.

All models

56 Refitting is a reversal of the removal procedure. On models up to 06/06, if a new ECU has been fitted, the following 'learning' procedure must be carried out if the MIL (engine management warning light) flashes after renewal:
a) *Run the engine until it reaches normal operating temperature.*
b) *Press the accelerator pedal at least 3 times, revving the engine to at least 6000 rpm each time, allowing the engine to return to idle speed between each press.*
c) *If the MIL is still flashing, the procedure must be repeated.*
d) *Once the MIL has stopped flashing, turn off the ignition and wait at least 1 minute to allow the ECU to permanently store the data.*
57 On models 07/06-on, if a new ECU is

fitted, it must be programmed using Fiat diagnostic equipment. Entrust this task to a Fiat dealer or suitably-equipped repairer.

Accelerator pedal potentiometer

58 The potentiometer is integral with the accelerator pedal assembly – see Section 4.

10 Intake manifold – removal and refitting

Note: *Refer to the warning given in Section 1 before proceeding.*

Removal

Models with throttle cable

1 Remove the throttle body as described in Section 9.
2 Drain the cooling system as described in Chapter 1A.
3 Note their fitted positions, then disconnect the various electrical wiring plugs and vacuum hoses from the manifold **(see illustration)**.
4 Undo the manifold retaining nuts/bolts, and remove the manifold from the cylinder head. Remove the sealing rings and obtain new rings for refitting.

Models without throttle cable

5 Remove the battery and battery tray as described in Chapter 5A.

6 Remove the air cleaner assembly as described in Section 2.
7 Raise the front of the vehicle and support it securely on axle stands (see *Jacking and vehicle support*).
8 Undo the bolts and remove the bracket securing the lower/rear engine mounting rod to the transmission – see Chapter 2A.
9 Release the rear silencer and central section of the exhaust system from the rubber mountings to facilitate manifold removal.
10 Release the wiring loom from the retaining clips on the underside of the intake manifold.
11 Remove the nuts/bolt securing the lower edge of the manifold to the cylinder head.
12 Depressurise the fuel system as described in Section 5, then disconnect the fuel supply pipe from the fuel rail **(see illustration 9.15)**.

10.3 Disconnect the various wiring plugs and hoses from the manifold

13 Note their fitted positions, then disconnect the various wiring plugs from the throttle body and manifold.

14 Disconnect the vapour hose from the EVAP purge valve **(see illustration)**.

15 Prise the servo check valve (complete with hose) from the servo.

16 Disconnect the HT leads from the middle two cylinders' spark plugs and ignition coils.

17 Undo the bolt/nuts securing the upper edge of the intake manifold to the cylinder head **(see illustration)**.

18 Position a workshop/trolley jack under the engine, then undo the nuts securing the right-hand engine mounting to the bracket on the cylinder head.

19 Carefully lower the engine, until the intake manifold assembly can be manoeuvred from place.

Refitting

20 Refitting is a reverse of the removal procedure, noting the following points:

a) *Ensure that the manifold and cylinder head mating surfaces are clean and dry, and fit new manifold sealing rings. Refit the manifold and securely tighten its retaining nuts/bolts.*

b) *Ensure all relevant hoses and wiring are reconnected to their original positions and are securely held (where necessary) by the retaining clips.*

c) *On completion, refill the cooling system (where applicable) as described in Chapter 1A.*

11 Exhaust manifold – removal and refitting

Removal

1 Disconnect the battery negative terminal as described in Chapter 5A.

2 Remove the air cleaner assembly as described in Section 2.

10.14 Pull back the collar (arrowed) and disconnect the EVAP pipe from the purge valve

3 Remove the exhaust system as described in Section 12.

4 Disconnect the oxygen sensors' wiring plugs as described in Section 9.

5 Soak the fasteners in releasing fluid, then undo the bolts/nuts and remove the heat shield from the manifold **(see illustrations)**.

6 Undo the upper and lower mounting bolt/nuts and manoeuvre the manifold from place.

Refitting

7 Refitting is a reversal of the removal procedure but use a new manifold gasket, and new front pipe flange gasket. Tighten all mounting and attachment nuts/bolts to the specified torque.

12 Exhaust system – general information and component renewal

General information

1 A 3-piece exhaust system is fitted comprising a centre pipe, catalytic converter and rear silencer. The centre pipe is connected to the exhaust manifold downpipe by means of a flange joint, and contains a flexible section to cater for engine movement. A

10.17 Undo the nuts (arrowed) at the top edge of the manifold

catalytic converter is fitted to all models, and is an integral part of the exhaust manifold.

2 The system is suspended throughout its entire length by rubber mountings.

Component renewal

Exhaust manifold and catalytic converter

3 Refer to Section 11.

Rear silencer

4 Firmly apply the handbrake, then jack up the front and rear of the car and support it securely on axle stands (see *Jacking and vehicle support*).

5 Undo the clamp securing the rear silencer to the centre pipe, and spray releasing fluid around the joint **(see illustration)**.

6 Free the silencer from the rubber mountings, and manoeuvre it from position.

Centre pipe

7 Remove the rear silencer as previously described.

8 Slacken the clamp securing the catalytic converter to the centre pipe, and spray releasing fluid around the joint.

9 Free the centre pipe from the rubber mounting and separate it from the catalytic converter.

11.5a Remove the heat shield (arrowed) from the exhaust manifold – pre-Euro 5 emissions engines . . .

11.5b . . . and Euro 5 emissions engines

12.5 Undo the clamp (arrowed) securing the rear silencer to the pipe

Notes

Chapter 4 Part B:
Fuel and exhaust systems – diesel engines

Contents

Degrees of difficulty

| **Easy,** suitable for novice with little experience | | **Fairly easy,** suitable for beginner with some experience | | **Fairly difficult,** suitable for competent DIY mechanic | | **Difficult,** suitable for experienced DIY mechanic | | **Very difficult,** suitable for expert DIY or professional | |

Specifications

General
System type:
70 bhp (51 kW) engines . . . . Magneti-Marelli 6JF high-pressure direct injection 'common-rail' system, electronically-controlled
75 bhp (55 kW) engines . . . . Magneti-Marelli 6F3 high-pressure direct injection 'common-rail' system, electronically-controlled
95 bhp (70 kW) engines . . . . Magneti-Marelli 8F2 high-pressure direct injection 'common-rail' system, electronically-controlled
Firing order. . . . . 1–3–4–2 (No 1 at timing chain end)
Fuel system operating pressure. . . . . 1600 bar max
Idle speed. . . . . 850 rpm – controlled by ECU
Maximum speed. . . . . 5200 rpm – controlled by ECU
Fuel level sensor:
Panda models:
Full . . . . 6 ± 3 ohms
Empty . . . . 310 ± 10 ohms
500 models:
Full . . . . 33 ± 3 ohms
Empty . . . . 299 ± 3 ohms

High-pressure fuel pump
Type . . . . Bosch CP1

Fuel supply pump
Type . . . . Electric, mounted in fuel tank
Delivery quantity. . . . . 2.25 litres/min
Delivery pressure . . . . 3.3 bar (maximum)

Torque wrench settings

	Nm	lbf ft
Camshaft position sensor retaining bolt.	7	5
Catalytic converter support bracket to sump reinforcement bracket . .	25	18
Catalytic converter-to-turbocharger bolts	25	18
Coolant pipe-to-heat exchanger bolts.	9	7
Crankshaft speed/position sensor retaining bolt	9	7
EGR valve bolts	22	16
Exhaust manifold nuts:*		
Stage 1	15	11
Stage 2	Angle-tighten a further 30°	
Exhaust system clamp nuts.	50	37
Front crossmember bolts.	40	30
Fuel injector clamp bracket nuts	20	15
Fuel pressure regulating valve to fuel rail.	9	7
Fuel pressure sensor to fuel rail	70	52
Fuel rail mounting bracket-to-camshaft housing bolts	25	18
Fuel rail-to-mounting bracket bolts	25	18
High-pressure fuel pipe unions:		
M12 union nuts.	25	18
M14 union nuts.	28	21
High-pressure fuel pump mounting bolts.	15	11
Injection pump-to-camshaft housing	15	11
Injector retaining clamp nut	20	15
Intake manifold bolts	25	18
Oil filter housing to cylinder block	9	7
Oxygen sensor	45	33
Turbocharger oil return pipe bolts	9	7
Turbocharger oil supply pipe banjo union bolts	12	9
Turbocharger to exhaust manifold	25	18

* Use new nuts

1 General information

The diesel engine covered in this manual is equipped with a high-pressure diesel injection system which incorporates the very latest in diesel injection technology. On this system, the high-pressure fuel pump is used purely to provide the pressure required for the injection system and has no control over the injection timing (unlike conventional diesel injection systems). The injection timing is controlled by the electronic control unit (ECU) via the electrically-operated injectors. The system operates as follows.

The fuel system consists of a fuel tank (which is mounted under the rear of the car, with an electric fuel supply pump immersed in it, a fuel filter with integral water separator, a high-pressure fuel pump, injectors and associated components.

Fuel is supplied by the tank-mounted supply pump to the fuel filter which is located in the engine compartment. The fuel filter removes all foreign matter and water, and ensures that the fuel supplied to the high-pressure pump is clean. Excess fuel is returned from the outlet on the filter housing lid to the tank via the fuel cooler. The fuel cooler is fitted to the underside of the vehicle and is cooled by the passing airflow to ensure the fuel is cool before it enters the fuel tank.

The fuel is heated to ensure no problems occur when the ambient temperature is very low. An electrically-operated fuel heater is fitted to the fuel filter housing, and the heater is controlled by the ECU.

The high-pressure fuel pump is driven directly from the rear of the exhaust camshaft. The high pressure required in the system (up to 1600 bar) is produced by the three pistons in the pump. The pump supplies high-pressure fuel to the fuel rail, which acts as a reservoir for the four injectors.

The electrical control system consists of the ECU, along with the following sensors:

a) *Accelerator pedal position sensor – informs the ECU of the accelerator pedal position, and the speed of pedal travel.*

b) *Coolant temperature sensor – informs the ECU of engine temperature.*

c) *Airflow meter – informs the ECU of the amount and temperature of air passing through the intake duct.*

d) *Crankshaft speed/position sensor – informs the ECU of the crankshaft position and speed of rotation.*

e) *Camshaft position sensor – informs the ECU of the positions of the pistons.*

f) *Fuel pressure sensor – informs the ECU of the fuel pressure present in the fuel rail.*

g) *Manifold pressure sensor – informs the ECU of the load on the engine.*

h) *ABS control unit – informs the ECU of the vehicle speed, based on wheel speed sensor signals (explained in greater detail in Chapter 9).*

All the above signals (in addition to signals from various other systems on the vehicle) are analysed by the ECU which selects the fuelling response appropriate to those values. The ECU controls the fuel injectors (varying the pulse width – the length of time the injectors are held open – to provide a richer or weaker mixture, as appropriate). The mixture is constantly varied by the ECU, to provide the best setting for cranking, starting (with either a hot or cold engine), warm-up, idle, cruising and acceleration.

The ECU also has full control over the fuel pressure present in the system via the pressure regulating valve located on the fuel rail. To reduce the fuel pressure, the ECU opens the pressure regulating valve which allows the excess fuel to return directly to the fuel tank.

The ECU also controls the exhaust gas recirculation (EGR) system, described in detail in Part C of this Chapter, and the engine cooling fan.

A turbocharger is fitted to increases engine efficiency. It does this by raising the pressure in the intake manifold above atmospheric pressure. Instead of the air simply being sucked into the cylinders, it is forced in.

Energy for the operation of the turbocharger comes from the exhaust gas. The gas flows through a specially-shaped housing (the turbine housing) and in so doing, spins the turbine wheel. The turbine wheel is attached to a shaft, at the end of which is another vaned wheel known as the compressor wheel. The compressor wheel spins in its own housing, and compresses the intake air on the way to the intake manifold. The turbo shaft is pressure-lubricated by an oil feed pipe from the main oil gallery. The shaft 'floats' on a cushion of oil. A drain pipe returns the oil to the sump. Boost pressure (the pressure in the intake manifold) is limited by a wastegate, which diverts the exhaust gas away from the turbine wheel in response to a pressure-sensitive actuator.

If there is an abnormality in any of the readings obtained from the various sensors, the ECU enters its back-up mode. In this event, it ignores the abnormal sensor signal and assumes a pre-programmed value which will allow the engine to continue running (albeit at reduced efficiency). If the ECU enters this back-up mode, the warning light on the instrument panel will come on, and the relevant fault code will be stored in the ECU memory. The fault code can be read using specialist test equipment.

2 High-pressure diesel injection system – special information

Warnings and precautions

1 It is essential to observe strict precautions when working on the fuel system components, particularly the high-pressure side of the system. Before carrying out any operations on the fuel system, refer to the precautions given in *Safety first!* at the beginning of this manual, and to the following additional information.

- *Do not carry out any repair work on the high-pressure fuel system unless you are competent to do so, have all the necessary tools and equipment required, and are aware of the safety implications involved.*
- *Before starting any repair work on the fuel system, wait at least 30 seconds after switching off the engine to allow the fuel circuit to return to atmospheric pressure.*
- *Never work on the high-pressure fuel system with the engine running.*
- *Keep well clear of any possible source of fuel leakage, particularly when starting the engine after carrying out repair*

2.4 Typical plastic plug and cap set for sealing disconnected fuel pipes and components

work. A leak in the system could cause an extremely high pressure jet of fuel to escape, which could result in severe personal injury.
- *Never place your hands or any part of your body near to a leak in the high-pressure fuel system.*
- *Do not use steam cleaning equipment or compressed air to clean the engine or any of the fuel system components.*

Repair procedures and general information

2 Strict cleanliness must be observed at all times when working on any part of the fuel system. This applies to the working area in general, the person doing the work, and the components being worked on.

3 Before working on the fuel system components, they must be thoroughly cleaned with a suitable degreasing fluid. Cleanliness is particularly important when working on the fuel system connections at the following components:
  a) Fuel filter.
  b) High-pressure fuel pump.
  c) Fuel rail.
  d) Fuel injectors.
  e) High-pressure fuel pipes.

4 After disconnecting any fuel pipes or components, the open union or orifice must be immediately sealed to prevent the entry of dirt or foreign material. Plastic plugs and caps in various sizes are available in packs from

2.6 Two crow-foot adapters will be necessary for tightening the fuel pipe unions

motor factors and accessory outlets, and are particularly suitable for this application **(see illustration)**. Fingers cut from disposable rubber gloves should be used to protect components such as fuel pipes, fuel injectors and wiring connectors, and can be secured in place using elastic bands.

5 Whenever any of the high-pressure fuel pipes are disconnected or removed, a new pipe(s) must be obtained for refitting.

6 The torque wrench settings given in the *Specifications* must be strictly observed when tightening component mountings and connections. This is particularly important when tightening the high-pressure fuel pipe unions. To enable a torque wrench to be used on the fuel pipe unions, two crow-foot adapters are required. Suitable types are available from motor factors and accessory outlets **(see illustration)**.

3 Air cleaner assembly – removal and refitting

Panda models

Pre-Euro 5 models

1 Disconnect the wiring connector from the airflow meter **(see illustration)**.

2 Release the clamp and disconnect the air outlet pipe from the airflow meter, then unclip the air intake pipe **(see illustrations)**.

3.1 Slide up the yellow clip (arrowed) and disconnect the airflow meter wiring plug

3.2a Release the clamp (arrowed) securing the air outlet pipe

3.2b Depress the clip above and below (arrowed) and disconnect the air intake pipe

3.3a Pull the air cleaner upwards to release the front mountings . . .

3.3b . . . then forwards to release the rear mounting

3.12a Prise up the edge (arrowed) of the cold air intake duct clamp to release it

3 Pull up the front edge of the air cleaner assembly, then pull it forwards to release the rear mounting (see illustrations).

Euro 5 models

4 Release the clamp securing the cold air intake duct to the air cleaner assembly, and disengage the air duct retaining pin (see illustration 3.12a and 3.12b).
5 Release the clamp securing the airflow meter to the air cleaner housing.
6 Disconnect the breather hose, then pull the air duct from the air cleaner housing.
7 Pull the air cleaner assembly upwards from its rubber mountings.

500 models

All except 95 bhp models

8 Disconnect the wiring connector from the airflow meter (see illustration 3.1).
9 Release the clamp and disconnect the air outlet pipe from the airflow meter.
10 Depress the retaining tab, and disconnect the cold air intake duct from the air cleaner housing (see illustration 3.2b).
11 Pull the up the front edge, and remove the housing.

95 bhp models

12 Release the clamp securing the cold air intake duct to the air cleaner assembly, and

disengage the air duct retaining pin (see illustrations). Remove the air duct.
13 Release the clamp securing the airflow meter to the air cleaner housing (see illustration).
14 Disconnect the breather hose from the rear of the housing, then release the clamp securing the hose at the front, right-hand corner of the housing (see illustrations). Pull the turbocharger air intake duct/airflow meter assembly from the housing.
15 Pull the air cleaner assembly upwards from its rubber mountings (see illustrations). If required, remove the foam insulation pad from the top of the engine.

3.12b Disengage the air intake duct retaining pin (arrowed)

3.13 Release the clamp (arrowed) securing the airflow meter to the air cleaner housing

3.14a Release the clamp securing the hose at the front, right-hand corner of the air cleaner housing . . .

3.14b . . . then squeeze together the sides of the collar (arrowed) and disconnect the breather hose from the rear of the air cleaner housing

3.15a Pull the up the front of the air cleaner housing . . .

3.15b . . . then forwards to release the rear mounting

4.2 Slide up the locking clip and disconnect the wiring plug

4.3 Accelerator pedal position sensor mounting nuts (arrowed)

4 Accelerator pedal position sensor – removal and refitting

Removal

1 Disconnect the battery negative terminal as described in Chapter 5A.
2 Working in the driver's footwell, disconnect the wiring connector from the top of the accelerator pedal position sensor (see illustration).
3 Unscrew the mounting nuts, and withdraw the sensor from the bulkhead (see illustration).

Refitting

4 Refitting is a reversal of removal.

5 Fuel system – priming and bleeding

1 After disconnecting part of the fuel supply system or running out of fuel, it is necessary to prime the fuel system and bleed off any air which may have entered the system components, as follows.
2 Prime the system by switching on the ignition three times for approximately 15 seconds each time. Operate the starter for a maximum of 30 seconds. If the engine does not start within this time, wait 5 seconds and repeat the procedure.
3 When the engine starts, run it at a fast idle speed for a minute or so to purge any trapped air from the fuel lines. After this time the engine should idle smoothly at a constant speed.
4 If the engine idles roughly, then there is still some air trapped in the fuel system. Increase the engine speed again for another minute or so then allow it to idle. Repeat this procedure as necessary until the engine is idling smoothly.

6 Fuel gauge sender unit – removal and refitting

Note 1: Refer to the information contained in Section 2 before proceeding.
Note 2: The fuel tank should be as empty as possible when carrying out this procedure.

Removal

1 Disconnect the battery negative terminal as described in Chapter 5A.
2 Remove the rear seat cushion as described in Chapter 11.
3 Lift the floor covering for access to the fuel pump cover.
4 Remove the cover from the aperture in the floor panel (see illustrations). On Panda models, the cover prises from place, whilst on the 500 models, the cover is retained by screws.
5 Release the locking catch and disconnect the wiring connector from the top of the fuel pump.
6 Bearing in mind the warning given in Section 2, disconnect the fuel supply line and return line quick-release fittings from the pump unit by pressing the tabs (see illustration). Plug the end of the supply line or cover it with adhesive tape.
7 Unscrew the large locking ring and remove it from the tank. This is best accomplished by making up a simple tool from two strips of metal, suitably drilled and bolted together with two lengths of threaded bar and locknuts. Engage the tool with the ribs of the locking

6.4a On Panda models, the fuel pump/ sender unit access panel prises up from place

6.4b On 500 models, the access panel is secured by screws (arrowed)

6.6 Depress the release tabs (arrowed) and disconnect the fuel feed and return hoses

6.7 Rotate the locking ring anti-clockwise and remove it

6.8a Carefully lift the pump/sender unit from the tank

6.8b Renew the sealing O-ring

ring, and turn the ring anti-clockwise until it can be unscrewed by hand **(see illustration)**.

8 Lift the fuel pump and sender unit assembly out of the fuel tank, taking great care not to damage the float arm. Recover the sealing O-ring and discard it – a new one must be used on refitting **(see illustrations)**.

9 Note that the fuel pump and sender unit is only available as a complete assembly – no components are available separately. However, the resistance of the fuel level sender unit can be checked by connecting a multimeter across the sender unit terminals at the plug socket. At full deflection (full tank) the resistance should be approximately 34 ohms, and zero deflection (empty tank) should be approximately 298 ohms **(see illustration)**. If the readings are significantly different than these, the unit may be faulty.

Refitting

10 Refitting is a reversal of the removal procedure using a new sealing ring, and aligning the lug on the pump cover with the cut-out on the tank **(see illustration)**. Prior to refitting the access cover, reconnect the battery, then start the engine and check the fuel line for signs of leakage.

7 Fuel tank –
removal and refitting

Note: *Refer to the warning given in Section 2 before proceeding.*

Removal

1 Before removing the fuel tank, all fuel must be drained from the tank. Since a fuel tank drain plug is not provided, it is therefore preferable to carry out the removal operation when the tank is nearly empty. Before proceeding, disconnect the battery negative terminal as described in Chapter 5A.

2 Working as described in Section 6, disconnect the fuel pump wiring connector and the fuel pipes from the top of the pump.

3 Chock the front wheels, then jack up the rear of the car and securely support it on axle stands (see *Jacking and vehicle support*). Remove the right-hand rear roadwheel.

Panda models

4 Release the rubber mountings and move the exhaust system to one side, for access to the fuel tank heat shield.

5 Undo the retaining nuts, extract the spring clip and remove the heat shield from under the fuel tank.

6 Loosen the clips and disconnect the filler pipe and vent pipe from the right-hand side of the fuel tank **(see illustration 7.10)**.

7 Place a trolley jack with an interposed block of wood beneath the tank, then raise the jack until it is supporting the weight of the tank.

8 Undo the fuel tank mounting bolts, then carefully lower the tank from its location. Move the exhaust system as far as possible to

one side to provide the necessary clearance for removal.

500 models

9 Remove the exhaust system as described in Section 20.

10 Loosen the clips and disconnect the filler pipe and vent pipe(s) from fuel tank **(see illustration)**.

11 Undo the retaining bolts and remove the fuel pipe shield from the vehicle underside.

12 Place a trolley jack with an interposed block of wood beneath the tank, then raise the jack until it is supporting the weight of the tank.

13 Undo the fuel tank mounting bolts, then carefully lower the tank from its location, unclipping any hoses from the top of the tank as it's lowered.

All models

14 If the tank is contaminated with sediment or water, remove the fuel pump/fuel gauge sender unit as described in Section 6, and swill the tank out with clean fuel. The tank is injection-moulded from a synthetic material – if seriously damaged, it should be renewed. However, in certain cases, it may be possible to have small leaks or minor damage repaired. Seek the advice of a specialist before attempting to repair the fuel tank.

Refitting

15 Refitting is a reversal of the removal procedure, ensuring that all pipes/hoses are correctly routed and securely reconnected.

6.9 Check the resistance of the sender unit at full, and zero deflection

6.10 Align the lug on the cover with the cut-out (arrowed) on the tank

7.10 Disconnect the fuel filler and vent hoses (arrowed)

9.2a Undo the screws (arrowed) and remove the panel . . .

9.2b . . . to access the diagnostic socket (arrowed) – Panda models

located behind the right-hand side of the facia **(see illustrations)**. Live data can also be captured from the various system sensors and actuators, indicating their operating parameters. This will allow the fault to be quickly and simply traced, alleviating the need to test all the system components individually, which is a time-consuming operation that carries a risk of damaging the ECU.

10 Injection system electrical components – removal and refitting

Note: *If any of the following components are renewed, there is a slim chance the ECU may need to be reprogrammed. Experience tells us that this is a very rare occurrence, but the possibility does exist. If, after renewing a part, the engine fails to respond as anticipated, have the ECU settings checked using suitable diagnostic equipment – usually found at a Fiat dealer or well-equipped repairer.*

Airflow meter

1 Disconnect the wiring from the airflow meter **(see illustration 3.1)**.
2 Slacken the retaining clamps/undo the bolts and remove the airflow meter from the air cleaner cover and upper air intake/outlet hose **(see illustrations)**.
3 Refitting is a reversal of removal, but ensure that the arrow on the airflow meter body points away from the air cleaner when refitting.

Throttle housing

4 Remove the air cleaner assembly as described in Section 3.
5 Remove the battery and battery tray as described in Chapter 5A.
6 Undo the two bolts/nuts securing the charge air pipe to the throttle housing.
7 Undo the bolt nut securing the charge air pipe to the transmission housing **(see illustration)**.
8 Release the clamp and detach the charge

9.2c On 500 models, starting at the lower edge, pull away the trim panel . . .

9.2d . . . to access the diagnostic plug (arrowed)

8 Fuel supply pump – removal and refitting

1 The diesel fuel supply pump is located in the tank module in the fuel tank. The removal and refitting procedures are the same as for the fuel gauge sender unit described in Section 6. The pump is integral with the tank module and cannot be renewed separately.

9 Injection system electrical components – testing

1 If a fault is suspected in the electronic control

side of the system, first ensure that all the wiring connectors are securely connected and free of corrosion. Ensure that the suspected problem is not of a mechanical nature, or due to poor maintenance; ie, check that the air cleaner filter element is clean, the engine breather hoses are clear and undamaged, and that the cylinder compression pressures are correct, referring to Chapter 1B and Chapter 2B.
2 If these checks fail to reveal the cause of the problem, the vehicle should be taken to a suitably-equipped Fiat dealer or engine management diagnostic specialist for testing. Using a fault code reader or similar diagnostic equipment, the engine management ECU can be interrogated, and any stored fault codes can be retrieved. The diagnostic plugs are

10.2a Airflow meter (arrowed) – pre-Euro 5 emissions engines . . .

10.2b . . . and Euro 5 emissions engines

10.7 Charge air pipe retaining nut (arrowed)

10.8 Release the clamp (arrowed) securing the charge air hose to the pipe

10.9a Throttle housing retaining bolts (upper bolts arrowed)

air pipe from the charge air hose (see illustration).

9 Undo the 3 retaining bolts and remove the throttle housing from the intake manifold. Note on some models, a support bracket is fitted to the underside of the housing (see illustrations). Disconnect the wiring plug as the housing is withdrawn.

10 Refitting is a reversal of removal, but thoroughly clean the mating faces and use a new seal on the charge air pipe.

Crankshaft speed/position sensor

11 On Euro 5 emissions level models, raise the front of the vehicle and support is securely on axle stands (see Jacking and vehicle support). On all other models, remove the air cleaner housing as described in Section 3.

12 The crankshaft speed/position sensor is located on the front of the cylinder block, in-line with the flywheel.

13 Disconnect the sensor wiring connector, then undo the retaining bolt and remove the sensor from the cylinder block (see illustration).

14 Refitting is a reversal of removal, tightening the retaining bolt securely.

10.9b Note the support bracket (arrowed) on the underside of the throttle housing

Camshaft position sensor

15 Remove the air cleaner assembly as described in Section 3.

16 The camshaft position sensor is located on the front right-hand side of the camshaft housing, above the exhaust side camshaft (see illustration).

17 Disconnect the sensor wiring connector, then undo the retaining bolt and remove the sensor from the camshaft housing.

18 Refitting is a reversal of removal, tightening the retaining bolt securely.

10.13 Crankshaft speed/position sensor (arrowed)

Fuel pressure sensor

19 Remove the air cleaner assembly as described in Section 3.

20 The fuel pressure sensor is located at the right-hand end of the fuel rail.

21 Disconnect the sensor wiring connector, then unscrew the sensor from the fuel rail.

22 Refitting is a reversal of removal, tightening the sensor to the specified torque.

Manifold pressure sensor

23 Remove the air cleaner assembly as described in Section 3.

24 The manifold pressure sensor is located on the intake manifold (see illustration).

25 Using a small screwdriver, lift up the locking catch and disconnect the sensor wiring connector.

26 Undo the retaining bolt and withdraw the sensor from the manifold. Recover the sealing O-ring.

27 Renew the sealing O-ring, then refit the sensor and tighten the retaining bolt securely. Reconnect the wiring connector and secure with the locking catch.

28 Refit the air cleaner as described in Section 3.

10.16 Camshaft position sensor (arrowed)

10.24 The manifold pressure sensor (arrowed) is located on the rear of the intake manifold

Electronic control unit (ECU)

Note: *If a new ECU is to be fitted, this work must be entrusted to a Fiat dealer or suitably-equipped specialist. It is necessary to initialise the new ECU after installation, which requires the use of dedicated Fiat diagnostic equipment.*

29 Disconnect the battery negative terminal as described in Chapter 5A.

Panda models

30 Lift the locking levers and disconnect the two wiring connectors from the ECU **(see illustrations)**.
31 Undo the nuts securing the ECU. Note the earth lead on pre-Euro 5 models **(see illustration)**.

500 models

32 The ECU is located on the rear of the battery tray. Lift the locking levers, and disconnect the wiring connectors from the ECU **(see illustration 10.30a and 10.30b)**.
33 Undo the retaining nuts and manoeuvre the ECU from the engine compartment **(see illustration)**.

All models

34 Refitting is a reversal of removal, ensuring that the wiring connectors are securely connected and locked with the locking levers.

Coolant temperature sensor

35 Refer to the procedures contained in Chapter 3.

11 High-pressure fuel pump – removal and refitting

Warning: Refer to the information contained in Section 2 before proceeding.

Note: *A new fuel pump-to-fuel rail*

10.30a Slide out the yellow locking tabs . . .

10.30b . . . then lift the locking levers and disconnect the ECU wiring plugs

10.31 ECU retaining nuts (arrowed). Note the earth lead (arrowed)

10.33 Note the earth lead (arrowed) under one of the ECU retaining nuts

high-pressure fuel pipe will be required for refitting.

Removal

1 Disconnect the battery negative terminal as described in Chapter 5A.
2 On models to Euro 5 emissions level, remove the battery and battery tray as described in Chapter 5A.
3 Remove the air cleaner assembly as described in Section 3.
4 Release the retaining clip and disconnect the fuel supply hose from the fuel pump **(see illustration)**. The hose will be disconnected as the pump is withdrawn.
5 Release the retaining clip securing the fuel return hose to the fuel pump **(see illustration)**.
6 Thoroughly clean the fuel pipe unions on the fuel pump and fuel rail. Using an open-ended spanner, unscrew the union nuts securing the high-pressure fuel pipe to the fuel pump and fuel rail. Counterhold the unions on the pump with a second spanner while unscrewing the

11.4 Fuel supply and return hose connections (arrowed) at the high-pressure fuel pump

11.5 Disconnect the return hose from the pump (arrowed)

11.6a Undo the unions (arrowed) and remove the high-pressure pipe between the pump and rail

11.6b Use a second spanner to counterhold the union nuts

11.7a Undo the mounting bolts (arrowed) . . .

11.7b . . . withdraw the fuel pump from the camshaft housing . . .

11.7c . . . and recover the sealing O-ring

union nuts **(see illustrations)**. Withdraw the high-pressure fuel pipe and plug or cover the open unions to prevent dirt entry. Note that the pipe must be renewed.

7 Disconnect the pump wiring connector, then unscrew the three mounting bolts and withdraw the pump from the camshaft housing. Recover the sealing O-ring **(see illustrations)**. Disconnect the return hose as the pump is withdrawn. Cover the hose end and the pump outlet to prevent dirt entry.

Caution: The high-pressure fuel pump is manufactured to extremely close tolerances and must not be dismantled in any way. No parts for the pump are available separately and if the unit is in any way suspect, it must be renewed.

Refitting

8 Thoroughly clean the fuel pump and camshaft housing mating faces.

9 Locate a new sealing O-ring on the pump flange and lubricate the O-ring with clean diesel fuel.

10 Align the pump drive dog with the slot on the camshaft, then place the pump in position, reconnecting the return hose as it's fitted. Refit the three mounting bolts and tighten them to the specified torque.

11 Remove the blanking plugs from the fuel pipe unions on the pump and fuel rail. Locate the new high-pressure fuel pipe over the unions and screw on the union nuts finger-tight at this stage.

12 Using a torque wrench and crow-foot adapter, tighten the fuel pipe union nuts to the specified torque. Counterhold the unions on the pump with an open-ended spanner while tightening the union nuts.

13 Reconnect the fuel return hose and supply hose and secure with the retaining clips.

14 Where applicable, refit the battery and battery tray.

15 Observing the precautions listed in Section 2, prime the fuel system as described in Section 5, then start the engine and allow it to idle. Check for leaks at the high-pressure fuel pipe unions with the engine idling. If satisfactory, increase the engine speed to 4000 rpm and check again for leaks. If any leaks are detected, obtain and fit a new high-pressure fuel pipe.

16 Refit the engine cover on completion.

12 Fuel rail – removal and refitting

⚠ *Warning: Refer to the information contained in Section 2 before proceeding.*

Note: *A complete set of high-pressure fuel pipes will be required for refitting.*

Removal

1 Disconnect the battery negative terminal as described in Chapter 5A.

2 Remove the air cleaner assembly as described in Section 3.

3 Undo the retaining bolts and release the pipe carrier assembly from above the high-pressure fuel pipes **(see illustration)**.

4 Disconnect the wiring connectors at the at the fuel pressure sensor and fuel pressure regulating valve (where fitted) on the fuel rail **(see illustrations)**.

12.3 Pipe carrier assembly retaining bolts (arrowed)

12.4a Disconnect the wiring plugs from the fuel pressure sensor . . .

12.4b . . . and the fuel pressure regulator

5 Thoroughly clean all the high-pressure fuel pipe unions on the fuel rail, fuel pump and injectors. Using two spanners, hold the unions and unscrew the union nuts securing the high-pressure fuel pipes to the fuel injectors. Unscrew the union nuts securing the high-pressure fuel pipes to the fuel rail, withdraw the pipes and plug or cover the open unions to prevent dirt entry **(see illustrations)**. It is advisable to label each fuel pipe (1 to 4) to avoid confusion when refitting.

6 Using an open-ended spanner, unscrew the union nuts securing the high-pressure fuel pipe to the fuel pump and fuel rail. Counterhold the unions on the pump with a second spanner, while unscrewing the union nuts **(see illustrations)**. Withdraw the high-pressure fuel pipe and plug or cover the open unions to prevent dirt entry.

7 Release the retaining clip and disconnect the fuel return hose from the fuel rail. Cover the hose end and the pump outlet to prevent dirt entry.

8 Undo the two retaining bolts and lift the fuel rail off the mounting bracket **(see illustration)**.

Refitting

9 Locate the fuel rail on the mounting bracket, refit the two retaining bolts and tighten them to the specified torque.

10 Refit the fuel return hose and secure with the retaining clip.

11 Working on one fuel injector at a time, remove the blanking plugs from the fuel pipe unions on the fuel rail and the relevant injector. Locate the new high-pressure fuel pipe over the unions and screw on the union nuts finger-tight. Tighten the union nuts to the specified torque using a torque wrench and crow-foot adapter **(see illustration)**. Counterhold the union on the injector with an open-ended spanner while tightening the union nut. Repeat this operation for the remaining three injectors.

12 Similarly, fit the high-pressure fuel pipe to the fuel pump and fuel rail, and tighten the

12.5a Unscrew the union nuts securing the high-pressure pipes to the injectors . . .

12.5b . . . and the fuel rail

12.6a Unscrew the union nuts securing the high-pressure pipes to the fuel pump . . .

12.6b . . . and fuel rail

union nuts to the specified torque. Counterhold the union on the pump with an open-ended spanner while tightening the union nut.

13 Reconnect the wiring connectors at the fuel pressure sensor and pressure regulating valve.

14 Refit the pipe carrier assembly and tighten the retaining bolts securely.

15 Refit the air cleaner assembly as described in Section 3.

16 Observing the precautions listed in Section 2, prime the fuel system as described in Section 5, then start the engine and allow it to idle. Check for leaks at the high-pressure

fuel pipe unions with the engine idling. If satisfactory, increase the engine speed to 4000 rpm and check again for leaks. If any leaks are detected, obtain and fit a new high-pressure fuel pipe(s).

17 Refit the engine cover on completion.

13 Fuel injectors – removal and refitting

⚠ *Warning: Refer to the information contained in Section 2 before proceeding.*

12.8 Undo the fuel rail retaining bolts (arrowed)

12.11 Tighten the fuel pipe union nuts using a torque wrench and crow-foot adapter

13.6a Slide out the yellow locking tab (arrowed) and disconnect the injector wiring plugs

13.6b On 95 bhp models, undo the bolts and move the wiring harness guide (arrowed) forwards a little

Note: *The following procedure describes the removal and refitting of the injectors as a complete set, however, the injectors may be removed in pairs if required. New copper sealing washers will be required for each disturbed injector when refitting.*

Removal

1 Disconnect the battery negative terminal as described in Chapter 5A.
2 Remove the air cleaner assembly as described in Section 3.

3 Undo the bolts and move the pipe carrier above the high-pressure fuel pipes to one side (see illustration 12.3).
4 Thoroughly clean all the high-pressure fuel pipe unions on the fuel rail and injectors.
5 Disconnect the wiring connector at the camshaft position sensor on the top of the camshaft housing.
6 Release the locking catches securing the wiring connectors to the four injectors, then disconnect the injector wiring, while at the same time moving the wiring harness guide forward. On 95 bhp models, undo the bolts

and move the loom guide forwards a little (see illustrations).
7 Using two spanners, hold the unions and unscrew the union nuts securing the high-pressure fuel pipes to the fuel injectors. Unscrew the union nuts securing the high-pressure fuel pipes to the fuel rail, withdraw the pipes and plug or cover the open unions to prevent dirt entry (see illustrations 12.5a and 12.5b). It is advisable to label each fuel pipe (1 to 4) to avoid confusion when refitting.
8 Disconnect the fuel leak-off hose connection at each injector by pushing in the locking clip and lifting out the hose fitting. Slip a plastic bag over the disconnected leak-off hose to prevent dirt entry (see illustrations).
9 Unscrew the retaining nut then remove the two washers from the injector clamp brackets (see illustrations). There are two clamp brackets, one securing injectors one and two, and the other securing injectors three and four.
10 Working on one pair of injectors at a time (one and two, or three and four) withdraw the two injectors together with the clamp bracket from the camshaft housing and cylinder head. If difficulty is experienced removing the injectors, liberally apply penetrating oil to

13.8a Disconnect the fuel leak-off hose connection at each injector . . .

13.8b . . . and clip a plastic bag over the disconnected leak-off hose to prevent contamination

13.9a Undo the retaining nut . . .

13.9b . . . then remove the upper washer . . .

13.9c . . . and lower washer from the injector clamp brackets

13.10a If necessary, use a slide hammer to release the injectors . . .

13.10b . . . then withdraw the two injectors together with the clamp bracket

13.10c The clamp bracket engages with the slots in the injector body

the base of each injector and allow time for the oil to penetrate. If the injectors are still reluctant to free, it will be necessary to use a small slide hammer engaged under the flange of the injector body casting, and gently tap them free. Note that it is not possible to twist the injectors from side-to-side to free them due to the design of the clamp bracket which positively engages in slots in the injector body **(see illustrations)**.

11 Once the injector pair has been removed, separate them from the clamp bracket and remove the copper washer from each injector **(see illustration)**. The copper washers may have remained in place at the base of the injector orifice in the cylinder head. If so, hook them out with a length of wire. Remove the upper injector seals from the camshaft housing.

12 Examine each injector visually for any signs of obvious damage or deterioration. If any defects are apparent, renew the injector(s).

Caution: The injectors are manufactured to extremely close tolerances and must not be dismantled in any way. Do not unscrew the fuel pipe union on the side of the injector, or separate any parts of the injector body. Do not attempt to clean carbon deposits from the injector nozzle or carry out any form of ultrasonic or pressure testing.

13 If the injectors are in a satisfactory condition, plug the fuel pipe union (if not already done) and suitably cover the electrical element and the injector nozzle.

14 Prior to refitting, obtain a new copper

13.11 Remove the copper washer from each injector

washer and camshaft housing seal for each removed injector.

Refitting

15 Locate a new copper washer on the base of each injector, and fit a new seal to the injector location in the camshaft housing.

16 Place the injector clamp bracket in the slot on each injector body and refit the injectors to the cylinder head in pairs. Guide the clamp bracket over the mounting stud as each injector pair is inserted.

17 Fit the two washers and the injector clamp bracket retaining nut to the mounting stud of each injector pair. Tighten the nuts finger-tight only at this stage.

18 Working on one fuel injector at a time, remove the blanking plugs from the fuel pipe unions on the fuel rail and the relevant injector. Locate the high-pressure fuel pipe over the unions and screw on the union nuts. Take care not to cross-thread the nuts or strain the fuel pipes as they are fitted. Once the union nut threads have started, tighten the nuts moderately tight only at this stage.

19 When all the fuel pipes are in place, tighten the injector clamp bracket retaining nuts to the specified torque.

20 Tighten the fuel pipe union nuts to the specified torque using a torque wrench and crow-foot adapter **(see illustration 12.11)**. Counterhold the union on the injector with an open-ended spanner, while tightening the union nut. Repeat this operation for the remaining three injectors.

21 Reconnect the fuel leak-off hose fittings to the injectors by pushing in the locking clip, attaching the fitting, then releasing the locking clip. Ensure that each fitting is securely connected and retained by the clip.

22 Reconnect the fuel injector wiring connectors and secure with the locking catches.

23 Refit the three bolts securing the plastic wiring harness guide to the top of the camshaft housing.

24 Reconnect the camshaft position sensor wiring connector.

25 Refit the air cleaner assembly as described in Section 3.

26 Observing the precautions listed in Section 2, prime the fuel system as described

in Section 5, then start the engine and allow it to idle. Check for leaks at the high-pressure fuel pipe unions with the engine idling. If satisfactory, increase the engine speed to 4000 rpm and check again for leaks. If any leaks are detected, obtain and fit a new high-pressure fuel pipe(s).

14 Fuel pressure regulating valve – removal and refitting

⚠ *Warning: Refer to the information contained in Section 2 before proceeding.*

Removal

1 The fuel pressure regulating valve is located on the left-hand end of the fuel rail.

2 Disconnect the battery negative terminal as described in Chapter 5A.

3 Remove the air cleaner assembly as described in Section 3.

4 Disconnect the pressure regulating valve wiring connector **(see illustration 12.4b)**.

5 Undo the two retaining bolts and remove the valve from the fuel rail. Recover the sealing O-ring.

Refitting

6 Thoroughly clean the fuel rail and pressure regulating valve mating faces.

7 Locate a new sealing O-ring on the pressure regulating valve and lubricate the O-ring with clean diesel fuel.

8 Refit the valve to the fuel rail and secure with the two retaining bolts tightened to the specified torque.

9 Reconnect the wiring connector and refit the air cleaner.

15 Intake manifold – removal and refitting

Removal

1 Disconnect the battery and battery tray as described in Chapter 5A.

2 Drain the cooling system as described in Chapter 1B.

15.4a Charge air hose (arrowed)

15.4b Rigid charge air pipe support bracket nut above the transmission (arrowed)

15.7 Disconnect the crankcase ventilation hose from the timing cover

15.8 Remove the bolts (arrowed) and detach the oil separator from the intake manifold

15.11a Intake manifold retaining bolts (arrowed)

3 Remove the air cleaner assembly as described in Section 3.

Panda models

4 Disconnect the charge air hose from the intake manifold, then undo the rigid charge air pipe support bracket nuts, and remove the hose **(see illustrations)**.
5 Slacken the clamps and disconnect the coolant hoses from the EGR cooler.
6 Slacken the clamp securing the EGR cooler to the EGR pipe, then undo the retaining bolts and remove the EGR cooler. Note that access at the rear of the cylinder head is extremely limited.
7 Undo the retaining bolt and detach the

crankcase ventilation hose attachment at the timing cover **(see illustration)**.
8 Undo the two bolts and free the crankcase ventilation system oil separator from the intake manifold **(see illustration)**.
9 Withdraw the engine oil dipstick, then undo the retaining bolt securing the dipstick guide tube to the intake manifold.
10 Check that all hoses, wiring and component attachments have been released to allow removal of the manifold.
11 Undo the retaining bolts (noting their different lengths) and remove the intake manifold from the cylinder head. Remove the rubber gasket from the manifold flange **(see illustrations)**.

500 models

12 Disconnect the wiring plugs from the fuel pressure regulator (where fitted) and sensor at the ends of the common fuel rail.
13 On 95 bhp models, remove the throttle housing as described in Section 10.
14 Remove the EGR cooler/valve assembly as described in Chapter 4C.
15 Disconnect the engine breather hose from the turbocharger air intake hose, from the cylinder head cover and the crankcase. Undo the hose support bracket bolts, and the oil separator retaining bolts and manoeuvre the breather hose/separator assembly from place **(see illustration)**. Release any wiring looms from the retaining clips as necessary. **Note:** *Given the extremely limited access, it may to easier to perform some of this procedure from under the vehicle.*
16 Withdraw the engine oil dipstick, then undo the retaining bolt securing the dipstick guide tube to the intake manifold. Free the wiring loom from the guide tube as it's withdrawn.
17 Remove both wiper arms as described in Chapter 12.
18 Remove the windscreen upper and lower base trims as described in Chapter 11.
19 Undo the retaining nuts, release the retaining clips and withdraw the rigid charge air pipe from the intake manifold **(see illustration)**.
20 Disconnect the wiring plug from the camshaft position sensor.

15.11b Renew the intake manifold flange rubber gasket

15.15 The oil separator (arrowed) is on the rear of the cylinder head – shown with the engine removed for clarity

15.19 Rigid charge air pipe (upper nut arrowed)

16.3 Intercooler intake and outlet hose clamps (arrowed)

16.4 Intercooler bracket-to-body bolts (arrowed)

16.6 Note the spacer (arrowed) fitted between the upper crossmember and the front panel

21 Check that all hoses, wiring and component attachments have been released to allow removal of the manifold.

22 Undo the retaining bolts (noting their different lengths) and remove the intake manifold from the cylinder head. Remove the rubber gasket from the manifold flange.

Refitting

23 Thoroughly clean the intake manifold and cylinder head mating faces, then locate a new rubber gasket on the intake manifold flange.

24 Locate the manifold in position and refit the retaining bolts. Diagonally and progressively, tighten the bolts to the specified torque.

25 The remainder of refitting is a reversal of removal, with reference to the Sections and Chapters indicated.

16 Intercooler –
removal and refitting

Removal

Panda models

1 Raise the front of the vehicle and support it securely on axle stands (see *Jacking and vehicle support*). Remove the left-hand from roadwheel.

2 Remove the fasteners, then pull back the front section of the left-hand front wheel arch liner.

3 Release the clamps securing the intake and outlet hoses to the intercooler **(see illustration)**.

4 Undo the nuts/bolts securing the intercooler bracket to the vehicle body, and manoeuvre it from position **(see illustration)**. Disconnect the intake and outlet hoses as the intercooler is withdrawn.

500 models

5 Remove the front bumper as described in Chapter 11.

6 Undo the retaining bolts and remove the front, upper crossmember **(see illustration)**.

7 Release the clamp and disconnect the air outlet hose from the top of the intercooler. If necessary, cut the clamp from the hose, and update it with a traditional 'worm-drive' type clamp.

8 Release the clamp and disconnect the air outlet hose from the base of the intercooler.

9 Drill out the rivets at the top of the intercooler mounting, then undo the bolts at the base, and manoeuvre the intercooler from place **(see illustrations)**.

Refitting

10 Refitting is a reversal of removal.

17 Exhaust manifold –
removal and refitting

Removal

1 Remove the turbocharger as described in Section 19.

2 Drain the coolant system as described in Chapter 1B.

3 Undo the bolts securing the rigid coolant inlet pipe to the oil cooler, then remove the support bracket bolt and move the pipe to one side **(see illustration)**.

4 On 95 bhp 500 models, remove the engine oil cooler as described in Chapter 2B, then remove the manifold heat shield.

5 Undo the securing the exhaust manifold to the cylinder head. Withdraw the manifold from the cylinder head studs and remove it from the engine. Recover the manifold gasket, noting that a new gasket and new manifold retaining nuts will be required for refitting.

Refitting

6 Thoroughly clean the mating faces of the exhaust manifold then locate the exhaust manifold over the cylinder head studs. Secure with the new nuts tightened progressively to the specified torque.

7 The remainder of refitting is a reversal of removal.

18 Turbocharger –
description and precautions

Description

1 The turbocharger increases engine efficiency by raising the pressure in the intake manifold above atmospheric pressure. Instead of the air simply being sucked into the cylinders, it is forced in.

16.9a Drill out the rivets at the top mounting of the intercooler (arrowed)

16.9b Undo the bolts (arrowed) at the base of the intercooler

17.3 Undo the bolts (arrowed) securing the rigid coolant pipe to the oil cooler

19.5 Turbocharger outlet pipe retaining bolts (arrowed)

19.6 Undo the bolts securing the turbocharger oil return pipe to the cylinder block

2 Energy for the operation of the turbocharger comes from the exhaust gas. The gas flows through a specially-shaped housing (the turbine housing) and, in so doing, spins the turbine wheel. The turbine wheel is attached to a shaft, at the end of which is another vaned wheel known as the compressor wheel. The compressor wheel spins in its own housing, and compresses the intake air on the way to the intake manifold.

3 Boost pressure (the pressure in the intake manifold) is limited by a wastegate, which diverts the exhaust gas away from the turbine wheel in response to a pressure-sensitive actuator.

4 The turbo shaft is pressure-lubricated by an oil feed pipe from the main oil gallery. The shaft 'floats' on a cushion of oil. A drain pipe returns the oil to the sump.

Precautions

5 The turbocharger operates at extremely high speeds and temperatures. Certain precautions must be observed, to avoid premature failure of the turbo, or injury to the operator.

- *Do not operate the turbo with any of its parts exposed, or with any of its hoses removed. Foreign objects falling onto the rotating vanes could cause excessive damage, and (if ejected) personal injury.*
- *Do not race the engine immediately after start-up, especially if it is cold. Give the oil a few seconds to circulate.*
- *Always allow the engine to return to idle*

speed before switching it off – do not blip the throttle and switch off, as this will leave the turbo spinning without lubrication.
- *Allow the engine to idle for several minutes before switching off after a high-speed run.*
- *Observe the recommended intervals for oil and filter changing, and use a reputable oil of the specified quality. Neglect of oil changing, or use of inferior oil, can cause carbon formation on the turbo shaft, leading to subsequent failure.*

19 Turbocharger – removal, inspection and refitting

Removal

1 Disconnect the battery negative terminal as described in Chapter 5A.

2 Remove the air cleaner assembly as described in Section 3.

3 Raise the front of the vehicle and support it securely on axle stands (see *Jacking and vehicle support*).

4 Referring to the procedures contained in Section 20, separate the exhaust system front section from the catalytic converter.

Panda models

5 Undo the bolts and detach the air outlet pipe from the turbocharger **(see illustration)**.

6 Undo the bolts securing the turbocharger oil return pipe to the cylinder block **(see illustration)**.

7 Release the clamp and disconnect the air intake hose from the turbocharger.

75 bhp 500 models

8 Working underneath the vehicle, release the clamps, undo the support bracket bolt and remove the intermediate air pipe and hose from the base of the intercooler **(see illustration)**.

9 Release the clamps and remove the air hose from the top of the intercooler.

10 Trace the oxygen sensor wiring loom back to the connector, and disconnect it, then unscrew the sensor from the catalytic converter.

11 Unclip the heater plug wiring loom, then disconnect the engine breather hose from the turbocharger air intake pipe.

12 Release the clamp and remove the turbocharger air intake pipe.

13 Undo the bolts securing the turbocharger oil return pipe to the cylinder block.

Panda and 75 bhp 500 models

14 Undo the retaining nuts and remove the exhaust manifold heat shield, complete with engine lifting bracket **(see illustration)**.

15 Where fitted, undo the bolts/nut and remove the shield above the oil filter housing.

16 Unscrew the two banjo union bolts and disconnect the turbocharger oil supply pipe from the oil filter housing and turbocharger **(see illustration)**. Recover the two copper washers from each banjo union, and suitable cover the ends of the pipe to prevent dirt entry. Note that new copper washers will be required for refitting.

17 From under the car, undo the bolt securing the catalytic converter support bracket to the sump reinforcement bracket.

18 Suitably support the catalytic converter from below, then undo the three retaining nuts and remove the turbocharger and catalytic converter from the exhaust manifold. Manipulate the assembly down and out from under the car.

19 Clamp the catalytic converter in a vice, then undo the bolt and three nuts, and remove the turbocharger heat shield (where fitted).

19.8 Intermediate air pipe support bracket bolt (arrowed)

19.14 Remove the heat shield complete with engine lifting bracket (arrowed)

19.16 Undo the turbocharger oil supply pipe banjo bolt (arrowed) from the oil filter housing

19.22a Undo the oil return pipe outer bolt, slacken the inner bolt and slide out the pipe flange

19.22b Undo the return pipe inner bolt and remove the gasket

19.25 Unscrew the oxygen sensor (arrowed)

20 Bend back the locking plate tabs and unscrew the three bolts securing the catalytic converter flange to the turbocharger. Remove the bolts and locking plate, noting that a new locking plate will be required for refitting.

21 Separate the catalytic converter from the turbocharger and recover the gasket. Note that a new gasket will be required for refitting.

22 If required, remove the oil return pipe from the turbocharger as follows. Undo the outer bolt, slacken the inner bolt and slide the pipe out from its location (the inner bolt hole in the pipe flange is slotted to allow removal). With the pipe removed, unscrew the inner bolt and recover the gasket **(see illustrations)**. Note that a new gasket will be required for refitting.

23 If required, unscrew the two bolts and remove the charge air pipe flange from the turbocharger and recover the gasket. Note that a new gasket will be required for refitting.

95 bhp 500 models

24 Drain the coolant as described in Chapter 1B.

25 Trace the oxygen sensor wiring loom back to the connector at the front of the transmission bellhousing, and disconnect it. Remove the heat shield, then unscrew the sensor from the catalytic converter **(see illustration)**.

26 Disconnect the wiring plug from the turbocharger vane position actuator solenoid valve, then undo the solenoid bracket mounting bolt and remove the solenoid, complete with bracket **(see illustrations)**. Note their fitted positions, and disconnect the vacuum hoses as the solenoid is withdrawn.

27 Undo the nuts, and remove the turbocharger heat shield **(see illustrations)**. Note that the retaining nut on the side only needs to be slackened, as the bracket is slotted.

28 Undo the banjo bolts and remove the oil supply pipe from the top of the turbocharger **(see illustrations)**. Discard the copper sealing washers – new ones must be fitted.

19.26a The vane position actuator solenoid (arrowed) is located on the rear face of the front panel, on the right-hand side

19.26b Note the routing of the various vacuum hoses

19.27a Undo the nuts (arrowed) on the top of the turbocharger . . .

19.27b . . . and slacken the nut (arrowed) on the side

19.28a Remove the oil feed pipe banjo bolt (arrowed) at the top of the turbocharger . . .

19.28b . . . and the bolt (arrowed) on the oil filter housing

19.29 Turbocharger air intake pipe clamp (arrowed)

19.30 Turbocharger oil return hose (arrowed)

19.33 Undo the air outlet pipe bolts (arrowed)

19.34 Slide out the yellow locking clip (arrowed) and disconnect the wiring plug from the vane position sensor

29 Release the clamps and disconnect the air intake pipe from the turbocharger (**see illustration**). Unclip the airflow meter wiring loom as the pipe is withdrawn.

30 Release the clamps and remove the oil return hose from the turbocharger to the engine block (**see illustration**).

31 Undo the union nuts, undo the support bracket bolt/nuts and disconnect the pressure

19.35 Turbocharger retaining nuts (arrowed)

pipe upstream and downstream pipe from the particulate filter (**see illustration 20.21**).

32 Remove the particulate filter as described in Section 20.

33 Undo the bolts securing the air outlet pipe to the turbocharger (**see illustration**).

34 Disconnect the wiring plug from the base of the variable geometry position sensor (**see illustration**).

35 Undo the retaining nuts and detach the turbocharger from the exhaust manifold (**see illustration**). Manoeuvre the turbocharger from place, and recover the gasket.

Inspection

36 With the turbocharger removed, inspect the housing for cracks or other visible damage.

37 Spin the turbine or the compressor wheel, to verify that the shaft is intact and to feel for excessive shake or roughness. Some play is normal, since in use, the shaft is 'floating' on a film of oil. Check that the wheel vanes are undamaged.

38 If oil contamination of the exhaust or induction passages is apparent, it is likely that turbo shaft oil seals have failed.

39 No DIY repair of the turbo is possible and none of the internal or external parts are available separately. If the turbocharger is suspect in any way a complete new unit must be obtained.

Refitting

40 Thoroughly clean the turbocharger and exhaust manifold mating faces, and renew any disturbed gaskets.

41 Refitting is a reversal of removal, noting the following points:

a) Tighten all fasteners to their specified torque where given.

b) Ensure all hoses/pipes are securely reconnected, and correctly routed.

c) Where applicable, refill the cooling system as described in Chapter 1B.

d) We recommend the engine oil and filter are renewed upon completion – see Chapter 1B.

20.7 Front exhaust pipe-to-tail pipe clamp (arrowed)

20.9a Exhaust front pipe clamp (arrowed)

20 Exhaust system – general information and component renewal

General information

1 The exhaust system is in two sections. The front section comprises the front pipe and flexible section and the rear section consists of the tailpipe and silencer.

2 Between the front section of the exhaust pipe and the turbocharger is a catalytic converter or particulate filter.

3 Periodically, the exhaust system should be checked for signs of leaks or damage. Also inspect the system rubber mountings, and renew if necessary.

4 Small holes or cracks can be repaired using proprietary exhaust repair products.

5 Before renewing an individual section of the exhaust system, it is wise to inspect the remaining section. If corrosion or damage is evident, it may prove more economical to renew the entire system.

Component renewal

Exhaust pipe sections

6 If either part of the system is to be renewed, it is important to ensure that the correct component is obtained.

7 To remove the rear tailpipe and silencer, chock the front wheels then jack up the rear of the vehicle and support on axle stands (see *Jacking and vehicle support*). Loosen the clamp securing the front pipe to the tailpipe, then release the rubber mountings and slide the tailpipe from the front pipe **(see illustration)**. If the tailpipe is rusted onto the front pipe, apply liberal amounts of penetrating oil and tap around the joint with a hammer to free it. Twist the tailpipe in both directions while holding the front pipe.

8 To remove the front section of the exhaust, jack up the front and rear of the vehicle and support it on axle stands (see *Jacking and vehicle support*). Undo the two bolts and remove the cross-brace from the front subframe.

9 Remove the tailpipe and silencer as described in paragraph 7. Loosen the clamp securing the exhaust front pipe to the catalytic converter then release the rubber mountings and slide the front pipe from the catalytic converter **(see illustrations)**. While doing this, take care to support the flexible section. **Note:** *Angular movement in excess of 10° can cause permanent damage to the flexible section.* If the front pipe is rusted onto the catalytic converter, apply liberal amounts of penetrating oil and tap around the joint with a hammer to free it. Twist the front pipe in both directions until free.

10 Refitting is a reversal of removal, tightening the clamp nuts to the specified torque.

Catalytic converter

11 Removal of the catalytic converter in included within the turbocharger removal procedure – refer to Section 19.

Particulate filter – 75 bhp models

12 Jack up the front of the vehicle and support it on axle stands (see *Jacking and vehicle support*).

13 Undo the 3 nuts securing the filter to the front section of the exhaust pipe.

14 Slacken the clamp securing the exhaust pipe. Free the filter from the rubber mountings, and slide it from the exhaust pipe.

Particulate filter – Euro 5 models

15 Jack up the front of the vehicle and support it on axle stands (see *Jacking and vehicle support*).

16 On 95 bhp 500 models, remove the radiator as described in Chapter 3.

17 Remove the air cleaner assembly as described in Section 3.

18 Working underneath, slacken the clamp bolt and disconnect the front section of the exhaust pipe. Slide the pipe rearwards a little.

19 Undo the bolt securing the particulate filter lower support bracket.

20 Disconnect the wiring plug, then unscrew the temperature sensor from the filter **(see illustration)**.

20.9b Release the exhaust pipe from the rubber mountings

20.20 Particulate filter temperature sensor (arrowed)

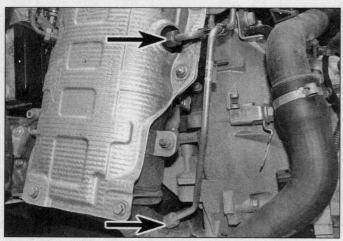

20.21 Pressure sensor upstream, and downstream pipe unions (arrowed)

20.22 Undo the nuts/bolts and remove the particulate filter heat shield

20.26 Particulate filter bracket nuts (arrowed)

21 Unscrew the upstream and downstream pressure sensor pipe unions from the particulate filter (see illustration).

22 Undo the retaining nuts/bolts and remove the heat shield from the filter (see illustration).

23 Undo the retaining nuts and remove the heat shield from the turbocharger (see illustrations 19.27a and 19.27b).

24 Slacken the clamps, undo the retaining bolts/nuts and remove the rigid air outlet pipe from the turbocharger to the intercooler.

25 Undo the nut securing the clamp between the turbocharger and the particulate filter.

26 Undo the retaining nuts and manoeuvre the filter from position (see illustration).

Chapter 4 Part C:
Emissions control systems

Contents

Degrees of difficulty

Easy, suitable for novice with little experience	**Fairly easy,** suitable for beginner with some experience	**Fairly difficult,** suitable for competent DIY mechanic	**Difficult,** suitable for experienced DIY mechanic	**Very difficult,** suitable for expert DIY or professional

Specifications

Torque wrench settings	Nm	lbf ft
EGR valve to cylinder head (diesel engines)	22	16
EGR valve to intake manifold (petrol engines)	20	15
Oxygen sensor	45	33
Particulate filter temperature sensor	45	33

1 General information and precautions

1 All petrol engine models use unleaded petrol and also have various other features built into the fuel/exhaust system to help minimise harmful emissions. All models are equipped with a crankcase emission control system, a catalytic converter and an evaporative emission control system to keep fuel vapour/ exhaust gas emissions down to a minimum.
2 Diesel engine models are also designed to meet strict emission requirements. A crankcase emission control system, a catalytic converter and, on some models, a diesel particulate filter are fitted to keep exhaust emissions down to a minimum. An exhaust gas recirculation (EGR) system is also used to further decrease exhaust emissions.
3 The emission control systems function as follows.

Petrol engines

Crankcase emissions control

4 To reduce the emission of unburned hydrocarbons from the crankcase into the atmosphere, the engine is sealed and the blow-by gases and oil vapour are drawn from the camshaft cover into the intake manifold to be burned by the engine during normal combustion.
5 The gases are forced out of the crankcase by the relatively higher crankcase pressure; if the engine is worn, the raised crankcase pressure (due to increased blow-by) will cause some of the flow to return under all manifold conditions.

Exhaust emission control

6 To minimise the amount of pollutants which escape into the atmosphere, all models are fitted with a catalytic converter which is integral with the exhaust manifold. The system is of the closed-loop type, in which oxygen sensors in the exhaust system provide the fuel injection/ignition system ECU with constant feedback, enabling the ECU to adjust the mixture to provide the best possible conditions for the converter to operate.
7 On all petrol engines covered by this manual, there are two heated oxygen sensors fitted to the exhaust system. The sensor on the top of the exhaust manifold/catalytic converter determines the residual oxygen content of the exhaust gases for mixture correction. The sensor in the exhaust front pipe (after the catalytic converter) monitors the function of the catalytic converter to give the driver a warning signal if there is a fault.
8 The oxygen sensor's tip is sensitive to oxygen and sends the ECU a varying voltage depending on the amount of oxygen in the exhaust gases. Peak conversion efficiency of all major pollutants occurs if the intake air/fuel mixture is maintained at the chemically-correct ratio for the complete combustion of petrol of 14.7 parts (by weight) of air to 1 part of fuel (the 'stoichiometric' ratio). The sensor output voltage alters in a large step at this point, the ECU using the signal change as a reference point and correcting the intake air/fuel mixture accordingly by altering the fuel injector pulse width.

Fuel evaporation emission control

9 To minimise the escape into the atmosphere of unburned hydrocarbons, a fuel evaporation emission control system is fitted. The fuel tank filler cap is sealed and a charcoal canister is mounted behind the wheel arch liner under the right-hand rear wing. The canister collects the petrol vapours generated in the tank when the car is parked and stores them until they can be cleared from the canister (under the control

of the fuel injection/ignition system ECU) via the purge valve into the intake manifold to be burned by the engine during normal combustion.

10 To ensure that the engine runs correctly when it is cold and/or idling and to protect the catalytic converter from the effects of an over-rich mixture, the purge control valve is not opened by the ECU until the engine has warmed-up, and the engine is under load; the valve solenoid is then modulated on and off to allow the stored vapour to pass into the intake manifold.

Diesel engines

Crankcase emission control

11 Refer to paragraphs 4 and 5.

Exhaust emission control

12 To minimise the level of exhaust pollutants released into the atmosphere, a catalytic converter and, on some models, a diesel particulate filter are fitted in the exhaust system.

13 The catalytic converter consists of a canister containing a fine mesh impregnated with a catalyst material, over which the hot exhaust gases pass. The catalyst speeds up the oxidation of harmful carbon monoxide and unburned hydrocarbons, effectively reducing the quantity of harmful products released into the atmosphere via the exhaust gases.

14 On engines without a diesel particulate filter, a heated oxygen sensor is fitted to the exhaust system, upstream of the primary catalytic converter. The sensor monitors the quality of the exhaust gases and provides a signal to the ECU which is then used for mixture correction.

15 On engines with a diesel particulate filter, the filter is incorporated in the exhaust system intermediate section and contains a silicon carbide honeycomb block containing microscopic channels in which the exhaust gases flow. As the gases flow through the honeycomb channels, soot particles are deposited on the channel walls. To prevent clogging of the honeycomb channels, the soot particles are burned off at regular intervals during what is known as a 'regeneration phase'. Under the control of the injection system ECU, the injection characteristics

are altered to raise the temperature of the exhaust gases to approximately 600°C. At this temperature, the soot particles are effectively burned off the honeycomb walls as the exhaust gases pass through. A differential pressure sensor and temperature sensor are used to inform the ECU of the condition of the particulate filter, and the temperature of the exhaust gases during the regeneration phase. When the ECU detects that soot build-up is reducing the efficiency of the particulate filter, it will instigate the regeneration process. This occurs at regular intervals under certain driving conditions and will normally not be detected by the driver.

Exhaust gas recirculation system

16 This system is designed to recirculate small quantities of exhaust gas into the intake manifold, and therefore into the combustion process. This reduces the level of unburnt hydrocarbons present in the exhaust gas before it reaches the catalytic converter. The system is controlled by the injection system ECU, using the information from its various sensors, via the electrically-operated EGR valve.

2 Petrol engine emissions control systems – testing and component renewal

Crankcase emission control

1 The components of this system require no attention other than to check that the hose(s) are clear and undamaged at regular intervals.

Evaporative emission control

2 If the system is thought to be faulty, disconnect the hoses from the charcoal canister and purge control valve and check that they are clear by blowing through them. Full testing of the system can only be carried out using specialist electronic equipment which is connected to the engine management system diagnostic wiring connector. If the purge control valve or charcoal canister are thought to be faulty, they must be renewed.

Charcoal canister

3 Chock the front wheels then jack up the

rear of the vehicle and support on axle stands (see *Jacking and vehicle support*). Remove the right-hand rear wheel.

4 Undo the fasteners and remove the right-hand rear wheel arch liner for access to the charcoal canister.

5 Disconnect the two vent hoses at the quick-release connectors on the charcoal canister **(see illustration)**. Suitably seal the vent hoses and canister unions to prevent dirt ingress.

6 Release the two disconnected vent hoses from the retaining clips around the charcoal canister.

7 Unscrew the retaining nuts and remove the canister from under the wheel arch **(see illustration)**.

8 Refitting is a reversal of the removal procedure. Make sure the hoses are correctly and securely reconnected.

Purge valve

9 The purge valve is mounted on the top of the intake manifold.

10 Remove the air cleaner assembly as described in Chapter 4A.

11 On Euro 5 emissions level models (with motorised throttle body), remove the throttle body as described in Chapter 4A.

12 Disconnect the wiring connector and vapour hose from the purge valve **(see illustration)**.

13 Extract the retaining spring clip, and remove the solenoid from the manifold.

14 Refitting is a reversal of the removal procedure.

Exhaust emission control

15 The performance of the catalytic converter can be checked only by measuring the exhaust gases using a good-quality, carefully-calibrated exhaust gas analyser.

16 If the CO level at the tailpipe is too high, the vehicle should be taken to a Fiat dealer or suitably-equipped repairer so that the complete fuel injection and ignition systems, including the oxygen sensors, can be thoroughly checked using the special diagnostic equipment. Once these have been checked and are known to be free from faults, the fault must be in the catalytic converter, which must be renewed.

2.5 Disconnect the hoses (arrowed) from the charcoal canister

2.7 Charcoal canister retaining nuts (arrowed)

2.12 Disconnect the hose and wiring plug (arrowed) from the purge valve

Catalytic converter

17 The catalytic converter is welded to the exhaust manifold, and the removal and refitting procedure is described in Chapter 4A.

Oxygen sensor

18 Refer to Section 9 of Chapter 4A.

3 Diesel engine emissions control systems – testing and component renewal

Crankcase emission control

1 The components of this system require no attention other than to check that the hose(s) are clear and undamaged at regular intervals.

Exhaust emission control

2 The performance of the catalytic converter and diesel particulate filter can only be checked using special diagnostic equipment. If a system fault is suspected, the vehicle should be taken to a Fiat dealer or suitably-equipped repairer so that the complete fuel injection system can be thoroughly checked.

Catalytic converter/ particulate filter

3 Refer to Chapter 4B for removal and refitting details.

Oxygen sensor

4 Warm the engine up to normal operating temperature then stop the engine and disconnect the battery negative terminal as described in Chapter 5A.
5 Remove the air cleaner assembly as described in Chapter 4B.
6 Firmly apply the handbrake, then jack up the front of the car and support it securely on axle stands (see *Jacking and vehicle support*).
7 Disconnect the oxygen sensor wiring connector, then unclip the wiring plug from the bracket on the front of the transmission.
8 Trace the wiring back to the sensor and release the wiring from the cable clips.
Caution: Take great care not burn yourself on the hot manifold/sensor.
9 Unscrew the sensor and remove it from the exhaust manifold (see illustration).
10 Refitting is a reverse of the removal procedure. Prior to installing the sensor, apply a smear of high-temperature grease to the sensor threads (Fiat recommend the use of a special grease available from your dealer). Tighten the sensor to the specified torque and ensure that the wiring is correctly routed and in no danger of contacting either the exhaust system or engine.

Particulate filter temperature sensor

11 Firmly apply the handbrake, then jack up the front of the car and support it securely on axle stands (see *Jacking and vehicle support*).

3.9 Unscrew the oxygen sensor (arrowed) from the exhaust pipe

12 Disconnect the sensor wiring connector, then trace the wiring back to the sensor and release the wiring from the cable clips.
13 Unscrew the sensor from the particulate filter (see illustration).
14 Refitting is a reverse of the removal procedure. Prior to installing the sensor, apply a smear of high-temperature grease to the sensor threads (Fiat recommend the use of a special grease available from your dealer). Tighten the sensor to the specified torque and ensure that the wiring is correctly routed and in no danger of contacting either the exhaust system or engine.

Exhaust gas recirculation system

15 Comprehensive testing of the system can only be carried out using specialist electronic equipment which is connected to the injection system diagnostic wiring connector (see Chapter 4B). If the EGR valve or solenoid valve are thought to be faulty, they must be renewed.

EGR valve/cooler

16 Remove the battery and battery tray as described in Chapter 5A.

Panda models

17 Remove the throttle body as described in Chapter 4B.
18 Undo the bolts and remove the hose/loom bracket to access the valve.
19 Disconnect the wiring connector from the

3.20 EGR valve/cooler retaining bolts (arrowed)

3.13 Particulate filter temperature sensor (arrowed)

top of the EGR valve. The valve is located on the rear of the cylinder head.
20 Undo the two mounting bolts and one support bracket bolt, then remove the EGR valve and heat exchanger assembly from the engine (see illustration). Recover the gasket.

500 models except 95 bhp

21 Remove the air cleaner assembly as described in Chapter 4B.
22 Remove both wiper arms as described in Chapter 12.
23 Remove the upper and lower windscreen base trims as described in Chapter 11.
24 Release the clamps, undo the bolts and remove the rigid air intake pipe from the intake manifold.
25 Disconnect the wiring from the EGR solenoid valve, and the starter motor. Move the wiring loom to one side.
26 Disconnect the heater coolant supply hose at the engine compartment bulkhead.
27 Release the clamps, undo the retaining bolts, and manoeuvre the EGR cooler and valve assembly from position.

95 bhp 500 models

Note: *Access to the EGR cooler is extremely limited with the engine fitted. If improved access is required, remove the engine as described in Chapter 2C.*
28 Disconnect the EGR valve wiring plug, then undo the bolts and remove the valve (see illustration).
29 Drain the cooling system as described in Chapter 1B.

3.28 EGR valve retaining bolts (arrowed)

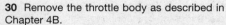

3.31 Prise out the clip (arrowed) a little, and disconnect the heater hose

3.33 EGR pipe-to intake manifold bolts (arrowed)

3.34 Coolant supply actuator solenoid wiring plug (arrowed)

30 Remove the throttle body as described in Chapter 4B.

31 Prise out the clip and disconnect the coolant hose from the heater pipe on the bulkhead **(see illustration)**.

32 Undo the retaining bolts and move the particulate filter pressure pipes to one side.

33 Undo the bolts and remove the EGR valve-to-intake manifold pipe **(see illustration)**.

34 Disconnect the EGR cooler coolant supply actuator solenoid wiring plug **(see illustration)**.

35 Disconnect the gearchange cables from the transmission levers as described in Chapter 7, then undo the bolts and move the cable support bracket to one side.

36 Undo the retaining bolts and manoeuvre the EGR cooler from place.

All models

37 Refitting is a reversal of removal, but bearing in mind the following points:

a) Thoroughly clean the mating faces and use a new gasket. It will be necessary to insert the mounting bolts into the valve prior to refitting, to retain the gasket in position.

b) Tighten the mounting bolts to the specified torque.

c) Where applicable, refill the coolant system as described in Chapter 1B.

4 Catalytic converter – general information and precautions

1 The catalytic converter is a reliable and simple device which needs no maintenance in itself, but there are some facts of which an owner should be aware if the converter is to function properly for its full service life.

Petrol engines

a) DO NOT use leaded petrol or LRP in a car equipped with a catalytic converter – the lead will coat the precious metals, reducing their converting efficiency and will eventually destroy the converter.

b) Always keep the ignition and fuel systems well-maintained in accordance with the manufacturer's schedule.

c) If the engine develops a misfire, do not drive the car at all (or at least as little as possible) until the fault is cured.

d) DO NOT push- or tow-start the car – this will soak the catalytic converter in unburned fuel, causing it to overheat when the engine does start.

e) DO NOT switch off the ignition at high engine speeds.

f) DO NOT use fuel or engine oil additives –

these may contain substances harmful to the catalytic converter.

g) DO NOT continue to use the car if the engine burns oil to the extent of leaving a visible trail of blue smoke.

h) Remember that the catalytic converter operates at very high temperatures. DO NOT, therefore, park the car in dry undergrowth, over long grass or piles of dead leaves after a long run.

i) Remember that the catalytic converter is FRAGILE – do not strike it with tools during servicing work.

j) In some cases a sulphurous smell (like that of rotten eggs) may be noticed from the exhaust. This is common to many catalytic converter-equipped cars and once the car has covered a few thousand miles the problem should disappear.

k) The catalytic converter, used on a well-maintained and well-driven car, should last for between 50 000 and 100 000 miles – if the converter is no longer effective it must be renewed.

Diesel engines

2 Refer to the information given in parts f, g, h, i and k of the petrol engines information given above.

Chapter 5 Part A:
Starting and charging systems

Contents

Degrees of difficulty

Easy, suitable for novice with little experience	**Fairly easy,** suitable for beginner with some experience	**Fairly difficult,** suitable for competent DIY mechanic	**Difficult,** suitable for experienced DIY mechanic	**Very difficult,** suitable for expert DIY or professional

Specifications

General
Electrical system type . . . .   12 volt negative earth

Battery
Type . . . .   Lead-acid, 'maintenance-free' (sealed for life)
Battery capacity . . . .   30, 40 or 50 Ah (depending on model)

Alternator
Type . . . .   Bosch or Magneti-Marelli
Regulated voltage . . . .   13.7 to 14.7 volts (approximately)

Starter motor
Type . . . .   Pre-engaged, Hitachi or Valeo

Torque wrench settings	Nm	lbf ft
Alternator:		
M8	25	18
M10	50	37
Glow plugs	10	7
Starter motor	25	18

1 General information and precautions

General information

The engine electrical system consists mainly of the charging and starting systems. Because of their engine-related functions, these components are covered separately from the body electrical devices such as the lights, instruments, etc (which are covered in Chapter 12). On petrol engine models refer to Part B for information on the ignition system.

The electrical system is of 12 volt negative earth type.

The battery is of the maintenance-free (sealed for life) type, and is charged by the alternator, which is belt-driven from the crankshaft pulley.

The starter motor is of pre-engaged type incorporating an integral solenoid. On starting, the solenoid moves the drive pinion into engagement with the flywheel ring gear before the starter motor is energised. Once the engine has started, a one-way clutch prevents the motor armature being driven by the engine until the pinion disengages.

Further details of the various systems are given in the relevant Sections of this Chapter. While some repair procedures are given, the usual course of action is to renew the component concerned.

Precautions

It is necessary to take extra care when working on the electrical system to avoid damage to semi-conductor devices (diodes and transistors), and to avoid the risk of personal injury. In addition to the precautions given in *Safety first!* at the beginning of this manual, observe the following when working on the system:

- *Always remove rings, watches, etc, before working on the electrical system. Even with the battery disconnected, capacitive discharge could occur if a component's live terminal is earthed through a metal object. This could cause a shock or nasty burn.*
- *Do not reverse the battery connections. Components such as the alternator, electronic control units, or any other components having semi-conductor circuitry could be irreparably damaged.*
- *If the engine is being started using jump leads and a slave battery, connect the batteries positive-to-positive and negative-to-negative (see 'Jump starting'). This also applies when connecting a battery charger but in this case both of the battery terminals should first be disconnected.*
- *Never disconnect the battery terminals, the alternator, any electrical wiring or any test instruments when the engine is running.*
- *Do not allow the engine to turn the alternator when the alternator is not connected.*
- *Never test for alternator output by flashing the output lead to earth.*
- *Never use an ohmmeter of the type incorporating a hand-cranked generator for circuit or continuity testing.*
- *Always ensure that the battery negative lead is disconnected when working on the electrical system.*
- *Before using electric-arc welding equipment on the car, disconnect the battery, alternator and components such as the fuel injection/ignition electronic control unit to protect them from the risk of damage.*

2 Electrical fault finding – general information

Refer to Chapter 12.

3 Battery – testing and charging

Testing

Traditional and low maintenance battery

1 If the vehicle covers a small annual mileage, it is worthwhile checking the specific gravity of the electrolyte every three months to determine the state of charge of the battery. Use a hydrometer to make the check and compare the results with the following table. Note that the specific gravity readings assume an electrolyte temperature of 15°C; for every 10°C below 15°C subtract 0.007. For every 10°C above 15°C add 0.007.

| | Ambient temperature | |
	above 25°C	below 25°C
Fully-charged	1.210 to 1.230	1.270 to 1.290
70% charged	1.170 to 1.190	1.230 to 1.250
Discharged	1.050 to 1.070	1.110 to 1.130

2 If the battery condition is suspect, first check the specific gravity of electrolyte in each cell. A variation of 0.040 or more between any cells indicates loss of electrolyte or deterioration of the internal plates.

3 If the specific gravity variation is 0.040 or more, the battery should be renewed. If the cell variation is satisfactory but the battery is discharged, it should be charged as described later in this Section.

Maintenance-free battery

4 Where a 'sealed for life' maintenance-free battery is fitted, topping-up and testing of the electrolyte in each cell is not possible. The condition of the battery can therefore only be tested using a battery condition indicator or a voltmeter.

3.5 Battery condition indicator (arrowed)

5 Later models are fitted with a maintenance-free battery with a built-in 'magic-eye' charge condition indicator. The indicator is located in the top of the battery casing, and indicates the condition of the battery from its colour **(see illustration)**. If the indicator shows green, then the battery is in a good state of charge. If the indicator turns darker, eventually to black, then the battery requires charging, as described later in this Section. If the indicator shows clear/yellow, then the electrolyte level in the battery is too low to allow further use, and the battery should be renewed. Do not attempt to charge, load or jump start a battery when the indicator shows clear/yellow.

All battery types

6 If testing the battery using a voltmeter, connect the voltmeter across the battery. The test is only accurate if the battery has not been subjected to any kind of charge for the previous six hours. If this is not the case, switch on the headlights for 30 seconds, then wait four to five minutes before testing the battery after switching off the headlights. All other electrical circuits must be switched off, so check that the doors and tailgate are fully shut when making the test.

7 If the voltage reading is less than 12.2 volts, then the battery is discharged, whilst a reading of 12.2 to 12.4 volts indicates a partially-discharged condition.

8 If the battery is to be charged, remove it from the vehicle (Section 4) and charge it as described later in this Section.

Charging

Note: *The following is intended as a guide only. Always refer to the manufacturer's recommendations (often printed on a label attached to the battery) before charging a battery.*

Traditional and low maintenance battery

9 Charge the battery at a rate of 3.5 to 4 amps and continue to charge the battery at this rate until no further rise in specific gravity is noted over a four hour period.

10 Alternatively, a trickle charger charging at the rate of 1.5 amps can safely be used overnight.

11 Specially rapid 'boost' charges which are

claimed to restore the power of the battery in 1 to 2 hours are not recommended, as they can cause serious damage to the battery plates through overheating.

12 While charging the battery, note that the temperature of the electrolyte should never exceed 38°C.

Maintenance-free battery

13 This battery type takes considerably longer to fully recharge than the standard type, the time taken being dependent on the extent of discharge, but it will take anything up to three days.

14 A constant voltage type charger is required, to be set, when connected, to 13.9 to 14.9 volts with a charger current below 25 amps. Using this method, the battery should be usable within three hours, giving a voltage reading of 12.5 volts, but this is for a partially-discharged battery and, as mentioned, full charging can take considerably longer.

15 If the battery is to be charged from a fully-discharged state (condition reading less than 12.2 volts), have it recharged by your Fiat dealer or local automotive electrician, as the charge rate is higher and constant supervision during charging is necessary.

4 Battery and battery tray – removal, disconnection and refitting

Battery disconnection

With battery monitor sensor

1 Depress the clip and disconnect the earth lead from the 'false pole' **(see illustration)**.

2 Depress the clip and disconnect the wiring plug from the battery monitor sensor **(see illustration)**.

3 Slacken the negative terminal clamp nut, rotate the clamp back and forth a little, to release it from the terminal post, and pull it upwards from place **(see illustration)**. Cover the terminal post, and position the clamp away from the battery to prevent accidental reconnection.

Without battery monitor sensor

4 On Type 1, slacken the negative lead clamp nut. On Type 2, push the over-centre clamp lever away from the battery to release it. On all types, rotate the negative (-) lead clamp back and forth a little, to release it from the battery terminal post, and pull it upwards from place **(see illustrations)**. Cover the battery terminal post, and position the lead clamp away from the battery to prevent accidental reconnection.

Removal

5 Disconnect the battery negative lead clamp as previously described.

4.1 Depress the clip (arrowed) and lift the earth terminal (-) from the 'false pole'

4.3 Slacken the negative terminal clamp nut (arrowed)

4.4b . . . twist the clamp back-and-forth and pull it upwards

4.6b . . . then slacken the positive (+) terminal clamp nut (arrowed)

4.2 Disconnect the wiring plug (arrowed) from the battery monitor sensor

4.4a Push the over-centre clamp lever away from the battery . . .

4.6a Pull up the plastic cover . . .

6 Remove the plastic cover over the positive (+) terminal lead clamp, then disconnect the lead at the battery positive (+) terminal by slackening the retaining nut and removing the terminal clamp **(see illustrations)**.

7 Undo the retaining nut, and remove the battery securing strap **(see illustration)**.

8 Carefully lift the battery from its location and remove from the car. Make sure the battery is kept upright at all times.

4.7 Undo the battery retaining strap nut (arrowed)

4.11 Pull the battery tray cover upwards, noting the drain hose routing (arrowed)

4.13a Disconnect the earth lead from the ECU (arrowed) – ECU mounted on the rear of the battery tray . . .

4.13b . . . and ECU mounted on the side of the battery tray (arrowed)

Refitting

Note: *As a precaution, before refitting the battery check that all doors are unlocked.*

9 Refitting is a reversal of removal, but smear petroleum jelly on the terminals after reconnecting the leads to reduce corrosion, and always reconnect the positive lead first, followed by the negative lead.

Battery tray

10 Remove the battery as described previously.

11 Pull the battery tray cover upwards from place **(see illustration)**. Note the drain tube.

12 Some models have the engine management ECU bolted to the side of the battery tray. Release the locking catches, and disconnect the wiring plugs from the engine management ECU – refer to Chapter 4A or 4B as applicable.

13 Where applicable, undo the bolt/nut securing the earth lead to the ECU **(see illustrations)**.

14 Undo the retaining bolts/nut, lift the battery tray and unclip the wiring loom(s) from the tray **(see illustrations)**. Manoeuvre the battery tray, complete with ECU (where applicable), from place.

15 Refitting is a reversal of removal.

5 Charging system – testing

Note: *Refer to the precautions given in 'Safety first!' and in Section 1 of this Chapter before starting work.*

1 If the ignition no-charge warning light fails to illuminate when the ignition is switched on, first check the alternator wiring connections for security. If all is satisfactory, the alternator is at fault, and should be renewed, or taken to an auto-electrician for testing and repair.

2 If the ignition warning light illuminates when the engine is running, stop the engine and check the condition of the auxiliary drivebelt (see Chapter 1A or 1B) and that the alternator connections are secure. If all is so far satisfactory, have the alternator checked by an auto-electrician for testing and repair.

3 If the alternator output is suspect even though the warning light functions correctly, the regulated voltage may be checked as follows.

4 Connect a voltmeter across the battery terminals, and start the engine.

5 Increase the engine speed until the voltmeter reading remains steady; the reading should be approximately 12 to 13 volts, and no more than 14 volts.

6 Switch on as many electrical accessories (eg, the headlights, heated rear window and heater blower) as possible, and check that the alternator maintains the regulated voltage at around 13.5 to 14.5 volts.

7 If the regulated voltage is not as stated, the fault may be due to worn brushes, weak brush springs, a faulty voltage regulator, a faulty diode, a severed phase winding, or worn or damaged slip-rings. The alternator should be renewed or taken to an auto-electrician for testing and repair.

6 Auxiliary drivebelt – removal and refitting

Refer to Chapter 1A or 1B.

7 Alternator – removal and refitting

Petrol engines

Removal

1 Disconnect the battery negative terminal as described in Section 4.

2 Remove the air cleaner assembly as described in Chapter 4A.

3 Remove the auxiliary drivebelt as described in Chapter 1A.

4 Remove the right-hand driveshaft as described in Chapter 8.

5 Unscrew the bolt securing the rear engine mounting assembly to the subframe.

6 Undo the retaining nuts and disconnect the cables from the rear of the alternator **(see illustration)**.

7 Unscrew the alternator upper and lower mounting bolts and withdraw the alternator from the engine. Note that it may be necessary to tip the engine forward slightly to gain access to the upper mounting bolt.

4.14a Battery tray retaining bolts/nut (arrowed) – 500 models . . .

4.14b . . . and Panda models (arrowed)

7.6 Disconnect the wiring (arrowed) from the rear of the alternator

7.12 Move the vacuum reservoir and bracket (arrowed) to one side

Refitting

8 Refitting is a reversal of removal, but tighten the mounting bolts to the specified torque. Refit the auxiliary drivebelt as described in Chapter 1A.

Diesel engines

Removal

9 The alternator is located on the rear of the cylinder block. First apply the handbrake, then jack up the front of the vehicle and support it on axle stands (see *Jacking and vehicle support*). Remove the right-hand front roadwheel and the wheel arch liner cover for access to the right-hand side of the engine.
10 Disconnect the battery negative terminal as described in Section 4.
11 Remove the auxiliary drivebelt as described in Chapter 1B.
12 Undo the retaining bolts and move the vacuum reservoir and bracket (where fitted) at the rear of the cylinder block to one side **(see illustration)**.
13 Unscrew the nuts and disconnect the wiring from the rear of the alternator.
14 Unscrew the upper mounting bolt and the two lower mounting bolts, then withdraw the alternator downwards from the block **(see illustrations)**.

Refitting

15 Refitting is a reversal of removal, but tighten the mounting bolts to the specified torque. Refit the auxiliary drivebelt as described in Chapter 1B.

8 Alternator – testing and overhaul

If the alternator is thought to be suspect, it should be removed from the vehicle and taken to an auto-electrician for testing. Most auto-electricians will be able to supply and fit brushes at a reasonable cost. However, check on the cost of repairs before proceeding as it may prove more economical to obtain a new or exchange alternator.

9 Starting system – testing

Note: *Refer to the precautions given in 'Safety first!' and in Section 1 of this Chapter before starting work.*
1 If the starter motor fails to operate when the ignition key is turned to the appropriate position, the possible causes are as follows:
 a) *The engine immobiliser is faulty.*
 b) *The battery is faulty.*
 c) *The electrical connections between the switch, solenoid, battery and starter motor are somewhere failing to pass the necessary current from the battery through the starter to earth.*
 d) *The solenoid is faulty.*
 e) *The starter motor is mechanically or electrically defective.*
2 To check the battery, switch on the headlights. If they dim after a few seconds, this indicates that the battery is discharged –

recharge (see Section 3) or renew the battery. If the headlights glow brightly, operate the starter switch while watching the headlights. If they dim, then this indicates that current is reaching the starter motor, therefore the fault must lie in the starter motor. If the lights continue to glow brightly (and no clicking sound can be heard from the starter motor solenoid), this indicates that there is a fault in the circuit or solenoid – see the following paragraphs. If the starter motor turns slowly when operated, but the battery is in good condition, then this indicates either that the starter motor is faulty, or there is considerable resistance somewhere in the circuit.
3 If a fault in the circuit is suspected, disconnect the battery leads (including the earth connection to the body), the starter/solenoid wiring and the engine/transmission earth strap – see Chapter 12. Thoroughly clean the connections, and reconnect the leads and wiring. Use a voltmeter or test light to check that full battery voltage is available at the battery positive lead connection to the solenoid. Smear petroleum jelly around the battery terminals to prevent corrosion – corroded connections are among the most frequent causes of electrical system faults.
4 If the battery and all connections are in good condition, check the circuit by disconnecting the switched feed wire from the solenoid (the thinner wire). Connect a voltmeter or test light between the wire end and a good earth (such as the battery negative terminal), and check that the wire is live when the ignition switch is turned to the 'start' position. If it is, then the circuit is sound – if not, there is a fault in the ignition/starter switch or wiring.
5 The solenoid contacts can be checked by connecting a voltmeter or test light between the battery positive feed connection on the starter side of the solenoid and earth. When the ignition switch is turned to the 'start' position, there should be a reading or lighted bulb, as applicable. If there is no reading or

7.14a Alternator upper and lower mounting bolts (arrowed)

7.14b Manoeuvre the alternator between the subframe and the driveshaft

10.4 Remove the bracket (arrowed) below the starter motor

10.6 Starter motor upper mounting bolts (arrowed)

10.7 Raise the plastic cover over the starter motor terminals

lighted bulb, the solenoid is faulty and should be renewed.

6 If the circuit and solenoid are proved sound, the fault must lie in the starter motor. In this event, it may be possible to have the starter motor overhauled by a specialist, but check on the cost of spares before proceeding, as it may prove more economical to obtain a new or exchange motor.

10 Starter motor – removal and refitting

Petrol engines

1 Disconnect the battery negative terminal as described in Section 4.

2 Firmly apply the handbrake, then jack up the front of the car and support it securely on axle stands (see *Jacking and vehicle support*).

Panda models

3 Remove the air cleaner assembly as described in Chapter 4A.

4 Undo the bolts and remove the engine-to-transmission support bracket from beneath the starter motor (see illustration).

500 models

5 Remove the battery and battery tray as described in Section 4.

All models

6 Unscrew and remove the starter motor upper mounting bolt located at the top of the transmission bellhousing (see illustration).

7 From under the car, raise the plastic cover over the starter solenoid wiring terminals (see illustration).

8 Unscrew the two nuts and disconnect the wiring from the solenoid terminal studs (see illustration).

9 Unscrew the lower mounting bolt(s), then withdraw the starter motor from the transmission (see illustration).

10 Refitting is a reversal of removal.

Diesel engines

11 Remove the battery and battery tray as describe in Section 4.

10.8 Disconnect the wiring (arrowed) from the terminal studs

12 Apply the handbrake, then jack up the front of the vehicle and support it on axle stands (see *Jacking and vehicle support*).

13 Undo the retaining bolts and move the vacuum reservoir and bracket (where fitted) at the rear of the cylinder block to one side (see illustration 7.12).

14 Using a long socket bit inserted through the access hole, unscrew and remove the upper mounting bolt (see illustration).

10.9 Starter motor lower mounting bolt (A), and on certain models, the additional bolt (B)

10.14 Starter motor upper mounting bolt (arrowed)

10.15a Prise open the plastic cover . . .

10.15b . . . remove the nut (arrowed) securing the outer lead . . .

10.15c . . . note the O-rings and washer (arrowed) . . .

10.15d . . . then slide the inner lead (arrowed) from place

10.15e When refitting, position the O-rings and washer (arrowed) on the plastic housing . . .

10.15f . . . followed by the inner lead

Take great care not to drop the bolt in the bellhousing.

15 Undo the two nuts and disconnect the wiring from the starter solenoid (see illustrations).

16 Unscrew the lower mounting bolt and withdraw the starter motor from the engine.

17 Refitting is a reversal of removal, but tighten the mounting bolts to the specified torque.

11 Starter motor – testing and overhaul

If the starter motor is thought to be suspect, it should be removed from the vehicle and taken to an auto-electrician for testing. Most auto-electricians will be able to supply and fit

brushes at a reasonable cost. However, check on the cost of repairs before proceeding as it may prove more economical to obtain a new or exchange motor.

12 Ignition switch/steering lock – removal and refitting

Removal

Switch

1 Remove the steering column combination switch assembly as described in Chapter 12.

2 Disconnect the ignition switch wiring plug.

3 Drill out the shear bolts, and remove the ignition switch/steering lock assembly (see illustration).

Lock barrel

4 Insert the ignition key, and turn it to the 1st position.

5 Press in the retaining clip, and pull the barrel from the switch (see illustrations).

6 Remove the circlip from the end of the barrel, press in the lever, rotate the barrel to align the lug and slot, then pull the tumbler assembly.

7 Refitting is a reversal of removal.

Refitting

8 Position the ignition switch/steering lock assembly, insert the new shear bolts, and tighten them until the heads shear off.

9 Reconnect the ignition switch wiring plug.

10 Refit the steering column combination switch assembly as described in Chapter 12.

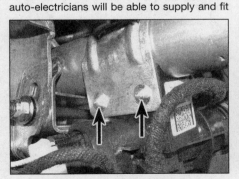

12.3 Ignition switch/steering lock shear bolts (arrowed)

12.5a Depress the clip (arrowed) . . .

12.5b . . . and pull the barrel from the switch

13 Pre/post-heating system (diesel engines) – description and testing

Description

1 Each cylinder of the engine is fitted with a heater plug (commonly called a glow plug) screwed into it. The plugs are electrically-operated before and during start-up when the engine is cold. Electrical feed to the glow plugs is controlled via the pre/post-heating system control unit.

2 A warning light in the instrument panel tells the driver that pre/post-heating is taking place. When the light goes out, the engine is ready to be started. The voltage supply to the glow plugs continues for several seconds after the light goes out. If no attempt is made to start, the timer then cuts off the supply, in order to avoid draining the battery and overheating the glow plugs.

3 The glow plugs also provide a 'post-heating' function, whereby the glow plugs remain switched on after the engine has started. The length of time 'post-heating' takes place is also determined by the control unit, and is dependent on engine temperature.

4 The fuel filter is fitted with a heating element to prevent the fuel 'waxing' in extreme cold temperature conditions and to improve combustion. The heating element is an integral part of the fuel filter housing and is controlled by the pre/post-heating system control unit.

Testing

5 If the system malfunctions, testing is ultimately by substitution of known good units, but some preliminary checks may be made as follows.

6 Connect a voltmeter or 12 volt test lamp between the glow plug supply cable and earth (engine or vehicle metal). Make sure that the live connection is kept clear of the engine and bodywork.

7 Have an assistant switch on the ignition, and check that voltage is applied to the glow plugs. Note the time for which the warning light is lit, and the total time for which voltage is applied before the system cuts out. Switch off the ignition.

8 At an underbonnet temperature of 20ºC, typical times noted should be approximately 3 seconds for warning light operation. Warning light time will increase with lower temperatures and decrease with higher temperatures.

9 If there is no supply at all, the control unit or associated wiring is at fault.

10 To locate a defective glow plug, disconnect the wiring connector from each plug.

11 Use a continuity tester, or a 12 volt test lamp connected to the battery positive terminal, to check for continuity between each glow plug terminal and earth. The resistance of a glow plug in good condition is very low (less than 1 ohm), so if the test lamp does not light or the continuity tester shows a high resistance, the glow plug is certainly defective.

12 If an ammeter is available, the current draw of each glow plug can be checked. After an initial surge of 15 to 20 amps, each plug should draw 12 amps. Any plug which draws much more or less than this is probably defective.

13 As a final check, the glow plugs can be removed and inspected as described in the following Section.

14 Glow plugs – removal, inspection and refitting

Caution: If the pre/post-heating system has just been energised, or if the engine has been running, the glow plugs will be very hot.

Removal

1 The glow plugs are located at the front of the cylinder head above the exhaust manifold.

2 Remove the air cleaner assembly as described in Chapter 4B.

3 On Euro 5 emissions level engines, undo the bolts and remove the turbocharger heat shield **(see illustration)**.

4 On 95 bhp 500 models, remove the turbocharger as described in Chapter 4B.

5 Disconnect the wiring plugs by pulling them from the glow plugs **(see illustration)**.

6 Unscrew the glow plugs and remove them from the cylinder head **(see illustration)**.

Inspection

7 Inspect each glow plug for physical damage. Burnt or eroded glow plug tips can be caused by a bad injector spray pattern. Have the injectors checked if this type of damage is found.

8 If the glow plugs are in good physical condition, check them electrically using a 12 volt test lamp or continuity tester as described in the previous Section.

9 The glow plugs can be energised by applying 12 volts to them to verify that they heat up evenly and in the required time. Observe the following precautions.

a) Support the glow plug by clamping it carefully in a vice or self-locking pliers. Remember it will become red-hot.

b) Make sure that the power supply or test lead incorporates a fuse or overload trip to protect against damage from a short-circuit.

c) After testing, allow the glow plug to cool for several minutes before attempting to handle it.

10 A glow plug in good condition will start to glow red at the tip after drawing current for 5 seconds or so. Any plug which takes much longer to start glowing, or which starts glowing in the middle instead of at the tip, is defective.

Refitting

11 Carefully refit the plugs and tighten to the specified torque. Do not overtighten, as this can damage the glow plug element. Push the electrical connectors firmly onto the glow plugs.

12 The remainder of refitting is a reversal of removal, checking the operation of the glow plugs on completion.

15 Pre/post-heating system control unit – removal and refitting

Removal

1 The pre/post-heating system control unit is located on the left-hand side of the engine compartment.

14.3 Undo the bolts (arrowed) and remove the heat shield

14.5 Glow plug wiring plug

14.6 Unscrew the glow plugs from the cylinder head (2 left-hand plugs arrowed)

2 Disconnect the battery negative terminal as described in Section 4.
3 Remove the cover, undo the retaining nut and manoeuvre the control unit from place **(see illustrations)**. Disconnect the wiring plugs as the unit is withdrawn.

Refitting

4 Refitting is a reversal of removal.

16 Stop/start system – component renewal

1 Some models are equipped with a stop/start fuel saving system, where the engine is turned off when neutral is selected in a traffic jam. The engine is restarted when the clutch is depressed, prior to selecting 1st gear.

Gear lever neutral sensor

2 Remove the centre console covers as described in Chapter 11.
3 Disconnect the wiring plug, prise the linkage rod from the gear lever, then remove the retaining clips and manoeuvre the sensor assembly from place **(see illustrations)**.
4 Refitting is a reversal of removal. Note that

if a new sensor has been fitted, it must be initialised using Fiat diagnostic equipment. Entrust this task to a suitably-equipped specialist.

Brake servo vacuum sensor

5 Remove the throttle body as described in Chapter 4B.
6 Disconnect the sensor wiring plug, then carefully prise the sensor from the servo **(see illustration)**.
7 Disconnect the vacuum hose from the vacuum pump/manifold **(see illustration)**. No further dismantling is recommended.
8 Refitting is a reversal of removal.

15.3a Undo the nuts (arrowed) . . .

15.3b . . . remove the pre/post-heating control unit cover . . .

15.3c . . . then undo the nut and disconnect the wiring plugs (arrowed)

16.3 Prise the neutral sensor linkage rod from the gearchange cable (arrowed)

16.6 Brake servo vacuum sensor (arrowed)

16.7 Depress the release button (arrowed) and disconnect the vacuum hose from the pump

Notes

Chapter 5 Part B:
Ignition system – petrol engines

Contents

Degrees of difficulty

Easy, suitable for novice with little experience	Fairly easy, suitable for beginner with some experience	Fairly difficult, suitable for competent DIY mechanic	Difficult, suitable for experienced DIY mechanic	Very difficult, suitable for expert DIY or professional

Specifications

General

System type	Static (distributorless) ignition system controlled by engine management ECU
Firing order..	1–3–4–2 (No 1 cylinder at timing belt end of engine)
Spark plugs	See Chapter 1A *Specifications*
Ignition timing...	Controlled by engine management ECU

Ignition coil
Resistances at 20°C (non-Euro 5 emissions only):

Primary windings	0.52 to 0.62 ohms
Secondary windings...................................	6.83 to 7.83 k ohms

Torque wrench setting

	Nm	lbf ft
Knock sensor securing bolt	25	18

1 General information

The ignition system is integrated with the fuel injection system to form a combined engine management system under the control of one ECU (see Chapter 4A for further information).

The ignition side of the system is of the static (distributorless) type, consisting (on pre-Euro 5 emissions level models only) of two twin-output ignition coils located on the left-hand side of the cylinder head. Each ignition coil supplies two cylinders (one coil supplies cylinders 1 and 4, and the other cylinders 2 and 3). Under the control of the ECU, the ignition coils operate on the wasted spark principle, ie, each spark plug sparks twice for every cycle of the engine, once on the compression stroke and once on the exhaust stroke. The spark voltage is greatest in the cylinder which is under compression, the other cylinder having a very weak spark which has no effect on the exhaust gases.

On Euro 5 emissions level models, 4 separate ignition coils are filled (one per cylinder) located in an assembly bolted to the cylinder head cover.

The ECU uses its inputs from the various sensors to calculate the required ignition advance setting and coil charging time depending on engine temperature, load and speed.

A knock sensor is also incorporated into the ignition system. Mounted onto the cylinder block, the sensor detects the high-frequency vibrations caused when the engine starts to pre-ignite, or 'pink'. Under these conditions, the knock sensor sends an electrical signal to the ECU which in turn retards the ignition advance setting in small steps until the 'pinking' ceases.

2 Ignition system – testing

Warning: Due to the high voltages produced by the electronic ignition system, extreme care must be taken when working on the system with the ignition switched on. Persons with surgically-implanted cardiac pacemaker devices should keep well clear of the ignition circuits, components and test equipment.

1 If a fault appears in the engine management (fuel injection/ignition) system first ensure that the fault is not due to a poor electrical connection or poor maintenance; ie, check that the air cleaner filter element is clean, the spark plugs are in good condition and correctly gapped, that the engine breather hoses are clear and undamaged,

referring to Chapter 1A for further information. Also check that the accelerator cable (where fitted) is correctly adjusted as described in Chapter 4A. If the engine is running very roughly, check the compression pressures and the valve clearances as described in Chapters 1A and 2A.

2 If these checks fail to reveal the cause of the problem, the vehicle should be taken to a suitably-equipped Fiat dealer for testing. A diagnostic connector is incorporated in the engine management wiring circuit into which a special electronic diagnostic tester can be plugged. The tester will locate the fault quickly and simply alleviating the need to test all the system components individually which is a time-consuming operation that carries a high risk of damaging the ECU.

3 The only ignition system checks which can be carried out by the home mechanic are those described in Chapter 1A, relating to the spark plugs, and the ignition coil test described in this Chapter. If necessary, the system wiring and wiring connectors can be checked as described in Chapter 12, ensuring that the ECU wiring connectors have first been disconnected.

---

3 Ignition HT coils – removal, testing and refitting

Removal

1 Remove the air cleaner assembly as described in Chapter 4A.

3.3 Disconnect the LT wiring plugs from the coils (arrowed)

3.5 Ignition coil mountings bolts

Pre-Euro 5 models

2 Remove the battery and battery tray as described in Chapter 5A.

3 Disconnect the LT wiring plug(s) from the top of the ignition coil **(see illustration)**.

4 Identify the HT leads for position then disconnect them from the coil HT terminals **(see illustration)**.

5 Unscrew the mounting bolts and remove the relevant ignition coil from the end of the cylinder head **(see illustration)**.

Euro 5 models

6 Disconnect the LT wiring plug from the ignition coil **(see illustration)**.

7 Identify the HT leads for position then disconnect them from the coil HT terminals.

8 Unscrew the mounting bolts and remove the ignition coil from the cylinder head cover **(see illustration)**.

Testing

9 Testing of the coil consists of using a multimeter set to its resistance function, to check the primary and secondary windings for continuity and resistance. Compare the results obtained to those given in the *Specifications* at the start of this Chapter. Note the resistance of the coil windings varies slightly according to the coil temperature and the figures in the *Specifications* are values for the coil at 20°C.

10 Check that there is no continuity between the HT lead terminals and the coil body/mounting bracket.

11 Note that with the ignition switched on and the engine stationary, voltage will only be

3.4 Identify the HT leads for position then disconnect them from the coil terminals

3.6 Lift the clip (arrowed) and disconnect the LT wiring plug

---

supplied to the ignition coils for approximately 2 seconds. However, when the engine is being cranked or running, voltage will be continually supplied.

12 If faulty, the coil should be renewed.

Refitting

13 Refitting is a reversal of the removal procedure ensuring that the wiring and HT leads are correctly reconnected.

---

4 Ignition timing – checking and adjustment

1 The ignition timing is constantly being monitored and adjusted by the engine management ECU, and nominal values cannot be given. Therefore, it is not possible for the home mechanic to check the ignition timing.

2 The only way in which the timing can be checked is using special electronic test equipment, connected to the engine management system diagnostic connector (refer to Chapter 4A for further information).

---

5 Knock sensor – removal and refitting

Removal

1 The knock sensor is screwed into the rear face of the cylinder block, under the intake manifold.

2 Firmly apply the handbrake, then jack up the front of the car and support it securely on axle stands (see *Jacking and vehicle support*).

3 Trace the wiring back from the sensor to its wiring connector, and disconnect it from the main loom.

4 From under the car, disconnect the knock sensor wiring connector.

5 Undo the sensor securing bolt and remove the sensor from the cylinder block.

Refitting

6 Refitting is a reversal of the removal procedure, ensuring that the sensor securing bolt is tightened to the specified torque.

3.8 Ignition coil mounting bolts (arrowed)

Chapter 6
Clutch

Contents

Degrees of difficulty

Easy, suitable for novice with little experience	**Fairly easy**, suitable for beginner with some experience	**Fairly difficult**, suitable for competent DIY mechanic	**Difficult**, suitable for experienced DIY mechanic	**Very difficult**, suitable for expert DIY or professional

Specifications

Type	Single dry plate with diaphragm spring, hydraulically-operated

Friction disc

Diameter:
Petrol engines	181 or 200 mm
Diesel engines	200 or 215 mm

New lining thickness:
Petrol engines	7.7 mm
Diesel engines	7.2 mm

Torque wrench settings	**Nm**	**lbf ft**
Master cylinder retaining nuts	15	10
Pressure plate retaining bolts*	15	10
Release cylinder mounting bolts:		
Externally mounted	5	4
Concentric internally mounted	15	11

* Do not re-use

1 General information

The clutch consists of a friction disc, a pressure plate assembly, and the hydraulic release cylinder (which incorporates the release bearing); all of these components are contained in a large cast-aluminium alloy bellhousing, sandwiched between the engine and the transmission.

The friction disc is fitted between the engine flywheel and the clutch pressure plate, and is allowed to slide on the transmission input shaft splines.

The pressure plate assembly is bolted to the engine flywheel. When the engine is running, drive is transmitted from the crankshaft, via the flywheel, to the friction disc (these components being clamped securely together by the pressure plate assembly) and from the friction disc to the transmission input shaft.

To interrupt the drive, the spring pressure must be relaxed. This is achieved using a hydraulic release mechanism which consists of the master cylinder, the release cylinder and the pipe/hose linking the two components. Depressing the pedal pushes on the master cylinder pushrod which hydraulically forces the release cylinder piston against the pressure plate spring fingers or against the release fork, which that acts upon the pressure plate spring fingers (model dependant). This causes the springs to deform and releases the clamping force on the friction disc.

The clutch is self-adjusting and requires no manual adjustment.

2 Clutch hydraulic system – bleeding

⚠ *Warning: Hydraulic fluid is poisonous; thoroughly wash off spills from bare skin without delay. Seek immediate medical advice if any fluid is swallowed or gets into the eyes. Certain types of hydraulic fluid are inflammable and may ignite when brought into contact with hot components; when servicing any hydraulic system, it is safest to assume that the fluid IS inflammable, and to take precautions against the risk of fire as though it were petrol that was being handled. Hydraulic fluid is an effective paint stripper and will also attack many plastics. If spillage occurs onto painted bodywork or fittings it should be washed off immediately, using copious quantities of fresh water. It is also hygroscopic – it can absorb moisture from the air, which then renders it useless. Old fluid may have suffered contamination, and should never be re-used. When topping-up or renewing the fluid, always use the recommended grade, and ensure that it comes from a new sealed container.*

2.8a Bleed nipple (arrowed) – external release cylinder

2.8b Press in the clip and pull the fluid pipe out one notch, fluid/bubbles will emerge from the bleed nipple (arrowed) – concentric release cylinder

General information

1 Whenever the clutch hydraulic lines are disconnected for service or repair, a certain amount of air will enter the system. The presence of air in any hydraulic system will introduce a degree of elasticity, and in the clutch system this will translate into poor pedal feel and reduced travel, leading to inefficient gearchanges and even clutch system failure. For this reason, after reconnection of the hydraulic lines, the system must be topped-up and bled to remove any air bubbles.

2 The most effective way of bleeding the clutch hydraulic system is to use a pressure brake bleeding kit. These are readily available in motor accessories shops and are extremely effective. The following procedure describes bleeding the clutch system using such a kit. The alternative method is to bleed the system by depressing the clutch pedal – refer to the brake hydraulic system bleeding procedures contained in Chapter 9 for details of this method.

3 Remove the battery and battery tray as described in Chapter 5A, then observe if the release cylinder which is located on the top of the transmission housing. On models without a visible release cylinder, the cylinder is in fact concentric with the transmission input shaft, within the gearbox bellhousing. On both types, a bleed nipple should be visible either on the release cylinder itself, or on the plastic connecting piece.

Bleeding

Note: *On some models the clutch shares the brake fluid reservoir; others have a separate reservoir.*

4 Remove the protective cap from the release cylinder bleed nipple, or from the connecting piece. Connect a length of clear plastic hose over the nipple or outlet and insert the other end into a clean container. Pour hydraulic fluid into the container, such that the end of the hose is covered.

5 Following the manufacturer's instructions, pour hydraulic fluid into the bleeding kit vessel.

6 Unscrew the brake or clutch fluid reservoir filler cap, then connect the bleeding kit fluid supply hose to the reservoir.

7 Connect the pressure hose to a supply of compressed air – a spare tyre is a convenient source.

Caution: Check that the pressure in the tyre does not exceed the maximum supply pressure quoted by the kit manufacturer, let some air escape to reduce the pressure, if necessary. Gently open the air valve and allow the air and fluid pressures to equalise. Check that there are no leaks before proceeding.

8 On models with an external release cylinder, slacken the nipple approximately half a turn. On models with a concentric (internal) release cylinder within the transmission bellhousing, press in the clip and pull the pressure pipe out one notch – fluid and bubbles will appear from the bleed nipple **(see illustrations)**.

9 Allow the hydraulic fluid to flow from the release cylinder, through the plastic hose and into the container. Maintain a steady flow until the emerging fluid is free of air bubbles; keep a watchful eye on the level of fluid in the bleeding kit vessel and the fluid reservoir – if it is allowed to drop too low, air may be forced into the system, defeating the object of the exercise. To refill the vessel, turn off the compressed air supply, remove the lid and pour in an appropriate quantity of fresh fluid – do not re-use the fluid collected in the receiving container. Repeat as necessary until the ejected fluid is bubble-free.

10 When clean hydraulic fluid, free from air bubbles, emerges from the plastic hose, tighten the bleed nipple, or press the pipe fully into the connector as applicable.

11 Pump the clutch pedal several times to assess its feel and travel. If firm, constant pedal resistance is not felt throughout the pedal stroke, it is probable that air is still present in the system – repeat the bleeding procedure until the pedal feel is restored.

12 Depressurise the bleeding kit and remove the kit, plastic hose and receiving container from the vehicle. Refit the protective cap to the bleed nipple. Discard the fluid expelled from the hydraulic system as it will be contaminated with moisture, air and dirt, making it unfit for further use.

13 Check the fluid level in the reservoir. At

3.3 Prise out the fluid pipe retaining clip (arrowed)

3.4 Clutch fluid supply hose (1), hose clamp (2) and master cylinder mounting nuts (3)

this point, the reservoir may be over-full; the excess should be removed using a *clean* pipette to reduce the level to the MAX mark.

14 Refit the battery and tray with reference to Chapter 5A.

15 Finally, road test the vehicle and check the operation of the clutch system whilst changing up and down through the gears, whilst pulling away from a standstill and from a hill start.

3 Master cylinder – removal and refitting

Removal

1 Unscrew the brake/clutch hydraulic fluid reservoir filler cap, and top-up the reservoir to the MAX mark (see *Weekly checks*). Place a piece of polythene over the filler neck, and secure the polythene with the filler cap. This will minimise fluid loss during subsequent operations. Alternatively, position a hose clamp on the fluid supply pipe above the master cylinder **(see illustration 3.4)**.

2 Remove all traces of dirt from the outside of

the master cylinder, then position some cloth beneath the cylinder to catch any spilt fluid.

3 Extract the retaining clip and disconnect the hydraulic pipe from the connector on the end of the master cylinder **(see illustration)**. Plug the pipe end and master cylinder port to minimise fluid loss and prevent the entry of dirt.

4 Disconnect the fluid supply hose from the clutch master cylinder **(see illustration)**.

5 Carefully prise the master cylinder pushrod from the clutch pedal **(see illustration)**.

6 Unscrew the two nuts securing the master cylinder to the engine compartment bulkhead and manoeuvre it from position. Be prepared for fluid spillage.

7 If the master cylinder is faulty it must be renewed; overhaul of the unit is not possible.

Refitting

8 Manoeuvre the master cylinder into position and refit the two retaining nuts. Tighten the nuts to the specified torque.

9 Press the end of the pushrod onto the pedal balljoint.

10 Connect the fluid supply hose to the master cylinder.

11 Press the hydraulic pipe back into the

connector on the end of the master cylinder and secure with the clip.

12 Bleed the clutch hydraulic system as described in Section 2.

4 Release cylinder – removal and refitting

Externally mounted cylinder

Note: *Refer to the warning at the beginning of Section 2 regarding the hazards of working with hydraulic fluid.*

Removal

1 Remove the battery and battery tray as described in Chapter 5A.

2 Remove the air cleaner assembly as described in Chapter 4A or 4B.

3 To minimise hydraulic fluid loss, remove the clutch master cylinder reservoir filler cap, then tighten it down onto a piece of polythene to obtain an airtight seal.

4 On diesel models, undo the retaining bolts, release the clips and detach the air intake pipe from the intake manifold – refer to Chapter 4B if necessary.

5 Place absorbent rags around the release cylinder, and be prepared for hydraulic fluid loss.

6 Extract the retaining clip and disconnect the hydraulic hose from the release cylinder.

7 Unscrew the release cylinder mounting bolts, release the cylinder pushrod from the release arm on the transmission, then remove the unit from the engine compartment **(see illustration)**.

8 It is not possible to obtain an overhaul kit from Fiat, however some motor factors may be able to supply one. Follow the instructions with the repair kit if obtained.

Refitting

9 Refitting is the reverse of the removal procedure, but bleed the clutch hydraulic system as described in Section 2 on completion.

3.5 Working under the facia, prise the clutch master cylinder pushrod (arrowed) from the pedal

4.7 External release cylinder mounting bolts (arrowed)

4.11 Release the rubber grommet (arrowed) from the transmission bellhousing

4.12 Concentric release cylinder retaining bolts (arrowed)

5.2 Clutch pedal pivot pin retaining circlip (arrowed)

Concentric internally mounted cylinder

Note 1: *Due to the amount of work necessary to remove and refit clutch components, it is usually considered good practice to renew the clutch friction disc, pressure plate assembly and release cylinder as a matched set, even if only one of these is actually worn enough to require renewal. It is also worth considering the renewal of the clutch components on a preventive basis if the engine and/or transmission have been removed for some other reason.*

Note 2: *Refer to the warning concerning the dangers of asbestos dust at the beginning of Section 6.*

Removal

10 Unless the complete engine/transmission unit is to be removed from the car and separated for major overhaul (see Chapter 2C), the clutch release cylinder can be reached by removing the transmission only, as described in Chapter 7.

11 Prise the square, rubber grommet from where the fluid pipe exits the transmission bellhousing **(see illustration)**.

12 Unscrew the retaining bolts and slide the release cylinder off from the transmission input shaft **(see illustration)**.

13 The release cylinder is a sealed unit and cannot be overhauled. If the cylinder seals are leaking or the release bearing is noisy or rough in operation, then the complete unit must be renewed.

Refitting

14 Ensure the release cylinder and transmission mating surfaces are clean and dry.

15 Carefully ease the cylinder along the input shaft and into position, then refit the release cylinder retaining bolts and tighten them to the specified torque.

16 Refit the square, rubber grommet to the aperture in the bellhousing.

17 Refit the transmission unit as described in Chapter 7.

18 Bleed the clutch hydraulic system as described in Section 2.

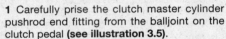

5 Clutch pedal – removal and refitting

1 Carefully prise the clutch master cylinder pushrod end fitting from the balljoint on the clutch pedal **(see illustration 3.5)**.

2 Remove the circlip from the left-hand end of the pivot pin **(see illustration)**.

3 Remove the clutch pedal position sensor (where fitted) as described in Chapter 12.

4 Slide the pivot to the right and remove the pedal.

5 Refitting is a reversal of removal.

6 Clutch assembly – removal, inspection and refitting

Warning: Dust created by clutch wear and deposited on the clutch components may contain asbestos, which is a health hazard. DO NOT blow it out with compressed air, or inhale any of it. DO NOT use petrol or petroleum-based solvents to clean off the dust. Brake system cleaner or methylated spirit should be used to flush the dust into a suitable receptacle. After the clutch components are wiped clean with rags, dispose of the contaminated rags and cleaner in a sealed, marked container.

Removal

1 Unless the complete engine/transmission unit is to be removed from the car and separated for major overhaul (see Chapter 2C), the clutch can be reached by removing the transmission as described in Chapter 7.

2 Before disturbing the clutch, use chalk or a marker pen to mark the relationship of the pressure plate assembly to the flywheel.

3 Progressively unscrew the pressure plate retaining bolts in diagonal sequence by half a turn at a time, until spring pressure is released and the bolts can be unscrewed by hand.

4 Remove the pressure plate assembly and

collect the friction disc, noting which way round the disc is fitted. It is recommended that new pressure plate retaining bolts are obtained.

Inspection

Note: *Due to the amount of work necessary to remove and refit clutch components, it is usually considered good practice to renew the clutch friction disc, pressure plate assembly and release cylinder as a matched set, even if only one of these is actually worn enough to require renewal. It is also worth considering the renewal of the clutch components on a preventive basis if the engine and/or transmission have been removed for some other reason.*

5 When cleaning clutch components, read first the warning at the beginning of this Section; remove dust using a clean, dry cloth, and working in a well-ventilated atmosphere.

6 Check the friction disc facings for signs of wear, damage or oil contamination. If the friction material is cracked, burnt, scored or damaged, or if it is contaminated with oil or grease (shown by shiny black patches), the friction disc must be renewed.

7 If the friction material is still serviceable, check that the centre boss splines are unworn, that the torsion springs are in good condition and securely fastened, and that all the rivets are tight. If any wear or damage is found, the friction disc must be renewed.

8 If the friction material is fouled with oil, this must be due to an oil leak from the crankshaft oil seal, from the sump-to-cylinder block joint, or from the release cylinder assembly (either the main seal or the sealing ring). Renew the crankshaft oil seal or repair the sump joint as described in the appropriate Part of Chapter 2, before installing the new friction disc. The clutch release cylinder is covered in Section 4.

9 Check the pressure plate assembly for obvious signs of wear or damage; shake it to check for loose rivets, or worn or damaged fulcrum rings, and check that the drive straps securing the pressure plate to the cover do not show signs of overheating (such as a deep

6.13 The side marked 'transmission side' or 'Getriebeseite' must point towards the transmission

6.14 Fit the pressure plate assembly over the friction disc

6.16 Centralise the friction disc using a clutch aligning tool or similar

yellow or blue discoloration). If the diaphragm spring is worn or damaged, or if its pressure is in any way suspect, the pressure plate assembly should be renewed.

10 Examine the machined bearing surfaces of the pressure plate and of the flywheel; they should be clean, completely flat, and free from scratches or scoring. If either is discoloured from excessive heat, or shows signs of cracks, it should be renewed – although minor damage of this nature can sometimes be polished away using emery paper.

11 Check that the release cylinder bearing rotates smoothly and easily, with no sign of noise or roughness. Also check that the surface itself is smooth and unworn, with no signs of cracks, pitting or scoring. If there is any doubt about its condition, the clutch

release cylinder should be renewed (it is not possible to renew the bearing separately).

Refitting

12 Lightly grease the teeth of the friction disc hub with high melting-point grease. Do not apply too much, otherwise it may eventually contaminate the friction disc linings.

13 Locate the friction disc on the flywheel, making sure that the lettering 'transmission side' or 'Getriebeseite' points towards the transmission (see illustration).

14 Refit the pressure plate assembly, aligning the marks made on dismantling (if the original pressure plate is re-used). Fit new pressure plate bolts, but tighten them only finger-tight so that the friction disc can still be moved (see illustration).

15 The friction disc must now be centralised

so that, when the transmission is refitted, its input shaft will pass through the splines at the centre of the friction disc.

16 Centralisation can be achieved by passing a screwdriver or other long bar through the friction disc and into the hole in the crankshaft. The friction disc can then be moved around until it is centred on the crankshaft hole. Alternatively, a clutch-aligning tool can be used to eliminate the guesswork; these can be obtained from most accessory shops (see illustration).

17 When the friction disc is centralised, tighten the pressure plate bolts evenly and in a diagonal sequence to the specified torque setting.

18 Refit the transmission as described in Chapter 7.

Chapter 7
Manual transmission

Contents

Degrees of difficulty

Easy, suitable for novice with little experience	Fairly easy, suitable for beginner with some experience	Fairly difficult, suitable for competent DIY mechanic	Difficult, suitable for experienced DIY mechanic	Very difficult, suitable for expert DIY or professional

Specifications

General

Type	Transversely-mounted, front wheel drive layout with integral transaxle differential/final drive. 5 forward speeds, 1 reverse speed
Designation:	
Petrol engines.	C.514
Diesel engines:	
Except 95 bhp (70 kW) models.	C.514R
95 bhp (70 kW) models.	C.510

Lubrication

Recommended oil type	Refer to *Lubricants and fluids*
Capacity	1.65 litres

Torque wrench settings

	Nm	lbf ft
Engine/transmission attachment bolts.	60	44
Engine/transmission mountings:		
Left-hand mounting bracket-to-transmission bolt	50	37
Left hand mounting-to-body nuts/bolt.	50	37
Transmission oil drain plug.	25	18
Transmission oil filler plug	20	15

2.2a Transmission oil filler plug (arrowed) . . .

2.2b . . . and drain plug (arrowed) – C.514 and C.514R transmissions

2.2c Transmission oil filler and drain plugs (arrowed) – C.510 transmission

1 General information

The transmission is contained in a cast-aluminium alloy casing bolted to the engine's left-hand end, and consists of the gearbox and final drive differential.

Drive is transmitted from the crankshaft via the clutch to the input shaft, which has a splined extension to accept the clutch friction plate and rotates in roller bearings at its right-hand end and ball-bearings at its left-hand end. From the input shaft, drive is transmitted to the output shaft which rotates in roller bearings at its right-hand end and ball-bearings at its left-hand end. From the output shaft, the drive is transmitted to the differential crownwheel which rotates with the differential case and gears in taper roller bearings, thus driving the sun gears and driveshafts. The rotation of the differential gears on their shaft allows the inner roadwheel to rotate at a slower speed than the outer roadwheel when the car is cornering.

The input and output shafts are arranged side-by-side, parallel to the crankshaft and driveshafts, so that their gear pinion teeth are in constant mesh. In the neutral position, the relevant input shaft and output shaft gear pinions rotate freely, so that drive cannot be transmitted to the output shaft and crownwheel.

Gear selection is via a floor-mounted lever and twin selector cable mechanism. The selector cables cause the appropriate selector fork to move its respective synchro-sleeve along the shaft, to lock the gear to the synchro-hub. Since the synchro-hubs are splined to the input and output shafts, this locks the gear to the shaft so that drive can be transmitted. To ensure that gearchanging can be made quickly and quietly, a synchromesh system is fitted to all forward gears.

2 Manual transmission oil – draining and refilling

1 Park the vehicle on a level surface, if possible over an inspection pit or on a ramp as the filler/level and drain plugs are accessed from under the engine compartment. If necessary jack up the vehicle and support on axle stands (see *Jacking and vehicle support*).
2 Wipe clean the area around the filler/level and drain plugs, which are on the front and bottom of the transmission (see illustrations).
3 Using an Allen key, unscrew the filler/level plug and clean it.
4 Position a suitable container beneath the transmission, then use the Allen key to unscrew the drain plug. Allow the oil to completely drain.
5 Wipe clean the drain plug then refit and tighten it to the specified torque.
6 Fill the transmission with the correct grade and quantity of oil, referring to Chapter 1A or 1B when checking the level. The oil level should be up to the lower edge of the filler plug opening. Refit and tighten the filler/level plug.
7 Where applicable lower the vehicle to the ground.

3 Gearchange selector cables – removal and refitting

Removal

1 Prise up the gear lever gaiter from the gear lever surround panel (see illustration).

Panda models

2 Remove the lower central panel from the facia as described in Chapter 11.
3 Undo the screws and remove the driver's side footwell kick panel from the side of the centre console (see illustration).

500 models

4 Remove the air cleaner assembly as described in Chapter 4A or 4B.
5 Remove the lower centre facia panel as described in Chapter 11.

All models

6 At the base of the console, undo the bolts and remove the support bracket between the facia crossmember and the floor (see illustration).

3.1 Prise up the gearchange lever gaiter

3.3 Undo the screws (arrowed) and remove the footwell kick panel

3.6 Remove the support bracket (arrowed) between the floor and the crossmember

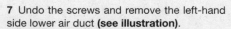

3.7 Remove the left-hand side floor air duct (arrowed)

3.8 Prise the selector cable end fittings from the lever attachments

3.9 Gently prise the neutral sensor linkage from the cable casing

7 Undo the screws and remove the left-hand side lower air duct **(see illustration)**.

8 Disconnect the selector cable end fittings from their attachments at the gear lever linkage **(see illustration)**.

9 Gently prise the neutral sensor linkage from the gearchange cable casing (where fitted) **(see illustration)**.

10 Extract the two retaining clips securing the selector cables to the gear lever housing **(see illustration)**.

11 Remove the battery and battery tray as described in Chapter 5A.

12 Disconnect the selector cable end fittings from their attachments at the transmission selector levers **(see illustration)**.

13 Pull back the collars, and pull the outer cables from the transmission support bracket **(see illustration)**.

14 Firmly apply the handbrake, then jack up the front of the car and support it securely on axle stands (see *Jacking and vehicle support*).

15 Release the gearchange cables from the bracket on the vehicle underside.

16 Release the rubber grommet from the vehicle floor, and manoeuvre the cables from position **(see illustration)**.

Refitting

17 Refitting is a reversal of removal, but before refitting the gear lever control panel, adjust the selector cable as follows. **Note:** *This adjustment procedure doesn't apply to 95 bhp diesel models – no adjustment facility is provided on these models.*

a) *With the transmission in Neutral, depress the selector cable locking clip, then press in the locking catch. This allows the end fitting to slide on the cable **(see illustration)**.*

b) *Place the gear lever in neutral and fit Fiat adjustment tool No 1.871.004.100 between the detent of the reverse inhibitor sleeve and the support barrier. In the absence of the tool, use an 8.0 mm thick spacer between the sleeve and barrier **(see illustration)**.*

c) *Hold the lever against the tool, then release the locking clip.*

d) *Check that all gears can be selected without stiffness or binding. If necessary, repeat the adjustment procedure.*

3.10 Slide out the cable retaining clips

3.12 Use an open-ended spanner to prise the end of the cables from the lever balljoints

3.13 Pull back the collars (arrowed) and detach the outer cables from the transmission bracket

3.16 Prise up the rubber gaiter from the floor – heater housing removed for clarity

3.17a Depress the locking clip, then press in the locking catch

3.17b There must be a gap of 8.0 mm between the reverse inhibitor sleeve and the support barrier

4.2 Gearchange lever/bracket assembly retaining bolt/nuts (arrowed)

5.21 Undo the bolt (arrowed) securing the mounting to the transmission/bracket

4 Gearchange lever assembly – removal and refitting

Removal

1 Disconnect the gearchange cables from the lever assembly as described in Section 3.
2 Undo the retaining bolts/nuts and remove the lever and bracket assembly **(see illustration)**. Where applicable, disconnect the neutral position sensor wiring plug as the assembly is withdrawn.

Refitting

3 Refitting is a reversal of removal.

5 Manual transmission – removal and refitting

Removal

1 Firmly apply the handbrake, then jack up the front of the car and support it securely on axle stands (see *Jacking and vehicle support*).
2 Remove both front wheels, then remove the left-hand wheel arch liner main and centre panels.
3 Remove the air cleaner assembly as described in Chapter 4A.
4 Remove the battery, battery tray and starter motor as described in Chapter 5A.
5 Disconnect the wiring connector from the reversing light switch on the front of the transmission, then unscrew the nut and disconnect the transmission earth lead from the top of the unit.

Diesel models

6 Remove the preheating system control unit as described in Chapter 5A.
7 Release the clamps, undo the retaining bolts, and remove the rigid air pipes to and

from the intercooler – refer to Chapter 4B.
8 On 500 diesel models, remove the electric radiator cooling fan assembly as described in Chapter 3.

All models

9 Disconnect the gearchange selector cable end fittings from the transmission lever ball-studs. Undo the bolts securing the selector cable support bracket to the transmission and move the bracket and cables to one side.
10 On models with an externally mounted release cylinder, unbolt the clutch release cylinder from the top of the transmission then fit a cable-tie around it to prevent the piston from being ejected. Position the cylinder to one side.
11 On models with an internal, concentric release cylinder, prise out the clip and disconnect the clutch fluid pressure pipe at the plastic pipe emerging from the transmission bellhousing – refer to Chapter 6. Plug the openings to prevent contamination.
12 On Panda models, remove the front grille as described in Chapter 11.
13 On 500 models, remove the front bumper as described in Chapter 11.
14 Remove both driveshafts as described in Chapter 8.
15 Detach the exhaust pipe support bracket, then undo the bolts and remove the cover plate (where fitted) from the base of the transmission bellhousing.
16 Working beneath the car, unscrew the bolts and nuts securing the rear engine mounting to the subframe and transmission, and withdraw the mounting.
17 On 500 models, undo the bolts and remove the transmission-to-engine support bracket above the right-hand driveshaft location.
18 Support the weight of the engine using a hoist attached to home-made brackets secured to suitable positions at the left-hand end of the engine.

19 Support the weight of the transmission on a trolley jack then unscrew the engine-to-transmission retaining bolts. Move aside all wiring and support brackets secured by the retaining bolts.
20 Unscrew the central bolt, and slacken the nuts securing the left-hand engine/transmission mounting to the body.
21 Undo the bolts securing the mounting bracket to the end of the transmission casing **(see illustration)**.
22 Check that all pipes, hoses and wiring are moved clear then carefully pull the transmission away from the engine. Lower the trolley jack and remove the transmission from under the car.

⚠ *Warning: Support the transmission to ensure that it remains steady on the jack head. Keep the transmission level until the input shaft is fully withdrawn from the clutch friction plate.*

Refitting

23 Refitting is a reversal of the removal procedure, bearing in mind the following points.
 a) Apply a smear of high-melting-point grease to the clutch friction plate splines; take care to avoid contaminating the friction surfaces.
 b) Tighten all bolts to the specified torque, referring to the Chapters indicated for components not covered in this Chapter.

6 Reversing light switch – testing, removal and refitting

Testing

1 The reversing light circuit is controlled by a plunger-type switch screwed into the front

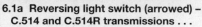

6.1a Reversing light switch (arrowed) –
C.514 and C.514R transmissions . . .

6.1b . . . and C.510 transmission (arrowed)

of the transmission casing **(see illustrations)**. If a fault develops, first ensure that the circuit fuse has not blown.

2 To test the switch, disconnect the wiring connector, and use a multimeter (set to the resistance function) or a battery-and-bulb test circuit to check that there is continuity between the switch terminals only when reverse gear is selected. If this is not the case, and there are no obvious breaks or other damage to the wires, the switch is faulty, and must be renewed.

Removal

3 Remove the battery and battery tray as described in Chapter 5A.
4 Disconnect the wiring connector, then unscrew the switch from the transmission casing.

Refitting

5 Refit and securely tighten the switch, then reconnect the wiring.

6 Refit the battery and tray as described in Chapter 5A.

7 Manual transmission overhaul – general information

Overhauling a manual transmission is a difficult and involved job for the DIY home mechanic. In addition to dismantling and reassembling many small parts, clearances must be precisely measured and, if necessary, changed by selecting shims and spacers. Internal transmission components are also often difficult to obtain, and in many instances, extremely expensive. Because of this, if the transmission develops a fault or becomes noisy, the best course of action is to have the unit overhauled by a specialist repairer, or to obtain an exchange reconditioned unit.

Nevertheless, it is not impossible for the more experienced mechanic to overhaul the transmission, provided the special tools are available, and the job is done in a deliberate step-by-step manner, so that nothing is overlooked.

The tools necessary for an overhaul include internal and external circlip pliers, bearing pullers, a slide hammer, a set of pin punches, a dial test indicator, and possibly a hydraulic press. In addition, a large, sturdy workbench and a vice will be required.

During dismantling of the transmission, make careful notes of how each component is fitted, to make reassembly easier and more accurate.

Before dismantling the transmission, it will help if you have some idea what area is malfunctioning. Certain problems can be closely related to specific areas in the transmission, which can make component examination and renewal easier. Refer to the *Fault finding* in the Reference Chapter for more information.

Chapter 8
Driveshafts

Contents

Degrees of difficulty

Easy, suitable for novice with little experience	**Fairly easy,** suitable for beginner with some experience	**Fairly difficult,** suitable for competent DIY mechanic	**Difficult,** suitable for experienced DIY mechanic	**Very difficult,** suitable for expert DIY or professional

Specifications

General

Type . . . . Unequal-length, solid steel shafts, splined to inner and outer constant velocity joints

Lubrication

Lubricant type . . . . Fiat specification grease (Tutela Allstar) or equivalent
Quantities:
   Wheel side joint 80g
   Differential side joint 100g

Torque wrench settings

	Nm	lbf ft
Driveshaft nut*	240	177
Roadwheel bolts:		
Steel wheel	85	63
Aluminium wheel	98	72
Suspension strut-to-swivel hub bolts	75	55
Track rod end-to-swivel hub nut	34	25

* Use a new nut.

1 General information

Power is transmitted from the differential to the roadwheels by the driveshafts, via inner and outer constant velocity (CV) joints.

The outer ball-and-cage type CV joints allow smooth transmission of drive to the wheels at all steering and suspension angles. Drive is transmitted by means of a number of radially static steel balls that run in grooves between the two halves of the joint.

The inner CV joints are of the tripod type. Drive is transmitted across the joint by means of three rollers, mounted on the driveshaft in a tripod arrangement, that are radially static but are free to slide in the grooved joint body.

The joints are protected by rubber gaiters, and are packed with grease to provide permanent lubrication. If wear is detected in the joint, it can be detached from the driveshaft and renewed. Normally, the CV joints do not require additional lubrication, unless they have been overhauled or the rubber gaiters have been damaged, allowing the grease to become contaminated. Refer to Chapter 1A or 1B for guidance in checking the condition of the driveshaft gaiters.

Both driveshafts are splined at their outer

2.7a Pull the swivel hub outwards at the top . . .

2.2 Tap up the staking securing the driveshaft retaining nut in position

ends, to accept the wheel hubs, and are threaded so that the hubs can be fastened to the driveshafts by means of a staked nut.

2 Driveshafts – removal and refitting

Note: *A balljoint separator tool will be required for this operation.*

Removal

1 Firmly apply the handbrake, then jack up the front of the car and support it securely on axle stands (see *Jacking and vehicle support*). Remove the appropriate roadwheel(s).

2 Using a hammer and chisel or similar tool, tap up the staking securing the driveshaft retaining nut in position **(see illustration)**.

3 The front wheel hub must be held stationary in order to loosen the driveshaft nut. Ideally, the hub should be held by a suitable tool bolted into place using two of the roadwheel bolts **(see Tool Tip)**. Alternatively, have an assistant firmly apply the footbrake to prevent the hub from rotating. Using a socket and extension bar, slacken and remove the driveshaft retaining nut.

⚠️ *Warning: The nut is extremely tight. Discard the nut – a new one must be used on refitting.*

HAYNES HiNT

H30004

A tool to hold the front hub stationary whilst the driveshaft nut is slackened can be fabricated from two lengths of steel strip (one long, one short) and a nut and bolt; the nut and bolt forming the pivot of a forked tool.

4 Release the brake caliper hydraulic hose (and, where applicable, the ABS wheel speed sensor cable and pad wear indicator sensor cable) from the brackets at the base of the suspension strut.

5 Unscrew the nut securing the track rod end to the swivel hub. Release the track rod end tapered shank using a balljoint separator tool.

6 Unscrew the two nuts and remove the bolts securing the top of the swivel hub to the base of the suspension strut. Note that the bolts are inserted from the rear.

7 Pull the swivel hub outwards at the top and withdraw the driveshaft outer constant velocity joint from the hub assembly **(see illustrations)**. If necessary, the joint can be tapped out of the hub using a soft-faced mallet. Support the end of the driveshaft – do not allow the end of the driveshaft to hang down as this will strain the joint components and gaiters.

Right-hand driveshaft with intermediate bearing

8 Undo the 3 bolts securing the intermediate bearing plate **(see illustration)**.

2.7b . . . and withdraw the driveshaft outer constant velocity joint from the hub assembly

2.8 The intermediate bearing is secured by 3 bolts (arrowed)

2.9a Gently tap the driveshaft and intermediate bearing from place

2.9b Recover the washer from the differential side of the driveshaft

9 Using a block of wood, carefully tap the driveshaft housing and bearing from place. Recover the rubber washer from the driveshaft as it's withdrawn **(see illustrations)**.

All other driveshafts

10 Insert a lever between the inner joint and the differential casing, and prise the driveshaft from place **(see illustration)**. Be prepared for oil spillage.

11 Remove the driveshaft from under the vehicle.

12 Loosely refit one of the strut lower mounting bolts to support the swivel hub while the driveshaft is removed.

Refitting

13 After removing the temporarily-fitted bolt from the strut mounting, pivot the swivel hub away from the car and engage the inner joint with the differential and the outer CV joint into the hub. On driveshafts with an intermediate bearing, feed the end of the driveshaft through the bearing housing, then refit the rubber washer before engaging it with the differential.

14 Screw on the new driveshaft retaining nut, but do not tighten it at this stage.

15 Refit and tighten the intermediate bearing bolts where applicable.

16 Refit the suspension strut-to-swivel hub bolts and tighten them to the specified torque.

17 Engage the track rod end with the swivel hub, refit the retaining nut and tighten the nut to the specified torque.

18 Refit the brake caliper hydraulic hose (and, where applicable, the ABS wheel speed sensor cable) to the bracket on the base of the suspension strut.

19 Using the method employed on removal to prevent rotation of the hub, tighten the driveshaft retaining nut to the specified torque. Secure the nut by tapping the staking into the grooves in the end of the CV joint using a hammer and chisel **(see illustration)**.

20 Refit the roadwheel and lower the car to the ground.

2.10 Lever between the inner joint and the differential casing

2.19 Stake the nut using a hammer and chisel

---

3   Driveshaft overhaul and rubber gaiter renewal

Outer joint

1 Remove the driveshaft as described in Section 2.

2 Release the rubber gaiter retaining clips by cutting them off with a pair of side-cutters **(see illustration)**. Remove the clips and slide the gaiter down the driveshaft away from the CV joint.

3 The outer joint is secured to the driveshaft by an external circlip. Use a soft metal drift

to drive the inner spider from the end of the driveshaft **(see illustration)**.

4 Slide the old gaiter off the end of the driveshaft.

5 With the constant velocity joint removed from the driveshaft, thoroughly clean the joint using paraffin, or a suitable solvent, and dry it thoroughly. Carry out a visual inspection of the joint.

6 Move the inner splined driving member from side-to-side, to expose each ball in turn at the top of its track. Examine the balls for cracks, flat spots, or signs of surface pitting.

7 Inspect the ball tracks on the inner and outer members. If the tracks have

3.2 Cut-through the clips securing the old rubber gaiter

3.3 Drive the inner spider from the end of the driveshaft

3.9a Slide the small clip onto the driveshaft, followed by the new gaiter . . .

3.9b . . . and the large clip

3.10 Renew the circlip on the end of the driveshaft

3.11 Pack the joint with the specified grease

3.14 Pliers are available specifically to fit/compress driveshaft boot clips

widened, the balls will no longer be a tight fit. At the same time, check the ball cage windows for wear or cracking between the windows.

8 If any of the constant velocity joint components are found to be worn or damaged, it will be necessary to renew the complete joint assembly as the internal parts are not available separately. If the joint is in satisfactory condition, obtain a new gaiter, retaining clips, circlip, and the correct type of grease. These components are all available

individually from Fiat dealers, but may be supplied as a complete repair kit from other sources.

9 Slide the smaller gaiter securing clip onto the driveshaft, followed by the gaiter and the large securing clip **(see illustrations)**. Note that the closed end of the clips must point in the direction of rotation (when the vehicle moves forwards).

10 Renew the circlip on the end of the shaft **(see illustration)**.

11 Pack the CV joint with the specified

grease, then twist the joint to ensure that all the recesses are filled **(see illustration)**.

12 Fit the CV joint to the driveshaft, and engage it with the shaft splines. Use a mallet to tap the joint onto the shaft until the circlip engages correctly.

13 Fill the gaiter with any remaining grease then slide the large end of the gaiter into position over the joint, ensuring that it is seated squarely over the joint body.

14 Locate the large securing clip over the gaiter and secure the clip in place by compressing the raised portion **(see illustration)**.

15 Check that the smaller end of the gaiter is located in the driveshaft groove then, using a small screwdriver, lift the lip of the gaiter to expel any air trapped inside **(see illustration)**.

16 Slide the smaller securing clip over the gaiter, and secure it as described previously **(see illustration)**.

17 Refit the driveshaft as described in Section 2.

Inner joint

18 Remove the driveshaft as described in Section 2.

19 Release the gaiter smaller and larger clips

3.15 Lift the inner lip to equalise air pressure in the boot

3.16 Fit and compress the smaller gaiter retaining clip

3.20a Pull back the gaiter . . .

3.20b . . . and slide the tripod from the end of the driveshaft

3.22 Remove the circlip (arrowed)

3.23 Make alignment marks between the tripod and shaft

3.27 The side of the tripod with the chamfer (arrowed) must fit against the driveshaft – not the circlip

3.28 Pack the joint with the specified grease

by cutting them off with a pair of side-cutters **(see illustration 3.2)**.

20 Pull back the gaiter and slide the outer housing from the tripod joint **(see illustrations)**.

21 Wipe off the excess grease from the tripod and the end of the driveshaft.

22 Using circlip pliers, remove the circlip securing the tripod to the end of the driveshaft **(see illustration)**. Discard the circlip – a new one should be used on refitting.

23 Make alignment marks between the tripod and the shaft, then withdraw the tripod and the gaiter from the end of the driveshaft **(see illustration)**.

24 Thoroughly clean the tripod and rollers, and the end of the driveshaft using paraffin, or a suitable solvent, and dry thoroughly. Carry out a visual inspection of the joint and renew any components as necessary. If the joint is in satisfactory condition, obtain a new gaiter, circlip, retaining clips, and the correct type of grease. These components are all available individually from Fiat dealers, but may be supplied as a complete repair kit from other sources.

25 Commence reassembly by sliding the smaller gaiter securing clip onto the driveshaft, followed by the gaiter.

26 Check that the gaiter is located in the driveshaft groove, then fit the securing clip

over the gaiter and secure the clip in place by compressing the raised portion.

27 Refit the tripod and fit a new circlip to secure the tripod to the driveshaft. Note the slight chamfer on the driveshaft side of the tripod **(see illustration)**.

28 Pack the specified grease around the tripod rollers and into the joint body **(see illustration)**.

29 Slide on the outer housing, position the gaiter and secure the outer clip in place by compressing the raised portion **(see illustration 3.14)**.

30 Refit the driveshaft as described in Section 2.

Chapter 9
Braking system

Contents

Degrees of difficulty

Easy, suitable for novice with little experience	Fairly easy, suitable for beginner with some experience	Fairly difficult, suitable for competent DIY mechanic	Difficult, suitable for experienced DIY mechanic	Very difficult, suitable for expert DIY or professional

Specifications

Front disc brakes

Type:	
Petrol models	Solid disc with single-piston sliding calipers
Diesel models	Ventilated disc with single-piston calipers
Disc diameter	240.0 mm
Disc thickness (new):	
Solid discs	10.8 to 11.1 mm
Ventilated discs	19.9 to 20.1 mm
Minimum disc thickness (wear limit):	
Solid discs	9.2 mm
Ventilated discs	18.2 mm
Maximum disc runout	0.15 mm
Brake pad friction material minimum thickness	1.5 mm

Rear drum brakes

Drum inner diameter (new)	180.0 to 180.2 mm
Maximum drum diameter (wear limit)	181.3 mm
Minimum brake shoe lining thickness	2.0 mm

Torque wrench settings

	Nm	lbf ft
Bleed screw	6	4
Brake disc screw	10	7
Brake drum locating studs	12	9
Brake pipe and hose unions	14	10
Front caliper:		
Guide pin bolts	27	20
Mounting bracket-to-swivel hub bolts:		
M10	60	44
M12	100	74
Rear wheel cylinder mounting bolts	10	7
Roadwheel bolts:		
Steel wheel	85	63
Aluminium wheel	98	72
Vacuum pump bolts	20	15

1 General information

The braking system is of the vacuum servo-assisted, dual-circuit hydraulic type. The arrangement of the hydraulic system is such that each circuit operates one front and one rear brake from a tandem master cylinder. Under normal circumstances, both circuits operate in unison. However, in the event of hydraulic failure in one circuit, full braking force will still be available at two diagonally-opposite wheels.

All models covered in this manual are fitted with front disc brakes and rear drum brakes. An anti-lock braking system (ABS) is fitted as standard to certain models and is offered as an option on all other models (refer to Section 17 for further information on ABS operation).

The front disc brakes are actuated by single-piston sliding type calipers, which ensure that equal pressure is applied to each brake pad.

The rear drum brakes incorporate leading and trailing shoes, which are actuated by twin-piston wheel cylinders. A self-adjust mechanism is incorporated, to automatically compensate for brake shoe wear. As the brake shoe linings wear, the footbrake operation automatically operates the adjuster mechanism to reduce the lining-to-drum clearance.

The mechanical handbrake linkage operates the brake shoes via a lever attached to the trailing brake shoe.

On models without ABS, load-sensitive proportioning valves operate on the rear brake hydraulic circuits, to prevent the possibility of the rear wheels locking before the front wheels under heavy braking. On models equipped with ABS, the hydraulic pressure applied to the rear brakes is regulated by the ABS hydraulic modulator under all braking conditions. On these models, the load-sensitive proportioning valves are not used.

Note: *When servicing any part of the system, work carefully and methodically; also observe scrupulous cleanliness when overhauling any part of the hydraulic system. Always renew components (in axle sets, where applicable) if in doubt about their condition, and use only genuine Fiat parts, or at least those of known good quality. Note the warnings given in 'Safety first!' and at relevant points in this Chapter concerning the dangers of asbestos dust and hydraulic fluid.*

2 Hydraulic system – bleeding

⚠ *Warning: Hydraulic fluid is poisonous; wash off immediately and thoroughly in the case of skin contact, and seek immediate*

medical advice if any fluid is swallowed, or gets into the eyes. Certain types of hydraulic fluid are inflammable, and may ignite when allowed into contact with hot components. When servicing any hydraulic system, it is safest to assume that the fluid IS inflammable, and to take precautions against the risk of fire as though it is petrol that is being handled. Hydraulic fluid is also an effective paint stripper, and will attack plastics; if any is spilt, it should be washed off immediately, using copious quantities of fresh water. Finally, it is hygroscopic (it absorbs moisture from the air) – old fluid may be contaminated and unfit for further use. When topping-up or renewing the fluid, always use the recommended type, and ensure that it comes from a freshly-opened sealed container.

Models without ABS

General

1 The correct operation of any hydraulic system is only possible after removing all air from the components and circuit; and this is achieved by bleeding the system.

2 During the bleeding procedure, add only clean, unused hydraulic fluid of the recommended type; never re-use fluid that has already been bled from the system. Ensure that sufficient fluid is available before starting work.

3 If there is any possibility of incorrect fluid being already in the system, the brake components and circuit must be flushed completely with uncontaminated, correct fluid, and new seals should be fitted throughout the system.

4 If hydraulic fluid has been lost from the system, or air has entered because of a leak, ensure that the fault is cured before proceeding further.

5 Park the car on level ground, switch off the engine and select first or reverse gear, then chock the wheels and release the handbrake.

6 Check that all pipes and hoses are secure, unions tight and bleed screws closed. Remove the dust caps (where applicable), and clean any dirt from around the bleed screws.

7 Unscrew the master cylinder reservoir cap, and top the master cylinder reservoir up to the MAX level line; refit the cap loosely. Remember to maintain the fluid level at least above the MIN level line throughout the procedure, otherwise there is a risk of further air entering the system.

8 There are a number of one-man, do-it-yourself brake bleeding kits currently available from motor accessory shops. It is recommended that one of these kits is used whenever possible, as they greatly simplify the bleeding operation, and also reduce the risk of expelled air and fluid being drawn back into the system. If such a kit is not available, the basic (two-man) method must be used, which is described in detail below.

9 If a kit is to be used, prepare the vehicle as described previously, and follow the kit manufacturer's instructions, as the procedure may vary slightly according to the type being

used; generally, they are as outlined below in the relevant sub-section.

10 Whichever method is used, the same sequence must be followed (paragraphs 11 and 12) to ensure the removal of all air from the system.

Bleeding sequence

11 If the system has been only partially disconnected, and suitable precautions were taken to minimise fluid loss, it should be necessary to bleed only that part of the system (ie, the primary or secondary circuit).

12 If the complete system is to be bled, then it should be done working in the following sequence:
   a) Left-hand rear wheel.
   b) Right-hand front wheel.
   c) Right-hand rear wheel.
   d) Left-hand front wheel.

Basic (two-man) bleeding method

13 Collect a clean glass jar, a suitable length of plastic or rubber tubing which is a tight fit over the bleed screw, and a ring spanner to fit the screw. The help of an assistant will also be required.

14 Remove the dust cap from the first screw in the sequence if not already done. Fit a suitable spanner and tube to the screw, place the other end of the tube in the jar, and pour in sufficient fluid to cover the end of the tube.

15 Ensure that the master cylinder reservoir fluid level is maintained at least above the MIN level line throughout the procedure.

16 Have the assistant fully depress the brake pedal several times to build-up pressure, then maintain it on the final downstroke.

17 While pedal pressure is maintained, unscrew the bleed screw (approximately one turn) and allow the compressed fluid and air to flow into the jar. The assistant should maintain pedal pressure, following the pedal down to the floor if necessary, and should not release the pedal until instructed to do so. When the flow stops, tighten the bleed screw again, have the assistant release the pedal slowly, and recheck the reservoir fluid level.

18 Repeat the steps given in paragraphs 16 and 17 until the fluid emerging from the bleed screw is free from air bubbles. If the master cylinder has been drained and refilled, and air is being bled from the first screw in the sequence, allow approximately five seconds between cycles for the master cylinder passages to refill.

19 When no more air bubbles appear, tighten the bleed screw securely, remove the tube and spanner, and refit the dust cap (where applicable). Do not overtighten the bleed screw.

20 Repeat the procedure on the remaining screws in the sequence, until all air is removed from the system, and the brake pedal feels firm again.

Bleeding using a one-way valve kit

21 As their name implies, these kits consist of a length of tubing with a one-way valve fitted to prevent expelled air and fluid being drawn back into the system; some kits include a translucent container, which can be positioned

2.22 Using a one-way valve kit to bleed the rear brake

so that the air bubbles can be more easily seen flowing from the end of the tube.

22 The kit is connected to the bleed screw, which is then opened **(see illustration)**. The user returns to the driver's seat, depresses the brake pedal with a smooth, steady stroke, and slowly releases it; this is repeated until the expelled fluid is clear of air bubbles.

23 Note that these kits simplify work so much that it is easy to forget the master cylinder reservoir fluid level; ensure that this is maintained at least above the MIN level line at all times.

Bleeding using a pressure-bleeding kit

24 These kits are usually operated by the reservoir of pressurised air contained in the spare tyre. However, note that it will probably be necessary to reduce the pressure to a lower level than normal; refer to the instructions supplied with the kit.

25 By connecting a pressurised, fluid-filled container to the master cylinder reservoir, bleeding can be carried out simply by opening each screw in turn (in the specified sequence), and allowing the fluid to flow out until no more air bubbles can be seen in the expelled fluid.

26 This method has the advantage that the large reservoir of fluid provides an additional safeguard against air being drawn into the system during bleeding.

27 Pressure-bleeding is particularly effective when bleeding 'difficult' systems, or when bleeding the complete system at the time of routine fluid renewal.

All methods

28 When bleeding is complete, and firm pedal feel is restored, wash off any spilt fluid, tighten the bleed screws securely, and refit their dust caps (where applicable).

29 Check the hydraulic fluid level in the master cylinder reservoir, and top-up if necessary.

30 Discard any hydraulic fluid that has been bled from the system; it will not be fit for re-use.

31 Check the feel of the brake pedal. If it feels at all spongy, air must still be present in the system, and further bleeding is required. Failure to bleed satisfactorily after a reasonable repetition of the bleeding procedure may be due to worn master cylinder seals.

Models with ABS

 Warning: On models equipped with ABS, ensure that the ignition is switched off before starting the bleeding procedure, to avoid any possibility of voltage being applied to the hydraulic modulator before the bleeding procedure is completed. Ideally, the battery should be disconnected. If voltage is applied to the modulator before the bleeding procedure is complete, this will effectively drain the hydraulic fluid in the modulator, rendering the unit unserviceable. Do not, therefore, attempt to 'run' the modulator in order to bleed the brakes.

32 A pressure-bleeding kit must be used for bleeding the hydraulic system on ABS models – see paragraphs 24 to 27.

33 Following the sequence given in paragraph 12, bleed each brake in turn until clean fluid, free of air bubbles, is seen to emerge. Pause between bleeding each brake to ensure that the fluid level in the reservoir is above the MIN level.

34 When bleeding is complete, and firm pedal feel is restored, wash off any spilt fluid, tighten the bleed screws, and refit their dust caps.

35 Check the hydraulic fluid level in the master cylinder reservoir, and top-up if necessary.

36 Discard any fluid that has been bled from the system; it will not be fit for re-use.

37 Check the feel of the brake pedal. If it feels at all spongy, air must still be present in the system, and further bleeding is required.

 Warning: Do not operate the vehicle if you are in doubt about the effectiveness of the braking system. If considerable air was present in the system prior to bleeding, it is possible for some of this air to remain trapped in the hydraulic modulator. If the pedal continues to feel spongy after repeated bleedings, or if any of the brake system warning lights remain on, have the vehicle towed to a Fiat dealer to be bled with the use of Fiat diagnostic equipment.

3 Hydraulic pipes and hoses – renewal

 Warning: Before starting work, refer to the warning at the beginning of Section 2 concerning the dangers of hydraulic fluid.

1 If any pipe or hose is to be renewed, minimise fluid loss by first removing the master cylinder reservoir cap, then tighten the cap down onto a piece of polythene to obtain an airtight seal. Alternatively, flexible hoses can be sealed, if required, using a proprietary brake hose clamp; metal brake pipe unions can be plugged (if care is taken not to allow dirt into the system) or capped immediately

they are disconnected. Place a wad of rag under any union that is to be disconnected, to catch any spilt fluid.

2 If a flexible hose is to be disconnected, unscrew the brake pipe union nut before removing the spring clip which secures the hose to its mounting bracket.

3 To unscrew the union nuts, it is preferable to obtain a brake pipe spanner of the correct size; these are available from most large motor accessory shops. Failing this, a close-fitting open-ended spanner will be required, though if the nuts are tight or corroded, their flats may be rounded-off if the spanner slips. In such a case, a self-locking wrench is often the only way to unscrew a stubborn union, but it follows that the pipe and the damaged nuts must be renewed on reassembly. Always clean a union and surrounding area before disconnecting it. If disconnecting a component with more than one union, make a careful note of the connections before disturbing any of them.

4 If a brake pipe is to be renewed, it can be obtained, cut to length and with the union nuts and end flares in place, from Fiat dealers. All that is then necessary is to bend it to shape, following the line of the original, before fitting it to the vehicle. Alternatively, most motor accessory shops can make up brake pipes from kits, but this requires very careful measurement of the original, to ensure that the new one is of the correct length. The safest answer is usually to take the original to the shop as a pattern.

5 On refitting, do not overtighten the union nuts. It is not necessary to exercise brute force to obtain a sound joint.

6 Ensure that the pipes and hoses are correctly routed, with no kinks, and that they are secured in the clips or brackets provided. After fitting, remove the polythene from the reservoir, and bleed the hydraulic system as described in Section 2. Wash off any spilt fluid, and check carefully for fluid leaks.

4 Front brake pads – renewal

 Warning: Renew both sets of front brake pads at the same time – never renew the pads on only one wheel, as uneven braking may result. Note that the dust created by wear of the pads may contain asbestos, which is a health hazard. Never blow it out with compressed air, and don't inhale any of it. An approved filtering mask should be worn when working on the brakes. DO NOT use petrol or petroleum-based solvents to clean brake parts; use brake cleaner or methylated spirit only.

1 Apply the handbrake, then slacken the front roadwheel bolts. Jack up the front of the vehicle and support it on axle stands (see *Jacking and vehicle support*). Remove both front roadwheels.

2 Two different designs of front caliper may be fitted. Follow the relevant accompanying photos for the actual pad renewal procedure. Diesel models are fitted with ventilated front discs **(from illustration 4.2v)**, and petrol models with solid discs **(from illustration 4.2a)**. Be sure to stay in order and read the caption under each illustration, and note the following points:

a) *New pads may have an adhesive foil on the backplates. Remove this foil prior to installation.*

b) *Gently clean the caliper guide surfaces, and apply a little brake assembly grease.*

c) *When pushing the caliper piston back to accommodate new pads, keep a close eye on the fluid level in the reservoir.*

4.2a Slide the brake pad wear sensor wiring plug (arrowed) upwards from the mounting bracket and disconnect it. Note that a wear sensor is only fitted to the left-hand caliper

4.2b Unclip the wear sensor wiring from the bracket

4.2c Pull out the retaining clip . . .

4.2d . . . and slide out the lower mounting pin

4.2e Pivot the caliper upwards . . .

4.2f . . . and secure it to the suspension spring to prevent straining the hose

4.2g Remove the inner brake pad . . .

4.2h . . . and pull out the wear sensor

4.2i Remove the outer brake pad

4.2j Measure the thickness of the friction material. If it's less than 1.5 mm, renew all 4 pads

4.2k Clean the caliper guide surfaces with a soft brush and some brake cleaner

4.2l Fit the outer brake pad. Ensure the fiction material is against the disc surface . . .

4.2m . . . followed by the inner pad

4.2n Fit the wear sensor (arrowed) to the inner brake pad

4.2o Use a piston retraction tool to force the piston back into the caliper body. Keep an eye on the fluid level in the master cylinder reservoir

4.2p Lower the caliper over the pads

4.2q Apply a little anti-seize grease to the pin, then slide it through the holes in the bracket and caliper . . .

4.2r . . . and secure it with the retaining clip (arrowed)

4.2s Fit the wiring retaining clip to the bracket . . .

4.2t . . . reconnect the wiring plug . . .

4.2u . . . and slide it onto the bracket

4.2v On diesel models, disconnect the brake pad wear sensor wiring plug . . .

4.2w . . . slide the plug up from the bracket . . .

4.2x . . . and release the wiring. The sensor is only fitted to the left-hand caliper

4.2y Remove the caliper lower guide pin bolt (arrowed) . . .

4.2z . . . and pivot the caliper upwards

4.2aa Secure the caliper to prevent it swinging down

4.2ab Remove the inner brake pad . . .

4.2ac . . . followed by the outer brake pad

4.2ad Prise up the shims from the caliper upper and lower mounting points on the bracket

4.2ae Measure the thickness of the friction material. If it's less than 1.5 mm, renew all 4 pads

4.2af Clean the caliper mounting surfaces with a soft brush and some brake cleaner

4.2ag Use a piston retraction tool to force the piston back into the caliper body. Keep an eye on the fluid level in the master cylinder reservoir

4.2ah Fit the shims to the lower mounting points . . .

4.2ai . . . and the upper mounting points

4.2aj Fit the outer brake pads, ensuring the friction material is against the disc surface . . .

4.2ak . . . followed by the inner brake pad (with wear indicator (arrowed) – left-hand side caliper only)

4.2al Lower the caliper over the pads . . .

4.2am . . . fit the lower guide pin bolt . . .

4.2an . . . and tighten it to the specified torque

4.2ao Secure the wear sensor wiring . . .

4.2ap . . . slide the plug onto the bracket . . .

4.2aq . . . and reconnect it

3 Depress the brake pedal repeatedly, until the pads are pressed into firm contact with the brake disc, and normal (non-assisted) pedal pressure is restored.
4 Repeat the above procedure on the remaining front brake caliper.
5 Apply the little anti-seize grease to the hub surface, then refit the roadwheels, lower the vehicle to the ground and tighten the roadwheel bolts to the specified torque.
6 Check the hydraulic fluid level as described in *Weekly checks*.
Caution: New pads will not give full braking efficiency until they have bedded-in. Be prepared for this, and avoid hard braking as far as possible for the first hundred miles or so after pad renewal.

5 Front brake caliper – removal, overhaul and refitting

⚠ *Warning: Before starting work, refer to the warnings at the beginning of Sections 2 and 4 concerning the dangers of hydraulic fluid and asbestos dust.*

Removal

1 Firmly apply the handbrake, then jack up the front of the car and support it securely on axle stands (see *Jacking and vehicle support*). Remove the appropriate front roadwheel.

2 Remove the brake pads as described in Section 4.
3 To minimise fluid loss during the following operations, remove the master cylinder reservoir filler cap, then tighten it down onto a piece of polythene, to obtain an airtight seal. Alternatively, use a brake hose clamp to seal off the flexible hydraulic hose running to the caliper.

⚠ *Warning: Do not use an ordinary G-clamp or mole grips for this purpose, as these can easily damage the hydraulic hose internally, possibly leading to failure.*

4 Clean the area surrounding the brake hose union, then slacken the union half a turn. It won't be possible to separate the union completely without twisting the hose at this stage.
5 Unscrew the caliper upper guide pin bolt, or slide out the upper pin, and remove the caliper body from the mounting bracket.
6 Hold the brake hose and rotate the caliper to unscrew the hose union from the caliper body. Cover the open ends of the union and the caliper fluid inlet, to prevent dirt ingress. Alternatively, the flexible brake hose may be separated from the rigid brake pipe at the bracket mounted on the inner wheel arch.
7 If desired, the caliper mounting bracket can be removed from the swivel hub after

5.7 Brake caliper mounting bracket bolts (arrowed)

unscrewing the two securing bolts **(see illustration)**.

Overhaul

Note: *Before commencing work, ensure that the appropriate caliper overhaul kit is obtained.*

8 With the caliper on the bench, wipe away all traces of dust and dirt, but *avoid inhaling the dust, as it is a health hazard.*

9 Place a small block of wood between the caliper body and the piston, to act as padding. Remove the piston by applying a jet of low pressure compressed air (such as that produced by a tyre foot pump) to the fluid inlet port.

⚠ *Warning: Protect your hands and eyes when using compressed air in this manner – brake fluid may be ejected under pressure when the piston is released.*

10 Peel the dust seal from the piston, then use a soft, blunt instrument (such as a knitting needle) to extract the piston seal from the caliper bore.

11 Thoroughly clean all components, using only methylated spirit or clean hydraulic fluid. Never use mineral-based solvents such as petrol or paraffin, which will attack the hydraulic system rubber components.

12 The caliper piston seal, the dust seal and the bleed nipple dust cap are only available as part of a seal kit. Since the manufacturers recommend that the piston seal and dust seal are renewed whenever they are disturbed, all of these components should be discarded on disassembly and new ones fitted on reassembly as a matter of course.

13 Carefully examine all parts of the caliper assembly, looking for signs of wear or damage. In particular, the cylinder bore and piston must be free from any signs of scratches, corrosion or wear. If there is any doubt about the condition of any part of the caliper, the relevant part should be renewed. Note that the piston surface is plated, and **must not** be polished with emery or similar abrasives to remove corrosion or scratches. In addition, the pistons are matched to the caliper bores and can only be renewed as a part of a complete caliper assembly.

14 Check that the threads in the caliper body and the mounting bracket are in good

condition. Check that the guide pin(s) are undamaged, and (when cleaned) a reasonably tight sliding fit in the mounting bracket bores.

15 Use compressed air to blow clear the fluid passages.

⚠ *Warning: Wear eye protection when using compressed air.*

16 Before commencing reassembly, ensure that all components are spotlessly-clean and dry.

17 Soak the new piston seal in clean hydraulic fluid, and fit it to the groove in the cylinder bore, using your fingers only (no tools) to manipulate it into place.

18 Fit the new dust seal inner lip to the cylinder groove, smear clean hydraulic fluid over the piston and caliper cylinder bore, and twist the piston into the dust seal. Press the piston squarely into the cylinder, then slide the dust seal outer lip to the groove in the piston.

Refitting

19 Where applicable, refit the caliper mounting bracket to the hub carrier. Coat the threads of the mounting bolts with thread-locking compound, then tighten them to the specified torque.

20 Hold the brake hose and rotate the caliper to screw the hose union back into the caliper body.

21 Place the caliper in position on the mounting bracket and tighten the caliper upper guide pin bolt to the specified torque, where applicable.

22 Refit the brake pads as described in Section 4.

23 On all models, tighten the brake hose-to-caliper union securely.

24 Check that the caliper slides smoothly on its guide pins.

25 Remove the polythene from the master cylinder reservoir filler cap, or remove the clamp from the fluid hose, as applicable.

26 Bleed the hydraulic fluid circuit as described in Section 2. Note that if no other part of the system has been disturbed, it should only be necessary to bleed the relevant front circuit.

27 Depress the brake pedal repeatedly to bring the pads into contact with the brake disc, and ensure that normal pedal pressure is restored.

28 Refit the roadwheel, and lower the car to the ground.

---

6 Brake disc – inspection, removal and refitting

Inspection

1 Firmly apply the handbrake, then jack up the front of the car and support it securely on axle stands (see *Jacking and vehicle support*). Remove the front roadwheels.

2 Rotate the brake disc by hand and examine

the whole of the surface area swept by the brake pads, on both sides of the disc. **Note:** *It will be necessary to remove the front brake pads to allow an adequate inspection of the disc's inner surface; refer to Section 4 for details.*

3 Typically, the disc surface will have a polished appearance and should be free from heavy scoring. Smooth rippling is produced by normal operation and does not indicate excessive wear. Deep scoring and cracks, however, are indications of more serious damage in need of correction.

4 If deep scoring is discovered, it may be possible to have the disc reground to restore the surface, depending on the extent of the damage. To determine whether this is a feasible course of action, it will be necessary to measure the thickness of the disc, as described later.

5 Check the whole surface of the disc for cracks, particularly around the roadwheel bolt holes. A cracked disc must be renewed.

6 A ridge of rust and brake dust at the inner and outer edges of the disc, beyond the pad contact area, is normal – this can be scraped away quite easily.

7 Raised ridges caused by the brake pads eroding the disc material, however, are an indication of excessive wear. If close examination reveals such ridges, the thickness of the disc must be measured, to assess whether it is still fit for use.

8 To measure the thickness of the disc, take readings at several points on the surface using a micrometer, in the area swept by the brake pads **(see illustration)**. Include any points where the disc has been scored; align the jaws of the micrometer with the deepest area of scoring, to get a true indication of the extent of the wear. Compare these measurements with the limits listed in the *Specifications*. If the disc has worn below its minimum thickness, at any point, it must be renewed.

9 If the discs are suspected of causing brake judder, check the disc runout, using one of the following methods:

DTI gauge runout measurement

10 Refit the four roadwheel bolts, together with one M14 plain washer per bolt – this will ensure adequate disc-to-hub contact. Tighten the bolts securely.

6.8 Measure the thickness of the disc using a micrometer

6.11 Use a dial test indicator (DTI) to measure brake disc runout

11 Clamp the DTI gauge to a stand and attach the stand, preferably via a magnetic base, to the strut mounting bracket. Align the gauge so that its pointer rests upon the area of the disc swept by the brake pads, on an arc 2.0 mm from the outer edge of the disc **(see illustration)**.

12 Zero the gauge and slowly rotate the disc through one revolution, observing the pointer movement. Note the maximum deflection recorded and compare the figure with that listed in *Specifications*.

Feeler blade runout measurement

13 Use the feeler blades to measure the clearance between the disc and a convenient fixed point, such as the caliper mounting bracket. Rotate the disc and measure the variation in clearance at several points around the disc. Compare the maximum figure with that listed in *Specifications*.

14 If the disc runout is outside of its specified tolerance, first check that the hub is not worn (see *Steering and suspension check* in Chapter 1A or 1B). If the hub is in good condition, remove the disc (as described later in this Section), rotate it through 180° and refit it. This may improve the seating and eradicate the excessive runout.

15 If the runout is still unacceptable, then it may be possible to restore the disc by regrinding; consult your Fiat dealer or a machine shop for a professional opinion – it may prove more economical to purchase a new disc. If the disc cannot be reground, then it must be renewed.

7.2 Undo the studs (arrowed) and remove the drum

6.18 Undo the studs (arrowed) and remove the disc

Removal

16 Mark the relationship between the disc and the hub with chalk or a marker pen, to allow correct refitting.

17 To allow the disc to be removed, undo the two bolts securing the brake caliper mounting bracket to the swivel hub **(see illustration 5.7)**. Withdraw the brake caliper and mounting bracket assembly, complete with brake pads, from the swivel hub, and suspend it from a rigid point on the suspension, using wire or a cable-tie. Do not allow it to hang unsupported as this will strain the brake hose.

18 Slacken and remove the disc locating studs. Support the disc as you do this and lift it off as it becomes free **(see illustration)**.

19 Remove the polished glaze from the surface of the disc with sand/emery paper. Use small, circular motions to avoid producing a directional finish on the surface.

Refitting

20 If a new disc is being fitted, remove the protective coating from the surface using an appropriate solvent.

21 Locate the disc on the hub so that the roadwheel bolt and locating stud holes are all correctly lined up; use the alignment marks made during removal. If the disc is being removed in an attempt to improve seating and hence runout, turn the disc through 180° and then refit it.

22 Refit the locating studs and tighten them securely.

23 Recheck the disc runout, using one of the methods described earlier in this Section.

7.3 Screw 2 M10 bolts into the threaded holes, and push the drum from the hub

24 Refit the brake caliper and mounting bracket assembly to the swivel hub. Coat the threads of the mounting bolts with thread-locking compound, then tighten them to the specified torque.

25 Depress the brake pedal several times to bring the brake pads into contact with the disc.

26 Refit the roadwheel and lower the car to the ground.

27 Check the hydraulic fluid level as described in *Weekly checks*.

---

7 Rear brake drums – removal, inspection and refitting

 Warning: Before starting work, refer to the warning at the beginning of Section 4 concerning the dangers of asbestos dust.

Removal

1 Chock the front wheels then jack up the rear of the car and securely support it on axle stands (see *Jacking and vehicle support*). Remove the appropriate rear roadwheel and fully release the handbrake.

2 If the original drum is to be refitted, mark the relationship between the drum and the hub. Slacken and remove the two locating studs and pull the drum from the hub **(see illustration)**.

3 If the drum is binding on the brake shoes, screw two M10 bolts into the locating stud threaded holes in the drum **(see illustration)**, and progressively tighten them against the hub flange to push the drum from the hub.

Inspection

Note: *If either drum requires renewal, BOTH should be renewed at the same time, to ensure even and consistent braking. New brake shoes should also be fitted.*

4 Working carefully, remove all traces of brake dust from the drum, but *avoid inhaling the dust, as it is a health hazard.*

5 Clean the outside of the drum, and check it for obvious signs of wear or damage, such as cracks around the roadwheel stud holes; renew the drum if necessary.

6 Carefully examine the inside of the drum. Light scoring of the friction surface is normal, but if heavy scoring is found, the drum must be renewed.

7 It is usual to find a lip on the drum's inboard edge which consists of a mixture of rust and brake dust; this should be carefully scraped away, to leave a smooth surface which can be polished with fine (120- to 150-grade) emery paper. If, however, the lip is due to the friction surface being recessed by excessive wear, then the drum must be renewed.

8 If the drum is thought to be excessively worn, or oval, its internal diameter must be measured at several points using an internal micrometer. Take measurements in pairs, the second at right-angles to the first, and compare the two, to check for signs of ovality. Provided that it does not enlarge the drum to beyond the specified maximum diameter, it may be possible to have the drum refinished by skimming or grinding; if this is not possible, the drums on both sides must be renewed. Note that if the drum is to be skimmed, BOTH drums must be refinished, to maintain a consistent internal diameter on both sides.

Refitting

9 If a new brake drum is to be installed, use a suitable solvent to remove any preservative coating that may have been applied to its internal friction surfaces. Note that it may also be necessary to shorten the adjuster strut length, by rotating the serrated strut wheel, to allow the drum to pass over the brake shoes – see Section 8 for details.
10 If the original drum is being refitted, align

8.5a Correct fitted position of the brake shoe upper return spring . . .

8.5b . . . and lower return spring

8.8 Depress the remaining clip and remove the pin

the marks made on the drum and hub before removal, then fit the drum over the hub. Refit the locating studs and tighten them to the specified torque.
11 Depress the footbrake repeatedly to expand the brake shoes against the drum, and ensure that normal pedal pressure is restored.
12 Check and if necessary adjust the handbrake as described in Section 12.
13 Refit the roadwheels, and lower the car to the ground.

8 Rear brake shoes – renewal

⚠ **Warning: Renew BOTH sets of rear brake shoes at the same time – NEVER renew the shoes on only one wheel, as uneven braking may result.**

● **Before starting work, refer to the warning given at the beginning of Section 4, concerning the dangers of asbestos dust.**
1 Remove the rear brake drums, as described in Section 7.
2 Working carefully, and taking the necessary precautions, remove all traces of brake dust from the brake drum, backplate and shoes.
3 Measure the thickness of the friction material of each brake shoe at several points; if either shoe is worn at any point to the specified minimum thickness or less, all four shoes must be renewed as a set. The shoes should also be renewed if any are fouled with hydraulic fluid, oil or grease; there is

8.6 Depress the shoe hold-down spring clip and slide it from under the pin head

8.9a Slide the handbrake cable end from the lever . . .

no satisfactory way of degreasing friction material, once contaminated.
4 If any of the brake shoes are worn unevenly, or contaminated, trace and rectify the cause before reassembly.
5 Note the position of each shoe, and the location of the return springs and self-adjuster mechanism to aid refitting later **(see illustrations)**.
6 Depress the leading brake shoe hold-down spring clip and slide the clip out from under the pin head, while holding the pin from the rear **(see illustration)**. Remove the pin from the rear of the backplate.
7 Pull out the leading shoe a little, and detach the lower return spring, pull the top of the leading shoe from the cylinder piston, then pivot the shoe upwards, remove the self-adjusting mechanism, and detach the upper return spring **(see illustration)**.
8 Remove the hold-down spring clip and pin from the trailing brake shoe, then withdraw the shoe from the backplate **(see illustration)**.
9 Slide the handbrake cable end out of the lever on the trailing shoe **(see illustrations)**. Remove the trailing brake shoe.
10 Retain the wheel cylinder pistons in the wheel cylinder using a cable-tie or a strong elastic band. Do not depress the brake pedal until the brakes are reassembled.
11 Carefully examine the self-adjuster mechanism for signs of wear or damage. Pay particular attention to the threads and the toothed adjuster wheel, and renew if necessary.
12 Check the condition of all return springs

8.7 Pull out the lower end of the shoe and detach the lower return spring

8.9b . . . on the trailing shoe – right-hand side brake assembly shown

8.16a Engage the upper return spring with the slots in the brake shoes . . .

8.16b . . . then engage the self-adjuster mechanism into the recess in the trailing shoe . . .

8.16c . . . and the other end with the leading shoe

and renew any that show signs of distortion or other damage.

13 Peel back the rubber protective caps, and check the wheel cylinder for fluid leaks or other damage; check that both cylinder pistons are free to move easily. Refer to Section 9, if necessary, for information on wheel cylinder overhaul.

14 Prior to installation, clean the backplate, and apply a thin smear of high-temperature brake grease or anti-seize compound to all those surfaces of the backplate which bear on the shoes, particularly the wheel cylinder pistons and lower pivot point. Do not allow the lubricant to foul the friction material.

15 Connect the handbrake cable to the lever on the trailing brake shoe, locate the trailing shoe on the backplate and secure in position with the pin and hold-down spring clip **(see illustration 8.8).**

16 Fit upper brake shoe return spring, and the self-adjuster mechanism into the recess in the trailing brake shoe, then engage the leading shoe with the other end of the adjuster mechanism **(see illustrations).**

17 Fit the lower brake shoe return spring, engaging it with the slots in the shoes **(see illustration).** Remove the elastic band or cable-tie from the wheel cylinder.

18 Manoeuvre the leading shoe into position and secure it with the hold-down pin and spring clip.

19 Turn the serrated wheel at the end of the self-adjuster mechanism, to retract the brake shoes – this will give additional clearance to allow the drum to pass over the shoes during refitting.

8.17 Refit the lower return spring

20 Refit the brake drum as described in Section 7.

21 Repeat the above procedure on the remaining rear brake.

22 Apply the brake pedal and handbrake lever several times to settle the self-adjusting mechanism. With both rear roadwheels refitted and the rear of the car still raised, turn the wheels by hand to check that the brake shoes are not binding. Check and if necessary adjust the operation of the handbrake, as described in Section 12.

23 On completion, check the brake hydraulic fluid level in the master cylinder reservoir as described in *Weekly checks.*

24 Note that new shoes will not give full braking efficiency until they have bedded-in. Be prepared for this, and avoid hard braking as far as possible for the first hundred miles or so after shoe renewal.

9 Rear wheel cylinder – removal, overhaul and refitting

⚠️ *Warning: Before starting work, refer to the warnings at the beginning of Sections 2 and 4 concerning the dangers of hydraulic fluid and asbestos dust.*

Removal

1 Remove the brake drum as described in Section 7.

2 Remove the brake shoes as described in Section 8.

9.4 Rear wheel cylinder hydraulic pipe union and securing bolts (arrowed)

3 To minimise fluid loss during the following operations, remove the master cylinder reservoir filler cap, then tighten it down onto a piece of polythene, to obtain an airtight seal.

4 Clean the brake backplate around the wheel cylinder mounting bolts and the hydraulic pipe union, then unscrew the union nut and disconnect the hydraulic pipe **(see illustration).** Cover the open ends of the pipe and the wheel cylinder to prevent dirt ingress.

5 Remove the two securing bolts, then withdraw the wheel cylinder from the backplate.

Overhaul

Note: *Before commencing work, ensure that the appropriate wheel cylinder overhaul kit is obtained.*

6 Clean the assembly thoroughly, using only methylated spirit or clean brake fluid.

7 Peel off both rubber dust covers, then use paint or similar to mark one of the pistons so that the pistons are not interchanged on reassembly.

8 Withdraw both pistons and the spring.

9 Discard the rubber piston cups and the dust covers. These components should be renewed as a matter of course, and are available as part of an overhaul kit, which also includes the bleed screw dust cap.

10 Check the condition of the cylinder bore and the pistons – the surfaces must be perfect and free from scratches, scoring and corrosion. It is advisable to renew the complete wheel cylinder if there is any doubt as to the condition of the cylinder bore or pistons.

11 Ensure that all components are clean and dry. The pistons, spring and cups should be fitted wet, using hydraulic fluid as a lubricant – soak them in clean fluid before installation.

12 Fit the cups to the pistons, ensuring that they are the correct way round. Use only your fingers (no tools) to manipulate the cups into position.

13 Fit the first piston to the cylinder, taking care not to distort the cup. If the original pistons are being re-used, the marks made on dismantling should be used to ensure that the pistons are refitted to their original bores.

14 Refit the spring and the second piston.

10.4a Disconnect the fluid level sender wiring plug (arrowed) . . .

10.4b . . . and the clutch fluid supply pipe (arrowed)

10.6 Brake master cylinder securing nuts (arrowed)

15 Apply a smear of rubber grease to the exposed end of each piston and to the dust cover sealing lips, then fit the dust covers to each end of the wheel cylinder.

Refitting

16 Refitting is a reversal of removal, bearing in mind the following points:
a) *Tighten the mounting bolts to the specified torque.*
b) *Refit the brake shoes as described in Section 8, and the brake drum as described in Section 7.*
c) *Before refitting the roadwheel and lowering the car to the ground, remove the polythene from the fluid reservoir, and bleed the hydraulic system as described in Section 2. Note that if no other part of the system has been disturbed, it should only be necessary to bleed the relevant rear circuit.*

10 Master cylinder –
removal and refitting

⚠️ **Warning: Before starting work, refer to the warning at the beginning of Section 2 concerning the dangers of hydraulic fluid.**

Removal

1 Remove the battery and battery tray as described in Chapter 5A.
2 Remove the air cleaner assembly as described in Chapter 4A or 4B.

10.7 Master cylinder reservoir retaining pin (arrowed)

3 Remove the master cylinder fluid reservoir filler cap, and siphon the hydraulic fluid from the reservoir. **Note:** *Do not siphon the fluid by mouth, as it is poisonous; use a syringe or an old poultry baster.* Alternatively, open any convenient bleed screw in the system, and gently pump the brake pedal to expel the fluid through a tube connected to the screw (see Section 2).
4 Disconnect the wiring connector from the brake fluid level sender unit, and, where applicable, the fluid supply pipe for the clutch master cylinder **(see illustrations)**.
5 Wipe clean the area around the brake pipe unions on the side of the master cylinder, and place absorbent rags beneath the pipe unions to catch any surplus fluid. Make a note of the correct fitted positions of the unions, then unscrew the union nuts and carefully withdraw the pipes. Plug or tape over the pipe ends and master cylinder orifices to minimise the loss of brake fluid, and to prevent the entry of dirt into the system. Wash off any spilt fluid immediately with cold water.
6 Slacken and remove the two nuts securing the master cylinder to the vacuum servo unit, then withdraw the unit from the engine compartment **(see illustration)**.
7 If required, pull out the retaining pin and separate the fluid reservoir from the master cylinder **(see illustration)**.

Refitting

8 Remove all traces of dirt from the master cylinder and servo unit mating surfaces and, where applicable, fit a new seal between the master cylinder body and the servo.

11.2 Disconnect the brake light switch wiring plug (arrowed)

9 Refit the reservoir to the master cylinder using new rubber grommets where necessary. Securely refit the retaining pin.
10 Fit the master cylinder to the servo unit, ensuring that the servo unit pushrod enters the master cylinder bore centrally. Refit the master cylinder mounting nuts, and tighten them securely.
11 Wipe clean the brake pipe unions, then refit them to the correct master cylinder ports, as noted before removal, and tighten the union nuts securely.
12 Reconnect the clutch master cylinder supply hose and the level warning sender wiring plug.
13 Refill the master cylinder reservoir with fresh hydraulic fluid of the specified type (see *Lubricants and fluids*), and bleed the complete hydraulic system as described in Section 2. Note that it may also be necessary to bleed the clutch hydraulic system as described in Chapter 6.
14 Refit the air cleaner assembly, battery and battery tray.
15 On completion, thoroughly check the operation of the brake and clutch systems.

11 Brake light switch –
removal and refitting

Note: *Fiat insist that if the switch is removed, it must be renewed.*

Removal

1 Disconnect the battery negative lead as described in Chapter 5A.
2 Reach up under the facia on the passenger's side, and disconnect the wiring connector from the switch **(see illustration)**.
3 Twist the switch anti-clockwise through about half a turn, and withdraw the switch from the pedal bracket.

Refitting

4 Depress the brake pedal and hold it in this position.
5 Insert the switch into its mounting bracket. Rotate the switch body clockwise through 90° until the locating lug is felt to engage in its recess.

12.9a Lift the mat from the cupholder, undo the nut (arrowed) . . .

12.9b . . . then remove the rear section of the centre console

6 Release the brake pedal and allow it to rest against the switch plunger – this adjusts the position of the switch body inside the bush.
7 Reconnect the wiring connector, then reconnect the battery lead and test the operation of the brake lights.

12 Handbrake –
checking and adjustment

Checking

1 The handbrake should be capable of holding the parked vehicle stationary, even on steep slopes, when applied with moderate force. The mechanism should be firm and positive in feel, with no trace of stiffness or sponginess from the cables, and the mechanism should release immediately the handbrake lever is released. If the mechanism does not operate satisfactorily, it should be checked immediately.
2 To check the operation of the handbrake, chock the front wheels then jack up the rear of the car and securely support it on axle stands (see *Jacking and vehicle support*). Release the handbrake lever.
3 Depress the brake pedal several times to

establish the correct shoe-to-drum clearance.
4 With the pedal released, check that the rear roadwheels can be rotated – slight dragging is acceptable, but it should be possible to turn each wheel easily.
5 Apply the handbrake lever and check that the rear roadwheels start to drag after one click of the ratchet mechanism, and are fully locked within 5 clicks of the ratchet.
6 Fully release the handbrake, and check that the rear roadwheels can again be rotated by hand.
7 If the handbrake does not operate as described, carry out the adjustment procedure as follows.

Adjustment

8 On Panda models, remove the centre console as described in Chapter 11.
9 On 500 models, lift the mat in the base of the rear cupholder, undo the retaining nut, and remove the rear section of the centre console **(see illustrations)**.
10 Using a spanner or suitable socket, turn the adjuster nut clockwise to apply tension to the cables, or anti-clockwise to release the tension on the cables, as necessary **(see illustration)**. Check the operation of the handbrake as described previously and repeat the adjustment procedure as required.

11 On completion, refit the centre console and lower the car to the ground.

13 Handbrake cables –
removal and refitting

Removal

1 There are two rear handbrake cables, one on each side of the car. To renew either rear cable, proceed as follows.
2 On Panda models, remove the centre console as described in Chapter 11.
3 On 500 models, lift the mat in the base of the rear cupholder, undo the retaining nut, and remove the rear section of the centre console **(see illustrations 12.9a and 12.9b)**.
4 At the base of the handbrake lever, fully slacken the handbrake adjuster nut to remove all tension from the cable draw bar, then disconnect the relevant handbrake inner cable from the draw bar.
5 Depress the retaining tabs and release the outer cables from the floorpan **(see illustration)**.
6 Chock the front wheels then jack up the rear of the car and securely support it on axle stands (see *Jacking and vehicle support*).
7 Remove the rear brake shoes and disconnect the end of the handbrake cable from the lever on the trailing shoe as described in Section 8. Withdraw the cable from the brake backplate.
8 Release the handbrake cable from the retaining clips on the rear axle mounting, exhaust heat shield, fuel tank support bracket and fuel tank, then remove the cable from under the car.

Refitting

9 Refitting is a reversal of removal, bearing in mind the following points:
 a) Ensure that the cable is securely fastened

12.10 Handbrake adjusting nut (arrowed)

13.5 Depress the tabs (arrowed) and release the outer cables

to the clips on the rear axle, heat shield, fuel tank and support bracket.
b) Connect the cable to the trailing brake shoe then refit the brake shoes as described in Section 8.
c) Refit the centre console as described in Chapter 11.
d) On completion, adjust the handbrake as described in Section 12.

14 Handbrake lever – removal and refitting

Removal

1 Remove the centre console as described in Chapter 11, then release the handbrake lever.
2 At the base of the handbrake lever, fully slacken the handbrake adjuster bolt, to remove all tension from the cable draw bar, then disconnect both handbrake inner cables from the draw bar.
3 Disconnect the wiring connector from the handbrake 'on' warning light switch located at the front of the handbrake lever base.
4 Undo the bolts securing the handbrake lever to the floor and remove the lever from the car (see illustration).

Refitting

5 Refitting is a reversal of removal, bearing in mind the following points:
a) Refit the centre console as described in Chapter 11.
b) On completion, adjust the handbrake as described in Section 12.

15 Handbrake 'on' warning light switch – removal and refitting

Removal

1 Remove the centre console as described in Chapter 11.
2 Disconnect the wiring connector from the switch located at the front of the handbrake lever base (see illustration).

14.4 Handbrake lever securing bolts (arrowed)

3 Release the retaining clip and remove the switch from its location.

Refitting

4 Refitting is a reversal of removal.

16 Vacuum servo unit – removal and refitting

Removal

1 Remove the master cylinder as described in Section 10.
2 Prise out the grommet and disconnect the vacuum hose from the front of the servo unit.
3 From inside the car, remove the plastic cover, then release the retaining clip securing the brake pedal reaction link to the servo unit pushrod (see illustrations).
4 Undo the nuts securing the servo unit to the bulkhead and withdraw the unit from within the engine compartment (see illustration).

Refitting

5 Refitting is a reversal of removal.

17 Anti-lock braking system (ABS) – general information

ABS is available as an option on 1.1 litre

15.2 Handbrake 'on' warning switch wiring plug and retaining clip (arrowed)

petrol models covered by this manual, and is fitted as standard equipment on all others. The purpose of the system is to prevent the wheels locking during heavy braking. This is achieved by automatic release of the brake on the relevant wheel, followed by modulated re-application of the brake. The system comprises an electronic control unit, a hydraulic modulator, hydraulic solenoid valves (located in the modulator unit), an electrically-driven fluid return pump, and four wheel speed sensors.

The solenoids (which control the fluid pressure to the calipers/wheel cylinders) are controlled by the electronic control unit, which itself receives signals from the wheel speed sensors. The wheel speed sensors monitor the speed of rotation of each wheel. By comparing the speed signals from the four wheels, the control unit can determine when a wheel is decelerating at an abnormal rate, compared to the speed of the of the other wheels. Using this information, the control unit can predict when a wheel is about to lock, and is able to reduce the fluid pressure to the brake on the relevant wheel to prevent it locking. Once the rotational speed of the monitored wheel returns to approximately that of the other wheels, the hydraulic fluid pressure is increased in stages, to enable braking to continue.

During normal operation, the system functions in the same way as a conventional non-ABS braking system.

16.3a Undo the screws (arrowed) and remove the plastic cover

16.3b Release the clips (arrowed) and disengage the servo unit pushrod from the reaction link

16.4 Servo unit securing nuts (arrowed)

18 Anti-lock braking system (ABS) components – removal and refitting

Hydraulic modulator

 Warning: Before starting work, refer to the warning at the beginning of Section 2 concerning the dangers of hydraulic fluid.

Removal

1 On models up to 06/06, remove the brake master cylinder as described in Section 10. On models 07/06-on, remove the battery and battery tray as described in Chapter 5A.
2 Release the locking clip and disconnect the ECU wiring harness connector.
3 Wipe clean the area around the brake pipe unions on the side of the modulator, and place absorbent rags beneath the pipe unions to catch any surplus fluid. Make a note of the correct fitted positions of the unions, then unscrew the union nuts and carefully withdraw the pipes. Plug or tape over the pipe ends and modulator orifices to minimise the loss of fluid, and to prevent the entry of dirt into the system.
4 Undo the retaining nuts/bolts, and remove the unit from the engine compartment.

Refitting

5 If a new modulator assembly is being fitted, it will be supplied prefilled with hydraulic fluid, and sealed with blanking plugs. Leave the plugs in position until just before connecting the brake pipes.
6 Locate the modulator in position and refit the retaining nuts/bolts.
7 Reconnect the brake pipes to their correct locations as noted during removal and tighten the union nuts securely.
8 Reconnect the ECU wiring connector.
9 Refit the brake master cylinder as described in Section 10, or the battery and tray as described in Chapter 5A (as applicable).

10 Bleed the complete brake hydraulic system as described in Section 2. Note that it may also be necessary to bleed the clutch hydraulic system as described in Chapter 6.

Electronic control unit

11 The electronic control unit is removed with the modulator assembly as described previously. The ECU is an integral part of the modulator and the two components cannot be separated.

Front wheel speed sensor

Removal

12 Firmly apply the handbrake, then jack up the front of the car and support it securely on axle stands (see *Jacking and vehicle support*). Remove the relevant front roadwheel and wheel arch liner.
13 Trace the wiring back from the sensor, and separate the two halves of the wiring connector. Note the routing of the wiring to aid correct refitting.
14 Unclip the wheel speed sensor wiring from the brackets on the suspension strut **(see illustration)**.
15 Unscrew the retaining bolt and withdraw the sensor from the swivel hub **(see illustrations)**.

18.14 Unclip the wheel speed sensor wiring (arrowed)

Refitting

16 Refitting is a reversal of removal, noting the following points:
a) *Ensure that the mating faces of the sensor and the swivel hub are clean, and apply a smear of high melting-point brake grease to the sensor location in the swivel hub before refitting.*
b) *Ensure that the end face of the sensor is clean.*
c) *Route the wiring as noted before removal.*

Rear wheel speed sensor

Removal

17 Chock the front wheels then jack up the rear of the car and securely support it on axle stands (see *Jacking and vehicle support*). Remove the appropriate rear roadwheel.
18 Trace the wiring back from the sensor to its wiring connector. Free the connector from its retaining clip, and disconnect the wiring from the main wiring loom.
19 Work back along the sensor wiring, and release it from the retaining clips. Note the routing of the wiring to aid correct refitting.
20 Slacken and remove the bolt securing the sensor unit to the rear stub axle, and remove the sensor and lead assembly **(see illustration)**.

18.15a Undo the retaining bolt (arrowed) . . .

18.15b . . . and withdraw the wheel speed sensor

18.20 Rear wheel speed sensor retaining bolt (arrowed)

19.3a Depress the release button (arrowed) and disconnect the servo unit vacuum hose

19.3b Disconnect the smaller vacuum hose (arrowed)

19.4 Vacuum pump mounting bolts (arrowed)

Refitting

21 Refitting is a reversal of removal, noting the following points:

a) *Ensure that the mating faces of the sensor and the stub axle are clean, and apply a smear of high melting-point brake grease to the sensor location in the stub axle before refitting.*

b) *Ensure that the end face of the sensor is clean.*

c) *Route the wiring as noted before removal.*

19 Vacuum pump – removal and refitting

Note: *A vacuum pump is only fitted to diesel models.*

Removal

1 Disconnect the battery and battery tray as described in Chapter 5A.

2 Remove the air cleaner assembly as described in Chapter 4B.

3 Disconnect the quick-release fitting and detach the vacuum servo unit vacuum hose from the pump. Disconnect the smaller vacuum hose from the outlet on the side of the pump **(see illustrations)**.

4 Undo the two mounting bolts and remove the pump from the camshaft housing **(see illustration)**. Recover the gasket.

Refitting

5 Refitting is a reversal of removal, but clean the mating faces of the pump and camshaft housing and fit a new gasket. Tighten the mounting bolts to the specified torque.

Chapter 10
Suspension and steering

Contents

Degrees of difficulty

Easy, suitable for novice with little experience	**Fairly easy,** suitable for beginner with some experience	**Fairly difficult,** suitable for competent DIY mechanic	**Difficult,** suitable for experienced DIY mechanic	**Very difficult,** suitable for expert DIY or professional

Specifications

Front suspension

Type . . . .   Independent, with MacPherson struts and transverse lower suspension arms. Anti-roll bar fitted to all models

Rear suspension

Type . . . .   Semi-independent torsion beam axle, with coil springs and telescopic shock absorbers

Steering

Type . . . .   Rack-and-pinion with electrically-operated power assistance
Toe setting (front):
  Panda models. . . . .   0° (parallel) ± 1°
  500 models. . . . .   0.5 ± 1.0 mm
Front camber setting:
  Panda models. . . . .   -52' ± 30'
  500 models. . . . .   -33' ± 30'

Torque wrench settings

	Nm	lbf ft
Front suspension		
Anti-roll bar:		
Mounting bolts	20	15
Link rod nut.	50	37
Driveshaft nut*	240	177
Front crossmember bolts	40	30
Lower arm balljoint-to-swivel hub:		
M8 bolt	32	24
M10 bolt	65	48
Lower arm front mounting securing bolt	120	89
Lower arm rear mounting securing bolt	120	89
Subframe bolts:		
Front	120	89
Rear/centre	160	118
Subframe extension strut bolts:		
M10 bolt	55	41
M12 bolt	90	66
Suspension strut piston rod top nut	65	48
Suspension strut-to-swivel hub bolts	75	55
Suspension strut upper mounting cup-to-piston rod nut	50	37
Rear suspension		
Hub nut*	280	207
Rear axle mounting brackets to axle	115	85
Rear axle mounting brackets to body	70	52
Shock absorber lower securing bolt:		
Panda models	70	52
500 models	85	63
Shock absorber upper securing bolt:		
Panda models	80	59
500 models	70	52
Stub axle-to-rear axle	65	48
Steering		
Steering column mounting nuts/bolts	15	11
Steering gear mounting bolts	80	59
Steering wheel nut*	50	37
Track rod end-to-swivel hub nut*	34	25
Universal joint clamp bolt*	33	24
Roadwheels		
Roadwheel bolts:		
Steel wheel	85	63
Aluminium wheel	98	72

* Do not re-use

1 General information

Front suspension

The front suspension is independent, comprising transverse lower wishbones, coil spring-over-damper MacPherson strut units and an anti-roll bar. The swivel hubs are bolted to the base of the strut units and are linked to the lower arms by means of balljoints. The entire front suspension assembly is mounted on a subframe, which is in turn bolted to the vehicle body.

Rear suspension

The rear suspension incorporates a torsion beam axle with trailing arms, coil springs and separate double-acting telescopic shock absorbers. The components form a discrete sub-assembly which can be unbolted from the underside of the vehicle separately or as a complete unit.

Steering

The two-piece steering shaft runs in a tubular column assembly, which is bolted to a bracket mounted on the vehicle bulkhead. The upper shaft is attached to the intermediate shaft by means of a universal joint and the intermediate shaft is similarly connected to the steering gear pinion by a second universal joint.

The rack-and-pinion steering gear is mounted on the front subframe, and is connected by means of track rods to the steering arms projecting rearwards from the swivel hubs. The track rods are fitted with balljoints at their inner and outer ends, to allow for suspension movement, and are threaded to facilitate adjustment.

Dualdrive electrically-operated power steering is fitted to all models. The power assistance is provided by an electric motor and gearbox assembly which is integral with the steering column. The system is controlled by an electronic control unit and provides the driver with two operating strategies – one for normal driving and one for 'city' driving. A control button on the facia is used to switch between the two functions. When the 'city' function is activated, a greater degree of power assistance is provided for ease of town driving and parking manoeuvres.

2 Front swivel hub assembly – removal and refitting

Note: *A balljoint separator tool will be required for this operation and a new driveshaft retaining nut will be required for refitting.*

Removal

1 Firmly apply the handbrake, then jack up the front of the car and support it securely on

axle stands (see *Jacking and vehicle support*). Remove the appropriate front roadwheel.

2 Using a hammer and chisel or similar tool, tap up the staking securing the driveshaft retaining nut in position.

3 The front wheel hub must be held stationary in order to loosen the driveshaft nut. Ideally, the hub should be held by a suitable tool bolted into place using two of the roadwheel bolts **(see Tool Tip)**. Alternatively, have an assistant firmly apply the footbrake to prevent the hub from rotating. Using a socket and extension bar, slacken and remove the driveshaft retaining nut.

⚠️ *Warning: The nut is extremely tight. Discard the nut – a new one must be used on refitting.*

4 Release the brake caliper hydraulic hose from the bracket at the base of the suspension strut **(see illustration)**.

5 Undo the two bolts securing the brake caliper mounting bracket to the swivel hub. Withdraw the caliper and mounting bracket assembly, complete with brake pads, off the disc **(see illustration)**. Suspend the caliper from a convenient place under the wheel arch using string or a cable-tie. Do not allow the caliper to hang unsupported from the brake hydraulic hose.

6 If the swivel hub is being removed for renewal of the bearing, mark the relationship between the brake disc and the hub with chalk or a marker pen, to allow correct refitting. Slacken and remove the disc locating studs, then remove the disc from the wheel hub.

A tool to hold the front hub stationary whilst the driveshaft nut is slackened can be fabricated from two lengths of steel strip (one long, one short) and a nut and bolt; the nut and bolt forming the pivot of a forked tool.

7 Undo the bolts and remove the disc backplate from the swivel hub assembly **(see illustration)**.

8 On models with ABS, release the wheel speed sensor cable from the brackets at the base of the suspension strut. Undo the sensor retaining bolt, withdraw the sensor from the swivel hub and suspend it away from the working area, to avoid the possibility of damage **(see illustration)**.

9 Unscrew the nut securing the track rod end to the swivel hub. Release the track rod end tapered shank using a balljoint separator tool.

10 Unscrew the two nuts and remove the

2.4 Release the clip (arrowed) and pull the hose from the strut bracket

bolts securing the top of the swivel hub to the base of the suspension strut **(see illustration)**.

11 Pull the swivel hub outwards at the top to release the driveshaft outer constant velocity joint from the wheel hub. If necessary, the joint can be tapped free using a soft-faced mallet.

12 Slacken and remove the nut, then withdraw the suspension lower arm balljoint clamp bolt from the swivel hub **(see illustration)**.

13 Tap a small chisel into the split on the swivel hub to spread the hub slightly, then lift the swivel hub assembly up and off the balljoint shank **(see illustration)**.

Refitting

14 Locate the swivel hub over the suspension lower arm balljoint, pushing it fully into engagement with the balljoint shank. Refit the

2.5 Undo the bolts (arrowed) and slide the caliper and bracket from the disc

2.7 Disc backplate retaining bolts (arrowed)

2.8 The wheel speed sensor (arrowed) is located on the top of the swivel hub

2.10 Swivel hub-to-suspension strut bolts/nuts (arrowed). Note that the bolts are inserted from the rear

2.12 Undo the nut and remove the balljoint clamp bolt (arrowed)

2.13 Use a chisel/screwdriver to spread the clamp slightly, and lift off the hub assembly

clamp bolt and secure with the nut tightened to the specified torque.

15 Engage the outer CV joint into the wheel hub, then pivot the top of the swivel hub back towards the car. Screw on the new driveshaft retaining nut, but do not tighten it at this stage.

16 Refit the suspension strut-to-swivel hub bolts, screw on the two nuts and tighten them to the specified torque.

17 Engage the track rod end with the swivel hub, refit the retaining nut and tighten the nut to the specified torque.

18 On models with ABS, ensure that the mating faces of the wheel speed sensor and the swivel hub are clean, and apply a smear of high melting-point brake grease to the sensor location in the swivel hub. Ensure that the end face of the sensor is clean, then locate it in position and secure with the retaining bolt. Refit the sensor cable to the brackets on the suspension strut.

19 Refit the backplate and tighten the retaining bolts securely.

20 Locate the brake disc on the hub so that the roadwheel bolt and locating stud holes are all correctly lined up; use the alignment marks made during removal. Refit the locating studs and tighten them securely.

21 Refit the brake caliper and mounting bracket assembly to the swivel hub. Coat the threads of the mounting bolts with thread-locking compound, then tighten them to the specified torque (see Chapter 9).

22 Refit the brake caliper hydraulic hose to the bracket at the base of the suspension strut.

23 Using the method employed on removal to prevent rotation of the hub, tighten the driveshaft retaining nut to the specified torque. Secure the nut by tapping the staking into the two grooves in the end of the CV joint using a hammer and chisel.

24 Refit the roadwheel, and lower the car to the ground. Depress the brake pedal several times to bring the brake pads into contact with the disc.

25 It is advisable to have the front wheel toe setting checked at the earliest opportunity.

3.7a The new bearing is supplied with one side protected by a plastic cap. This indicates which side has the magnetic pulse wheel embedded in the oil seal, which must face inwards against the wheel speed sensor

3.2 Press the hub flange from the bearing

3 Front hub bearings – renewal

Note: *Various special tools, including a hydraulic press, will be required for this operation (see text). If the necessary tools are not available, the swivel hub assembly should be removed as described in Section 2 and taken to a suitably-equipped engineering works for renewal of the bearing.*

1 Remove the swivel hub assembly as described in Section 2.

2 Press the wheel hub flange from the bearing and extract the hub, together with the bearing inner race **(see illustration)**.

3 The bearing inner race must now be removed from the wheel hub using a suitable puller. To provide sufficient clearance for the puller legs, force the inner race away from the hub flange using a hammer and small chisel inserted between the inner race and the hub flange. When sufficient clearance exists, engage the puller legs behind the inner race and draw the race off the wheel hub.

4 Using a large screwdriver, extract the bearing retaining circlip from the swivel hub **(see illustration)**.

5 Mount the swivel hub on the press bed and press the bearing out of the hub. Note that a flange on the outboard side of the swivel hub means that the bearing can only be removed in one direction.

6 Before installing the new bearing, thoroughly clean the bearing location in the swivel hub.

3.7b Press the new bearing from the inboard side of the hub

3.4 Extract the circlip

7 Fit the new bearing from the inboard side the swivel hub and press it fully into position, applying pressure only to the bearing outer race. Note that one side of the bearing is fitted with a seal which has a magnetic pulse wheel embedded. This side of the bearing must face inwards, against the wheel speed sensor location **(see illustrations)**.

8 Fit the bearing retaining circlip to its groove in the swivel hub so that the circlip's gap is aligned with the aperture for the ABS wheel speed sensor (otherwise the sensor will not function correctly and the ABS failure warning lamp will illuminate) **(see illustration)**.

9 Suitably support the bearing inner race on the press bed and press the wheel hub into the bearing.

10 On completion, check that the wheel hub rotates freely in the bearing without resistance or roughness.

11 Refit the swivel hub assembly as described in Section 2.

4 Front suspension strut – removal and refitting

Removal

1 Firmly apply the handbrake, then jack up the front of the car and support it securely on axle stands (see *Jacking and vehicle support*). Remove the appropriate roadwheel(s).

2 Release the brake caliper hydraulic hose (and, where applicable, the ABS wheel speed

3.8 Locate the new circlip so its ends are either side of the wheel speed sensor location (arrowed)

Suspension and steering 10•5

4.3 Counterhold the anti-roll bar link with an Allen key

4.7 Undo the strut mounting nut, counterholding with an Allen key/bit

5.2 Use spring compressors to relieve the tension on the top mounting

sensor cable) from the brackets at the base of the suspension strut.

3 Undo the nut and detach the anti-roll bar link rod from the strut **(see illustration)**. If necessary, counterhold the link rod balljoint shank with an Allen key.

4 Unscrew the two nuts and remove the bolts securing the base of the suspension strut to the top of the swivel hub.

5 Pull the swivel hub outwards at the top to release it from the suspension strut.

6 On 500 models, remove the upper and lower windscreen base trim panels as described in Section 22 of Chapter 11.

7 Have an assistant support the strut from underneath the wheel arch. Working in the engine compartment, unscrew the nut securing the upper mounting cup to the strut piston rod while counterholding the piston rod with a suitable Allen key. Lift off the upper mounting cup and withdraw the assembly from under the wheel arch **(see illustration)**.

Refitting

8 Manoeuvre the strut assembly into position under the wheel arch and locate the upper mounting cup over the strut piston. Refit the retaining nut and moderately tighten it at this stage. Final tightening of this nut is carried out with the car resting on its roadwheels.

9 Engage the lower end of the strut with the swivel hub, then fit the securing bolts and nuts. Tighten the nuts to the specified torque.

10 Refit the brake caliper hydraulic hose (and where applicable, the ABS wheel speed

sensor cable) to the bracket at the base of the suspension strut.

11 Refit the roadwheel, and lower the car to the ground.

12 With the car resting on its roadwheels, tighten the suspension strut upper mounting cup retaining nut to the specified torque.

5 Front suspension strut – overhaul

Note: *Suitable coil spring compressor tools will be required for this operation.*

1 Remove the front suspension strut as described in Section 4.

2 Fit suitable spring compressors to the coil spring, and compress the spring sufficiently to enable the upper mounting to be turned by hand **(see illustration)**.

⚠ *Warning: Ensure that the coil spring is compressed sufficiently to remove all the tension from the upper mounting before attempting to remove the piston rod nut.*

3 Unscrew the nut securing the strut piston rod to the upper mounting, while counterholding the piston with a suitable Allen key **(see illustration)**.

4 Withdraw the upper mounting and upper spring seat, then withdraw the spring, complete with the compressors **(see illustration)**.

5 Withdraw the dust cover and bump rubber **(see illustration)**.

6 With the strut assembly now dismantled, examine all the components for wear, damage or deformation. Renew any components as necessary.

7 Examine the strut body for signs of fluid leakage or damage and the piston rod for signs of pitting or scoring. While holding it in an upright position, test the operation of the strut by moving the piston rod through a full stroke, and then through short strokes of 50 to 100 mm. In both cases, the resistance felt should be smooth and continuous. If the resistance is jerky, or uneven, or if there is any visible sign of wear or damage to the strut, renewal is necessary.

8 If any doubt exists about the condition of the coil spring, carefully remove the spring compressors, and check the spring for distortion and signs of cracking. Renew the spring if it is damaged or distorted, or if there is any doubt about its condition.

⚠ *Warning: Coil springs are classified by their height when under load – this is indicated by a coloured paint marking on the side of the coil windings. All coil springs fitted to the vehicle must be of the same classification to ensure the correct ride height.*

9 Begin reassembly by refitting the dust cover and bump rubber.

10 Ensure that the coil spring is compressed sufficiently to enable the upper mounting components to be fitted, then fit the spring over the piston rod, ensuring that the lower end

5.3 Undo the piston rod nut, counterholding with an Allen key/bit

5.4 Withdraw the mounting and upper spring seat (arrowed)

5.5 Withdraw the dust cover and bump rubber

5.10 Ensure the spring end is located against the recess on the lower seat (arrowed)

5.11 The raised projection on the spring seat (arrowed) must align with the swivel hub mounting brackets (arrowed)

5.12 The pointer on the mounting (arrowed) must face the rear of the vehicle

of the spring is correctly located in the recess on the lower spring seat (see illustration).

11 Locate the upper spring seat over the piston rod, ensuring that the raised projection on the spring seat is on the same side as the swivel hub mounting bracket at the base of the strut (see illustration).

12 Refit the upper mounting and position it so that the pointer on the seat flange will be facing the rear of the car when the strut is installed (see illustration).

13 Fit the piston rod top nut, then tighten the nut to the specified torque, counterholding the piston rod in a manner similar to that used during dismantling. Note that a suitable crows-foot adapter or flange-drive socket (Vortex) will be required to tighten the piston rod top nut to the specified torque.

14 Remove the spring compressors and refit the strut to the car as described in Section 4.

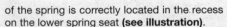

6 Front suspension lower arm – removal and refitting

Removal

1 Firmly apply the handbrake, then jack up the front of the car and support it securely on axle stands (see Jacking and vehicle support). Remove the relevant roadwheel.

500 models

2 Remove the front bumper as described in Chapter 11.

3 Remove the support bracket between the front subframe and the vehicle body, then remove inner wheel arch liner panel (see illustration).

4 Undo the retaining bolts and remove the lower, front crossmember (see illustration).

5 Undo the retaining bolts and remove the extension strut from the front of the subframe on the relevant side (see illustration).

All models

6 Slacken and remove the nut, then withdraw the suspension lower arm balljoint clamp bolt from the swivel hub.

7 Tap a small chisel into the split on the swivel hub to spread the hub slightly, then lever the end of the suspension lower arm down to release it from the base of the swivel hub.

8 Unscrew the bolt securing the suspension lower arm rear mounting to the subframe (see illustration).

9 Slacken and remove the nut from the through-bolt at the lower arm front mounting (see illustrations). Withdraw the bolt.

6.3 Remove the support bracket and wheel arch liner panel (arrowed)

6.4 Remove the front, lower crossmember (arrowed)

6.5 Undo the bolts (arrowed) and remove the subframe extension strut – 500 models only

6.8 Lower arm rear mounting bolt (arrowed)

6.9a Lower arm front mounting bolt (arrowed) – 500 models . . .

6.9b . . . and Panda models (arrowed)

6.16 Raise the lower arm so the distance between the lower edge and the subframe upper edge is 187 mm

10 Manoeuvre the suspension lower arm from its mounting locations and remove it from under the car.
11 With the lower arm removed, examine the arm itself, and the mounting bushes, for wear, cracks or damage.
12 Check the balljoint for wear, excessive play, or stiffness. Also check the balljoint dust boot for cracks or damage.
13 The mounting bushes and balljoint assembly are integral with the suspension lower arm, and cannot be renewed independently. If either the bushes or the balljoint are worn or damaged, the complete suspension lower arm assembly must be renewed.

Refitting

14 Locate the suspension lower arm in its mountings. Fit the through-bolt to the front mounting bracket and engage it with the lower arm bush. Fit the securing nut, but do not fully-tighten it at this stage.
15 Refit the rear mounting bolt, but do not fully-tighten the bolt at this stage.
16 Using a trolley jack, raise the outer end of the lower arm until it's positioned as shown **(see illustration)**, then tighten the front and rear mounting bolts to the specified torque.

17 Engage the lower arm balljoint with the swivel hub, then refit the balljoint clamp bolt and nut. Tighten the clamp bolt nut to the specified torque.

500 models

18 Refit the subframe extension struts, and tighten the retaining bolts to their specified torque.
19 Refit the front crossmember, then tighten the retaining bolts to the specified torque.
20 Refit the wheel arch liner panel, bracket and bumper as described in Chapter 11.

All models

21 Refit the roadwheel, and lower the car to the ground.
22 On completion, have the front wheel toe setting checked at the earliest opportunity.

7 Front suspension lower arm balljoint – renewal

The balljoint is integral with the suspension lower arm. If the balljoint is worn or damaged, the complete lower arm must be renewed, as described in Section 6.

8 Front anti-roll bar – removal and refitting

Removal

1 Firmly apply the handbrake, then jack up the front of the car and support it securely on axle stands (see *Jacking and vehicle support*). Remove both front roadwheels.
2 Undo the nut each side, securing the link rods to the ends of the anti-roll bar. Use an Allen key in the balljoint shank to counterhold the nut **(see illustration)**.
3 On 500 models, undo the bolts and remove

the front subframe-to-body bracket each side **(see illustration 6.3)**.
4 Undo the bolts securing the anti-roll bar clamps to the front subframe **(see illustration)**.
5 Undo the bolts securing the steering rack to the subframe **(see illustration 15.10)**.
6 Paint alignment marks between the subframe and vehicle body to aid refitting.
7 Place a workshop/trolley jack under the front subframe, then slacken the retaining bolts and lower the front subframe slightly **(see illustration 9.7)**.
8 Manoeuvre the anti-roll bar assembly through the wheel arch aperture.
9 Inspect the rubber bushes for cracks or deterioration. If renewal is necessary, at the time of writing, it would appear that the complete anti-roll bar must be renewed – the bushes are not available separately. Check with a Fiat dealer or parts specialist.
10 Check the anti-roll bar for signs of damage, wear or serious corrosion.

Refitting

11 Refitting is a reversal of removal, bearing in mind the following points:
a) *Moderately tighten the anti-roll bar mountings initially, then tighten them all to the specified torque after the car has been lowered to the ground and is resting on its roadwheels.*
b) *Tighten all fasteners to their specified torque where given.*
c) *Align the previously-made marks prior to tightening the subframe mounting bolts.*

9 Front subframe – removal and refitting

Removal

1 Remove both front suspension lower arms as described in Section 6.

8.2 Undo the nut (arrowed) securing the anti-roll bar to the link rod

8.4 Anti-roll bar clamp bolts (arrowed)

9.7 Front subframe mounting bolt locations (arrowed)

10.4 Prise off the dust cap

2 Undo the bolts and remove the rear, lower engine/transmission link rod.

3 Remove the rear silencer and centre exhaust pipe as described in Chapter 4A or 4B.

4 Undo the bolts securing the anti-roll bar clamps to the subframe (see illustration 8.4).

5 Undo the bolts securing the steering rack to the subframe (see illustration 15.10).

6 Paint alignment marks between the subframe and vehicle body to aid refitting.

7 Position a workshop/trolley jack under the subframe, then undo the retaining bolts and lower the subframe from place (see illustration).

Refitting

8 Raise the subframe into position, align the previously-made marks, then tighten the retaining bolts to the specified torque.

9 The remainder of refitting is a reversal of removal, noting the following points:

 a) Tighten all fasteners to their specified torque where given.

 b) Moderately tighten the anti-roll bar mountings initially, then tighten them all to the specified torque after the car has been lowered to the ground and is resting on its roadwheels.

 c) Have the front wheel alignment checked at the earliest opportunity.

10 Rear hub assembly – removal and refitting

Note: A new rear hub retaining nut must be used on refitting.

Removal

1 The rear hub bearings are integral with the hubs themselves, and cannot be renewed separately. If the bearings require renewal, the complete hub assembly must be renewed.

2 Chock the front wheels, then jack up the rear of the vehicle and support securely on axle stands (see Jacking and vehicle support). Remove the appropriate rear roadwheel.

3 Remove the brake drum as described in Chapter 9. **Do not** depress the brake pedal whilst the brake drum is removed.

4 Prise the dust cap from the hub, using a mallet and chisel (see illustration).

5 Slacken and remove the hub nut and recover the spacer.

Caution: The nut is tightened to a very high torque. Use a long extension bar to remove the nut and ensure that you have access to torque wrench capable of tightening

the new nut to the specified torque before removing the existing nut.

6 Withdraw the hub and bearing assembly from the stub axle, and recover the inner spacer. Discard the hub nut – a new one must be used on refitting.

7 Thoroughly clean the stub axle, then slide the inner spacer and the hub assembly into position.

8 Fit the outer spacer, then thread a new hub nut onto the end of the stub axle.

9 Tighten the hub nut to the specified torque, then check that the hub spins smoothly and freely. Carefully tap the dust cap into position over the nut.

10 Refit the brake drum as described in Chapter 9.

11 Refit the roadwheel and lower the car to the ground.

11 Rear suspension components – removal and refitting

1 Chock the front wheels then jack up the rear of the car and securely support it on axle stands (see Jacking and vehicle support). Remove the relevant rear roadwheel(s).

Shock absorber

Removal

2 Using a trolley jack positioned under the rear axle trailing arm, raise the trailing arm to take the strain from the shock absorber.

3 Slacken and withdraw the shock absorber lower retaining bolt (see illustration).

4 Lower the jack and allow the shock absorber to separate from the trailing arm. Take care to avoid displacing the coil spring.

5 Slacken and withdraw the shock absorber upper retaining bolt (see illustration).

6 Withdraw the shock absorber from its upper mounting and remove it from under the car.

7 Examine the shock absorber for signs of

11.3 Rear shock absorber lower mounting bolt . . .

11.5 . . . and upper mounting bolt

fluid leakage or damage. While holding it in an upright position, test the operation of the shock absorber by moving the piston through a full stroke, and then through short strokes of 50 to 100 mm. In both cases, the resistance felt should be smooth and continuous. If the resistance is jerky, or uneven, or if there is any visible sign of wear or damage, renewal is necessary.

Refitting

8 Refitting is a reversal of removal. Tighten the shock absorber upper and lower retaining bolts to the specified torque, but delay this operation until the full weight of the car is resting on its roadwheels.

Coil spring

Removal

9 Using a trolley jack positioned under the rear axle trailing arm, raise the trailing arm to take the strain from the shock absorbers.
10 Slacken and withdraw the shock absorber lower retaining bolts on both sides.
11 Lower the trailing arm gradually using a trolley jack, until the coil spring is released from its lower seat on the trailing arm and its upper seat on the underbody. Make a note of the orientation of the coil spring, to aid correct refitting later.

Refitting

12 Refitting is a reversal of removal. Tighten the shock absorber retaining bolts to the specified torque, but delay this operation until the full weight of the car is resting on its roadwheels.

Stub axle

Removal

13 Remove the rear hub assembly as described in Section 9.
14 Remove the rear brake shoes as described in Chapter 9.
15 Using a brake hose clamp, clamp the brake flexible hydraulic hose located adjacent to the rear axle mounting.
16 Clean the brake backplate around the wheel cylinder hydraulic pipe union, then unscrew the union nut and disconnect the hydraulic pipe. Cover the open ends of the pipe and the wheel cylinder to prevent dirt ingress.
17 On models with ABS, slacken and remove the bolt securing the rear wheel speed sensor to the rear of the stub axle and withdraw the sensor from its location. Suspend the sensor away from the working area, to avoid the possibility of damage.
18 Undo the two bolts and remove the brake backplate from the stub axle.
19 Undo the four nuts, withdraw the bolts and remove the stub axle from the rear axle bracket **(see illustration)**.

Refitting

20 Ensure that the stub axle and rear axle bracket mating faces are clean, then locate

the stub axle in position. Refit the retaining bolts and nuts and tighten the nuts to the specified torque.
21 Locate the brake backplate on the stub axle, refit the bolts and tighten them securely. Connect the brake pipe to the wheel cylinder and securely tighten the union nut. Remove the brake hose clamp from the flexible hydraulic hose.
22 Refit the rear brake shoes as described in Chapter 9.
23 Refit the rear hub assembly as described in Section 9.
24 Ensure that the mating faces of the wheel speed sensor and the stub axle are clean, and apply a smear of high melting-point brake grease to the sensor location in the stub axle. Clean the end face of the sensor, locate it in place and secure with the retaining bolt.
25 On completion, bleed the brake hydraulic system as described in Chapter 9. Note that if no other part of the system has been disturbed, it should only be necessary to bleed the relevant rear circuit.

Rear axle assembly

Note: *On Panda models, at the time of writing, the rubber-in-torsion pivot bushes at the front end of the rear axle assembly are not available separately. If either is worn or damaged, the complete rear axle assembly must be renewed.*

Removal

26 Remove the rear brake shoes on both sides as described in Chapter 9.
27 Using brake hose clamps, clamp the brake flexible hydraulic hoses located adjacent to each rear axle mounting.
28 Clean the area around the brake pipe-to-flexible hose union nuts, and unscrew the pipe unions on each side. Extract the retaining clips and detach the flexible hoses from the brackets on the rear axle. Cover the open ends of the pipes and hoses to prevent dirt ingress.
29 On models with ABS, slacken and remove the bolts securing the rear wheel speed sensors to the rear of the stub axles and withdraw the sensors from their location. Suspend the sensors away from the working area, to avoid the possibility of damage.
30 Release the handbrake cables, and where

11.19 Stub axle retaining nuts (arrowed)

applicable, the rear wheel speed sensor cables, from their clips on the rear axle.
31 Remove both rear coil springs as described previously in this Section.
32 Suitably support the rear axle assembly on a trolley jack and engage the help of an assistant.
33 Undo the bolts securing the rear axle mounting brackets to the underbody on both sides. Slowly lower the jack and guide the axle assembly down and out from under the car.
34 On 500 models, it is possible to renew the axle mounting bushes. Undo the nuts/bolts and remove the mounting bracket from the front end of the axle.
35 Note the fitted position of the bushes, then using a combination of washers, spacers, a length of threaded rod and nuts, draw the bush from place each side. Note that Fiat special tool No 2.000.025.600 may be available for this task.
36 Using soapy water as a lubricant, position the new bushes on the axle, and draw them into place using the same method as removal.
37 Refit the mounting brackets and tighten the nuts/bolts to the specified torque.

Refitting

38 Guide the axle assembly into position, refit the mounting bracket retaining bolts and tighten them to the specified torque.
39 Refit the rear coil springs as described previously in this Section.
40 Ensure that the mating faces of the wheel speed sensors and the stub axles are clean, and apply a smear of high melting-point brake grease to the sensor locations in the stub axles. Clean the end face of the sensors, locate them place and secure with the retaining bolts.
41 Refit the flexible brake hydraulic hoses to their mounting brackets and secure with the retaining clips. Reconnect the brake pipe union to each hose and tighten the union nut securely. Remove the brake hose clamps from the hoses.
42 Secure the handbrake cables, and where applicable, the rear wheel speed sensor cables, in their clips on the rear axle.
43 Refer to Chapter 9 and refit the rear brake shoes then bleed the brake hydraulic system. Note that if no other part of the system has been disturbed, it should only be necessary to bleed the rear circuits.

---

12 Steering wheel –
  removal and refitting

Removal

1 Remove the airbag unit from the steering wheel as described in Chapter 12.
2 Turn the steering wheel to its centre position, so that the roadwheels are pointing straight-ahead.
3 Lift off the protective seal over the steering

12.3 Lift the protective seal over the retaining nut

12.5 There should already be alignment marks between the steering wheel and column shaft (arrowed)

12.6 Disconnect the horn switch wiring plug

wheel retaining nut **(see illustration)**.

4 Slacken and remove the steering wheel retaining nut. Discard the nut as a new item must be used on refitting.

5 If no marks are visible, make alignment marks between the steering wheel and the end of the steering column shaft, to aid correct refitting later **(see illustration)**.

6 Disconnect the horn switch wiring connector and lift the steering wheel off the column splines. If it is tight, twist it from side-to-side, whilst pulling upwards to release it from the shaft splines **(see illustration)**. Once the wheel is free, feed the airbag and horn switch wiring through the aperture in the steering wheel and remove the wheel from the car.

7 With the steering wheel removed, the clock spring assembly should be locked in place. It is advisable to secure the moving and fixed portions of the clock spring together using

tape to prevent rotation with the steering wheel removed.

Refitting

8 Check that the airbag clock spring is still centred correctly as described in paragraph 7. Remove the tape used to secure the clock spring moving and fixed portions together.

9 Feed the airbag and horn switch wiring through the steering wheel and locate the wheel on the column splines. Ensure that the marks made on the steering wheel and column shaft are aligned.

10 Screw on a new steering wheel retaining nut and tighten the nut to the specified torque. Refit the protective seal over the retaining nut.

11 Reconnect the horn switch wiring connector.

12 Refit the airbag unit as described in Chapter 12.

13 Steering column – removal and refitting

Removal

1 Remove the steering wheel as described in Section 11.

2 Remove the steering column combination switch assembly as described in Chapter 12.

Panda models

3 Undo the retaining bolts and remove the metal guard plate beneath the power steering electric motor (where fitted) **(see illustration)**.

500 models

4 Remove the complete facia as described in Chapter 11.

5 Undo the retaining bolts/nut and remove the bracket beneath the steering column **(see illustration)**.

All models

6 Note their fitted positions and loom routing, then disconnect the various wiring plugs from the column.

7 Working in the driver's footwell, unscrew the clamp bolt on the intermediate shaft lower universal joint **(see illustration)**. The joint and rack pinion are equipped with a master spline, so they will only align in one position. Discard the bolt – a new one must be fitted.

8 Undo the steering column retaining nuts/bolts and manoeuvre the assembly away from the bulkhead bracket **(see illustrations)**.

9 Disconnect the universal joint from the

13.3 Undo the bolts (arrowed) and remove the metal guard plate

13.5 Remove the metal bracket (arrowed) beneath the column

13.7 Intermediate shaft lower clamp bolt (arrowed)

13.8a Steering column upper mounting retaining nuts (arrowed)

13.8b Manoeuvre the steering column assembly away from the bulkhead

steering gear pinion, and remove the steering column from the car.

Refitting

10 Refitting is a reversal of removal, bearing in mind the following points.
 a) *Ensure that the roadwheels are in the straight-ahead position then engage the universal joint with the steering gear pinion, aligning the marks made on removal.*
 b) *Tighten all retaining nuts and bolts to the specified torque.*
 c) *Refit the steering column stalk switches and airbag clock spring as described in Chapter 12.*
 d) *Refit the steering wheel as described in Section 11.*

14 Power steering electric motor – removal and refitting

It would appear at the time of writing, that no separate parts are available for the steering column (except for the ignition switch/steering lock assembly – see Chapter 5A). Consequently, if faulty, the complete steering column assembly must be renewed. Consult a Fiat parts specialist.

15 Rack-and-pinion steering gear assembly – removal and refitting

Removal

1 Turn the steering wheel to its centre position, so that the roadwheels are pointing straight-ahead.
2 Firmly apply the handbrake, then jack up the front of the car and support it securely on axle stands (see *Jacking and vehicle support*). Remove both front roadwheels.

500 models
3 Remove the front bumper as described in Chapter 11.
4 Remove the support bracket between the front subframe and the vehicle body, then remove inner wheel arch liner panel (see illustrations 6.3).
5 Undo the retaining bolts and remove the lower, front crossmember (see illustration 6.4).
6 Undo the retaining bolts and remove the extension strut from the front of the subframe on the relevant side (see illustration 6.5).

All models
7 Working in the driver's footwell, unscrew the clamp bolt securing the intermediate shaft lower universal joint. Make suitable alignment marks on the steering gear pinion and universal joint to ensure correct orientation when refitting. Discard the bolt – a new one must be fitted.
8 Unscrew the nut securing the track rod end to the swivel hub. Release the track rod end tapered shank using a balljoint separator tool.
9 Undo the bolt securing the rear engine/transmission mounting to the subframe.

10 Undo the bolts securing the steering rack to the subframe (see illustration).
11 Paint alignment marks between the subframe and vehicle body to aid refitting.
12 Place a workshop/trolley jack under the front subframe, then slacken the retaining bolts and lower the front subframe slightly (see illustration 9.7).
13 Rotate the steering gear downwards to release it from the bulkhead, then withdraw the steering gear through the wheel arch.

Refitting

14 Refitting is a reversal of removal, bearing in mind the following points.
 a) *Centralise the steering gear by turning the pinion so that the rack moves to full left lock. Now move the rack to full right lock, counting the number of turns of the pinion. Turn the pinion back by half the number of turns counted.*
 b) *Ensure that the roadwheels are in the straight-ahead position then engage steering gear pinion with the universal joint, aligning the marks made on removal.*
 c) *Align the previously-made marks prior to tightening the subframe mounting bolts.*
 d) *Tighten all retaining nuts and bolts to the specified torque.*
 e) *Have the front wheel toe setting checked at the earliest opportunity.*

16 Steering gear rubber gaiters – renewal

Note: *New gaiter retaining clips should be used on refitting.*
1 Remove the relevant track rod end as described in Section 17.
2 Make an alignment mark between the track rod end locknut and the track rod, to allow the locknut to be accurately positioned when refitting. Unscrew the locknut from the end of the track rod.
3 Mark the correct fitted position of the gaiter on the track rod, then release the gaiter securing clips. Slide the gaiter from the steering gear, and off the track rod.
4 Thoroughly clean the track rod and the steering gear housing, using fine abrasive paper to polish off any corrosion, burrs or sharp edges

17.3 Use a separator tool to detach the track rod end balljoint from the swivel hub

15.10 Steering rack mounting bolts (arrowed)

which might damage the new gaiter sealing lips on installation. Scrape off all the grease from the old gaiter, and apply it to the track rod inner balljoint. (This assumes that grease has not been lost or contaminated as a result of damage to the old gaiter. Use fresh grease if in doubt.)
5 Carefully slide the new gaiter onto the track rod, and locate it on the steering gear housing. Align the outer edge of the gaiter with the mark made on the track rod prior to removal, then secure it in position with new retaining clips.
6 Screw the track rod end locknut onto the end of the track rod and position it accurately in accordance with the mark made on removal.
7 Refit the track rod end as described in Section 17.

17 Track rod end – removal and refitting

Removal

1 Firmly apply the handbrake, then jack up the front of the car and support it securely on axle stands (see *Jacking and vehicle support*). Remove the relevant front roadwheel.
2 Hold the track rod, and unscrew the track rod end locknut by a quarter of a turn. Do not move the locknut from this position, as it will serve as a handy reference mark on refitting.
3 Partially unscrew the nut securing the track rod end to the steering arm (see illustration).
4 Using a balljoint separator tool, separate the track rod end from the steering arm (see illustration). Remove the nut and lift the track rod end from the arm.

17.4 Track rod end locking nut (arrowed)

5 Counting the **exact** number of turns necessary to do so, unscrew the track rod end from the track rod.

Refitting

6 Carefully clean the track rod end and the track rod threads.

7 Renew the track rod end if the rubber dust cover is cracked, split or perished, or if the movement of the balljoint is either sloppy or too stiff. Also check for other signs of damage such as worn threads.

8 Screw the track rod end onto the track rod by the number of turns noted during removal. This should bring it to within a quarter of a turn from the locknut. Hold the track rod and securely tighten the locknut.

18.1 Steering geometry details

9 Ensure that the balljoint taper is clean, then engage the taper with the steering arm on the swivel hub.

10 Refit the track rod end retaining nut, and tighten the nut to the specified torque.

11 Refit the roadwheel, and lower the car to the ground.

12 Have the front wheel toe setting checked at the earliest opportunity.

18 Wheel alignment and steering angles – general information

Definitions

1 A car's steering and suspension geometry is defined in four basic settings **(see illustration)** – all angles are usually expressed in degrees (toe settings are also expressed as a measurement); the steering axis is defined as an imaginary line drawn through the axis of the suspension strut, extended where necessary to contact the ground.

Camber

2 Camber is the angle between each roadwheel and a vertical line drawn through its centre and tyre contact patch, when viewed from the front or rear of the car. Positive camber is when the roadwheels are tilted outwards from the vertical at the top; negative camber is when they are tilted inwards.

3 The front camber angle is not adjustable, and is given for reference only (see paragraph 5). The rear camber angle is adjustable and can be adjusted using a camber angle gauge.

Castor

4 Castor is the angle between the steering axis and a vertical line drawn through each roadwheel's centre and tyre contact patch, when viewed from the side of the car. Positive castor is when the steering axis is tilted so that it contacts the ground ahead of the vertical; negative castor is when it contacts the ground behind the vertical.

5 Castor is not adjustable, and is given for reference only; while it can be checked using a castor checking gauge, if the figure obtained is significantly different from that specified, the car must be taken for careful checking by a professional, as the fault can only be caused by wear or damage to the body or suspension components.

Toe

6 Toe is the difference, viewed from above, between lines drawn through the roadwheel centres and the car's centre-line. 'Toe-in' is when the roadwheels point inwards, towards each other at the front, while 'toe-out' is when they splay outwards from each other at the front.

7 The front wheel toe setting is adjusted by screwing the right-hand track rod in or out of its balljoint, to alter the effective length of the track rod assembly.

8 Rear wheel toe setting is also adjustable. The toe setting is adjusted by slackening the trailing arm mounting bracket bolts and repositioning the bracket.

Checking and adjustment

Front wheel toe setting

9 Due to the special measuring equipment necessary to check the wheel alignment, and the skill required to use it properly, the checking and adjustment of these settings is best left to a Fiat dealer or similar expert. Note that most tyre-fitting shops now possess sophisticated checking equipment.

10 To check the toe setting, a tracking gauge must first be obtained. Two types of gauge are available, and can be obtained from motor accessory shops. The first type measures the distance between the front and rear inside edges of the roadwheels, as previously described, with the car stationary. The second type, known as a 'scuff plate', measures the actual position of the contact surface of the tyre, in relation to the road surface, with the car in motion. This is achieved by pushing or driving the front tyre over a plate, which then moves slightly according to the scuff of the tyre, and shows this movement on a scale. Both types have their advantages and disadvantages, but either can give satisfactory results if used correctly and carefully.

11 Make sure that the steering is in the straight-ahead position when making measurements.

12 If adjustment is necessary, apply the handbrake then jack up the front of the car and support it securely on axle stands.

13 First clean the track rod threads; if they are corroded, apply penetrating fluid before starting adjustment. Release the rubber gaiter outer clips, peel back the gaiters and apply a smear of grease so that both are free and will not be twisted or strained as their respective track rods are rotated.

14 Retain the track rod with a suitable spanner and slacken the locknut. Alter the length of the track rod, by screwing them into or out of the balljoints by rotating the track rod using an open-ended spanner fitted to the track rod flats provided; shortening the track rods (screwing them onto their balljoints) will reduce toe-in/increase toe-out.

15 When the setting is correct, hold the track rod and tighten the locknut to the specified torque setting. If after adjustment, the steering wheel spokes are no longer horizontal when the wheels are in the straight-ahead position, remove the steering wheel and reposition it (see Section 17).

16 Check that the toe setting has been correctly adjusted by lowering the car to the ground and rechecking the toe setting; re-adjust if necessary. Ensure that the rubber gaiters are seated correctly and are not twisted or strained, and secure them in position with the retaining clips; where necessary fit a new retaining clip.

Chapter 11
Bodywork and fittings

Contents

Degrees of difficulty

Easy, suitable for novice with little experience	⚙	**Fairly easy,** suitable for beginner with some experience	⚙	**Fairly difficult,** suitable for competent DIY mechanic	⚙	**Difficult,** suitable for experienced DIY mechanic	⚙	**Very difficult,** suitable for expert DIY or professional	⚙

Specifications

Torque wrench settings	Nm	lbf ft
Front seat belt inertia reel	40	30
Rear seat belt inertia reel	40	30
Rear seat belt lower anchor on wheel arch	20	15
Rear seat belt stalk	40	30

1 General information

The bodyshell is composed of pressed-steel sections which are welded together, although some use of structural adhesives is made. In addition, the front wings are bolted on.

The bonnet, door and some other panels vulnerable to corrosion are fabricated from zinc-coated metal. A coating of anti-chip primer, applied prior to paint spraying provides further protection.

Extensive use is made of plastic materials, mainly in the interior, but also in exterior components. The outer sections of the front and rear bumpers are injection-moulded from a synthetic material which is very strong, and yet light. Plastic components such as wheel arch liners are fitted to the underside of the vehicle, to improve the body's resistance to corrosion.

2 Maintenance – bodywork and underframe

The general condition of a vehicle's bodywork is the one thing that significantly affects its value. Maintenance is easy, but needs to be regular. Neglect, particularly after minor damage, can lead quickly to further deterioration and costly repair bills. It is important also to keep watch on those parts of the vehicle not immediately visible, for instance the underside, inside all the wheel arches, and the lower part of the engine compartment.

The basic maintenance routine for the bodywork is washing – preferably with a lot of water, from a hose. This will remove all the loose solids which may have stuck to the vehicle. It is important to flush these off in such a way as to prevent grit from scratching the finish. The wheel arches and underframe need washing in the same way, to remove any accumulated mud, which will retain moisture and tend to encourage rust. Paradoxically enough, the best time to clean the underframe and wheel arches is in wet weather, when the mud is thoroughly wet and soft. In very wet weather, the underframe is usually cleaned of large accumulations automatically, and this is a good time for inspection.

Periodically, except on vehicles with a wax-based underbody protective coating, it is a good idea to have the whole of the underframe of the vehicle steam-cleaned, engine compartment included, so that a thorough inspection can be carried out to see what minor repairs and renovations are necessary. Steam-cleaning is available at many garages, and is necessary for the removal of the accumulation of oily grime, which sometimes is allowed to become thick in certain areas. If steam-cleaning facilities are not available, there are some excellent grease solvents available which can be brush-applied; the dirt can then be simply hosed off. Note that these methods should not be used on vehicles with wax-based underbody protective coating, or the coating will be removed. Such vehicles should be inspected annually, preferably just prior to Winter, when the underbody should be washed down, and any damage to the wax coating repaired. Ideally, a completely fresh coat should be applied. It would also be worth considering the use of such wax-based protection for injection into door panels, sills, box sections, etc, as an additional safeguard against rust damage, where such protection is not provided by the vehicle manufacturer.

After washing paintwork, wipe off with a chamois leather to give an unspotted clear finish. A coat of clear protective wax polish will give added protection against chemical pollutants in the air. If the paintwork sheen has dulled or oxidised, use a cleaner/polisher combination to restore the brilliance of the shine. This requires a little effort, but such dulling is usually caused because regular washing has been neglected. Care needs to be taken with metallic paintwork, as special non-abrasive cleaner/polisher is required to avoid damage to the finish. Always check that the door and ventilator opening drain holes and pipes are completely clear, so that water can be drained out. Brightwork should be treated in the same way as paintwork. Windscreens and windows can be kept clear of the smeary film which often appears, by the use of proprietary glass cleaner. Never use any form of wax or other body or chromium polish on glass.

3 Maintenance –
upholstery and carpets

Mats and carpets should be brushed or vacuum-cleaned regularly, to keep them free of grit. If they are badly stained, remove them

from the vehicle for scrubbing or sponging, and make quite sure they are dry before refitting. Seats and interior trim panels can be kept clean by wiping with a damp cloth. If they do become stained (which can be more apparent on light-coloured upholstery), use a little liquid detergent and a soft nail brush to scour the grime out of the grain of the material. Do not forget to keep the headlining clean in the same way as the upholstery. When using liquid cleaners inside the vehicle, do not over-wet the surfaces being cleaned. Excessive damp could get into the seams and padded interior, causing stains, offensive odours or even rot.

4 Minor body damage – repair

Minor scratches

If the scratch is very superficial, and does not penetrate to the metal of the bodywork, repair is very simple. Lightly rub the area of the scratch with a paintwork renovator, or a very fine cutting paste, to remove loose paint from the scratch, and to clear the surrounding bodywork of wax polish. Rinse the area with clean water.

Apply touch-up paint to the scratch using a fine paint brush; continue to apply fine layers of paint until the surface of the paint in the scratch is level with the surrounding paintwork. Allow the new paint at least two weeks to harden, then blend it into the surrounding paintwork by rubbing the scratch area with a paintwork renovator or a very fine cutting paste. Finally, apply wax polish.

Where the scratch has penetrated right through to the metal of the bodywork, causing the metal to rust, a different repair technique is required. Remove any loose rust from the bottom of the scratch with a penknife, then apply rust-inhibiting paint to prevent the formation of rust in the future. Using a rubber or nylon applicator, fill the scratch with bodystopper paste. If required, this paste can be mixed with cellulose thinners to provide a very thin paste which is ideal for filling narrow scratches. Before the stopper-paste in the scratch hardens, wrap a piece of smooth cotton rag around the top of a finger. Dip the finger in cellulose thinners, and quickly sweep it across the surface of the stopper-paste in the scratch; this will ensure that the surface of the stopper-paste is slightly hollowed. The scratch can now be painted over as described earlier in this Section.

Dents

When deep denting of the vehicle's bodywork has taken place, the first task is to pull the dent out, until the affected bodywork almost attains its original shape. There is little point in trying to restore the original shape completely, as the metal in the damaged area

will have stretched on impact, and cannot be reshaped fully to its original contour. It is better to bring the level of the dent up to a point which is about 3 mm below the level of the surrounding bodywork. In cases where the dent is very shallow anyway, it is not worth trying to pull it out at all. If the underside of the dent is accessible, it can be hammered out gently from behind, using a mallet with a wooden or plastic head. Whilst doing this, hold a suitable block of wood firmly against the outside of the panel, to absorb the impact from the hammer blows and thus prevent a large area of the bodywork from being 'belled-out'.

Should the dent be in a section of the bodywork which has a double skin, or some other factor making it inaccessible from behind, a different technique is called for. Drill several small holes through the metal inside the area – particularly in the deeper section. Then screw long self-tapping screws into the holes, just sufficiently for them to gain a good purchase in the metal. Now the dent can be pulled out by pulling on the protruding heads of the screws with a pair of pliers.

The next stage of the repair is the removal of the paint from the damaged area, and from an inch or so of the surrounding 'sound' bodywork. This is accomplished most easily by using a wire brush or abrasive pad on a power drill, although it can be done just as effectively by hand, using sheets of abrasive paper. To complete the preparation for filling, score the surface of the bare metal with a screwdriver or the tang of a file, or alternatively, drill small holes in the affected area. This will provide a really good 'key' for the filler paste.

To complete the repair, see the Section on filling and respraying.

Rust holes or gashes

Remove all paint from the affected area, and from an inch or so of the surrounding 'sound' bodywork, using an abrasive pad or a wire brush on a power drill. If these are not available, a few sheets of abrasive paper will do the job most effectively. With the paint removed, you will be able to judge the severity of the corrosion, and therefore decide whether to renew the whole panel (if this is possible) or to repair the affected area. New body panels are not as expensive as most people think, and it is often quicker and more satisfactory to fit a new panel than to attempt to repair large areas of corrosion.

Remove all fittings from the affected area, except those which will act as a guide to the original shape of the damaged bodywork (eg headlight shells etc). Then, using tin snips or a hacksaw blade, remove all loose metal and any other metal badly affected by corrosion. Hammer the edges of the hole inwards, in order to create a slight depression for the filler paste.

Wire-brush the affected area to remove the powdery rust from the surface of the remaining metal. Paint the affected area with rust-inhibiting paint, if the back of the rusted area is accessible, treat this also.

Before filling can take place, it will be necessary to block the hole in some way. This can be achieved by the use of aluminium or plastic mesh, or aluminium tape.

Aluminium or plastic mesh, or glass-fibre matting, is probably the best material to use for a large hole. Cut a piece to the approximate size and shape of the hole to be filled, then position it in the hole so that its edges are below the level of the surrounding bodywork. It can be retained in position by several blobs of filler paste around its periphery.

Aluminium tape should be used for small or very narrow holes. Pull a piece off the roll, trim it to the approximate size and shape required, then pull off the backing paper (if used) and stick the tape over the hole; it can be overlapped if the thickness of one piece is insufficient. Burnish down the edges of the tape with the handle of a screwdriver or similar, to ensure that the tape is securely attached to the metal underneath.

Filling and respraying

Before using this Section, see the Sections on dent, deep scratch, rust holes and gash repairs.

Many types of bodyfiller are available, but generally speaking, those proprietary kits which contain a tin of filler paste and a tube of resin hardener are best for this type of repair. A wide, flexible plastic or nylon applicator will be found invaluable for imparting a smooth and well-contoured finish to the surface of the filler.

Mix up a little filler on a clean piece of card or board – measure the hardener carefully (follow the maker's instructions on the pack), otherwise the filler will set too rapidly or too slowly. Using the applicator, apply the filler paste to the prepared area; draw the applicator across the surface of the filler to achieve the correct contour and to level the surface. As soon as a contour that approximates to the correct one is achieved, stop working the paste – if you carry on too long, the paste will become sticky and begin to 'pick-up' on the applicator. Continue to add thin layers of filler paste at 20-minute intervals, until the level of the filler is just proud of the surrounding bodywork.

Once the filler has hardened, the excess can be removed using a metal plane or file. From then on, progressively-finer grades of abrasive paper should be used, starting with a 40-grade production paper, and finishing with a 400-grade wet-and-dry paper. Always wrap the abrasive paper around a flat rubber, cork, or wooden block – otherwise the surface of the filler will not be completely flat. During the smoothing of the filler surface, the wet-and-dry paper should be periodically rinsed in water. This will ensure that a very smooth finish is imparted to the filler at the final stage.

At this stage, the dent should be surrounded by a ring of bare metal, which in turn should be encircled by the finely 'feathered' edge of the good paintwork. Rinse the repair area with clean water, until all of the dust produced by the rubbing-down operation has gone.

Spray the whole area with a light coat of primer – this will show up any imperfections in the surface of the filler. Repair these imperfections with fresh filler paste or bodystopper, and once more smooth the surface with abrasive paper. Repeat this spray-and-repair procedure until you are satisfied that the surface of the filler, and the feathered edge of the paintwork, are perfect. Clean the repair area with clean water, and allow to dry fully.

The repair area is now ready for final spraying. Paint spraying must be carried out in a warm, dry, windless and dust-free atmosphere. This condition can be created artificially if you have access to a large indoor working area, but if you are forced to work in the open, you will have to pick your day very carefully. If you are working indoors, dousing the floor in the work area with water will help to settle the dust which would otherwise be in the atmosphere. If the repair area is confined to one body panel, mask off the surrounding panels; this will help to minimise the effects of a slight mis-match in paint colours. Bodywork fittings (eg chrome strips, door handles etc) will also need to be masked off. Use genuine masking tape, and several thicknesses of newspaper, for the masking operations.

Before commencing to spray, agitate the aerosol can thoroughly, then spray a test area (an old tin, or similar) until the technique is mastered. Cover the repair area with a thick coat of primer; the thickness should be built up using several thin layers of paint, rather than one thick one. Using 400-grade wet-and-dry paper, rub down the surface of the primer until it is really smooth. While doing this, the work area should be thoroughly doused with water, and the wet-and-dry paper periodically rinsed in water. Allow to dry before spraying on more paint.

Spray on the top coat, again building up the thickness by using several thin layers of paint. Start spraying at one edge of the repair area, and then, using a side-to-side motion, work until the whole repair area and about 2 inches of the surrounding original paintwork is covered. Remove all masking material 10 to 15 minutes after spraying on the final coat of paint.

Allow the new paint at least two weeks to harden, then, using a paintwork renovator, or a very fine cutting paste, blend the edges of the paint into the existing paintwork. Finally, apply wax polish.

Plastic components

With the use of more and more plastic body components by the vehicle manufacturers (eg bumpers. spoilers, and in some cases major body panels), rectification of more serious damage to such items has become a matter of either entrusting repair work to a specialist in this field, or renewing complete components. Repair of such damage by the DIY owner is not really feasible, owing to the cost of the equipment and materials required for effecting such repairs. The basic technique involves making a groove along the line of the crack in the plastic, using a rotary burr in a power drill. The damaged part is then welded back together, using a hot-air gun to heat up and fuse a plastic filler rod into the groove. Any excess plastic is then removed, and the area rubbed down to a smooth finish. It is important that a filler rod of the correct plastic is used, as body components can be made of a variety of different types (eg polycarbonate, ABS, polypropylene).

Damage of a less serious nature (abrasions, minor cracks etc) can be repaired by the DIY owner using a two-part epoxy filler repair material. Once mixed in equal proportions, this is used in similar fashion to the bodywork filler used on metal panels. The filler is usually cured in twenty to thirty minutes, ready for sanding and painting.

If the owner is renewing a complete component himself, or if he has repaired it with epoxy filler, he will be left with the problem of finding a suitable paint for finishing which is compatible with the type of plastic used. At one time, the use of a universal paint was not possible, owing to the complex range of plastics encountered in body component applications. Standard paints, generally speaking, will not bond to plastic or rubber satisfactorily. However, it is now possible to obtain a plastic body parts finishing kit which consists of a pre-primer treatment, a primer and coloured top coat. Full instructions are normally supplied with a kit, but basically, the method of use is to first apply the pre-primer to the component concerned, and allow it to dry for up to 30 minutes. Then the primer is applied, and left to dry for about an hour before finally applying the special-coloured top coat. The result is a correctly-coloured component, where the paint will flex with the plastic or rubber, a property that standard paint does not normally possess.

5 Major body damage – repair

Where serious damage has occurred, or large areas need renewal due to neglect, it means that complete new panels will need welding-in, and this is best left to professionals. If the damage is due to impact, it will also be necessary to check completely the alignment of the bodyshell, and this can only be carried out accurately by a Fiat dealer using special jigs. If the alignment of the bodyshell is not corrected, the car's handling may be seriously affected. In addition, excessive stress may be imposed on the steering, suspension, tyres or transmission, causing abnormal wear or even complete failure.

6.3 Undo the bolts (arrowed) at the top edge of the bumper

6.4 Undo the bolts at the lower edge of the bumper (right-hand side bolts arrowed)

6.5 Undo the screws (arrowed) securing the wheel arch liner . . .

6 Bumpers – removal and refitting

Front bumper

1 For improved access, firmly apply the handbrake, then jack up the front of the car and support it securely on axle stands (see *Jacking and vehicle support*).

Panda models

2 Remove the front grille as described in Section 7.
3 Remove the retaining bolts at the top edge of the bumper (see illustration).
4 Undo the retaining bolts at the lower edge of the bumper (see illustration).

5 Undo the screws and pull back the front section of the wheel arch liner each side (see illustration).
6 Remove the screws each side securing the edge of the bumper to the front wing (see illustration).
7 Where applicable, unplug the wiring from the rear of the foglight units.
8 Unclip any electrical cabling secured to the rear side of the bumper then, with the help of an assistant, carefully draw the bumper away from the front of the car.
9 Refitting is a reversal of removal.

500 models

10 Undo the fasteners securing the front section of the wheel arch liner each side. For improved access, remove the front wheels.
11 Pull back the front section of the wheel

arch liner, then undo the bolts each side securing the lower, outer edge of the bumper in the wheel arch areas (see illustration).
12 Undo the screws at the top edge of the bumper (see illustration).
13 Undo the screws at the lower edge of the bumper (see illustration).
14 With the help of an assistant, pull out the rear edges, then carefully draw the bumper away from the front of the car (see illustrations). Disconnect the wiring plugs as the bumper is withdrawn.
15 Refitting is a reversal of removal.

Rear bumper

16 For improved access, chock the front wheels, then jack up the rear of the car and support it securely on axle stands (see *Jacking*

6.6 . . . then pull back the wheel arch liner and undo the screws (arrowed) securing the bumper to the wing

6.11 Undo the bolt (arrowed) each side securing the bumper to the wing

6.12 Remove the screws (arrowed) at the top edge of the bumper . . .

6.13 . . . and the lower edge (arrowed)

6.14a Pull out the rear edges of the bumper . . .

6.14b . . . disconnect the main beam units wiring plugs, and manoeuvre the bumper forwards

6.17a Undo the fasteners (arrowed) . . .

6.17b . . . and remove the rear section of the wheel arch liner each side

6.18 Undo the bolts (arrowed) securing the bumper to the wing

and vehicle support). For improved access, remove rear wheels.

Panda models

17 Undo the fasteners, and remove the rear section of the wheel arch liner each side **(see illustrations)**.

18 Reach up and remove the fasteners securing the upper edge of the bumper to the rear wing on each side **(see illustration)**.

19 From below, undo the bolts securing the rear bumper lower mountings to the brackets on the vehicle underbody **(see illustration)**.

20 Support the bumper, then undo the bolts from the upper edge of the bumper **(see illustration)**.

21 With the help of an assistant, carefully draw the bumper away from the car **(see illustration)**.

22 Refitting is a reversal of removal.

500 models

23 Remove the rear lights as described in Chapter 12.

24 Undo the fasteners securing the wheel arch liner to the bumper each side, then pull forwards the liner and remove the bumper-to-wing screw **(see illustrations)**.

25 Undo the screws on the underside of bumper **(see illustration)**.

26 Undo the fasteners on the upper edge of the bumper **(see illustration)**.

27 With the help of an assistant, carefully

6.19 Undo the bolts on the underside of the bumper (right-hand side bolt arrowed)

6.20 Remove the bolts (arrowed) along the upper edge . . .

6.21 . . . then withdrawn the bumper from the vehicle

6.24a Undo the wheel arch liner-to-bumper screws (arrowed) . . .

6.24b . . . then pull the liner forwards and remove the bumper-to-wing screw each side (arrowed)

6.25 Undo the screws on the bumper underside (arrowed) . . .

6.26 . . . and on the top edge (arrowed) each side

6.27 Pull out the edges, and withdraw the bumper

7.1 Undo the bolts (arrowed) . . .

7.2 . . . and lift the radiator grille upwards

draw the bumper away from the car (see illustration). Unclip the lower edge of the wheel arch liner as the bumper is withdrawn.
28 Refitting is a reversal of removal.

7 Radiator grille – removal and refitting

1 Open the bonnet, then remove the bolts at the upper edge (see illustration).
2 Remove the grille upwards (see illustration).
3 Refitting is a reversal of removal.

8 Tailgate – removal and refitting

Removal

1 Disconnect the battery negative terminal as described in Chapter 5A.
2 Remove the tailgate inner trim panel as described in Section 25.
3 On Panda models, undo the screws and remove the cover from the high-level brake light (see illustration). Disconnect the wiring plug.
4 On 500 models, prise out the caps, undo the bolts and remove the high-level brake light (see illustrations). Disconnect the wiring plug.
5 Disconnect the various wiring connectors for the tailgate lock, number plate light and

tailgate wiper motor then unbolt any earth leads. Check for any other wiring connectors which must be disconnected to facilitate tailgate removal. **Note:** *Carefully label each wiring harness connector to aid correct refitting.*
6 Tie a length of cord to the wiring harness, then bind the loose ends of the cabling together using PVC tape. Prise the wiring harness grommet from the upper edge of the tailgate, then feed the wiring through the aperture in the tailgate. Untie the cord from the harness, but leave it in place in the tailgate, to aid refitting later.
7 Disconnect the fluid hose from the tailgate washer nozzle, then tie a length of cord to the hose and draw it out of the tailgate, using the same procedure carried out on the wiring harness.
8 Have an assistant support the tailgate in the open position.
9 Detach the upper ends of the support struts from the tailgate as described in Section 9.
10 Slacken and unscrew the nuts or bolts (as applicable) securing the hinges to the tailgate, then lift the tailgate from the vehicle.

Refitting

11 Refitting is a reversal of removal, bearing in mind the following points.
 a) *Tie the cord to the wiring harness and use it to pull the harness through the aperture and into the tailgate. Repeat the procedure on the washer fluid hose.*
 b) *Do not fully tighten the hinge bolts/nuts until the tailgate adjustment has been*

checked, as described in the following paragraphs.

Adjustment

12 Close the tailgate **carefully**, in case the alignment is incorrect, which may cause scratching on the tailgate or the body as the tailgate is closed, and check for alignment with the adjacent panels. If necessary, slacken the bolts/nuts that secure the hinges to the bodywork and re-align the tailgate to suit. Once the tailgate is correctly aligned, tighten the hinge bolts/nuts securely.
13 Check that the tailgate fastens and releases in a satisfactory manner. If adjustment is necessary, slacken the striker plate retaining bolts, and adjust the position of the striker to suit. Once the lock is operating correctly, securely tighten the striker plate retaining bolts.
14 If necessary, adjust the protrusion of the rubber buffers at the lower edge of the tailgate by screwing them in or out, as appropriate.

9 Tailgate strut – removal and refitting

Removal

1 Open the tailgate and support it using suitable wooden props.
2 At the upper end of each strut, lever out the balljoint spring clip a little. Compress the strut slightly by hand and then prise the strut

8.3 Brake light cover screws (arrowed) – Panda models

8.4a Prise out the covers, undo the bolts (arrowed) . . .

8.4b . . . and pull the high-level brake light from the tailgate – 500 models

9.2 Prise out the spring clip a little

10.2 Unclip the linkage rod from the lock barrel assembly

10.3 Lock retaining bolts and wiring plug (arrowed)

balljoint from the stud on the tailgate (see illustration).

 Warning: The strut may still be under tension and could extend suddenly once detached from its mountings.

3 Release the lower end of each strut from the studs on the rear wings in the same way.

Refitting

4 Refitting is a reversal of removal.

10 Tailgate lock components – removal and refitting

Lock

1 Remove the tailgate inner trim panel as described in Section 25.

Panda models

2 Unclip the linkage rod from the lock barrel assembly (see illustration).
3 Disconnect the wiring plug, then slacken and unscrew the two bolts securing the lock assembly to the lower edge of the tailgate (see illustration).
4 Carefully withdraw the lock assembly a little, then disconnect the wiring plug from the lock motor, and disconnect the linkage rod from the lock lever, leaving it in place (see illustration). Remove the lock.
5 Refitting is the reversal of removal.

500 models

6 Undo the retaining bolts and manoeuvre the lock unit back into the tailgate, disconnecting the wiring plug as the lock is withdrawn (see illustration).
7 Refitting is a reversal of removal.

Exterior handle assembly

8 Remove the tailgate inner trim panel as described in Section 25.

Panda models

9 Disconnect the wiring plug from the number plate light, and disconnect the linkage rod from the lock barrel.
10 Prise out the clips and remove the plastic bracket around the lock barrel assembly (see illustration).
11 Undo the 4 retaining nuts, release the clip and remove the handle assembly (see illustrations).
12 Refitting is a reversal of removal.

500 models

13 Disconnect the wiring plug, undo the 4 retaining nuts and remove the handle assembly (see illustration).
14 Refitting is a reversal of removal.

10.4 Disconnect the linkage rod from the lock (arrowed)

10.6 Lock retaining bolts (arrowed) – 500 models

10.10 Prise out the centre pins, lever out the clips (arrowed) and remove the plastic bracket

10.11a Undo the retaining nuts (centre nuts arrowed) . . .

10.11b . . . and remove the exterior handle

10.13 Exterior handle retaining nuts (arrowed) – 500 models

10.16a Prise out the retaining clip . . .

10.16b . . . and pull the barrel from position

Lock barrel

Panda models

15 Remove the exterior handle assembly as described previously.

16 Insert the key into the lock barrel, then prise out the retaining clip and pull the barrel from place **(see illustrations)**.

17 Refitting is the reversal of removal.

Striker plate

18 With the tailgate open, mark the position of the striker plate in relation to the bodywork using a pencil or marker pen, to aid accurate refitting.

19 Slacken and unscrew the bolts securing the striker plate to the body.

20 Remove the striker plate from its aperture, and on Panda models, disconnect the remote release cable and remove the striker.

21 Refitting is a reversal of removal. Use the markings made during removal to give the correct alignment.

22 Check that the tailgate fastens and releases in a satisfactory manner. If adjustment is necessary, slacken the striker plate retaining bolts, and adjust the position of the plate to suit. Once the lock is operating correctly, securely tighten the striker plate retaining bolts.

11 Bonnet – removal and refitting

Removal

1 Open the bonnet and prop it up with a stout pole.

2 Mark the relationship between the hinges and the edge of the bonnet using a soft pencil or marker pen. Slacken and unscrew the bolts or nuts (as applicable); have an assistant support the bonnet as the last bolts/nuts are removed.

3 With the help of an assistant, lift off the bonnet and set it down on its edge, using a dust sheet to protect the paintwork.

Refitting

4 Refit the bonnet and retaining bolts/nuts, using the markings made during removal to achieve the correct alignment. Note that the bolt mounting holes are slotted to allow adjustment if required. On completion, tighten the bolts/nuts securely.

5 If necessary, adjust the bonnet lock assembly, as described in Section 12.

12 Bonnet lock assembly – removal and refitting

Removal

1 Open the bonnet and mark the relationship between the lock assembly and the front body panel using a soft pencil or marker pen.

2 Slacken and unscrew the two bolts and withdraw the lock assembly from its location **(see illustrations)**.

3 Disconnect the lock release cable and remove the lock assembly **(see illustration)**.

Refitting

4 Refitting is a reversal of removal. Use the alignment markings made during removal to aid accurate refitting. Check that the bonnet fastens and releases in a satisfactory manner, noting that the mounting holes are slotted to allow adjustment of the lock, if required. On completion, tighten the bolts securely.

5 If necessary, adjust the protrusion of the rubber buffers on the front body panel (located above each headlamp unit) by screwing them in or out, as appropriate. When the rubber

12.2a Bonnet lock retaining bolts (arrowed) – Panda models . . .

12.2b . . . and 500 models

12.3 Pull the outer cable (arrowed) from the bracket, then disengage the end of the inner cable

buffers are correctly adjusted, there should be just enough free movement to allow the bonnet to be closed and locked easily, without using excessive force, but not enough to allow the bonnet to rattle when secured in the locked position.

13 Bonnet release cable –
removal and refitting

Removal

1 Disconnect the release cable from the bonnet lock assembly as described in Section 12.
2 Working around the engine bay, extract the release cable from its securing clips.
3 In the passenger's footwell, remove the side kick panel, then undo the two bolts securing the release handle mounting bracket to the body **(see illustrations)**.
4 Disconnect the cable from the release lever assembly **(see illustration)**.
5 Tie a length of string to the end of the cable in the engine compartment, then carefully pull the cable through the bulkhead grommet into the passenger's compartment. Untie the string from the cable, but leave it in place in the bulkhead, to aid refitting.

Refitting

6 Refitting is a reversal of removal, using the string to draw the cable through the bulkhead into the engine compartment. Reconnect the cable to the bonnet lock and adjust the lock position as described in Section 12.

14 Door inner trim panel –
removal and refitting

Front door

Panda models

1 Carefully prise out the panels surrounding the interior release handle, and undo the screw(s) revealed **(see illustrations)**.
2 Where a manually-adjustable exterior mirror is fitted, prise the rubber cover off the

14.2 Pull off the rubber cover to expose the mirror adjustment lever nut

13.3a Prise out the clip, undo the screw, and remove the kick panel

13.4a Pull the outer cable from the bracket . . .

adjustment lever, then unscrew and remove the locking collar using pointed-nose pliers **(see illustration)**.
3 Carefully pull away the exterior mirror inner trim panel **(see illustration)**.

14.1a Prise out the 'tweeter' panel, undo the screw exposed . . .

14.3 Carefully prise away the mirror trim panel

13.3b Release handle retaining bolts (arrowed)

13.4b . . . then disengage the end fitting

4 Undo the 3 retaining screws – 1 below the armrest, and 2 at the lower edge of the panel **(see illustration)**.
500 models
5 Carefully prise away the interior release

14.1b . . . then prise out the rear panel, and undo the screw (arrowed)

14.4 Undo the panel retaining screws (arrowed)

14.5a Starting at the rear, prise away the interior release handle trim . . .

14.5b . . . and undo the screw (arrowed)

14.6 Starting at the front, prise away the trim, and undo the screws (arrowed)

14.7a Use a flat-bladed plastic tool to release the push-in clips around the edge of the trim panel

14.7b Disconnect the release cable from the inside of the trim panel

14.8a Undo the speaker screws (arrowed) – Panda models

handle surround trim, and undo the screw revealed **(see illustrations)**.
6 Prise up the cover in the door pull handle recess, and undo the 2 screws **(see illustration)**.

All models

7 Using a suitable forked tool inserted between the door and the trim panel, release the press-stud clips located around the edge of the panel, then lift the trim panel upwards. Disconnect the release cable and any

wiring plugs as the panel is withdrawn **(see illustrations)**.
8 If work is to be carried out on the door internal components, it will be necessary to remove the plastic sealing sheet from the inside of the door. Disconnect the speaker wiring plug, drill out the retaining rivets/undo the retaining screws, and remove the speaker. Start at one corner of the sheet and carefully peel it away, using a sharp blade to split the sealant bead, if necessary **(see illustrations)**.

9 Refitting is a reversal of removal, bearing in mind the following points:
a) Ensure that the sealing sheet is correctly refitted, press it on firmly to ensure that it is adequately sealed around its edges. It should be possible to use the original sealant, but if necessary, new sealant can be obtained from a Fiat dealer.
b) Make sure that the weatherstrip engages securely with the edge of the door as the panel is refitted.

14.8b Drill out the speaker rivets (arrowed) – 500 models

14.8c Use a sharp blade to carefully cut through the sealant

14.10a Prise out the panel in front of the interior handle and undo the screw (arrowed)

14.10b Prise out the rear panel and undo the screw (arrowed)

14.10c Undo the remaining panel screws (arrowed)

14.11a Squeeze a screwdriver between the handle and washer, and push the retaining clip out

14.11b Regulator handle retaining clip (arrowed) – shown with the handle removed for clarity

14.11c Note the lug and cut-out (arrowed)

Rear door

10 Carefully prise out the trim panel adjacent to the interior release handle, then undo the 5 panel retaining screws (see illustrations).

11 Prise out the clip and remove the window regulator handle (see illustrations). Recover the handle spacer.

12 Using a suitable forked tool inserted between the door and the trim panel, release the press-stud clips located around the edge of the panel, then pull the top of the panel from the door. Disconnect the release cable from the handle as the panel is withdrawn (see illustrations).

13 If work is to be carried out on the door internal components, remove the door speaker (see Chapter 12), then remove the plastic sealing sheet as described in paragraph 8.

14 Refitting is a reversal of removal, bearing in mind the following points:
a) Ensure that the sealing sheet is correctly refitted, press it on firmly to ensure that it is adequately sealed around its edges. It should be possible to use the original sealant, but if necessary, new sealant can be obtained from a Fiat dealer.
b) Make sure that the weatherstrip engages securely with the edge of the door as the panel is refitted.

15 Door – removal and refitting

Note: This procedure is applicable both to the front and rear doors.

Removal

1 Disconnect the battery negative lead as described in Chapter 5A.

2 Undo the screw/clip and remove the footwell kick panel. If removing the passenger's side door, undo the bolts and move the bonnet release lever to one side (see illustrations 13.3a and 13.3b).

3 Unplug the multiway electrical connector from the inner edge of the pillar, and detach the wiring loom rubber gaiter from the outer edge.

4 Undo the bolt and release the check strap attachment on the door pillar.

5 Have an assistant support the door, then unscrew the door hinge retaining bolts, and lift the door from the car (see illustration).

14.12a Prise between the door and panel to release the press-stud clips around the edge

14.12b Disconnect the release cable as the panel is withdrawn

15.5 Undo the hinge pin bolts (arrowed)

16.3a Drill out the rivets (arrowed) . . .

16.3b . . . and remove the anti-theft partition

Refitting

6 Refitting is a reversal of removal. On completion, tighten the hinge bolts securely.

Adjustment

7 Close the door **carefully**, in case the alignment is incorrect, which may cause scratching on the door or the body as the door is closed, and check the fit of the door with the surrounding panels.
8 If adjustment is required, loosen the hinge-to-body securing bolts (the bolt holes are elongated to allow for adjustment) and move the hinges as required to achieve satisfactory alignment. Tighten the securing bolts securely on completion.

9 Check the operation of the door lock. If necessary, slacken the securing bolts, and adjust the position of the lock striker on the body pillar to achieve satisfactory alignment. Tighten the bolts securely on completion.

16 Door handle and lock components – removal and refitting

Front door exterior handle

1 Ensure that the door window glass is in the fully closed position.
2 Remove the door inner trim panel and sealing sheet as described in Section 14.

Panda models

3 Drill out the rivets securing the anti-theft partition to the door panel **(see illustrations)**. Manipulate the partition out through the door panel aperture.
4 Prise out the clips and remove the polystyrene damper unit from the door (where fitted) **(see illustration)**.
5 Undo the 2 bolts at the door edge and manoeuvre the rear window guide/cover from the door **(see illustrations)**.
6 Working inside the door space, disconnect the exterior handle link rod from the handle, and the link rod from the lock cylinder **(see illustration)**.
7 Undo the retaining bolts and manoeuvre the handle from the door **(see illustrations)**.

16.4 Unclip and remove the polystyrene damper

16.5a Undo the bolts (arrowed) . . .

16.5b . . . and remove the window rear guide

16.6 Disconnect the link rod (1) from the handle, and (2) from the lock

16.7a Undo the retaining bolts (arrowed) . . .

16.7b . . . and manoeuvre the handle from the door

16.8a Disconnect the link rod from the lock (arrowed) . . .

16.8b . . . and the rod from the lock cylinder (arrowed – lock removed for clarity)

16.9a Undo the bolt (arrowed) at the door edge . . .

500 models

8 Working inside the door space, disconnect the exterior handle link rod from the handle, and the link rod from the lock cylinder **(see illustrations)**.

9 Undo the retaining bolt at the edge of the door, and the retaining nut inside the door space **(see illustrations)**.

10 Pull the front of the handle outwards a little, then pull it forwards and manoeuvre it from the door **(see illustration)**.

All models

11 Refitting is the reversal of removal.

Front door lock cylinder

Note: *This procedure only applies to Panda models. On 500 models, the lock cylinder*

appears to be integral with the handle – consult a Fiat dealer.

12 Remove the exterior handle as previously described.

13 Insert the ignition key, release the metal retaining clip from the rear of the cylinder, then extract the lock cylinder from the door handle **(see illustrations)**.

14 Locate the lock cylinder in the handle and secure with the retaining clip.

15 Refit the door exterior handle as previously described.

Front door interior handle

16 Remove the door inner trim panel and sealing sheet as described in Section 14.

17 Undo the retaining screws and withdraw the handle from the door **(see illustration)**.

18 Refitting is a reversal of removal. Refit the

door inner trim panel and sealing sheet as described in Section 14.

Front door lock mechanism

19 Disconnect the battery negative lead as described in Chapter 5A.

20 Remove the door inner trim panel as described in Section 14, then drill out the rivets and remove the anti-theft panel (where fitted) **(see illustrations 16.3a and 16.3b)**.

21 Undo the 2 retaining nuts and remove the window guide from rear of the door space **(see illustrations 16.5a and 16.5b)**.

22 Detach the lock cylinder link rod and exterior handle link rod from the door lock mechanism.

23 At the trailing edge of the door, remove the three screws that secure the lock mechanism to the door **(see illustration)**.

16.9b . . . the nut (arrowed) in the door space . . .

16.10 . . . then manoeuvre the handle from the door

16.13a Prise out the clip . . .

16.13b . . . and pull the lock cylinder from place

16.17 Interior handle retaining screws (arrowed)

16.23 Undo the lock screws (arrowed) at the door edge

16.24a Disconnect the wiring plug as the lock is withdrawn

16.24b Prise up the cover and disconnect the release cable

16.27a Disconnect the link rod (arrowed) . . .

24 Manoeuvre the lock mechanism, complete with interior handle release cable out through the door aperture **(see illustrations)**. Disconnect the central locking wiring connectors from the lock motor as the lock is withdrawn. If required, disconnect the release cable.

25 Refitting is a reversal of removal. On completion, refit the door inner trim panel and sealing sheet as described in Section 14.

Rear door exterior handle

26 Remove the door inner trim panel and sealing sheet as described in Section 14.

27 Disconnect the link rod from the lever on the lock assembly, then undo the retaining bolts and manoeuvre the exterior handle from the door **(see illustrations)**.

28 Locate the handle in position and secure with the retaining bolts.

29 Reconnect the link rod, then refit the door inner trim panel and sealing sheet as described in Section 14.

Rear door interior handle

30 Remove the door inner trim panel and sealing sheet as described in Section 14.

31 Undo the retaining screws and withdraw the handle from the door **(see illustration)**.

32 Detach the lock mechanism link rod from the handle lever and remove the handle.

33 Refitting is a reversal of removal. Refit the door inner trim panel and sealing sheet as described in Section 14.

Rear door lock mechanism

34 Remove the door inner trim panel and sealing sheet as described in Section 14.

35 Drill out the 3 rivets and remove the plastic shield to access the lock assembly **(see illustration)**.

36 Undo the two retaining bolts and remove the window glass lower rear guide channel **(see illustration)**. Unclip the wiring loom as the guide channel is removed.

37 At the trailing edge of the door, remove the three screws that secure the lock mechanism to the door **(see illustration)**.

38 Manoeuvre the lock mechanism, complete with release cable, out through the door aperture and disconnect the wiring plug.

39 Refitting is a reversal of removal. On completion, refit the door inner trim panel and sealing sheet as described in Section 14.

16.27b . . . undo the bolts (arrowed) . . .

16.27c . . . and manoeuvre the handle from the door

16.31 Interior handle retaining screws (arrowed)

16.35 Drill out the rivets (arrowed) and remove the plastic panel

16.36 Rear window guide bolts (arrowed)

16.37 Rear door lock retaining screws (arrowed)

17.4 Undo the mirror retaining nut (arrowed)

17.6 Prise the cover from the mirror arm

17.7 Mirror retaining bolts (arrowed)

17 Mirror components – removal and refitting

Door mirror assembly

Panda models

1 Remove the mirror inner trim panel as described in Section 14.
2 Disconnect the mirror wiring connector (where applicable).
3 Remove the foam insulation for access to the mirror retaining nut.
4 Using pointed-nose pliers engaged with the slots in the mirror retaining nut, unscrew the nut and withdraw the mirror from the door **(see illustration)**.
5 Refitting is a reversal of removal.

500 models

6 Fold the mirror assembly towards the door, then carefully prise up the lower cover from the mirror arm **(see illustration)**.
7 Disconnect the wiring plug (where applicable), undo the retaining bolts and remove the mirror assembly **(see illustration)**.
8 Refitting is a reversal of removal.

Door mirror glass

9 Push the lower edge of the glass inwards to create an opening between the upper edge of the glass and the mirror body.

17.10 Prise between the top of the glass and the mirror body

10 Insert a blunt, flat-bladed tool between the mirror glass and the mirror body, and carefully release the mirror glass securing clips **(see illustration)**.

⚠️ **Warning: Protect your hands and eyes from glass splinters.**

11 Where applicable, disconnect the heater element wiring from the rear of the glass, and withdraw the glass from the mirror assembly.
12 Where applicable, reconnect the wires to the rear of the mirror glass, then push the glass into position to engage the securing clips.

Interior mirror

13 Slide the mirror mounting arm upwards from the bonded base on the windscreen **(see illustration)**.
14 Refitting is a reversal of removal.

17.13 Slide the mirror arm upwards from the base

18 Door window glass and regulator – removal and refitting

Front window glass

Panda models

1 Remove the door inner trim panel and the plastic sealing sheet, as described in Section 14.
2 Operate the window regulator mechanism, so that the glass-to-regulator retaining clip is accessible through the door aperture, then release the clip **(see illustration)**.
3 Undo the screws and remove the front **(see illustration)** and rear **(see illustrations 16.5a and 16.5b)** window guide channels.
4 Prise up the inner weatherstrip from the window aperture **(see illustration)**.

18.2 Pull the clip strap (arrowed) downwards to release the glass from the regulator

18.3 Front window guide screws (arrowed)

18.4 Pull up the inner weatherstrip

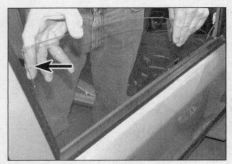

18.5 Release the plastic slide (arrowed) from the channel

18.6 Lift the rear of the window and manoeuvre it from the door

18.13 Rear window guide nuts (arrowed)

18.14 Front window guide nuts (arrowed)

18.15 Prise up the inner weatherstrip

5 Fully lower the glass, then pull the glass out of the rear guide channel to disengage the plastic slider **(see illustration)**. If the slider is reluctant, pull the rubber channel from the door frame and release the slider.
6 Lift the glass upwards at the rear and remove it from the inside of the door frame **(see illustration)**.
7 Locate the glass in the door and engage the plastic slider with the rear guide channel. Push the glass rearwards until the slider is heard to engage with the channel.
8 Engage the front edge of the glass with the front guide channel, then move the glass upwards to its mid position.
9 Engage the regulator mechanism with the

hole at the base of the glass, then reach up behind and reconnect the plastic fastener.
10 Refit the front and rear guide channels and tighten the bolts securely.
11 Check the operation of the glass and regulator then refit the door inner trim panel and plastic sheet as described in Section 14.

500 models

12 Remove window regulator assembly as described in this Section.
13 Undo the retaining nuts and remove the rear window guide **(see illustration)**.
14 Undo the retaining nuts and remove the front window guide **(see illustration)**. Unclip the wiring loom from the guide as it's withdrawn.

15 Carefully prise up the internal weatherstrip from the base of the window aperture **(see illustration)**.
16 Slide the window glass fully downwards, lift the rear of the glass clear of the guide and manoeuvre it from the door frame **(see illustration)**.
17 Refit the glass down into the door, and engage the clip on the upper, rear edge of the glass with the window guide.
18 Slide the glass upwards squarely to the top of the door frame, and secure it with tape.
19 The remainder of refitting is a reversal of removal.

Front window regulator

Panda models

20 Separate the window glass from the regulator mechanism, as described in paragraphs 1 and 2.
21 Fully raise the window glass, and secure the glass in position using suitable tape, or by wedging the glass in position using rags between the glass and the edge of the door – ensure that the glass cannot drop into the door.
22 Unscrew the 5 nuts securing the regulator/motor assembly to the door **(see illustration)**.
23 Lower the assembly down to the bottom of the door and disconnect the motor wiring connector.

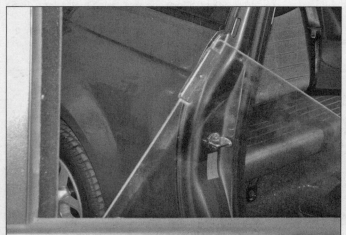

18.16 Lower the glass, then lift the rear corner clear of the guide

18.22 Front window regulator nuts (arrowed)

18.26a Press in the catch securing the glass to the regulator . . .

18.26b . . . then slide up the glass and secure it with tape

18.27 Regulator retaining nuts (arrowed)

24 Manipulate the complete regulator assembly out through the aperture in the door.

500 models

25 Remove the door inner trim panel and the plastic sealing sheet, as described in Section 14.

26 Lower the window glass approximately 200 mm until the glass securing catch is visible through the access hole, then press in the catch, slide the glass upwards and secure it in place with tape **(see illustrations)**.

27 Disconnect the wiring plug from the regulator motor, then undo the 3 retaining nuts and manoeuvre the regulator from the door **(see illustration)**.

All models

28 Refitting is a reversal of removal, bearing in mind the following points:

a) *Attach the window glass to the regulator as described previously, before tightening the regulator retaining nuts.*

b) *Check the operation of the window mechanism before refitting the door inner trim panel.*

c) *Refit the door inner trim panel and plastic sheet as described in Section 14.*

Rear window glass

29 Remove the door inner trim panel and the plastic sealing sheet, as described in Section 14.

30 Carefully prise the lower window aperture inner weatherstrip upwards from its location, and remove it from the door frame **(see illustration)**.

18.30 Prise up the weatherstrip

31 Operate the window regulator mechanism to move the glass to the fully closed position.

32 Undo the two retaining bolts and remove the window glass lower rear guide channel **(see illustration 16.36)**.

33 Operate the window regulator mechanism until the glass-to-regulator retaining clip is accessible through the door aperture.

34 Support the glass, then unclip the plastic fastener that secures the window glass to the regulator mechanism. To do this, pull the strap at the base of the fastener downwards. This will release the fastener from its retaining peg **(see illustration 18.2)**.

35 With the plastic fastener released, disengage the regulator mechanism from the hole at the base of the window glass. To improve access, undo the 4 nuts and remove the regulator assembly **(see illustration 18.47)**.

36 Lower the glass to the bottom of the guide

18.36 Pull the rear of the rubber channel from the door frame

channels, and pull the rear channel out of the door aperture **(see illustration)**.

37 Move the glass rearwards to disengage the plastic slider from the front guide channel, then pull the front channel out of the door aperture **(see illustrations)**.

38 Lift the glass upwards and remove it from the outside of the door frame **(see illustration)**.

39 Locate the glass in the door and refit the front guide channel.

40 Engage the plastic slider with the front guide channel and push the glass forwards until the slider is heard to engage with the channel.

41 Locate the rear guide channel over the glass and push the channel down into its location in the door aperture.

42 Engage the regulator mechanism with the hole at the base of the glass, then reach up behind and reconnect the plastic fastener.

18.37a Disengage the plastic slider (arrowed) from the front channel . . .

18.37b . . . then pull the channel from the door frame

18.38 Lift the rear, and manoeuvre the glass from the door

18.47 Window regulator nuts (arrowed)

18.48 Manoeuvre the regulator from the door aperture

43 Refit the window aperture outer weatherstrip.

44 Check the operation of the glass and regulator, then refit the door inner trim panel and plastic sheet as described in Section 14.

Rear window regulator

45 Separate the window glass from the regulator mechanism, as described in paragraphs 29 and 33 to 35.

46 Fully raise the window glass, and secure the glass in position using suitable tape, or by wedging the glass in position using rags between the glass and the edge of the door – ensure that the glass cannot drop into the door. Alternatively, lift the glass panel out through the window aperture.

47 Unscrew the four nuts securing the regulator assembly to the door **(see illustration)**.

48 Disengage the regulator shaft from the door, then lower the assembly and manipulate it out through the door aperture **(see illustration)**.

49 Refitting is a reversal of removal, bearing in mind the following points:

a) *Attach the window glass to the regulator as described previously, before tightening the regulator retaining nuts.*

b) *Check the operation of the window mechanism before refitting the door inner trim panel.*

c) *Refit the door inner trim panel and plastic sheet as described in Section 14.*

19 Side window glass – removal and refitting

These areas of glass are secured by the tight fit of the weatherstrip in the body aperture, and are bonded in position with a special adhesive. Renewal of such fixed glass is a difficult, messy and time-consuming task, which is considered beyond the scope of the home mechanic. It is difficult, unless one has plenty of practice, to obtain a secure, waterproof fit. Furthermore, the task carries a high risk of breakage. In view of this, owners are strongly advised to have this sort of work carried out by one of the many specialist windscreen fitters.

20 Windscreen and tailgate glass – general information

These areas of glass are secured by the tight fit of the weatherstrip in the body aperture, and are bonded in position with a special adhesive. Renewal of such fixed glass is a difficult, messy and time-consuming task, which is considered beyond the scope of the home mechanic. It is difficult, unless one has plenty of practice, to obtain a secure, waterproof fit. Furthermore, the task carries a high risk of breakage; this applies especially to the laminated glass windscreen. In view of this, owners are strongly advised to have this sort of work carried out by one of the many specialist windscreen fitters.

21 Sunroof – general information

1 Due to the complexity of the sunroof mechanism, considerable expertise is needed to repair, renew or adjust the sunroof components successfully. Removal of the roof first requires the headlining to be removed, which is a complex and tedious operation, and not a task to be undertaken lightly. Therefore, any problems with the sunroof should be referred to a Fiat dealer.

2 If the sunroof motor fails to operate, first check the relevant fuse. If the fault cannot be traced and rectified, the sunroof can be opened and closed manually, using the special

crank handle supplied in the vehicle tool kit to turn the motor spindle.

3 To gain access to the motor spindle, ensure that the ignition key is in the 'off' position, then carefully prise plastic cap from the headlining. Engage the crank handle with the spindle, and turn the handle to open or close the sunroof.

4 Once the roof is closed, remove the crank handle, and clip the overhead console back into place.

22 Body exterior fittings – removal and refitting

Windscreen scuttle grille panel

1 Open and support the bonnet.

2 Remove the windscreen wiper arms as described in Chapter 12.

Panda models

3 Undo the centre retaining screw and the two outer screws securing the panel to the scuttle **(see illustration)**.

4 Release the end of weatherstrip from its location at each side of the panel.

5 Lift the panel up at the front then move it forward to disengage the rear locating clips

22.3 Remove the scuttle grille panel screws (centre and left-hand screws arrowed)

22.5 Pull the panel forwards to release the clips

22.6a Remove the upper trim panel fasteners (centre and right-hand fasteners arrowed) . . .

22.6b . . . by prising up the centre pins . . .

(see illustration). Disconnect the washer hose as the panel is withdrawn.

500 models

6 Release the fasteners, then pull forwards the outer edges, and slide the windscreen upper base trim panel downwards from the windscreen. Disconnect the washer jet hose as the panel is withdrawn (see illustrations).
7 Undo the fasteners, unclip the weatherstrip at each end, and remove the windscreen lower base trim panel (see illustration).

All models

8 Before refitting, take the opportunity to clear any leaves/debris from the drain tubes/holes in the base of the scuttle area (see illustration). Refitting is a reversal of removal.

Wheel arch liners

9 The wheel arch liners are secured by self-tapping screws/fasteners and removal is self-evident and straightforward. Multiple liner panels are used which overlap each other at their edges. In some instances it may be necessary to move aside adjoining panels for access to a specific panel.

Body trim strips and badges

10 The various body trim strips and badges are held in position with a special adhesive tape. Removal requires the trim/badge to be heated, to soften the adhesive, and then cut away from the surface. Due to the high risk of

22.6c . . . and pulling out the plastic expansion rivets

damage to the vehicle paintwork during this operation, it is recommended that this task should be entrusted to a Fiat dealer.

23 Seats – removal and refitting

Front seat

⚠️ **Warning: Certain models are equipped with side airbags built into the outer sides of the front seats. Refer to Chapter 12 for the precautions which should be observed when dealing with an airbag system. Do**

22.6d Pull the trim and clips (arrowed) upwards from the studs (arrowed) at the base of the windscreen

not tamper with the airbag unit in any way, and do not attempt to test any airbag system components. Note that the airbag is triggered if the mechanism is supplied with an electrical current (including via an ohmmeter), or if the assembly is subjected to a temperature of greater than 100°C.
1 On models with side airbags in the front seats, de-activate the airbag system, as described in Chapter 12, before attempting to remove the seat.
2 The front seats rails are secured to the floorpan by four bolts.
3 Slide the seat towards the rear of the car to gain access to the two bolts at the front, then slacken and remove them (see illustration).
4 Slide the seat fully forwards and remove the

22.7 Pull up the weatherstrip (arrowed) then undo the screws (right-hand screws arrowed)

22.8 Clear any debris from the drain holes (arrowed)

23.3 Undo the bolts at the front of the seat rails (arrowed) . . .

23.4a . . . and at the rear (arrowed) –
Panda models . . .

23.4b . . . and 500 models

23.7a Undo the bolt . . .

23.7b . . . and remove the centre mounting
cover

23.8 Undo the 2 bolts each side securing
the seat backrests

23.11 Rear backrest bolts – 500 models

two rearmost bolts **(see illustrations)**. Where applicable, disconnect the airbag, and/or seat heater wiring connectors, then remove the seat from the car

5 Refitting is a reversal of removal.

Rear seat backrest

Panda models – fixed rear seat

6 Release the seat back from its locking catches and tip it forwards.

7 Undo the retaining bolt and lift up the centre hinge locking cover. Disengage the seat pivot from the centre mounting **(see illustrations)**.

8 Undo the two bolts securing the side hinges to the body and remove the seat back from the car **(see illustration)**.

Panda models – sliding rear seat

9 The sliding rear seat backrests are integral with the seat cushion – see later in this Section.

500 models

10 Remove the rear parcel shelf.

11 Release the catches and fold the backrest forwards, then undo the bolts each side and manoeuvre the backrest from the vehicle **(see illustration)**.

All models

12 Refitting is a reversal of removal.

Rear seat cushion

Panda models – fixed rear seat

13 Remove the rear seat backrest as previously described.

14 Undo the bolts at the front lower edge of the cushion, and the 3 bolts at the rear edge. Lift the luggage compartment carpet to access the outer bolts **(see illustrations)**. Lift out the cushion.

23.14a Undo the bolt (arrowed) each side at the front of the seat
cushion . . .

23.14b . . . and the 3 (arrowed) at the rear

23.17a Undo the 4 bolts (arrowed) . . .

23.17b . . . and pull the centre bracket rearwards

Panda models – sliding rear seat

15 Undo the bolt each side underneath the front of the seat cushion (see illustration 23.14a).

16 Slide the seat fully forwards, then lift out the luggage compartment floor carpet.

17 Undo the 4 bolts at the rear of the cushion, then pull the centre bracket rearwards (see illustrations).

18 Undo the bolt securing the seat belt each side, then lift out the seat with the help of an assistant.

500 models

19 Undo the bolts at the front lower edge of the cushion, and release the retainers at the rear edge (see illustration). Manoeuvre the cushion from the vehicle.

All models

20 Refitting is a reversal of removal.

24 Seat belt components – removal and refitting

Note: *Record the positions of the washers and spacers on the seat belt anchors, and ensure they are refitted in their original positions.*

Front seat belt

⚠ **Warning: On certain models, the front seat belt inertia reels are equipped with a pyrotechnic pretensioner mechanism. Refer to the airbag system precautions contained in Chapter 12 which apply equally to the seat belt pretensioners. Do not tamper with the inertia reel pretensioner unit in any way, and do not attempt to test the unit.**

500 models

1 De-activate the airbag system (which will also de-activate the pyrotechnic pretensioner

23.19 Rear cushion retaining bolts (arrowed) – 500 models

mechanism, where fitted), as described in Chapter 12, before attempting to remove the seatbelt.

2 Remove the side trim panel as described in Section 25.

3 Release the locking catch and disconnect the pretensioner wiring plug (see illustration).

4 Undo the inertia reel retaining bolt and withdraw the inertia reel from the centre pillar (see illustration).

5 Refitting is a reversal of removal, ensuring

24.6 Inertia reel retaining bolt (arrowed)

24.3 Press in the clip (arrowed) each side and disconnect the pretensioner wiring plug

that all mounting bolts are tightened to the specified torque.

Panda models

6 De-activate the airbag system (which will also de-activate the pyrotechnic pretensioner mechanism, where fitted), as described in Chapter 12, before attempting to remove the seatbelt.

7 Remove the B-pillar trim panels as described in Section 25.

8 Disconnect the pretensioner wiring plug (see illustration).

24.8 Disconnect the pretensioner wiring plug (arrowed) . . .

24.9 . . . and remove the inertia reel bolt (arrowed) – Panda models

24.12 Prise the backrest angle adjustment knob from place

24.13 Undo the screws and remove the height adjustment lever

9 Undo the inertia reel retaining bolt and withdraw the inertia reel from the centre pillar **(see illustration)**.
10 Refitting is a reversal of removal, ensuring that all mounting bolts are tightened to the specified torque.

Front seat belt stalk

11 Set the seat cushion in its highest position (where possible), then remove the relevant front seat as described in Section 23.
12 Prise the backrest angle adjustment knob from the base of the backrest **(see illustration)**.
13 On the driver's seat, undo the screws, and remove the seat height adjustment lever **(see illustration)**.

14 Carefully pull the front and rear edges of the seat cushion side trim panel from place, then manoeuvre the panel upwards from the retaining clips **(see illustration)**.
15 Release the wiring loom from any retaining clips, then undo the bolt and remove the seat belt stalk **(see illustration)**.
16 Refitting is a reversal of removal, ensuring that all mounting bolts are tightened securely.

Rear seat outer belt

500 models

17 Remove the luggage compartment trim panel as described in Section 25.
18 Undo the inertia reel retaining bolt, upper anchorage bolt and lower anchorage bolt.

Remove the seat belt assembly from the car **(see illustrations)**.
19 Refitting is a reversal of removal, ensuring that all mounting bolts are tightened to the specified torque

Panda models

20 Remove the rear parcel shelf support panel as described in Section 25.
21 Remove the foam cover from the seat belt inertia reel.
22 Undo the inertia reel retaining bolt and remove the seat belt assembly from the car **(see illustration)**.
23 Refitting is a reversal of removal, but tighten the seat belt anchor bolts to the specified torque.

24.14 Pull out the front and rear edges, then slide the panel upwards from the seat base

24.15 Seat belt stalk retaining bolt (arrowed)

24.18a Rear seat belt inertia reel retaining bolt (arrowed) . . .

24.18b . . . upper anchorage bolt . . .

24.18c . . . and lower anchorage bolt – 500 models

24.22 Remove the foam cover, and undo the inertia reel retaining bolt (arrowed)

Rear seat belt stalk

500 models

24 Remove the rear seat cushion as described in Section 23.
25 Undo the retaining bolts and remove the seat belt stalks **(see illustration)**.
26 Refitting is a reversal of removal, ensuring that all mounting bolts are tightened to the specified torque.

Panda models

27 Remove the rear seat cushion as described in Section 23.
28 Undo the retaining bolts and remove the seat belt stalks **(see illustration)**.
29 Refitting is a reversal of removal, ensuring that all mounting bolts are tightened to the specified torque.

24.25 Rear seat belt stalks retaining bolts (arrowed) – 500 models

24.28 Rear seat belt stalks retaining bolts (arrowed) – Panda models

25 Interior trim panels – removal and refitting

General

1 The interior trim panels are secured by a combination of metal and plastic clips and screws. When releasing certain types of securing clips, a suitable forked tool will prove invaluable to avoid damage to the panel and clips. A degree of force will be necessary to pull some of the panels from their locations, especially where numerous internal retaining clips are used. Be prepared for some of the plastic clips to break when their relevant panel is being removed.

Door inner trim panels

2 Refer to Section 14.

Tailgate inner trim panel

Panda models

3 Prise out the push-in clips securing the inner trim panel to the tailgate **(see illustration)**.

4 Undo the screw securing the pull-down handle, and remove the panel from the tailgate **(see illustration)**.
5 To refit the panel, locate it in position, and push the clips into place.

500 models

6 Use a blunt, flat-bladed tool to prise out the panel retaining clips **(see illustration 25.3)**.
7 Undo the screw securing the pull-down handle, and lower the tailgate panel from position leaving the upper edge attached to the base of the screen **(see illustrations)**. Note that in order the completely remove the trim panel, it must be unbonded from the plastic hinge pieces. It is possible to access all of the tailgate components with the

panel hinged down. The panel must only be completely removed for tailgate or trim panel renewal.
8 Refitting is a reversal of removal.

Sill front trim panels

Panda models

9 Undo the retaining screw at the rear end of the panel **(see illustration)**.
10 Carefully pull the panel upwards from the sill to release the securing clips.
11 To refit the panel, locate it in position, ensuring that the retaining clips engage, and secure with the screw.

500 models

12 Undo the screw at the front of the sill

25.3 Prise out the various push-in clips around the edge of the tailgate panel . . .

25.4 . . . then undo the pull-down handle screw (arrowed)

25.7a Undo the pull-down handle screw (arrowed) – 500 models

25.7b Leave the tailgate panel bonded to the plastic hinge (arrowed)

25.9 Undo the screw (arrowed) and pull up the sill to release the clips

25.12a Undo the screw at the rear (arrowed) . . .

25.12b . . . and front (arrowed) of the sill trim panel

25.17 Pull the A-pillar trim panel inwards to release the clips

25.21 Undo the screw (arrowed) at the rear of the B-pillar trim panel

25.22a Lift the cap and undo the upper anchorage bolt

25.22b Remove the anchorage, complete with spacer

trim panel, and the one at the rear **(see illustrations)**.

13 Pull the sill trim panel upwards to release the retaining clips.

14 Refitting is a reversal of removal.

A-pillar trim panels

15 On models with headlining airbags, de-activate the airbag system as described in Chapter 12.

16 Locally remove the front door weatherstrip from the edge of the panel.

17 Carefully pull the panel away from the pillar to release the securing clips **(see illustration)**. Disconnect the tweeter wiring plug (where fitted)

18 Refitting is a reversal of removal, ensuring the weatherstrip is correctly seated.

B-pillar trim panels

Panda models

19 Remove the sill trim panel as described previously, then undo the seat belt lower anchorage bolt.

20 Locally remove the front and rear door weatherstrip from the edges of the centre pillar.

21 Undo the screw securing the side trim panel to the base of the centre pillar trim panel **(see illustration)**.

22 Lift up the trim cap over the seat belt upper anchor bolt. Undo the upper anchor bolt and release the seat belt from the height adjuster **(see illustrations)**. Record the positions of the washers and spacers on the upper anchor bolt to ensure correct refitting.

23 Pull the upper section of the B-pillar trim panel inwards to release the retaining clips **(see illustration)**.

24 Pull the base of the trim panel upwards to disengage the lower locating pins **(see illustration)**.

25 Refitting is a reversal of removal, ensuring that all retaining clips are fully engaged. Refit the seat belt anchor bolts with the washers and spacers correctly positioned as noted during removal. Tighten the anchor bolts to the specified torque.

500 models

26 Locally remove the front door weatherstrip from the edge of the B-pillar.

27 Lift up the trim cap over the seat belt upper anchor bolt. Undo the upper anchor bolt and release the seat belt **(see illustration)**. Record

25.23 Pull the upper B-pillar trim panel inwards to release the clips

25.24 Lift the lower B-pillar trim panel to disengage the locating pins from the holes (arrowed)

25.27 Lift up the cap and undo the upper anchorage bolt – 500 models

25.28a Prise the lower edge of the trim panel away from the B-pillar . . .

25.28b . . . then lower it to release the upper lugs (arrowed)

25.33 Undo the side trim panel screw and prise out the clip (arrowed)

the positions of the washers and spacers on the upper anchor bolt to ensure correct refitting.

28 Carefully pull the lower edge B-pillar trim panel away from the pillar to release the securing clips, then lower it from the headlining **(see illustrations)**.

29 Refitting is a reversal of removal, ensuring that all retaining clips are fully engaged. Refit the seat belt upper anchor bolt with the washers and spacers correctly positioned as noted during removal. Tighten the upper anchor bolt to the specified torque.

Side trim panels

Panda models

30 Remove the rear seat cushion as described in Section 23.

31 Undo the rear seat belt lower anchor bolt. Record the positions of the washers and spacers on the lower anchor bolt to ensure correct refitting.

32 Undo the screw securing the lower front corner of the side trim panel to the base of the B-pillar trim panel **(see illustration 25.21)**.

33 Undo the screw securing the upper rear corner of the panel to the body above the inner wheel arch, and prise out the clip **(see illustration)**.

34 Carefully pull the panel upwards from the body to release the securing clips.

35 Refitting is a reversal of removal, ensuring that all retaining clips are fully engaged. Refit the rear seat belt anchor bolt with the washers and spacers correctly positioned as noted

25.41a Undo the screws at the lower front edge of the side trim panel (arrowed) . . .

during removal. Tighten the anchor bolt to the specified torque.

500 models

36 Remove the sill trim panel as described previously.

37 Locally remove the front door weatherstrip from the edge of the centre pillar.

38 Remove the rear seat cushion and seat back as described in Section 23.

39 Remove the C-pillar trim panel as described in this Section.

40 Remove the B-pillar trim panel as described in this Section.

41 Undo the 2 screws at the lower front edge of the side trim panel, and the screw at the upper front edge **(see illustrations)**.

42 Rotate the locking device anti-clockwise and pull the seat belt fitting from the anchorage **(see illustration)**.

43 Carefully prise the panel away from

25.41b . . . and the screw (arrowed) at the top front edge

the body to release the securing clips **(see illustrations)**. Unclip the guide, and feed the seat belt anchorage through the incision as the panel is withdrawn.

44 Refitting is a reversal of removal, ensuring that all retaining clips are fully engaged. Refit the seat belt anchor bolts with the washers and spacers correctly positioned as noted during removal. Tighten the anchor bolts to the specified torque.

Parcel shelf supports

Panda models

45 Remove the parcel shelf from the luggage compartment.

46 Remove the side trim panel as described previously.

47 Prise out the belt guide trim from the support panel **(see illustration)**. Remove the guide trim from the seat belt.

25.42 Rotate the locking device anti-clockwise and detach the seat belt

25.43 Pull the panel inwards to release the clips

25.47 Prise out the seal belt guide trim

25.48 Undo the screws (arrowed) beneath the support panel

25.49 Pull the support panel inwards to release the clips (arrowed)

25.54a Undo the C-pillar screws (arrowed) . . .

25.54b . . . then pull the panel inwards to release the clips

25.57a Undo the screws (arrowed) . . .

48 Undo the screws on the underside of the parcel shelf supports (see illustration).
49 Pull the panel inwards to release the retaining clips (see illustration).
50 Withdraw the seat belt through the opening, and remove the support from the car.
51 Refitting is a reversal of removal, ensuring that all retaining clips are fully engaged. Refit the rear seat belt lower anchor bolt with the washers and spacers correctly positioned as noted during removal. Tighten the anchor bolt to the specified torque.

C-pillar trim panels

500 models

52 Remove the rear parcel shelf, and fold the rear seat backrest forwards.
53 Locally remove the tailgate weatherstrip from the edge of the rear pillar.
54 Undo the retaining screws at the lower edge of the pillar trim panel (see illustrations). Pull the panel inwards to release the retaining clips.
55 If required, undo the rear seat belt lower anchorage bolt and feed the belt through the aperture in the pillar trim panel.
56 Refitting is a reversal of removal, ensuring that all retaining clips are fully engaged. Refit the rear seat belt lower anchor bolt with the

washers and spacers correctly positioned as noted during removal. Tighten the anchor bolt to the specified torque.

Luggage compartment trim panel

500 models

57 Undo the 2 screws and pull the lock striker trim panel upwards from the tailgate sill (see illustrations).
58 Lift out the luggage compartment floor covering.
59 Locally remove the tailgate weatherstrip from the edge of the trim panel.
60 Remove the side panel trim as described in this Section.
61 Remove the retaining clip, and manoeuvre the luggage compartment trim panel from place (see illustration).
62 Refitting is a reversal of removal.

26 Centre console –
removal and refitting

Removal

1 Disconnect the battery negative terminal as described in Chapter 5A.

25.57b . . . and pull the tailgate sill trim panel upwards

25.61 Prise out the clips and remove the luggage compartment trim panel

26.2 Prise up the cigarette light/power socket/mirror switch panel

26.3 Lift out the mats at the front, and undo the nuts

26.4 Lift the cover at the rear and undo the nut

Panda models

2 Carefully prise the cigarette lighter/power socket/mirror switch panel from place, and disconnect the wiring plug (see illustration).

3 Lift the mats from the base of the front cupholders, and undo the nuts exposed (see illustration).

4 Prise open the cover at the rear of the console and undo the nut beneath (see illustration).

5 Open the cover in the centre of the console, and undo the nut beneath (see illustration).

6 Manoeuvre the console from the vehicle.

500 models

7 Undo the screws and remove the footwell kick panel each side (see illustrations).

8 Lift the mat from the rear cupholder, and undo the retaining nut beneath (see illustration).

9 Manoeuvre the rear section of the centre console from place (see illustration).

10 Lift out the mats in the base of the front cupholders, and undo the nuts beneath (see illustration).

11 Undo the bolt in front of the handbrake lever (see illustration).

12 Undo the screw each side at the front of the console (see illustration).

26.5 Lift the cover in front of the handbrake lever, and undo the nut

26.7a Undo the screws (arrowed) and remove the footwell kick panel on the driver's side . . .

26.7b . . . and passenger's side (arrowed)

26.8 Lift out the cupholder mat, and undo the nut (arrowed) beneath

26.9 Lift out the rear section of the console

26.10 Lift out the front cupholder mat and undo the nuts beneath

26.11 Undo the bolt (arrowed) in front of the handbrake lever

26.12 Undo the screw (arrowed) each side at the front of the console

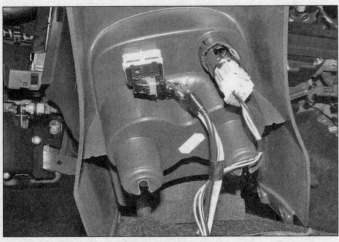

26.13 Disconnect the wiring plugs on the underside of the console

27.1a Undo the screws (arrowed) inside the glovebox . . .

13 Fully raise the handbrake lever, then lift the console from place. Disconnect the wiring plugs on the underside as the console is withdrawn (see illustration).

Refitting

14 Refitting is a reversal of removal.

27 Facia panels –
removal and refitting

27.1b . . . the 2 underneath (arrowed) . . .

27.1c . . . and pull the glovebox from the facia

⚠ *Warning: All models are equipped with an airbag system. The driver's airbag is mounted in the steering wheel centre pad and, where fitted, the passenger's airbag is mounted in the passenger's side of the facia. Make sure that the safety precautions given in Chapter 12 are followed, to prevent personal injury.*

Glovebox/oddments tray

Panda models

1 Open the glovebox, prise out the airbag de-activation switch (where fitted), disconnect the wiring plug, then undo the 5 retaining screws and pull the glovebox from the facia (see illustrations).

2 Refitting is a reversal of removal.

500 models

3 Remove the door sill trim panel as described in Section 25.
4 Undo the 2 retaining screws at the base of the tray (see illustration).
5 Undo the 3 screws at the top edge of the tray (see illustration).

27.4 Undo the screws (arrowed) at the base of the tray . . .

27.5 . . . the screws (arrowed) at the top of the tray . . .

27.6 . . . remove the screw in the document holder . . .

27.7a . . . the screw under the fusebox cover . . .

27.7b . . . and withdrawn the oddments tray

27.9 Fusebox/lower panel screws (arrowed)

27.11 Prise the coin tray from the facia . . .

27.12 . . . followed by the vent panel

6 Open the document tray, and undo the screw exposed **(see illustration)**.
7 Release the clip, open the fusebox cover, undo the screw and manoeuvre the tray from place **(see illustrations)**.
8 Refitting is a reversal of removal.

Driver's side lower facia/ fusebox panel

Panda models

9 Release the two screws, and remove the panel from the facia **(see illustration)**.
10 Refitting is a reversal of removal.

Facia vent panels

500 models

11 Carefully prise the coin tray/EOBD connector holder trim panel from below the vent panel **(see illustration)**.
12 Prise the facia vent panel from place **(see illustration)**.
13 Refitting is a reversal of removal.

Steering column shrouds

14 Remove the steering wheel as described in Chapter 10.
15 Undo the retaining screws and remove the lower shroud from the underside of the steering column **(see illustrations)**.
16 Undo the two screws securing the front of the upper shroud to the steering column switch assembly. Manipulate the shroud out from under the instrument panel and remove

27.15a Steering column lower shroud screws (arrowed) – Panda models . . .

27.15b . . . and 500 models (arrowed)

27.16a Upper steering column shroud screws (arrowed) – 500 models . . .

27.16b . . . and Panda models (arrowed)

27.16c Note the shroud retaining clips (arrowed)

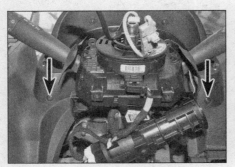

27.18 Undo the screws (arrowed) at the lower edge . . .

27.19a . . . two screws (arrowed) at the upper edge . . .

the shroud from the column (see illustrations).

17 Refitting is a reversal of removal, referring to Chapter 10 for steering wheel refitting procedures.

Instrument panel surround

Panda models

18 Undo the two lower retaining screws, one on each side of the surround (see illustration).

19 Undo the two upper screws in the centre of the surround, then withdraw the surround from the facia (see illustrations).

20 Refitting is a reversal of removal.

500 models

21 Remove the steering column combination switch assembly as described in Chapter 12.

22 Undo the 3 retaining bolts and remove the instrument panel surround (see illustration).

23 Refitting is a reversal of removal.

27.19b . . . and remove the instrument panel surround

27.22 Instrument panel surround retaining screws (arrowed) – 500 models

Lower centre panel

Panda models

24 Carefully prise up the gearchange lever gaiter from the panel (see illustration).

25 Undo the retaining screws, and pull up the gearchange lever surround panel (see illustrations).

26 Undo the 2 retaining screws and remove

27.24 Prise up the gearchange lever gaiter

27.25a Undo the screws (arrowed) . . .

27.25b . . . and pull up the gearchange lever surround panel

27.26 Footwell kick panel retaining screws (arrowed)

27.27a Undo the screw (arrowed) each side at the front, lower corner . . .

27.27b . . . the two screws (arrowed) at the top . . .

the footwell kick panel adjacent to the heater housing on the driver's side **(see illustration)**.

27 Undo the 4 screws and manoeuvre the lower centre panel from place **(see illustrations)**.

28 Refitting is a reversal of removal.

500 models

29 Remove the centre console as described in Section 26.

30 Prise up the gearchange emblem from the knob, undo the retaining bolt, then prise the gearchange lever gaiter upwards from the panel **(see illustrations)**.

31 Undo the screws and pull the gearchange lever surround panel upwards **(see illustrations)**.

32 Undo the screws at the top edge then remove the lower centre panel **(see illustrations)**.

33 Refitting is a reversal of removal.

27.27c . . . and pull the lower centre panel rearwards

27.30a Prise the emblem from the gearchange knob, undo the retaining bolt (arrowed) . . .

27.30b . . . pull off the knob . . .

27.30c . . . and prise up the gaiter

27.31a Undo the retaining screws (arrowed) . . .

27.31b . . . then prise up the gearchange lever surround panel

27.32a Undo the retaining screws (arrowed) . . .

27.32b . . . and remove the lower centre panel

27.42 Prise out the facia vents each side

27.43a The facia is secured by a bolt (arrowed) each side in the vent apertures ...

27.43b ... a bolt each side in the lower, outer corners (arrowed) ...

Complete facia assembly

Note: *This is an involved operation entailing the removal of numerous components and assemblies, and the disconnection of a multitude of wiring connectors. Make notes on the location of all disconnected wiring, or attach labels to the connectors, to avoid confusion when refitting.*

34 Disconnect the battery negative terminal as described in Chapter 5A.

35 Remove the A-pillar trim panels on both sides as described in Section 25.

Panda models

36 Remove the heater/air conditioning control knobs/trim as described in Chapter 3.

37 Remove the steering column as described in Chapter 10.

38 Remove all the facia panels described previously in this Section.

39 If not already done so, remove the audio unit and instrument cluster as described in Chapter 12.

40 Remove the central switch panel and electric window switches as described in Chapter 12.

41 Where fitted, undo the passenger's airbag retaining bolts, and disconnect the wiring plug – refer to Chapter 12.

42 Prise out the facia demister vents each side (see illustration).

43 Undo the 12 facia retaining bolts (see illustrations).

27.43c ... a bolt (arrowed) each side of the heater housing ...

27.43d ... a bolt in the audio unit aperture (arrowed) ...

27.43e ... 2 bolts (arrowed) in the switch aperture ...

27.43f ... and 3 bolts (arrowed) in the centre

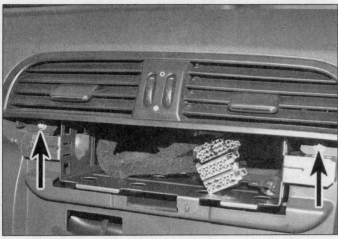

27.50 Undo the screws (arrowed) and prise out the central air vent

27.51a Prise up the central . . .

27.51b . . . and side demister vents

27.52 Steering column adjustment lever surround trim screws (arrowed)

44 With the help of an assistant, manoeuvre the facia from the vehicle.

500 models

45 Remove the steering column combination switch assembly and driver's side knee airbag as described in Chapter 12.

46 Remove the centre console as described in Section 26.

47 Remove all the facia panels described previously in this Section.

48 Remove the instrument cluster, and facia switches as described in Chapter 12.

49 Remove the audio unit as described in Chapter 12.

50 Undo the retaining screws and remove the facia central vent (see illustration).

51 Carefully prise up the windscreen central

and side demister vents from the facia (see illustrations).

52 Undo the 2 screws securing the steering column adjustment lever surround trim to the facia (see illustration).

53 The facia is now secured by 4 screws at the top edge (in the demister vents apertures), 1 screw each side in the lower, outer corners, 2 screws above the heater/air conditioning

27.53a The facia is secured by a screw in each upper vent aperture (arrowed) . . .

27.53b . . . side vent aperture (arrowed) . . .

27.53c . . . a screw (arrowed) each side at the lower, outer corner . . .

27.53d . . . 2 screws (arrowed) above the heater control location . . .

27.53e . . . a screw (arrowed) in each window switch aperture . . .

27.53f . . . a screw (arrowed) in the audio unit aperture . . .

27.53g . . . a screw (arrowed) each side of the heater housing . . .

27.53h . . . and a screw (arrowed) in the gearchange lever aperture

control location, 1 screw each side in the electric window switch apertures, 1 screw in the audio unit aperture, 1 screw on the lower facia adjacent to the heater distribution housing each side, and 1 screw in the gearchange lever aperture **(see illustrations)**. Remove the screws.

All models

54 Carefully pull the whole facia moulding away from the bulkhead slightly. Label all remaining wiring connectors to aid correct refitting later, then disconnect them. Check that nothing remains connected between the facia and bulkhead, then draw the facia moulding away and remove it from the car.

55 Refitting is a reversal of removal, noting the following points:

a) *Reinstate all electrical connections according to the labels made during removal and ensure that cables are* secured in their clips, using the original routing.

b) *Refer to the Chapters indicated and refit all components disturbed during the removal process.*

c) *On completion, reconnect the battery negative terminal and check the operation of all controls, gauges and instruments disturbed during the removal process, including the heating/air conditioning system.*

Chapter 12
Body electrical systems

Contents

Degrees of difficulty

Easy, suitable for novice with little experience	**Fairly easy,** suitable for beginner with some experience	**Fairly difficult,** suitable for competent DIY mechanic	**Difficult,** suitable for experienced DIY mechanic	**Very difficult,** suitable for expert DIY or professional

Specifications

Bulb ratings

	Watts
Brake light:	
Panda models	21/5
500 models	21
High-level	5, capless
Courtesy light	5, festoon
Front direction indicator light	21, amber
Front direction indicator repeater light	5, capless
Front foglight	55, H1
Front sidelight/running light:	
Panda models	5, capless
500 models	21/5, capless
Headlights:	
Panda models	60/55, H4
500 models:	
Main beam	55, H1
Dipped beam	55, H7
Luggage compartment light	5, capless
Number plate light	5, festoon
Rear direction indicator light	21
Rear foglight	21
Reversing light	21
Tail light:	
Panda models	With brake light
500 models	10

1 General information and precautions

The electrical system is of 12 volt negative earth type. Power for the lights and all electrical accessories is supplied by a lead-acid type battery, which is charged by the alternator.

This Chapter covers repair and service procedures for the various electrical components not associated with the engine. Information on the battery, alternator and starter motor can be found in Chapter 5A.

It should be noted that, prior to working on any component in the electrical system, the battery negative terminal should first be disconnected, to prevent the possibility of electrical short-circuits and/or fires as described in Chapter 5A.

⚠️ *Warning: Before carrying out any work on the electrical system, read through the precautions given in 'Safety first!' at the beginning of this manual, and in Chapter 5A.*

⚠️ *Warning: Certain models are equipped with an airbag system and may also have pyrotechnic seat belt pretensioners. When working on the electrical system, refer to the precautions given in Section 19, to avoid the possibility of personal injury.*

2 Electrical fault finding – general information

Note: *Refer to the precautions given in 'Safety first!' and in Section 1 of this Chapter before starting work. The following tests relate to testing of the main electrical circuits, and should not be used to test delicate electronic circuits (such as engine management systems and anti-lock braking systems), particularly where an electronic control unit is used.*

General

1 A typical electrical circuit consists of an electrical component, any switches, relays, motors, fuses, fusible links or circuit breakers related to that component, and the wiring and connectors which link the component to both the battery and the chassis. To help to pinpoint a problem in an electrical circuit, wiring diagrams are included at the end of this Chapter.

2 Before attempting to diagnose an electrical fault, first study the appropriate wiring diagram, to obtain a more complete understanding of the components included in the particular circuit concerned. The possible sources of a fault can be narrowed down by noting whether other components related to the circuit are operating properly. If several components or circuits fail at one time, the problem is likely to be related to a shared fuse or earth connection.

3 Electrical problems usually stem from simple causes, such as loose or corroded connections, a faulty earth connection, a blown fuse, a melted fusible link, or a faulty relay (refer to Section 3 for details of testing relays). Visually inspect the condition of all fuses, wires and connections in a problem circuit before testing the components. Use the wiring diagrams to determine which terminal connections will need to be checked, in order to pinpoint the trouble-spot.

4 The basic tools required for electrical fault-finding include a circuit tester or voltmeter (a 12 volt bulb with a set of test leads can also be used for certain tests); a self-powered test light (sometimes known as a continuity tester); an ohmmeter (to measure resistance); a battery and set of test leads; and a jumper wire, preferably with a circuit breaker or fuse incorporated, which can be used to bypass suspect wires or electrical components. Before attempting to locate a problem with test instruments, use the wiring diagram to determine where to make the connections.

5 To find the source of an intermittent wiring fault (usually due to a poor or dirty connection, or damaged wiring insulation), a wiggle test can be performed on the wiring. This involves wiggling the wiring by hand, to see if the fault occurs as the wiring is moved. It should be possible to narrow down the source of the fault to a particular section of wiring. This method of testing can be used in conjunction with any of the tests described in the following sub-Sections.

6 Apart from problems due to poor connections, two basic types of fault can occur in an electrical circuit – open-circuit or short-circuit.

7 Open-circuit faults are caused by a break somewhere in the circuit, which prevents current from flowing. An open-circuit fault will prevent a component from working, but will not cause the relevant circuit fuse to blow.

8 Short-circuit faults are normally caused by a breakdown in wiring insulation, which allows a feed wire to touch either another wire, or an earthed component such as the bodyshell. This allows the current flowing in the circuit to 'escape' along an alternative route, usually to earth. As the circuit does not now follow its original complete path, it is known as a 'short' circuit. A short-circuit fault will normally cause the relevant circuit fuse to blow.

Finding an open-circuit

9 To check for an open-circuit, connect one lead of a circuit tester or voltmeter to either the negative battery terminal or a known good earth.

10 Connect the other lead to a connector in the circuit being tested, preferably nearest to the battery or fuse.

11 Switch on the circuit, bearing in mind that some circuits are live only when the ignition switch is moved to a particular position.

12 If voltage is present (indicated either by the tester bulb lighting or a voltmeter reading, as applicable), this means that the section of the circuit between the relevant connector and the battery is problem-free.

13 Continue to check the remainder of the circuit in the same fashion.

14 When a point is reached at which no voltage is present, the problem must lie between that point and the previous test point with voltage. Most problems can be traced to a broken, corroded or loose connection.

Finding a short-circuit

15 To check for a short-circuit, first disconnect the load(s) from the circuit (loads are the components which draw current from a circuit, such as bulbs, motors, heating elements, etc).

16 Remove the relevant fuse from the circuit, and connect a circuit tester or voltmeter to the fuse connections.

17 Switch on the circuit, bearing in mind that some circuits are live only when the ignition switch is moved to a particular position.

18 If voltage is present (indicated either by the tester bulb lighting or a voltmeter reading, as applicable), this means that there is a short-circuit.

19 If no voltage is present, but the fuse still blows with the load(s) connected, this indicates an internal fault in the load(s).

Finding an earth fault

20 The battery negative terminal is connected to 'earth' – the metal of the engine/transmission and the car body – and most systems are wired so that they only receive a positive feed, the current returning via the metal of the car body. This means that the component mounting and the body form part of that circuit. Loose or corroded mountings can therefore cause a range of electrical faults, ranging from total failure of a circuit, to a puzzling partial fault. In particular, lights may shine dimly (especially when another circuit sharing the same earth point is in operation), motors (eg, wiper motors or the radiator cooling fan motor) may run slowly, and the operation of one circuit may have an apparently-unrelated effect on another. Note that on many vehicles, earth straps are used between certain components, such as the engine/transmission and the body, usually where there is no metal-to-metal contact between components, due to flexible rubber mountings, etc. Earth connections are made in various places **(see illustrations)**.

2.20a Some of the earth connections are behind the rear side trim panel (arrowed) . . .

2.20b . . . in front of the bonnet release lever (arrowed) . . .

2.20c . . . camshaft cover (arrowed) . . .

2.20d . . . left-hand rear of the engine compartment (arrowed) . . .

2.20e . . . under the heater housing (arrowed) . . .

2.20f . . . and the left-hand front chassis leg in the engine compartment (arrowed – main earth strap to transmission casing) – Panda models . . .

2.20g . . . and 500 models (arrowed)

21 To check whether a component is properly earthed, disconnect the battery, and connect one lead of an ohmmeter to a known good earth point. Connect the other lead to the wire or earth connection being tested. The resistance reading should be zero; if not, check the connection as follows.
22 If an earth connection is thought to be faulty, dismantle the connection, and clean back to bare metal both the bodyshell and the wire terminal or the component earth connection mating surface. Be careful to remove all traces of dirt and corrosion, then use a knife to trim away any paint, so that a clean metal-to-metal joint is made. On reassembly, tighten the joint fasteners securely; if a wire terminal is being refitted,

use serrated washers between the terminal and the bodyshell, to ensure a clean and secure connection. When the connection is remade, prevent the onset of corrosion in the future by applying a coat of petroleum jelly or silicone-based grease, or by spraying on (at regular intervals) a proprietary ignition sealer.

3 Fuses and relays –
general information

Fuses

1 Fuses are designed to break a circuit when a predetermined current is reached, in order

to protect the components and wiring which could be damaged by excessive current flow. Any excessive current flow will be due to a fault in the circuit, usually a short-circuit (see Section 2).
2 The main fuses are located in the fusebox under the facia on the driver's side (Panda models) or passenger's side (500 models).
3 To gain access to the fuses on Panda models, release the two screws located at the base of the facia lower panel, then remove the panel from the facia. On 500 models, unclip the panel in front of the oddments tray **(see illustrations)**.
4 Additional fuses and circuit breakers are located in the fuse/relay box in the engine

3.3a Undo the screws (arrowed) and remove the fusebox cover – Panda models

3.3b On 500 models, unclip the panel (arrowed) in the oddment tray . . .

3.3c . . . to access the fusebox

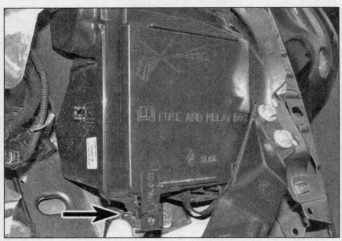

3.4a Release the clip at the base . . .

3.4b . . . and slide up the engine compartment fuse/relay box cover – 500 models

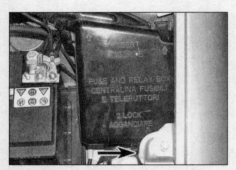

3.4c Release the clip (arrowed) and pivot the fuse/relay box cover upwards – Panda models

compartment; release the clip and lift off the cover to gain access (see illustration).

5 A blown fuse can be recognised from its melted or broken wire.

6 To remove a fuse, first ensure that the relevant circuit is switched off.

7 Using the plastic tool clipped to the main fusebox, pull the fuse from its location.

8 Spare fuses are provided in the main fusebox.

9 Before renewing a blown fuse, trace and rectify the cause, and always use a fuse of the correct rating (fuse ratings are specified on the inside of the fusebox cover panel). Never substitute a fuse of a higher rating, or make temporary repairs using wire or metal foil; more serious damage, or even fire, could result.

10 Note that the fuses are colour-coded as follows. Refer to the wiring diagrams for details of the fuse ratings used and the circuits protected.

Colour	Rating
Orange	5A
Red	10A
Blue	15A
Yellow	20A
Clear or White	25A
Green	30A

Relays

11 A relay is an electrically-operated switch, which is used for the following reasons:

a) A relay can switch a heavy current remotely from the circuit in which the current is flowing, therefore allowing the use of lighter-gauge wiring and switch contacts.

b) A relay can receive more than one control input, unlike a mechanical switch.

c) A relay can have a timer function – for example, the intermittent wiper relay.

12 The main and optional equipment relays are primarily located in the engine compartment fuse/relay box (see Fuses). Additional relays may be fitted, depending on model and specification and these are generally mounted adjacent to the component being controlled.

13 If a circuit or system controlled by a relay develops a fault, and the relay is suspect, operate the system. If the relay is functioning, it should be possible to hear it click as it is energised. If this is the case, the fault lies with the components or wiring of the system. If the relay is not being energised, then either the relay is not receiving a main supply or a switching voltage, or the relay itself is faulty. Testing is by the substitution of a known good unit, but be careful – while some relays

4.3 Lever over the clip and remove the plastic cover

are identical in appearance and in operation, others look similar but perform different functions.

14 To remove a relay, first ensure that the relevant circuit is switched off. The relay can then simply be pulled out from the socket, and pushed back into position.

4 Bulbs (exterior lights) – renewal

General

1 Whenever a bulb is renewed, note the following points:

a) Ensure that the relevant electrical circuit is isolated before removing a bulb. If in doubt, disconnect the battery negative terminal (refer to Disconnecting the battery in the Chapter 5A) before starting work.

b) Remember that, if the circuit has just been in use, the bulb may be extremely hot.

c) Always check the bulb contacts and holder, ensuring that there is clean metal-to-metal contact between the bulb and its live contact(s) and earth. Clean off any corrosion or dirt before fitting a new bulb.

d) Wherever bayonet-type bulbs are fitted, ensure that the live contact(s) bear firmly against the bulb contact.

e) Always ensure that the new bulb is of the correct rating (see Specifications), and that it is completely clean before fitting it; this applies particularly to headlight/ foglight bulbs (see following paragraphs).

Headlight

2 Open and support the bonnet.

Panda models

3 Lever over the retaining clip and remove the plastic cover from the rear of the headlight (see illustration).

4.4 Pull the connector from the rear of the bulb

4.5a Push the ends of the clip (arrowed) outwards to disengage it . . .

4.5b . . . then withdraw the bulb. Note the locating lugs (arrowed)

4 Disconnect the bulb's wiring connector **(see illustration)**.

5 Push the bulb's wire retaining clip sideways at the top, and hinge it down. Remove the bulb from the headlight **(see illustrations)**.

6 When handling the new bulb, use a tissue or clean cloth to avoid touching the glass with the fingers; moisture and grease from the skin can cause blackening and rapid failure of this type of bulb. If the glass is accidentally touched, wipe it clean using methylated spirit. Avoid knocking or shaking the bulb as this may weaken the filament.

7 Install the new bulb, using a reversal of the removal procedure, ensuring that its locating tabs are correctly located in the light unit

cut-outs. Secure the bulb in position with the retaining clip.

500 models – dipped beam bulb

8 Pull off the rubber cover from the dipped beam bulb – this is the lower rubber cover on the back of the headlight **(see illustration)**.

9 Lift the retaining tab, and remove the bulbholder/bulb assembly from the reflector **(see illustrations)**.

10 Remove the bulb from the holder **(see illustration)**.

11 When handling the new bulb, use a tissue or clean cloth to avoid touching the glass with the fingers; moisture and grease from the skin

can cause blackening and rapid failure of this type of bulb. If the glass is accidentally touched, wipe it clean using methylated spirit. Avoid knocking or shaking the bulb as this may weaken the filament.

12 Install the new bulb, using a reversal of the removal procedure, ensuring that its locating tabs are correctly located in the light unit cut-outs.

500 models – main beam bulb

13 Unclip the access flap in the relevant front wheel arch **(see illustration)**.

14 Pull off the rubber cover from the headlight **(see illustration)**.

4.8 Pull the lower rubber cover from the dipped beam headlight

4.9a Lift the retaining tab (arrowed) . . .

4.9b . . . and withdraw the bulb/holder assembly

4.10 Pull the bulb from the holder

4.13 Unclip the main beam headlight access flap

4.14 Pull off the main beam headlight bulb cover

4.15 Pull the connector from the bulb

4.16a Push the ends of the retaining clips (arrowed) outwards . . .

4.16b . . . and withdraw the main beam bulb

15 Pull the wiring connector from the bulb (see illustration).

16 Push the bulb's wire retaining clips outwards at the base. Remove the bulb from the headlight (see illustrations).

17 When handling the new bulb, use a tissue or clean cloth to avoid touching the glass with the fingers; moisture and grease from the skin can cause blackening and rapid failure of this type of bulb. If the glass is accidentally touched, wipe it clean using methylated spirit. Avoid knocking or shaking the bulb as this may weaken the filament.

18 Install the new bulb, using a reversal of the removal procedure. Ensure that its locating tabs are correctly located in the light unit cut-outs and secure the bulb in position with the retaining clip.

Sidelight/running light

Panda models

19 Open and support the bonnet.

20 Lever over the retaining clip and remove the plastic cover from the rear of the headlight (see illustration 4.3).

21 Twist and withdraw the sidelight bulbholder from the headlight unit (see illustration).

22 Remove the push-fit bulb from the bulbholder (see illustration).

23 Fit the new bulb using a reversal of the removal procedure.

500 models

24 Unclip the access flap in the relevant front wheel arch (see illustration 4.13).

25 Pull off the rubber cover from the rear of the headlight (see illustration 4.14).

26 Twist and withdraw the sidelight bulbholder from the headlight unit (see illustration).

27 Remove the push-fit bulb from the bulbholder (see illustration).

28 Fit the new bulb using a reversal of the removal procedure.

Front direction indicator

29 Open and support the bonnet.

Panda models

30 Lever over the retaining clip and remove the plastic cover from the rear of the headlight (see illustration 4.3).

31 Twist and withdraw the bulbholder from the headlight unit (see illustration).

32 The bulb is a bayonet fit in the bulbholder (see illustration). Push and twist it anti-clockwise.

4.21 Twist the sidelight bulbholder (arrowed) anti-clockwise and withdraw it

4.22 Pull the sidelight bulb from the holder

4.26 Twist the side/running light bulbholder (arrowed) anti-clockwise and withdraw it

4.27 Pull the side/running light bulb from the holder

4.31 Twist the direction indicator bulbholder (arrowed) anti-clockwise

4.32 Push and twist the bulb anti-clockwise

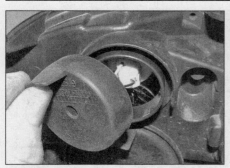

4.34 Pull off the upper rubber cover from the dipped beam headlight

4.35 Twist the direction indicator bulbholder anti-clockwise and withdraw it

4.38a Push the side repeater forwards to compress the clip (arrowed) – Panda models . . .

33 Fit the new bulb using a reversal of the removal procedure.

500 models

34 Pull off the rubber cover from the dipped beam bulb – this is the upper rubber cover on the back of the headlight (see illustration).
35 Twist and withdraw the bulbholder from the headlight unit (see illustration).
36 Pull the capless bulb from the bulbholder.
37 Fit the new bulb using a reversal of the removal procedure.

Indicator side repeater

38 Push the light unit towards the front of the vehicle slightly, then insert a screwdriver

behind the opposite edge of the unit and lever it out of the wing aperture (see illustrations). Take great care not to damage the vehicle paintwork. If the light unit is reluctant to release, undo the rearmost nut and bolt, then pull the rear section of the wheel arch liner forwards, reach up behind the wing and release the light unit. If this is the case, it may be preferable to detach the bulbholder, leaving the light unit in place.
39 Withdraw the light unit, then twist the bulbholder anti-clockwise to release it from the light unit (see illustration).
40 The bulb is a push-fit in the bulbholder.
41 Fit the new bulb using a reversal of the removal procedure.

Front foglight

42 Remove the foglight as described in Section 6.
43 Unscrew the plastic cover clockwise from the rear of the foglight, and disconnect the wiring connector from the bulb (see illustrations).
44 Release the retaining clip, hinge it downwards/upwards as applicable, and remove the bulb (see illustrations).
45 Fit the new bulb using a reversal of the removal procedure.

Rear light cluster bulbs
Panda models

46 Remove the rear light cluster as described in Section 6.

4.38b . . . and 500 models

4.39 Twist the bulbholder anti-clockwise and withdraw it

4.43a Twist clockwise to remove the foglight cover – Panda models . . .

4.43b . . . and 500 models (arrowed)

4.44a Press apart the ends of the retaining clip (arrowed) – Panda models . . .

4.44b . . . and 500 models (arrowed)

4.47 Undo the screws (arrowed) and remove the bulbholder

4.51 Release the bulbholder clips (arrowed)

4.52 Remove the relevant bulb from the holder

4.54 Starting on the right-hand side, prise the number plate light from place

4.58 Release the clip (arrowed) at the end of the bulbholder

47 Undo the 4 retaining screws and remove the bulbholder assembly from the light unit **(see illustration)**.

48 Remove the relevant bulb by pushing it in slightly, and rotating it anti-clockwise.

49 Fit the new bulb using a reversal of the removal procedure.

500 models

50 Remove the rear light cluster as described in Section 6.

51 Release the 4 retaining clips and remove the bulbholder from the light unit **(see illustration)**.

52 Remove the relevant bulb by pushing it in slightly, and rotating it anti-clockwise **(see illustration)**.

53 Fit the new bulb using a reversal of the removal procedure.

Number plate light

54 Using a small screwdriver, carefully prise the right-hand side of the light unit from its location **(see illustration)**

55 Pull the festoon bulb from its contacts.

56 Fit the new bulb using a reversal of the removal procedure.

High-level brake light

57 Remove the light unit as described in Section 6.

58 Release the plastic retaining clip at the end of the bulbholder and lift it from the light unit **(see illustration)**.

59 Remove the relevant push-fit bulb from the bulbholder.

60 Fit the new bulb using a reversal of the removal procedure.

5 Bulbs (interior lights) – renewal

General

1 Whenever a bulb is renewed, note the following points:

a) *Ensure that the relevant electrical circuit is isolated before removing a bulb. If in doubt, disconnect the battery negative terminal (refer to Disconnecting the battery in the Chapter 5A) before starting work.*

b) *Remember that, if the light has just been in use, the bulb may be extremely hot.*

c) *Always check the bulb contacts and holder, ensuring that there is clean metal-to-metal contact between the bulb and its live contact(s) and earth. Clean off any corrosion or dirt before fitting a new bulb.*

d) *Wherever bayonet-type bulbs are fitted, ensure that the live contact(s) bear firmly against the bulb contact.*

e) *Always ensure that the new bulb is of the correct rating (see Specifications), and that it is completely clean before fitting it.*

Courtesy light

2 Using a small screwdriver, carefully prise the light unit from its location **(see illustration)**.

5.2 Prise the courtesy light unit from the headlining

5.4 Lift the cover (arrowed) and pull out the festoon bulb

5.13 Pull the capless bulbs (arrowed) from the heater control assembly

5.14 Prise the heater control panel from the facia

3 Insert the screwdriver under the tab on the light unit rear cover and open the cover.

4 Remove the relevant festoon bulb from the bulbholder contacts **(see illustration)**.

5 Fit the new bulb using a reversal of the removal procedure.

Luggage compartment light

6 The light unit (where fitted) is located under the right-hand parcel shelf support panel.

7 Using a small screwdriver, carefully prise the light unit from the support panel.

8 Open the bulbholder and remove the push-fit bulb.

9 Fit the new bulb using a reversal of the removal procedure.

Instrument panel illumination

10 The instrument panel illumination and warning light bulbs are an integral part of the instrument panel cluster and cannot be renewed separately.

Switch illumination

11 The bulbs that illuminate the facia-mounted switches are integral with the switch body and cannot be renewed separately.

Heater/ventilation control illumination

Panda models

12 Remove the heater control knobs and surrounds as described in Chapter 3.

13 Remove the relevant push-fit bulb from its location in the ventilation control panel **(see illustration)**.

500 models

14 Carefully prise the heater control panel from the facia **(see illustration)**.

15 Pull the relevant capless bulb from place **(see illustration)**.

All models

16 Fit the new bulb using a reversal of the removal procedure.

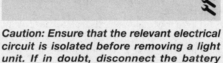

6 Exterior light units – removal and refitting

Caution: Ensure that the relevant electrical circuit is isolated before removing a light unit. If in doubt, disconnect the battery negative terminal as described in Chapter 5A.

Headlight

1 Raise the front of the vehicle and support it securely on axle stands (see *Jacking and vehicle support*). Remove both front wheels.

Panda models

2 Remove the front bumper and radiator grille as described in Chapter 11.

3 Disconnect the wiring plug from the rear of the headlight **(see illustration)**.

4 Undo the 3 retaining bolts and remove the headlight **(see illustration)**.

5 Refitting is a reversal of removal. On

5.15 Pull the illumination bulbs (arrowed) from place

completion, it is advisable to have the headlight beam alignment checked with reference to Section 8.

500 models – dipped beam unit

6 Remove the front bumper as described in Chapter 11.

7 Disconnect the wiring plug from the rear of the unit.

8 Unscrew the headlight's three securing bolts – one on top, one to the inside, and one at the outer side **(see illustration)**.

9 Withdraw the headlight from the car.

10 Refitting is a reversal of removal. On completion, it is advisable to have the headlight beam alignment checked with reference to Section 8.

500 models – main beam unit

11 Remove the front bumper as described in Chapter 11.

6.3 Depress the clip and disconnect the headlight wiring plug

6.4 Headlight retaining bolts (arrowed)

6.8 Dipped beam headlight retaining bolts (arrowed)

6.12 Main beam headlight retaining bolts (arrowed)

6.14 Foglight retaining screws (arrowed) – Panda models

12 Undo the retaining bolts and remove the light unit **(see illustration)**.

13 Refitting is a reversal of removal. On completion, it is advisable to have the headlight beam alignment checked with reference to Section 8.

Foglights

Panda models

14 Undo the 3 retaining screws and manoeuvre the foglight assembly forwards from the bumper **(see illustration)**. Disconnect the wiring plug as the unit is withdrawn.

15 If required, undo the screws and detach the foglight from the panel.

16 Refitting is a reversal of removal. The aim of the foglights can be adjusted by means of the adjustment screw accessible through a hole in the underside of the bumper **(see illustrations)**.

500 models

17 Unclip the foglight surround panel **(see illustration)**.

18 Undo the retaining bolts, rotate the foglight unit slightly and manoeuvre it from the bumper **(see illustrations)**. Disconnect the wiring plug as the unit is withdrawn.

19 Refitting is a reversal of removal. The aim of the foglights can be adjusted by means of the adjustment screw accessible through a hole in the underside of the foglight surround panel **(see illustration)**.

Indicator side repeater light

20 The procedure is described as part of the bulb renewal procedure in Section 4.

Rear light cluster

21 Open the tailgate, undo the retaining screws, and pull the light unit rearwards to

6.16a Adjust the foglight aim by inserting a socket through the hole (arrowed) . . .

6.16b . . . onto the adjustment screw (arrowed)

6.17 Unclip the foglight surround panel

6.18a Undo the foglights retaining bolts (arrowed) . . .

6.18b . . . then rotate the foglight slightly to disengage the adjustment screw

6.19 Foglight adjustment screw (arrowed)

6.21a Undo the retaining screws (arrowed) . . .

6.21b . . . and prise the rear light cluster rewards to release the push-in clips – Panda models

6.21c Undo the retaining screws (arrowed) . . .

6.21d . . . and pull the rear light cluster rearwards to release the push-in clips (arrowed) – 500 models

6.23a Prise out the caps . . .

6.23b . . . undo the retaining screws (arrowed) . . .

release the clips (see illustrations). Disconnect the wiring plug as the unit is withdrawn.
22 Refitting is a reversal of removal.

High-level brake light

23 Prise out the plastic caps (where fitted), undo the 2 screws and remove the high-level brake light (see illustrations). Pull the trim rearwards to release the clips. Disconnect the wiring plug as the light unit is withdrawn.
24 Refitting is a reversal of removal.

7 Instrument panel – removal and refitting

Removal

1 Disconnect the battery negative terminal as described in Chapter 5A.

6.23c . . . and remove the high-level brake light – 500 models

Panda models

2 Undo the 4 retaining screws and manoeuvre the instrument panel surround from the facia (see illustrations).
3 Undo the 3 screws and remove the panel

7.2a The instrument panel surround is secured by 2 screws underneath (arrowed) . . .

7.2b . . . and 2 screws at the top (arrowed)

6.23d High-level brake light screws (arrowed) – Panda models

from the facia (see illustration). Disconnect the wiring plug as the panel is withdrawn.
4 The instrument panel cannot be dismantled and the individual components are not available separately.

7.3 Instrument cluster retaining screws (arrowed)

7.6 Prise the facia vent panel from place

7.7a Undo the screws (arrowed) . . .

7.7b . . . and remove the instrument panel surround

7.8 Instrument panel retaining screws (arrowed)

8.2a Headlight beam adjustment screws (arrowed) – Panda models

8.2b Dipped beam headlight adjustment screws (arrowed) – 500 models

500 models

5 Remove the steering column combination switch assembly as described in Section 13.

6 Carefully prise the driver's side facia vent panel from place **(see illustration)**.

7 Undo the 3 retaining screws and remove the instrument panel surround from the facia **(see illustrations)**.

8 Undo the 4 retaining screws and manoeuvre the instrument panel from place **(see illustration)**. Disconnect the wiring plug as the panel is withdrawn.

Refitting

9 Refitting is a reversal of removal. **Note:** *If a new instrument panel has been fitted, it must be programmed using Fiat diagnostic equipment. Entrust this task to a Fiat dealer or suitably-equipped repairer.*

8 Headlight beam alignment – general information

1 Accurate adjustment of the headlight beam is only possible using optical beam-setting equipment, and this work should therefore be carried out by a Fiat dealer or suitably-equipped workshop. Incorrectly adjusted headlamps can dazzle other drivers and cause accidents.

2 For reference, the headlights can be adjusted using the adjuster screws, accessible via the top of each light unit **(see illustrations)**.

9 Horn – removal and refitting

Removal

Panda models

1 Remove the radiator grille as described in Chapter 11.

500 models

2 Raise the front of the vehicle and support it securely on axle stands (see *Jacking and vehicle support*).

All models

3 Undo the nut securing the horn to the mounting bracket **(see illustrations)**. Disconnect the wiring connector as the horn is withdrawn.

9.3a On Panda models, the horn is located above the radiator on the front panel

8.2c The main beam headlight adjustment screw (arrowed) is just accessible behind and below the dipped beam headlight – 500 models

Refitting

4 Refitting is a reversal of removal.

9.3b On 500 models, the horn is located at the left-hand end of the front panel

10.2a On Panda models, the door speaker is retained by screws (arrowed) . . .

10.2b . . . whilst on 500 models, rivets are used (arrowed)

12.2 Insert the extraction tools and pull the audio unit from the facia

10 Loudspeakers – removal and refitting

Removal

Front door speaker

1 Remove the door inner trim panel as described in Chapter 11.
2 Undo the retaining screws/drill out the rivets (as applicable) and remove the speaker (see illustrations). Disconnect the wiring plug as the speaker is withdrawn.

Front tweeter

3 Remove the A-pillar trim panel as described in Chapter 11.
4 Rotate the speaker anti-clockwise and remove it from the panel.

Rear door speaker

5 Remove the rear door inner trim panel as described in Chapter 11.
6 Undo the retaining screws and remove the speaker. Disconnect the wiring plug as the speaker is withdrawn.

Rear speaker

7 Remove the rear side panel as described in Chapter 11.
8 Drill out the rivets and remove the speaker. Disconnect the wiring plug as the speaker is withdrawn.

Refitting

9 Refitting is a reversal of removal.

11 Radio aerial – removal and refitting

Removal

1 Unscrew the aerial antenna from the mounting base.
2 Removal of the aerial base requires removal of the headlining. This is considered outside the scope of this manual, as successful refitting of the headlining requires experience, patience and dexterity. We recommend this task is entrusted to a Fiat dealer or suitably-experienced repairer.

Refitting

3 Refitting is a reversal of removal.

12 Audio unit – removal and refitting

Removal

1 Disconnect the battery negative terminal as described in Chapter 5A.

Panda models

2 Insert the special extraction tools into the

holes on either side of the audio unit. Press them home until the internal clips can be felt to release (see illustration). Note that extraction tools can be obtained from motor accessory outlets.

500 models

3 Carefully prise the blank covers from the audio unit switches, then insert the extraction tools into the holes on either side of the audio unit. Press them home until the internal clips can be felt to release (see illustrations). Note that if the original extraction tools are not available, new ones can be obtained from motor accessory outlets.

All models

4 Pull the unit from the facia, then disconnect the aerial lead and wiring connector from the rear of the unit (see illustration).

Refitting

5 Refitting is a reversal of removal, ensuring that the wiring is routed freely behind the unit.

13 Switches – removal and refitting

Steering column combination switches

1 Remove the steering wheel as described in Chapter 10.

12.3a Prise out the covers . . .

12.3b . . . insert the tools and extract the audio unit

12.4 Disconnect the wiring from the rear of the audio unit

13.3 Slacken the clamp ring Allen bolt (arrowed)

13.4a Disconnect the wiring plugs above the combination switch (arrowed) . . .

2 Remove the steering column shrouds as described in Chapter 11, Section 27.

3 Using an Allen key, slacken the clamp ring bolt at the underside of the switch unit **(see illustration)**.

4 Disconnect the switch unit wiring plugs **(see illustrations)**.

5 Withdraw the stalk switch unit off the steering column.

6 Refitting is a reversal of removal. Refit the steering column shrouds and steering wheel with reference to the Chapters and Sections indicated.

Facia switches

Panda models

7 Disconnect the battery negative lead as described in Chapter 5A.

8 Carefully prise the switch assembly from the facia **(see illustration)**. Disconnect the wiring plug as the switch assembly is withdrawn.

9 Refitting is a reversal of removal.

500 models

10 Remove the instrument cluster as described in Section 7.

11 Remove the heater control panel as described in Chapter 3.

12 Undo the decorative trim panel retaining screws in the centre, and pull the panel from place **(see illustrations)**. Disconnect any wiring plugs as the panel is withdrawn.

13 Undo the retaining screws and detach the switch assembly from the panel **(see illustration)**.

14 Refitting is a reversal of removal.

Brake light switch

15 Refer to the information contained in Chapter 9.

13.4b . . . below the switch . . .

13.4c . . . then slide the switch from the column

13.8 Prise the switch assembly from the facia

13.12a Undo the screws (arrowed) . . .

13.12b . . . then pull the decorative trim panel rearwards to release the clips

13.13 Switch retaining screws (arrowed)

13.17 Prise up the cover . . .

13.18 . . . then prise the window switch from place

13.21a Prise the mirror adjustment switch from the armrest . . .

13.21b . . . or centre console

13.24 Prise out the locking element

13.25a Rotate the locking arm forwards . . .

Electric window switches

16 Disconnect the battery negative lead as described in Chapter 5A.
17 Carefully prise the switch cover from the facia (see illustration).
18 Prise the switch from the facia (see illustration). Disconnect the wiring pug from the switch as it's withdrawn.
19 Refitting is a reversal of removal.

Door mirror adjustment switch

20 Disconnect the battery negative lead as described in Chapter 5A.
21 Carefully prise the switch panel from the centre console/armrest (see illustrations). Disconnect the wiring as the panel is withdrawn.
22 Refitting is a reversal of removal.

Clutch pedal position switch

23 Working under the driver's side of the facia, disconnect the switch wiring plug.
24 Prise out the locking element securing the switch arm to the pedal lug (see illustration).
25 Rotate the locking pin arm forwards, withdraw the lower retaining pin, and disengage the upper locating lug. Manoeuvre the switch from position (see illustrations).
26 Refitting is a reversal of removal.

Steering wheel switches

27 Remove the driver's airbag as described in Section 20 of this Chapter.
28 Disconnect the switch assembly wiring plug, then gently prise the switches from the steering wheel.
29 Refitting is a reversal of removal.

Ignition switch/steering lock

30 Refer to Chapter 5A.

14 Tailgate wiper motor – removal and refitting

Removal

1 Disconnect the battery negative terminal as described in Chapter 5A.
2 Remove the tailgate inner trim panel as described in Chapter 11, Section 25.
3 Remove the wiper arm with reference to Section 17.
4 Working inside the tailgate, disconnect the tailgate wiper motor wiring connector.

13.25b . . . withdrawn the locking pin . . .

13.25c . . . and disengage the upper locating lug (arrowed)

13.25d Upper locating lug (arrowed)

14.5 Tailgate wiper motor retaining bolts (arrowed)

5 Unscrew the three bolts securing the motor to the tailgate and remove the motor assembly (see illustration).

Refitting

6 Refitting is a reversal of removal. Refit the wiper arm with reference to Section 17.

15 Windscreen/tailgate washer system components – removal and refitting

Washer fluid reservoir

Removal

1 Firmly apply the handbrake, then jack up the front of the car and support it securely on axle stands (see *Jacking and vehicle support*). Remove the right-hand front roadwheel.
2 On Panda models, undo the screws and fold back the front section of the wheel arch liner.
3 On 500 models, undo the bolts securing the support bracket between the front subframe and the vehicle body, then undo the fasteners and remove the wheel arch liner.
4 From under the wheel arch undo the two reservoir retaining bolts. Where applicable, release any retaining clips securing the reservoir.
5 Lower the reservoir from its location and disconnect the washer pump wiring connectors and the fluid hoses. Remove the reservoir from under the wheel arch (see illustration).

15.15 Squeeze together the clips (arrowed) and pull the jet from the tailgate

15.5 Disconnect the washer pump hoses and wiring plug

15.12b Squeeze together the clips and pull the jet from the trim panel

Refitting

6 Refitting is a reversal of removal.

Washer pump(s)

Removal

7 On Panda models, remove the washer fluid reservoir, as described in the previous sub-Section.
8 On 500 models, partially remove the wheel arch liner to access the pump, fitted into the reservoir.
9 Pull the washer pump from the reservoir. Where applicable, recover the grommet.

Refitting

10 Refitting is a reversal of removal.

Windscreen washer nozzles

Removal

11 Remove the windscreen scuttle grille panel as described in Section 22 of Chapter 11.

16.4 Lift the cover and disconnect the wiper motor wiring plug

15.12a Disconnect the hose from the base of the jet

15.13 Adjust the jet vertical aim by rotating the screw

12 Disconnect the hose from the base of the nozzle, then release the retaining clips and pull the nozzle from place (see illustrations).

Refitting

13 Refitting is a reversal of removal. If necessary, the vertical aim of the nozzles can be adjusted using a screwdriver (see illustration).

Tailgate washer nozzle

Removal

14 Remove the high level brake light as described in Section 6.
15 Squeeze together the clips and prise the washer nozzle from place (see illustration).
16 Disconnect the washer fluid hose from the nozzle.

Refitting

17 Refitting is a reversal of removal.

16 Windscreen wiper motor and linkage – removal and refitting

Removal

1 Disconnect the battery negative terminal as described in Chapter 5A.
2 Refer to Section 17 and remove both wiper arms.
3 Remove the windscreen scuttle grille panel as described in Chapter 11, Section 22.
4 Lift the wiper motor protective cover (where fitted) and disconnect the motor wiring connector (see illustration).

5 Undo the two wiper motor and linkage retaining bolts and withdraw the assembly from the scuttle. Note the lug at the front (Panda models) or rear (500 models) of the motor that engages with a grommet in the scuttle **(see illustrations)**.

Refitting

6 Refitting is a reversal of removal.

17 Wiper arm –
removal and refitting

Removal

Windscreen wiper

1 Operate the wiper motor, then switch it off so that the wiper arm returns to the at-rest/parked position.

2 The at-rest position of the blades is indicated by marks on the windscreen **(see illustrations)**. If these marks are not visible, stick a length of masking tape on the glass below the edge of the wiper blade, to use as an alignment aid on refitting.

3 On 500 models, carefully prise the plastic cover from the front windscreen scuttle trim panel to expose the wiper spindle **(see illustration)**.

4 Prise off the wiper arm spindle nut cover, then slacken and remove the spindle nut **(see illustration)**.

5 Lift the blade off the glass, and pull the wiper arm off its spindle. If necessary, the arm

16.5a Windscreen wiper motor retaining bolts (arrowed) – Panda models . . .

16.5c Note the lug (arrowed) on the front of the motor – Panda models . . .

can be carefully removed using a puller **(see illustrations)**. If both windscreen wiper arms are removed, note their locations, as different arms are fitted to the driver's and passenger's sides.

16.5b . . . and 500 models (arrowed)

16.5d . . . or rear (arrowed) – 500 models

Tailgate wiper

6 Lift up the cover and undo the spindle nut **(see illustration)**.

7 Pull the wiper arm from the spindle.

17.2 The blade 'at rest' position may be marked by a circle or 3 dots on the glass

17.3 On 500 models, prise out the left-hand end (arrowed) of the plastic cover first

17.4 Prise up the spindle cover, and undo the nut beneath

17.5a Pull the wiper arm from the spindle

17.5b If necessary, use a puller to release the wiper arm

17.6 Lift the cover and undo the spindle nut

17.11 Align the blade with the mark (arrowed) on the glass

Refitting

Windscreen wiper

8 Ensure that the wiper arm and spindle splines are clean and dry.
9 When refitting a wiper arm, refit the arm to the spindle, aligning the wiper blade with the tape fitted before removal. If both windscreen wiper arms have been removed, ensure that the arms are refitted to their correct positions as noted before removal.
10 Refit the spindle nut, tighten it securely, and refit the nut cover.

Tailgate wiper

11 Fit the wiper arm over the spindle and align the blade with the mark on the screen **(see illustration)**.
12 Tighten the spindle nut and fold over the plastic cover.

18 Anti-theft system and engine immobiliser – general information

All models in the range are equipped as standard with a central locking system incorporating an electronic engine immobiliser function.

The electronic engine immobiliser is operated by a transponder fitted to the ignition key, in conjunction with an analogue module fitted around the ignition switch.

When the ignition key is inserted in the switch and turned to the ignition 'on' position, the control module sends a pre-programmed recognition code signal to the module on the ignition switch. If the recognition code signal matches that of the transponder on the ignition key, an unlocking request signal is sent to the engine management ECU allowing the engine to be started. If the ignition key signal is not recognised, the engine management system remains immobilised.

When the ignition is switched off, a locking signal is sent to the ECU and the engine is immobilised until the unlocking request signal is again received.

19 Airbag system – general information, precautions and system de-activation

General information

A driver's airbag is fitted as standard on all models, with passenger's airbag, side airbags, and side window airbags available as optional equipment on most models. The driver's airbag is located in the steering wheel centre pad and the passenger's airbag is located above the glovebox in the facia. The side airbags are located in the front seat backs, and the side window airbags are located in the roof headlining on both sides of the car. In addition, pyrotechnic seat belt pretensioners are fitted to the inertia reels of the front seat belts.

The airbag and seat belt pyrotechnic safety systems are armed only when the ignition is switched on, however, a reserve power source maintains a power supply to the systems in the event of a break in the main electrical supply. The airbags are activated by a 'g' sensor (deceleration sensor), and controlled by an electronic control unit located under the centre of the facia. The side airbags and side window airbags are activated by severe side impact and operate in conjunction with the main system. The pyrotechnic seat belt pretensioners operate independently of the main system.

The airbags are inflated by a gas generator, which forces the bag out from its location in the steering wheel, facia, seat back frame or roof headlining.

Precautions

 Warning: The following precautions must be observed when working on vehicles equipped with an airbag system, to prevent the possibility of personal injury. Many of the precautions are equally applicable to the pyrotechnic seat belt pretensioners and should be similarly observed.

General

The following precautions **must** be observed when carrying out work on a vehicle equipped with an airbag:
a) *Do not disconnect the battery with the engine running.*
b) *Before carrying out any work in the vicinity of the airbag, removal of any of the airbag components, or any welding work on the vehicle, de-activate the system as described in the following sub-Section.*
c) *Do not attempt to test any of the airbag system circuits using test meters or any other test equipment.*
d) *If the airbag warning light comes on, or any fault in the system is suspected, consult a Fiat dealer without delay. **Do not** attempt to carry out fault diagnosis, or any dismantling of the components.*

When handling an airbag
a) *Transport the airbag by itself, bag upward.*
b) *Do not put your arms around the airbag.*
c) *Carry the airbag close to the body, bag outward.*
d) *Do not drop the airbag or expose it to impacts.*
e) *Do not attempt to dismantle the airbag unit.*
f) *Do not connect any form of electrical equipment to any part of the airbag circuit.*

When storing an airbag unit
a) *Store the unit in a cupboard with the airbag upward.*
b) *Do not expose the airbag to temperatures above 80°C.*
c) *Do not expose the airbag to flames.*
d) *Do not attempt to dispose of the airbag – consult a Fiat dealer.*
e) *Never refit an airbag which is known to be faulty or damaged.*

De-activation of airbag system

The system must be de-activated before carrying out any work on the airbag components or surrounding area:
a) *Switch on the ignition and check the operation of the airbag warning light on the instrument panel. The light should illuminate when the ignition is switched on, then extinguish.*
b) *Switch off the ignition.*
c) *Remove the ignition key.*
d) *Switch off all electrical equipment.*
e) *Disconnect the battery negative terminal as described in Chapter 5A.*
f) *Insulate the battery negative terminal and the end of the battery negative lead to prevent any possibility of contact.*
g) *Wait for at least ten minutes before carrying out any further work.*

Activation of airbag system

To activate the system on completion of any work, proceed as follows:
a) *Ensure that there are no occupants in the vehicle, and that there are no loose objects around the vicinity of the steering wheel. Close the vehicle doors and windows.*
b) *Ensure that the ignition is switched off then reconnect the battery negative terminal.*
c) *Open the driver's door and switch on the ignition, without reaching in front of the steering wheel. Check that the airbag warning light illuminates briefly then extinguishes.*
d) *Switch off the ignition.*
e) *If the airbag warning light does not operate as described in paragraph c), consult a Fiat dealer before driving the vehicle.*

20 Airbag system components – removal and refitting

⚠️ **Warning: Refer to the precautions given in Section 19 before attempting to carry out work on any of the airbag components. Any suspected faults with the airbag system should be referred to a Fiat dealer – under no circumstances attempt to carry out any work other than removal and refitting of the front airbag unit(s) and/or the airbag clockspring, as described in the following paragraphs.**

Electronic control unit

1 The airbag ECU is located under the centre of the facia and is accessible after removal of the footwell kick panels adjacent to the heater air distribution housing.

20.3a Insert a screwdriver . . .

20.3c . . . and push the wire clips (arrowed) outwards to release the airbag

20.6b . . . and disconnect the wiring plug

Driver's airbag unit

2 De-activate the airbag system as described in Section 19.

Panda models

3 Release the 3 airbag retaining clips (**see illustrations**).

500 models

4 With the front wheels in the straight-ahead position, rotate the steering wheel 90° left or right to access the hole in the wheel boss.

5 Insert a flat-bladed screwdriver and release the airbag retaining clip, by twisting it one way or the other. With the first clip released, turn the steering wheel as necessary to release the other 2 clips, noting which way the wheel is rotated, so that it can be returned to the straight-ahead position (**see illustration**).

All models

6 Carefully lift the airbag unit from the steering

20.3b . . . through the 3 holes in the steering wheel boss (arrowed) . . .

20.5 On 500 models, insert a screwdriver and twist it to force the wire clips outwards

20.6c On 500 models, depress the clip each side . . .

wheel and disconnect the wiring connector(s) (**see illustrations**).

7 If the airbag unit is to be stored for any length of time, refer to the storage precautions given in Section 19.

8 Refitting is a reversal of removal, bearing in mind the following points:
 a) Do not strike the airbag unit, or expose it to impacts during refitting.
 b) On completion of refitting, activate the airbag system as described in Section 19.

Airbag clockspring

9 The airbag clockspring is integral with the steering column combination switch assembly. Remove the switch assembly as described in Section 13.

10 Refitting is a reversal of removal, bearing in mind the following points:
 a) Ensure that the centre position indicator window on the outer moving portion of the clockspring is centred over the red indicator tab on the fixed portion.
 b) Ensure that the roadwheels are in the straight-ahead position before refitting the clockspring and steering wheel.
 c) Refit the steering wheel as described in Chapter 10, and refit the airbag unit as described previously in this Section.

Passenger's airbag unit

11 De-activate the airbag system as described in Section 19.

Panda models

12 The passenger's airbag is fitted to the upper part of the facia, above the glovebox.

13 Remove the glovebox as described in Chapter 11, Section 27.

20.6a On Panda models, prise up the locking clip . . .

20.6d . . . and disconnect the wiring plugs

20.14a Undo the airbag mounting bolts (arrowed) . . .

20.14b . . . manoeuvre the airbag from the facia . . .

20.14c . . . and disconnect the wiring plug

14 Working in the glovebox aperture, undo the bolts securing the airbag assembly to the facia crossmember brackets (see illustrations). Carefully withdraw the airbag from the facia and disconnect the wiring connector.
15 If the airbag unit is to be stored for any length of time, refer to the storage precautions given in Section 19.
16 Refitting is a reversal of removal, bearing in mind the following points:
  a) Do not strike the airbag unit, or expose it to impacts during refitting.
  b) On completion of refitting, activate the airbag system as described in Section 19.

500 models

17 Remove the complete facia as described in Chapter 11.
18 Disconnect the airbag wiring plugs, and release it from the retainers (see illustrations). Manoeuvre the airbag from place.

19 Refitting is a reversal of removal, bearing in mind the following points:
  a) Do not strike the airbag unit, or expose it to impacts during refitting.
  b) On completion of refitting, activate the airbag system as described in Section 19.

Knee airbag

20 Remove the lower steering column shroud as described in Section 27 of Chapter 11.
21 Undo the bolts beneath the driver's side of the facia, and carefully slide the airbag rearwards. Disconnect the wiring plug as the airbag is removed (see illustrations).
22 Refitting is a reversal of removal, bearing in mind the following points:
  a) Do not strike the airbag unit, or expose it to impacts during refitting.
  b) On completion of refitting, activate the airbag system as described in Section 19.

Side and side window airbags

23 The side, and side window, airbags are located respectively within the front seat backs and roof headlining, and no attempt should be made to remove them. Any suspected problems with the side airbag system should be referred to a Fiat dealer.

Crash sensors

24 On Panda models, remove the B-pillar trim panel as described in Chapter 11.
25 On 500 models, remove the rear side panel as described in Chapter 11.
26 Undo the retaining bolt/nut and remove the sensor from the pillar (see illustration). Disconnect the wiring plug as the sensor is withdrawn.
27 Refitting is a reversal of removal. Activate the airbag system as described in Section 19.

20.18a Passenger's airbag mounting bolt (arrowed)

20.18b Squeeze together the sides (arrowed) to release the clips and disconnect the wiring plugs from each end of the airbag

20.21a Undo the knee airbag retaining bolts (arrowed) . . .

20.21b . . . pull the airbag rearwards . . .

20.21c . . . then squeeze the sides together to disconnect the wiring plug

20.26 Side crash sensor retaining nut (arrowed)

Fiat 500 wiring diagrams

Diagram 1

At the time of writing, certain wiring diagram technical information was unavailable. As a result these diagrams are intended as a representative set covering most major electrical systems typically encountered on this model range.

 WARNING: This vehicle is fitted with a supplemental restraint system (SRS) consisting of a combination of driver (and passenger) airbag(s), side impact protection airbags and seatbelt pre-tensioners. The use of electrical test equipment on any SRS wiring systems may cause the seatbelt pre-tensioners to abruptly retract and airbags to explosively deploy, resulting in potentially severe personal injury. Extreme care should be taken to correctly identify any circuits to be tested to avoid choosing any of the SRS wiring in error.
For further information see airbag system precautions in body electrical systems chapter.
Note: The SRS wiring harness can normally be identified by yellow and/or orange harness or harness connectors.

Key to symbols

Solenoid actuator	
Earth point and location	(E7)
Wire colour (red with black tracer)	R/N
Dashed outline denotes part of a larger item, containing in this case an electronic or solid state device.	B 22 30 (k)
B/22 refers to connector B pin 22.	
30 refers to standard DIN terminal designation, in this instance for permanent battery supply.	

Bulb	⊗
Switch	
Fuse/Fusible link	**F26**
Resistor	
Variable resistor	
Variable resistor	
Heating element	

Wire splice, soldered joint, or unspecified connector	
Connecting wires	
Diode	
Light-emitting diode	
Item number	*12*
Motor/pump	(M)

Engine compartment fusebox ④

F08	30A	Heater blower motor
F09	15A	Trailer
F10	15A	Horn
F11	10A	Engine control system
F14	15A	Main beam
F15	20A	Sunroof motor
F16	7.5A	Engine control unit, automatic gearbox
F17	10A	Engine control unit
F18	7.5A	Engine control unit
F19	7.5A	Air conditioning compressor
F20	30A	Heated rear window and mirrors
F21	15A	Fuel pump
F22	15A	Ignition coil, injectors (1.2 8v)
F22	20A	Engine control unit (1.3 multijet)
F23	20A	Braking system
F24	7.5A	Braking system, power steering
F30	15A	Foglights
F84	10A	Automatic gearbox
F85	15A	Front accessory socket/cigar lighter
F87	7.5A	Reversing lights

R2	Main beam relay
R3	Horn relay
R5	Air conditioning compressor relay
R6	Single /low speed cooling fan relay
R7	High speed cooling fan relay
R8	Air con/heater blower relay relay
R9	Engine management main relay
R10	Spare
R14	Foglight relay
R17	Fuel pump relay
R19	Heated rear window & mirror relay
R20	Automatic gearbox inhibitor relay
R30	Automatic gearbox relay
R31	Accessory socket/cigar lighter relay

Passenger compartment fusebox ⑤

F12	7.5A	RH dip beam
F13	7.5A	LH dip beam, headlight levelling
F31	5A	Engine compartment shunt control unit
F32	7.5A	Interior lights, luggage compartment and door courtesy lights
F36	10A	Diagnostic connector, audio system and climate control
F37	5A	Stop lights, instrument cluster
F38	20A	Central locking
F43	15A	Front and rear wash/wipe
F47	20A	Driver's electric window
F48	20A	Passenger's electric window
F49	5A	Parking sensors, switch illumination and electric mirrors
F50	7.5A	Air bag
F51	7.5A	Audio system, climate control, stop lights and clutch
F53	5A	Instrument cluster

Earth locations

H47371

Colour codes

B	White	C	Orange
L	Blue	R	Red
H	Grey	S	Pink
G	Yellow	V	Green
M	Brown	Z	Purple
N	Black	A	Lt. Blue
W	Dk. Brown		

Key to items

1 Battery
2 Starter motor
3 Alternator
4 Engine compartment fusebox
 R3 = horn relay
 R6 = single/low speed cooling fan relay
 R7 = high speed cooling fan relay
 R31 = accessory socket/cigar lighter relay
5 Passenger compartment fusebox
6 Ignition switch

7 Engine management control unit
8 Steering wheel clock spring
 (horn switch)
9 Horn
10 Engine cooling fan
11 Coolant temperature sensor
12 Cooling fan resistor
13 Refrigerant pressure sensor
14 Cigar lighter/accessory socket
15 Reversing light switch

16 LH rear light unit
 a = reversing light
18 Instrument cluster

Diagram 2

H47372

Starting & charging

Horn

Engine cooling fan - models without air conditioning

Engine cooling fan - models with air conditioning

Cigar lighter/accessory socket

Reversing light

Colour codes

B	White	**C**	Orange
L	Blue	**R**	Red
H	Grey	**S**	Pink
G	Yellow	**V**	Green
M	Brown	**Z**	Purple
N	Black	**A**	Lt. Blue
W	Dk. Brown		

Key to items

1 Battery
4 Engine compartment fusebox
    R14 = foglight relay
5 Passenger compartment fusebox
6 Ignition switch
16 LH rear light unit
    b = stop light
    c = tail light
17 RH rear light unit
    b = stop light
    c = tail light
    d = fog light

18 Instrument cluster
20 Stop light switch
21 High level stop light
22 Steering column switch unit
    a = main lighting switch
    b = dip/main/flash switch
23 LH main beam unit
    a = daytime running light
    b = side light
24 RH main beam unit
    (as above)
25 Number plate light/tailgate switch

36 Dashboard switch
    a = foglights
37 LH front foglight
38 RH front foglight

Diagram 3

H47373

Stop lights

Front foglights

Side, tail, number plate & daytime running lights

Rear foglights

Colour codes

B	White	C	Orange
L	Blue	R	Red
H	Grey	S	Pink
G	Yellow	V	Green
M	Brown	Z	Purple
N	Black	A	Lt. Blue
W	Dk. Brown		

Key to items

1 Battery
4 Engine compartment fusebox
  R2 = main beam relay
5 Passenger compartment fusebox
6 Ignition switch
16 LH rear light unit
  d = direction indicator
17 RH rear light unit
  d = direction indicator
18 Instrument cluster
22 Steering column switch unit
  a = main lighting
  b = dip/main/flash
  c = direction indicator
23 LH main beam unit
  c = main beam
24 RH main beam unit
  c = main beam
36 Dashboard switch
  b = hazard warning lights
40 LH dip beam unit
  a = headlight levelling
  b = dip beam
  c = direction indicator
41 RH dip beam unit
  (as above)
42 LH indicator side repeater
43 RH indicator side repeater

Diagram 4

H47374

Headlights & headlight levelling

Direction indicators & hazard warning lights

Colour codes

B	White	**C**	Orange
L	Blue	**R**	Red
H	Grey	**S**	Pink
G	Yellow	**V**	Green
M	Brown	**Z**	Purple
N	Black	**A**	Lt. Blue
W	Dk. Brown		

Key to items

1 Battery
4 Engine compartment fusebox
5 Passenger compartment fusebox
6 Ignition switch
18 Instrument cluster
22 Steering column switch unit
   d = trip computer
   e = front wiper
   f = front/rear washer
   g = rear wiper

45 Front interior light
46 LH front door lock
47 RH front door lock
48 Tailgate lock
49 Luggage compartment light
50 Passenger's vanity mirror light
51 Fuel gauge sender/fuel pump
52 Handbrake switch
53 LH pad wear sensor
54 Low brake fluid switch

55 Sunroof motor
56 Sunroof switch
   a = open
   b = close
57 Front wiper motor
58 Rear wiper motor
59 Front/rear washer pump

Diagram 5

H47375

Interior lighting

Wash/wipe

Instrument cluster

Sunroof

Colour codes

B	White	C	Orange
L	Blue	R	Red
H	Grey	S	Pink
G	Yellow	V	Green
M	Brown	Z	Purple
N	Black	A	Lt. Blue
W	Dk. Brown		

Key to items

1 Battery
4 Engine compartment fusebox
  R8 = air conditioning and heater blower relay
  R19 = heater rear window/ mirror relay
5 Passenger compartment fusebox
6 Ignition switch
62 Heated rear window switch
63 Heated rear window
64 LH mirror assembly
  a = heating element
  b = horizontal sdjustment
  c = vertical adjustment
65 RH mirror assembly
  (as above)
66 Heated mirror fuse
67 Electric mirror switch
68 Air conditioning control switch
69 Heater blower resistor pack
70 Evaporator temperature sensor
71 Heater blower motor
72 Heater control illumination

Diagram 6

H47376

Heated rear window and mirrors

Electric mirrors

Air conditioning

Colour codes

B	White	**C**	Orange
L	Blue	**R**	Red
H	Grey	**S**	Pink
G	Yellow	**V**	Green
M	Brown	**Z**	Purple
N	Black	**A**	Lt. Blue
W	Dk. Brown		

Key to items

1 Battery
4 Engine compartment fusebox
5 Passenger compartment fusebox
6 Ignition switch
18 Instrument cluster
25 Number plate light/tailgate switch
36 Dashboard switch
  c = power steering city

46 LH front door lock
47 RH front door lock
48 Tailgate lock
75 LH front electric window switch
76 RH front electric window switch
77 LH front electric window motor
78 RH front electric window motor
79 Central locking/alarm receiver aerial
80 Power steering control unit

Diagram 7

H47362

Electric windows

Power steering

Central locking

Fiat Panda wiring diagrams

Diagram 8

At the time of writing, certain wiring diagram technical information was unavailable. As a result these diagrams are intended as a representative set covering most major electrical systems typically encountered on this model range.

 WARNING: This vehicle is fitted with a supplemental restraint system (SRS) consisting of a combination of driver (and passenger) airbag(s), side impact protection airbags and seatbelt pre-tensioners. The use of electrical test equipment on any SRS wiring systems may cause the seatbelt pre-tensioners to abruptly retract and airbags to explosively deploy, resulting in potentially severe personal injury. Extreme care should be taken to correctly identify any circuits to be tested to avoid choosing any of the SRS wiring in error.
For further information see airbag system precautions in body electrical systems chapter.
Note: The SRS wiring harness can normally be identified by yellow and/or orange harness or harness connectors.

Key to symbols

Solenoid actuator	Bulb	Wire splice, soldered joint, or unspecified connector
Earth point and location	Switch	Connecting wires
Wire colour (red with black tracer)	Fuse/Fusible link **F26**	Diode
Dashed outline denotes part of a larger item, containing in this case an electronic or solid state device.	Resistor	Light-emitting diode
B/22 refers to connector B pin 22 .	Variable resistor	Item number *12*
30 refers to standard DIN terminal designation, in this instance for permanent battery supply.	Variable resistor	Motor/pump
	Heating element	

Engine compartment fusebox ④

F08	30A	Heater blower motor
F09	20A	Headlight washer
F10	15A	Horn
F11	15A	Engine control system
F14	15A	Main beam
F15	15A	Trailer
F16	7.5A	Engine control unit, auto. gearbox
F17	10A	Engine control unit
F18	15A	Engine control unit
F19	7.5A	Air conditioning compressor
F20	-	Spare
F21	15A	Fuel pump
F22	20A	Engine management
F23	20A	Braking system
F24	10A	Power steering
F30	15A	Foglights
F84	15A	Automatic gearbox

F85	20A	Front accessory socket/cigar lighter
F87	7.5A	ABS & stop lights
R2		Main beam relay
R3		Horn relay
R5		Air conditioning compressor relay
R6		Single /low speed cooling fan relay
R7		High speed cooling fan relay
R8		Air con/heater blower relay
R9		Engine management main relay
R10		Fuel pump relay (multijet)
R14		Foglight relay
R17		Headlight washer relay
R19		Fuel pump relay
R20		Automatic gearbox inhibitor relay
R30		Automatic gearbox relay
R31		Accessory socket/cigar lighter relay

Passenger compartment fusebox ⑤

F31	5A	Reversing light
F35	7.5A	Audio
F37	10A	Stop lights
F41	7.5A	Heated mirrors
F45	15A	Heated seats
F46	15A	Sunroof
F49	7.5A	Climate control, tyre pressure monitor, water in fuel sensor
F50	7.5A	Air bag
F51	5A	Body control unit, instrument cluster
F54	15A	Subwoofer
FA	-	Spare
FB	-	Spare

Body control unit ⑦

F12	7.5A	RH dip deam
F13	7.5A	LH dip beam, headlight levelling
F38	20A	Central locking
F39	10A	Diagnostic connector, audio, climate control, tyre pressure monitor, body control unit
F40	30A	Heated rear window
F43	30A	Front and rear wash/wipe
F47	20A	Driver's electric window
F48	20A	Passenger's electric window
F52	15A	Rear wiper
F53	15A	Front/rear washer

Earth locations

H47378

Colour codes

B	White	C	Orange
L	Blue	R	Red
H	Grey	S	Pink
G	Yellow	V	Green
M	Brown	Z	Purple
N	Black	A	Lt. Blue
W	Dk. Brown		

Key to items

1 Battery
2 Starter motor
3 Alternator
4 Engine compartment fusebox
  R3 = horn relay
  R6 = single/low speed cooling fan relay
  R7 = high speed cooling fan relay
  R8 = air con/heater blower relay
5 Passenger compartment fusebox

6 Ignition switch
7 Body control unit
8 Engine management control unit
9 Short circuit coupling
10 Steering wheel clock spring (horn switch)
11 Horn
12 Engine cooling fan
13 Coolant temperature sensor

14 Cooling fan resistor
15 Refrigerant pressure sensor
16 Cigar lighter/accessory socket
17 Reversing light switch
18 LH rear light unit
  a = reversing light

Diagram 9

H47379

Starting & charging

Horn

Engine cooling fan - models without air conditioning

Engine cooling fan - models with air conditioning

Cigar lighter/accessory socket

Reversing light

Colour codes

B	White	**C**	Orange
L	Blue	**R**	Red
H	Grey	**S**	Pink
G	Yellow	**V**	Green
M	Brown	**Z**	Purple
N	Black	**A**	Lt. Blue
W	Dk. Brown		

Key to items

1 Battery
4 Engine compartment fusebox
   R14 = foglight relay
5 Passenger compartment fusebox
6 Ignition switch
7 Body control unit
9 Short circuit coupling

18 LH rear light unit
   b = stop light
   c = tail light
19 RH rear light unit
   b = stop light
   c = tail light
   d = fog light

20 Stop light switch
21 High level stop light
22 Steering column switch unit
   a = main lighting switch
   b = dip/main beam switch
23 LH headlight unit
   a = side light

24 RH headlight unit
   (as above)
25 Number plate light
26 Dashboard switch
   a = foglights
27 LH front foglight
28 RH front foglight

Diagram 10

H47380

Stop lights

Front foglights

Side, tail, number plate & daytime running lights

Rear foglights

Colour codes

B	White	C	Orange
L	Blue	R	Red
H	Grey	S	Pink
G	Yellow	V	Green
M	Brown	Z	Purple
N	Black	A	Lt. Blue
W	Dk. Brown		

Key to items

1 Battery
4 Engine compartment fusebox
  R2 = main beam relay
5 Passenger compartment fusebox
6 Ignition switch
7 Body control unit
18 LH rear light unit
  d = direction indicator
19 RH rear light unit
  d = direction indicator

22 Steering column switch unit
  a = main lighting
  b = dip/main/flash
  c = direction indicator
  d = headlight flasher
23 LH headlight unit
  b = headlight levelling
  c = dip/main beam
  d = direction indicator

24 RH headlight unit
  (as above)
26 Dashboard switch
  b = hazard warning lights
30 LH indicator side repeater
31 RH indicator side repeater
32 Instrument cluster

Diagram 11

H47381

Headlights & headlight levelling

Direction indicators & hazard warning lights

Colour codes

B	White	C	Orange
L	Blue	R	Red
H	Grey	S	Pink
G	Yellow	V	Green
M	Brown	Z	Purple
N	Black	A	Lt. Blue
W	Dk. Brown		

Key to items

1 Battery
4 Engine compartment fusebox
5 Passenger compartment fusebox
6 Ignition switch
7 Body control unit
9 Short circuit coupling
22 Steering column switch unit
  d = front wash/wiper
  e = rear wiper
  f = rear washer

e = trip computer
35 Front interior light
36 LH front door lock
37 RH front door lock
38 LH rear door lock
39 RH rear door lock
40 Luggage compartment light
41 Tailgate handle switch
42 Fuel gauge sender/fuel pump
43 Handbrake switch

44 Low brake fluid switch
45 Instrument cluster
46 Sunroof assembly
47 Front wiper motor
48 Rear wiper motor
49 Front/rear washer pump
53 LH mirror assembly
  d = outside air temp. sensor

Diagram 12

H47382

Interior lighting

Wash/wipe

Instrument cluster

Sunroof

Colour codes

B	White	C	Orange
L	Blue	R	Red
H	Grey	S	Pink
G	Yellow	V	Green
M	Brown	Z	Purple
N	Black	A	Lt. Blue
W	Dk. Brown		

Key to items

1 Battery
4 Engine compartment fusebox
 R8 = air con/heater blower relay
5 Passenger compartment fusebox
6 Ignition switch
7 Body control unit
8 Engine management control unit
9 Short circuit coupling
26 Dashboard switch
 c = heated rear window switch
52 Heated rear window
53 LH mirror assembly
 a = heating element
 b = horizontal adjustment
 c = vertical adjustment
54 RH mirror assembly
 (as above)
55 Electric mirror switch
56 Air conditioning control switch
57 Heater blower resistor pack
58 Evaporator temperature sensor
59 Heater blower motor
60 Heater control illumination

Diagram 13

H47383

Heated rear window and mirrors

Electric mirrors

Air conditioning

Colour codes

B	White	C	Orange
L	Blue	R	Red
H	Grey	S	Pink
G	Yellow	V	Green
M	Brown	Z	Purple
N	Black	A	Lt. Blue
W	Dk. Brown		

Key to items

1 Battery
4 Engine compartment fusebox
5 Passenger compartment fusebox
6 Ignition switch
7 Body control unit
9 Short circuit coupling
26 Dashboard switch
   c = power steering city

65 Driver's door lock
66 Passenger's door lock
67 LH rear door lock
68 RH rear door lock
69 Tailgate lock motor
70 Driver's electric window switch
71 Passenger's electric window switch
72 Driver's electric window motor

73 Passenger's electric window motor
74 Power steering control unit
75 Vehicle speed sensor

Diagram 14

H47384

Electric windows

Power steering

Central locking

Dimensions and weights

Note: *All figures are approximate, and may vary according to model. Refer to manufacturer's data for exact figures.*

Dimensions

Overall length:
Panda models	3538 mm
500 models	3546 mm

Overall width (excluding mirrors):
Panda models	1578 mm
500 models	1627 mm

Overall height:

Panda models:
Without roof bars	1540 mm
With roof bars	1578 mm
500 models	1488 mm

Wheelbase:
Panda models	2299 mm
500 models	2300 mm

Weights

Kerb weight (depending on model)	840 kg to 980 kg
Maximum roof rack load	50 kg

Fuel economy

Although depreciation is still the biggest part of the cost of motoring for most car owners, the cost of fuel is more immediately noticeable. These pages give some tips on how to get the best fuel economy.

Working it out

Manufacturer's figures

Car manufacturers are required by law to provide fuel consumption information on all new vehicles sold. These 'official' figures are obtained by simulating various driving conditions on a rolling road or a test track. Real life conditions are different, so the fuel consumption actually achieved may not bear much resemblance to the quoted figures.

How to calculate it

Many cars now have trip computers which will

display fuel consumption, both instantaneous and average. Refer to the owner's handbook for details of how to use these.

To calculate consumption yourself (and maybe to check that the trip computer is accurate), proceed as follows.

1. Fill up with fuel and note the mileage, or zero the trip recorder.
2. Drive as usual until you need to fill up again.
3. Note the amount of fuel required to refill the tank, and the mileage covered since the previous fill-up.
4. Divide the mileage by the amount of fuel used to obtain the consumption figure.

For example:

Mileage at first fill-up (a) = 27,903
Mileage at second fill-up (b) = 28,346
Mileage covered (b - a) = 443
Fuel required at second fill-up = 48.6 litres

The half-completed changeover to metric units in the UK means that we buy our fuel

in litres, measure distances in miles and talk about fuel consumption in miles per gallon. There are two ways round this: the first is to convert the litres to gallons before doing the calculation (by dividing by 4.546, or see Table 1). So in the example:

48.6 litres ÷ 4.546 = 10.69 gallons
443 miles ÷ 10.69 gallons = 41.4 mpg

The second way is to calculate the consumption in miles per litre, then multiply that figure by 4.546 (or see Table 2).

So in the example, fuel consumption is:

443 miles ÷ 48.6 litres = 9.1 mpl
9.1 mpl x 4.546 = 41.4 mpg

The rest of Europe expresses fuel consumption in litres of fuel required to travel 100 km (l/100 km). For interest, the conversions are given in Table 3. In practice it doesn't matter what units you use, provided you know what your normal consumption is and can spot if it's getting better or worse.

Table 1: conversion of litres to Imperial gallons

litres	1	2	3	4	5	10	20	30	40	50	60	70
gallons	0.22	0.44	0.66	0.88	1.10	2.24	4.49	6.73	8.98	11.22	13.47	15.71

Table 2: conversion of miles per litre to miles per gallon

miles per litre	5	6	7	8	9	10	11	12	13	14
miles per gallon	23	27	32	36	41	46	50	55	59	64

Table 3: conversion of litres per 100 km to miles per gallon

litres per 100 km	4	4.5	5	5.5	6	6.5	7	8	9	10
miles per gallon	71	63	56	51	47	43	40	35	31	28

Maintenance

A well-maintained car uses less fuel and creates less pollution. In particular:

Filters

Change air and fuel filters at the specified intervals.

Oil

Use a good quality oil of the lowest viscosity specified by the vehicle manufacturer (see *Lubricants and fluids*). Check the level often and be careful not to overfill.

Spark plugs

When applicable, renew at the specified intervals.

Tyres

Check tyre pressures regularly. Under-inflated tyres have an increased rolling resistance. It is generally safe to use the higher pressures specified for full load conditions even when not fully laden, but keep an eye on the centre band of tread for signs of wear due to over-inflation.

When buying new tyres, consider the 'fuel saving' models which most manufacturers include in their ranges.

Driving style

Acceleration

Acceleration uses more fuel than driving at a steady speed. The best technique with modern cars is to accelerate reasonably briskly to the desired speed, changing up through the gears as soon as possible without making the engine labour.

Air conditioning

Air conditioning absorbs quite a bit of energy from the engine – typically 3 kW (4 hp) or so. The effect on fuel consumption is at its worst in slow traffic. Switch it off when not required.

Anticipation

Drive smoothly and try to read the traffic flow so as to avoid unnecessary acceleration and braking.

Automatic transmission

When accelerating in an automatic, avoid depressing the throttle so far as to make the transmission hold onto lower gears at higher speeds. Don't use the 'Sport' setting, if applicable.

When stationary with the engine running, select 'N' or 'P'. When moving, keep your left foot away from the brake.

Braking

Braking converts the car's energy of motion into heat – essentially, it is wasted. Obviously some braking is always going to be necessary, but with good anticipation it is surprising how much can be avoided, especially on routes that you know well.

Carshare

Consider sharing lifts to work or to the shops. Even once a week will make a difference.

Electrical loads

Electricity is 'fuel' too; the alternator which charges the battery does so by converting some of the engine's energy of motion into electrical energy. The more electrical accessories are in use, the greater the load on the alternator. Switch off big consumers like the heated rear window when not required.

Freewheeling

Freewheeling (coasting) in neutral with the engine switched off is dangerous. The effort required to operate power-assisted brakes and steering increases when the engine is not running, with a potential lack of control in emergency situations.

In any case, modern fuel injection systems automatically cut off the engine's fuel supply on the overrun (moving and in gear, but with the accelerator pedal released).

Gadgets

Bolt-on devices claiming to save fuel have been around for nearly as long as the motor car itself. Those which worked were rapidly adopted as standard equipment by the vehicle manufacturers. Others worked only in certain situations, or saved fuel only at the expense of unacceptable effects on performance, driveability or the life of engine components.

The most effective fuel saving gadget is the driver's right foot.

Journey planning

Combine (eg) a trip to the supermarket with a visit to the recycling centre and the DIY store, rather than making separate journeys.

When possible choose a travelling time outside rush hours.

Load

The more heavily a car is laden, the greater the energy required to accelerate it to a given speed. Remove heavy items which you don't need to carry.

One load which is often overlooked is the contents of the fuel tank. A tankful of fuel (55 litres / 12 gallons) weighs 45 kg (100 lb) or so. Just half filling it may be worthwhile.

Lost?

At the risk of stating the obvious, if you're going somewhere new, have details of the route to hand. There's not much point in achieving record mpg if you also go miles out of your way.

Parking

If possible, carry out any reversing or turning manoeuvres when you arrive at a parking space so that you can drive straight out when you leave. Manoeuvering when the engine is cold uses a lot more fuel.

Driving around looking for free on-street parking may cost more in fuel than buying a car park ticket.

Premium fuel

Most major oil companies (and some supermarkets) have premium grades of fuel which are several pence a litre dearer than the standard grades. Reports vary, but the consensus seems to be that if these fuels improve economy at all, they do not do so by enough to justify their extra cost.

Roof rack

When loading a roof rack, try to produce a wedge shape with the narrow end at the front. Any cover should be securely fastened – if it flaps it's creating turbulence and absorbing energy.

Remove roof racks and boxes when not in use – they increase air resistance and can create a surprising amount of noise.

Short journeys

The engine is at its least efficient, and wear is highest, during the first few miles after a cold start. Consider walking, cycling or using public transport.

Speed

The engine is at its most efficient when running at a steady speed and load at the rpm where it develops maximum torque. (You can find this figure in the car's handbook.) For most cars this corresponds to between 55 and 65 mph in top gear.

Above the optimum cruising speed, fuel consumption starts to rise quite sharply. A car travelling at 80 mph will typically be using 30% more fuel than at 60 mph.

Supermarket fuel

It may be cheap but is it any good? In the UK all supermarket fuel must meet the relevant British Standard. The major oil companies will say that their branded fuels have better additive packages which may stop carbon and other deposits building up. A reasonable compromise might be to use one tank of branded fuel to three or four from the supermarket.

Switch off when stationary

Switch off the engine if you look like being stationary for more than 30 seconds or so. This is good for the environment as well as for your pocket. Be aware though that frequent restarts are hard on the battery and the starter motor.

Windows

Driving with the windows open increases air turbulence around the vehicle. Closing the windows promotes smooth airflow and

reduced resistance. The faster you go, the more significant this is.

And finally . . .

Driving techniques associated with good fuel economy tend to involve moderate acceleration and low top speeds. Be considerate to the needs of other road users who may need to make brisker progress; even if you do not agree with them this is not an excuse to be obstructive.

Safety must always take precedence over economy, whether it is a question of accelerating hard to complete an overtaking manoeuvre, killing your speed when confronted with a potential hazard or switching the lights on when it starts to get dark.

Conversion factors

Length (distance)
Inches (in)	x 25.4	=	Millimetres (mm)	x 0.0394	= Inches (in)
Feet (ft)	x 0.305	=	Metres (m)	x 3.281	= Feet (ft)
Miles	x 1.609	=	Kilometres (km)	x 0.621	= Miles

Volume (capacity)
Cubic inches (cu in; in³)	x 16.387	=	Cubic centimetres (cc; cm³)	x 0.061	= Cubic inches (cu in; in³)
Imperial pints (Imp pt)	x 0.568	=	Litres (l)	x 1.76	= Imperial pints (Imp pt)
Imperial quarts (Imp qt)	x 1.137	=	Litres (l)	x 0.88	= Imperial quarts (Imp qt)
Imperial quarts (Imp qt)	x 1.201	=	US quarts (US qt)	x 0.833	= Imperial quarts (Imp qt)
US quarts (US qt)	x 0.946	=	Litres (l)	x 1.057	= US quarts (US qt)
Imperial gallons (Imp gal)	x 4.546	=	Litres (l)	x 0.22	= Imperial gallons (Imp gal)
Imperial gallons (Imp gal)	x 1.201	=	US gallons (US gal)	x 0.833	= Imperial gallons (Imp gal)
US gallons (US gal)	x 3.785	=	Litres (l)	x 0.264	= US gallons (US gal)

Mass (weight)
Ounces (oz)	x 28.35	=	Grams (g)	x 0.035	= Ounces (oz)
Pounds (lb)	x 0.454	=	Kilograms (kg)	x 2.205	= Pounds (lb)

Force
Ounces-force (ozf; oz)	x 0.278	=	Newtons (N)	x 3.6	= Ounces-force (ozf; oz)
Pounds-force (lbf; lb)	x 4.448	=	Newtons (N)	x 0.225	= Pounds-force (lbf; lb)
Newtons (N)	x 0.1	=	Kilograms-force (kgf; kg)	x 9.81	= Newtons (N)

Pressure
Pounds-force per square inch (psi; lbf/in²; lb/in²)	x 0.070	=	Kilograms-force per square centimetre (kgf/cm²; kg/cm²)	x 14.223	= Pounds-force per square inch (psi; lbf/in²; lb/in²)
Pounds-force per square inch (psi; lbf/in²; lb/in²)	x 0.068	=	Atmospheres (atm)	x 14.696	= Pounds-force per square inch (psi; lbf/in²; lb/in²)
Pounds-force per square inch (psi; lbf/in²; lb/in²)	x 0.069	=	Bars	x 14.5	= Pounds-force per square inch (psi; lbf/in²; lb/in²)
Pounds-force per square inch (psi; lbf/in²; lb/in²)	x 6.895	=	Kilopascals (kPa)	x 0.145	= Pounds-force per square inch (psi; lbf/in²; lb/in²)
Kilopascals (kPa)	x 0.01	=	Kilograms-force per square centimetre (kgf/cm²; kg/cm²)	x 98.1	= Kilopascals (kPa)
Millibar (mbar)	x 100	=	Pascals (Pa)	x 0.01	= Millibar (mbar)
Millibar (mbar)	x 0.0145	=	Pounds-force per square inch (psi; lbf/in²; lb/in²)	x 68.947	= Millibar (mbar)
Millibar (mbar)	x 0.75	=	Millimetres of mercury (mmHg)	x 1.333	= Millibar (mbar)
Millibar (mbar)	x 0.401	=	Inches of water (inH₂O)	x 2.491	= Millibar (mbar)
Millimetres of mercury (mmHg)	x 0.535	=	Inches of water (inH₂O)	x 1.868	= Millimetres of mercury (mmHg)
Inches of water (inH₂O)	x 0.036	=	Pounds-force per square inch (psi; lbf/in²; lb/in²)	x 27.68	= Inches of water (inH₂O)

Torque (moment of force)
Pounds-force inches (lbf in; lb in)	x 1.152	=	Kilograms-force centimetre (kgf cm; kg cm)	x 0.868	= Pounds-force inches (lbf in; lb in)
Pounds-force inches (lbf in; lb in)	x 0.113	=	Newton metres (Nm)	x 8.85	= Pounds-force inches (lbf in; lb in)
Pounds-force inches (lbf in; lb in)	x 0.083	=	Pounds-force feet (lbf ft; lb ft)	x 12	= Pounds-force inches (lbf in; lb in)
Pounds-force feet (lbf ft; lb ft)	x 0.138	=	Kilograms-force metres (kgf m; kg m)	x 7.233	= Pounds-force feet (lbf ft; lb ft)
Pounds-force feet (lbf ft; lb ft)	x 1.356	=	Newton metres (Nm)	x 0.738	= Pounds-force feet (lbf ft; lb ft)
Newton metres (Nm)	x 0.102	=	Kilograms-force metres (kgf m; kg m)	x 9.804	= Newton metres (Nm)

Power
Horsepower (hp)	x 745.7	=	Watts (W)	x 0.0013	= Horsepower (hp)

Velocity (speed)
Miles per hour (miles/hr; mph)	x 1.609	=	Kilometres per hour (km/hr; kph)	x 0.621	= Miles per hour (miles/hr; mph)

Fuel consumption*
Miles per gallon, Imperial (mpg)	x 0.354	=	Kilometres per litre (km/l)	x 2.825	= Miles per gallon, Imperial (mpg)
Miles per gallon, US (mpg)	x 0.425	=	Kilometres per litre (km/l)	x 2.352	= Miles per gallon, US (mpg)

Temperature

Degrees Fahrenheit = (°C x 1.8) + 32   Degrees Celsius (Degrees Centigrade; °C) = (°F - 32) x 0.56

It is common practice to convert from miles per gallon (mpg) to litres/100 kilometres (l/100km), where mpg x l/100 km = 282

Spare parts are available from many sources, including maker's appointed garages, accessory shops, and motor factors. To be sure of obtaining the correct parts, it will sometimes be necessary to quote the vehicle identification number. If possible, it can also be useful to take the old parts along for positive identification. Items such as starter motors and alternators may be available under a service exchange scheme – any parts returned should be clean.

Our advice regarding spare parts is as follows.

Officially appointed garages

This is the best source of parts which are peculiar to your car, and which are not otherwise generally available (eg, badges, interior trim, certain body panels, etc). It is also the only place at which you should buy parts if the car is still under warranty.

Accessory shops

These are very good places to buy materials and components needed for the maintenance of your car (oil, air and fuel filters, light bulbs, drivebelts, greases, brake pads, touch-up paint, etc). Components of this nature sold by a reputable shop are usually of the same standard as those used by the car manufacturer.

Besides components, these shops also sell tools and general accessories, usually have convenient opening hours, charge lower prices, and can often be found close to home. Some accessory shops have parts counters where components needed for almost any repair job can be purchased or ordered.

Motor factors

Good factors will stock all the more important components which wear out comparatively quickly, and can sometimes supply individual components needed for the overhaul of a larger assembly (eg, brake seals and hydraulic parts, bearing shells, pistons, valves). They may also handle work such as cylinder block reboring, crankshaft regrinding, etc.

Engine reconditioners

These specialise in engine overhaul and can also supply components. It is recommended that the establishment is a member of the Federation of Engine Re-Manufacturers, or a similar society.

Tyre and exhaust specialists

These outlets may be independent, or members of a local or national chain. They frequently offer competitive prices when compared with a main dealer or local garage, but it will pay to obtain several quotes before making a decision. When researching prices, also ask what extras may be added – for instance fitting a new valve, balancing the wheel and tyre disposal all both commonly charged on top of the price of a new tyre.

Other sources

Beware of parts or materials obtained from market stalls, car boot sales, on-line auctions or similar outlets. Such items are not invariably sub-standard, but there is little chance of compensation if they do prove unsatisfactory. In the case of safety-critical components such as brake pads, there is the risk not only of financial loss, but also of an accident causing injury or death.

Second-hand components or assemblies obtained from a car breaker can be a good buy in some circumstances, but this sort of purchase is best made by the experienced DIY mechanic.

Vehicle identification numbers

The VIN is stamped into the right-hand side luggage compartment floor panel (arrowed) . . .

. . . and is repeated on the model plate (arrowed)

Modifications are a continuing and unpublicised process in vehicle manufacture, quite apart from major model changes. Spare parts manuals and lists are compiled upon a numerical basis, the individual vehicle identification numbers being essential to correct identification of the component concerned.

When ordering spare parts, always give as much information as possible. Quote the vehicle type and year, vehicle identification number (VIN), and engine number, as appropriate.

The vehicle identification number (VIN) is stamped into the right-hand side of the luggage compartment floor, and is repeated on the model plate affixed to the left-hand side of the luggage compartment floor (see illustrations). The model plate also gives vehicle loading details, engine type, and various trim and colour codes.

The engine number is stamped on the right-hand end of the cylinder block.

The transmission identification numbers are located on a plate attached to the top of the transmission casing, or cast into the casing itself.

Whenever servicing, repair or overhaul work is carried out on the car or its components, observe the following procedures and instructions. This will assist in carrying out the operation efficiently and to a professional standard of workmanship.

Joint mating faces and gaskets

When separating components at their mating faces, never insert screwdrivers or similar implements into the joint between the faces in order to prise them apart. This can cause severe damage which results in oil leaks, coolant leaks, etc upon reassembly. Separation is usually achieved by tapping along the joint with a soft-faced hammer in order to break the seal. However, note that this method may not be suitable where dowels are used for component location.

Where a gasket is used between the mating faces of two components, a new one must be fitted on reassembly; fit it dry unless otherwise stated in the repair procedure. Make sure that the mating faces are clean and dry, with all traces of old gasket removed. When cleaning a joint face, use a tool which is unlikely to score or damage the face, and remove any burrs or nicks with an oilstone or fine file.

Make sure that tapped holes are cleaned with a pipe cleaner, and keep them free of jointing compound, if this is being used, unless specifically instructed otherwise.

Ensure that all orifices, channels or pipes are clear, and blow through them, preferably using compressed air.

Oil seals

Oil seals can be removed by levering them out with a wide flat-bladed screwdriver or similar implement. Alternatively, a number of self-tapping screws may be screwed into the seal, and these used as a purchase for pliers or some similar device in order to pull the seal free.

Whenever an oil seal is removed from its working location, either individually or as part of an assembly, it should be renewed.

The very fine sealing lip of the seal is easily damaged, and will not seal if the surface it contacts is not completely clean and free from scratches, nicks or grooves. If the original sealing surface of the component cannot be restored, and the manufacturer has not made provision for slight relocation of the seal relative to the sealing surface, the component should be renewed.

Protect the lips of the seal from any surface which may damage them in the course of fitting. Use tape or a conical sleeve where possible. Where indicated, lubricate the seal lips with oil before fitting and, on dual-lipped seals, fill the space between the lips with grease.

Unless otherwise stated, oil seals must be fitted with their sealing lips toward the lubricant to be sealed.

Use a tubular drift or block of wood of the appropriate size to install the seal and, if the seal housing is shouldered, drive the seal down to the shoulder. If the seal housing is unshouldered, the seal should be fitted with its face flush with the housing top face (unless otherwise instructed).

Screw threads and fastenings

Seized nuts, bolts and screws are quite a common occurrence where corrosion has set in, and the use of penetrating oil or releasing fluid will often overcome this problem if the offending item is soaked for a while before attempting to release it. The use of an impact driver may also provide a means of releasing such stubborn fastening devices, when used in conjunction with the appropriate screwdriver bit or socket. If none of these methods works, it may be necessary to resort to the careful application of heat, or the use of a hacksaw or nut splitter device. Before resorting to extreme methods, check that you are not dealing with a left-hand thread!

Studs are usually removed by locking two nuts together on the threaded part, and then using a spanner on the lower nut to unscrew the stud. Studs or bolts which have broken off below the surface of the component in which they are mounted can sometimes be removed using a stud extractor.

Always ensure that a blind tapped hole is completely free from oil, grease, water or other fluid before installing the bolt or stud. Failure to do this could cause the housing to crack due to the hydraulic action of the bolt or stud as it is screwed in.

For some screw fastenings, notably cylinder head bolts or nuts, torque wrench settings are no longer specified for the latter stages of tightening, "angle-tightening" being called up instead. Typically, a fairly low torque wrench setting will be applied to the bolts/nuts in the correct sequence, followed by one or more stages of tightening through specified angles.

When checking or retightening a nut or bolt to a specified torque setting, slacken the nut or bolt by a quarter of a turn, and then retighten to the specified setting. However, this should not be attempted where angular tightening has been used.

Locknuts, locktabs and washers

Any fastening which will rotate against a component or housing during tightening should always have a washer between it and the relevant component or housing.

Spring or split washers should always be renewed when they are used to lock a critical component such as a big-end bearing retaining bolt or nut. Locktabs which are folded over to retain a nut or bolt should always be renewed.

Self-locking nuts can be re-used in non-critical areas, providing resistance can be felt when the locking portion passes over the bolt or stud thread. However, it should be noted that self-locking stiffnuts tend to lose their effectiveness after long periods of use, and should then be renewed as a matter of course.

Split pins must always be replaced with new ones of the correct size for the hole.

When thread-locking compound is found on the threads of a fastener which is to be re-used, it should be cleaned off with a wire brush and solvent, and fresh compound applied on reassembly.

Special tools

Some repair procedures in this manual entail the use of special tools such as a press, two or three-legged pullers, spring compressors, etc. Wherever possible, suitable readily-available alternatives to the manufacturer's special tools are described, and are shown in use. In some instances, where no alternative is possible, it has been necessary to resort to the use of a manufacturer's tool, and this has been done for reasons of safety as well as the efficient completion of the repair operation. Unless you are highly-skilled and have a thorough understanding of the procedures described, never attempt to bypass the use of any special tool when the procedure described specifies its use. Not only is there a very great risk of personal injury, but expensive damage could be caused to the components involved.

Environmental considerations

When disposing of used engine oil, brake fluid, antifreeze, etc, give due consideration to any detrimental environmental effects. Do not, for instance, pour any of the above liquids down drains into the general sewage system, or onto the ground to soak away. Many local council refuse tips provide a facility for waste oil disposal, as do some garages. You can find your nearest disposal point by calling the Environment Agency on 08708 506 506 or by visiting www.oilbankline.org.uk.

Note: It is illegal and anti-social to dump oil down the drain. To find the location of your local oil recycling bank, call 08708 506 506 or visit www.oilbankline.org.uk.

The jack available as a Fiat accessory should **only** be used for changing the roadwheels in an emergency. When carrying out any other kind of work, raise the vehicle using a heavy-duty hydraulic (or 'trolley') jack, and always supplement the jack with axle stands positioned under the vehicle jacking points. If the roadwheels do not have to be removed, consider using wheel ramps – if wished, these can be placed under the wheels once the vehicle has been raised using a hydraulic jack, and the vehicle lowered onto the ramps so that it is resting on its wheels.

Only ever jack the vehicle up on a solid, level surface. If there is even a slight slope, take great care that the vehicle cannot move as the wheels are lifted off the ground. Jacking up on an uneven or gravelled surface is not recommended, as the weight of the vehicle will not be evenly distributed, and the jack may slip as the vehicle is raised.

As far as possible, do not leave the vehicle unattended once it has been raised, particularly if children are playing nearby.

Before jacking up the front of the car, ensure that the handbrake is firmly applied. When jacking up the rear of the car, place wooden chocks in front of the front wheels, and engage first gear.

When using a hydraulic jack or axle stands, always position the jack head or axle stand head under the relevant jacking points. These are situated directly underneath the vehicle jack location marks in the sill **(see illustrations)**.

The jack supplied with the vehicle locates in the holes provided in the sill. Ensure that the jack head is correctly engaged before attempting to raise the vehicle.

Never work under, around, or near a raised vehicle, unless it is adequately supported in at least two places.

When jacking or supporting the vehicle at these points, always use a block of wood between the jack head or axle stand, and the vehicle body. It is also considered good practice to use a large block of wood when supporting under other areas, to spread the load over a wider area, and reduce the risk of damage to the underside of the car (it also helps to prevent the underbody coating from being damaged by the jack or axle stand). **Do not** jack the vehicle under any other part of the sill, engine sump, floor pan, subframe, or directly under any of the steering or suspension components.

Never work under, around, or near a raised vehicle, unless it is adequately supported on stands. Do not rely on a jack alone, as even a hydraulic jack could fail under load. Makeshift methods should not be used to lift and support the car during servicing work.

Two jacking points are provided on each side

H48452

Heavy duty jacking points

Introduction

A selection of good tools is a fundamental requirement for anyone contemplating the maintenance and repair of a motor vehicle. For the owner who does not possess any, their purchase will prove a considerable expense, offsetting some of the savings made by doing-it-yourself. However, provided that the tools purchased meet the relevant national safety standards and are of good quality, they will last for many years and prove an extremely worthwhile investment.

To help the average owner to decide which tools are needed to carry out the various tasks detailed in this manual, we have compiled three lists of tools under the following headings: *Maintenance and minor repair*, *Repair and overhaul*, and *Special*. Newcomers to practical mechanics should start off with the *Maintenance and minor repair* tool kit, and confine themselves to the simpler jobs around the vehicle. Then, as confidence and experience grow, more difficult tasks can be undertaken, with extra tools being purchased as, and when, they are needed. In this way, a *Maintenance and minor repair* tool kit can be built up into a *Repair and overhaul* tool kit over a considerable period of time, without any major cash outlays. The experienced do-it-yourselfer will have a tool kit good enough for most repair and overhaul procedures, and will add tools from the *Special* category when it is felt that the expense is justified by the amount of use to which these tools will be put.

Maintenance and minor repair tool kit

The tools given in this list should be considered as a minimum requirement if routine maintenance, servicing and minor repair operations are to be undertaken. We recommend the purchase of combination spanners (ring one end, open-ended the other); although more expensive than open-ended ones, they do give the advantages of both types of spanner.
- [ ] *Combination spanners:*
  Metric - 8 to 19 mm inclusive
- [ ] *Adjustable spanner - 35 mm jaw (approx.)*
- [ ] *Spark plug spanner (with rubber insert) - petrol models*
- [ ] *Spark plug gap adjustment tool - petrol models*
- [ ] *Set of feeler gauges*
- [ ] *Brake bleed nipple spanner*
- [ ] *Screwdrivers:*
  Flat blade - 100 mm long x 6 mm dia
  Cross blade - 100 mm long x 6 mm dia
  Torx - various sizes (not all vehicles)
- [ ] *Combination pliers*
- [ ] *Hacksaw (junior)*
- [ ] *Tyre pump*
- [ ] *Tyre pressure gauge*
- [ ] *Oil can*
- [ ] *Oil filter removal tool (if applicable)*
- [ ] *Fine emery cloth*
- [ ] *Wire brush (small)*
- [ ] *Funnel (medium size)*
- [ ] *Sump drain plug key (not all vehicles)*

Repair and overhaul tool kit

These tools are virtually essential for anyone undertaking any major repairs to a motor vehicle, and are additional to those given in the *Maintenance and minor repair* list. Included in this list is a comprehensive set of sockets. Although these are expensive, they will be found invaluable as they are so versatile - particularly if various drives are included in the set. We recommend the half-inch square-drive type, as this can be used with most proprietary torque wrenches.

The tools in this list will sometimes need to be supplemented by tools from the *Special* list:
- [ ] *Sockets to cover range in previous list (including Torx sockets)*
- [ ] *Reversible ratchet drive (for use with sockets)*
- [ ] *Extension piece, 250 mm (for use with sockets)*
- [ ] *Universal joint (for use with sockets)*
- [ ] *Flexible handle or sliding T "breaker bar" (for use with sockets)*
- [ ] *Torque wrench (for use with sockets)*
- [ ] *Self-locking grips*
- [ ] *Ball pein hammer*
- [ ] *Soft-faced mallet (plastic or rubber)*
- [ ] *Screwdrivers:*
  Flat blade - long & sturdy, short (chubby), and narrow (electrician's) types
  Cross blade – long & sturdy, and short (chubby) types
- [ ] *Pliers:*
  Long-nosed
  Side cutters (electrician's)
  Circlip (internal and external)
- [ ] *Cold chisel - 25 mm*
- [ ] *Scriber*
- [ ] *Scraper*
- [ ] *Centre-punch*
- [ ] *Pin punch*
- [ ] *Hacksaw*
- [ ] *Brake hose clamp*
- [ ] *Brake/clutch bleeding kit*
- [ ] *Selection of twist drills*
- [ ] *Steel rule/straight-edge*
- [ ] *Allen keys (inc. splined/Torx type)*
- [ ] *Selection of files*
- [ ] *Wire brush*
- [ ] *Axle stands*
- [ ] *Jack (strong trolley or hydraulic type)*
- [ ] *Light with extension lead*
- [ ] *Universal electrical multi-meter*

Sockets and reversible ratchet drive

Brake bleeding kit

Torx key, socket and bit

Hose clamp

Angular-tightening gauge

Special tools

The tools in this list are those which are not used regularly, are expensive to buy, or which need to be used in accordance with their manufacturers' instructions. Unless relatively difficult mechanical jobs are undertaken frequently, it will not be economic to buy many of these tools. Where this is the case, you could consider clubbing together with friends (or joining a motorists' club) to make a joint purchase, or borrowing the tools against a deposit from a local garage or tool hire specialist.

The following list contains only those tools and instruments freely available to the public, and not those special tools produced by the vehicle manufacturer specifically for its dealer network. You will find occasional references to these manufacturers' special tools in the text of this manual. Generally, an alternative method of doing the job without the vehicle manufacturers' special tool is given. However, sometimes there is no alternative to using them. Where this is the case and the relevant tool cannot be bought or borrowed, you will have to entrust the work to a dealer.

- [ ] *Angular-tightening gauge*
- [ ] *Valve spring compressor*
- [ ] *Valve grinding tool*
- [ ] *Piston ring compressor*
- [ ] *Piston ring removal/installation tool*
- [ ] *Cylinder bore hone*
- [ ] *Balljoint separator*
- [ ] *Coil spring compressors (where applicable)*
- [ ] *Two/three-legged hub and bearing puller*
- [ ] *Impact screwdriver*
- [ ] *Micrometer and/or vernier calipers*
- [ ] *Dial gauge*
- [ ] *Tachometer*
- [ ] *Fault code reader*
- [ ] *Cylinder compression gauge*
- [ ] *Hand-operated vacuum pump and gauge*
- [ ] *Clutch plate alignment set*
- [ ] *Brake shoe steady spring cup removal tool*
- [ ] *Bush and bearing removal/installation set*
- [ ] *Stud extractors*
- [ ] *Tap and die set*
- [ ] *Lifting tackle*

Buying tools

Reputable motor accessory shops and superstores often offer excellent quality tools at discount prices, so it pays to shop around.

Remember, you don't have to buy the most expensive items on the shelf, but it is always advisable to steer clear of the very cheap tools. Beware of 'bargains' offered on market stalls, on-line or at car boot sales. There are plenty of good tools around at reasonable prices, but always aim to purchase items which meet the relevant national safety standards. If in doubt, ask the proprietor or manager of the shop for advice before making a purchase.

Care and maintenance of tools

Having purchased a reasonable tool kit, it is necessary to keep the tools in a clean and serviceable condition. After use, always wipe off any dirt, grease and metal particles using a clean, dry cloth, before putting the tools away. Never leave them lying around after they have been used. A simple tool rack on the garage or workshop wall for items such as screwdrivers and pliers is a good idea. Store all normal spanners and sockets in a metal box. Any measuring instruments, gauges, meters, etc, must be carefully stored where they cannot be damaged or become rusty.

Take a little care when tools are used. Hammer heads inevitably become marked, and screwdrivers lose the keen edge on their blades from time to time. A little timely attention with emery cloth or a file will soon restore items like this to a good finish.

Working facilities

Not to be forgotten when discussing tools is the workshop itself. If anything more than routine maintenance is to be carried out, a suitable working area becomes essential.

It is appreciated that many an owner-mechanic is forced by circumstances to remove an engine or similar item without the benefit of a garage or workshop. Having done this, any repairs should always be done under the cover of a roof.

Wherever possible, any dismantling should be done on a clean, flat workbench or table at a suitable working height.

Any workbench needs a vice; one with a jaw opening of 100 mm is suitable for most jobs. As mentioned previously, some clean dry storage space is also required for tools, as well as for any lubricants, cleaning fluids, touch-up paints etc, which become necessary.

Another item which may be required, and which has a much more general usage, is an electric drill with a chuck capacity of at least 8 mm. This, together with a good range of twist drills, is virtually essential for fitting accessories.

Last, but not least, always keep a supply of old newspapers and clean, lint-free rags available, and try to keep any working area as clean as possible.

Micrometers

Dial test indicator ("dial gauge")

Oil filter removal tool (strap wrench type)

Compression tester

Bearing puller

This is a guide to getting your vehicle through the MOT test. Obviously it will not be possible to examine the vehicle to the same standard as the professional MOT tester. However, working through the following checks will enable you to identify any problem areas before submitting the vehicle for the test.

It has only been possible to summarise the test requirements here, based on the regulations in force at the time of printing. Test standards are becoming increasingly stringent, although there are some exemptions for older vehicles.

An assistant will be needed to help carry out some of these checks.

The checks have been sub-divided into four categories, as follows:

1 Checks carried out **FROM THE DRIVER'S SEAT**

2 Checks carried out **WITH THE VEHICLE ON THE GROUND**

3 Checks carried out **WITH THE VEHICLE RAISED AND THE WHEELS FREE TO TURN**

4 Checks carried out on **YOUR VEHICLE'S EXHAUST EMISSION SYSTEM**

---

1 Checks carried out **FROM THE DRIVER'S SEAT**

Handbrake (parking brake)

☐ Test the operation of the handbrake. Excessive travel (too many clicks) indicates incorrect brake or cable adjustment.
☐ Check that the handbrake cannot be released by tapping the lever sideways. Check the security of the lever mountings.

☐ If the parking brake is foot-operated, check that the pedal is secure and without excessive travel, and that the release mechanism operates correctly.
☐ Where applicable, test the operation of the electronic handbrake. The brake should engage and disengage without excessive delay. If the warning light does not extinguish when the brake is disengaged, this could indicate a fault which will need further investigation.

Footbrake

☐ Depress the brake pedal and check that it does not creep down to the floor, indicating a master cylinder fault. Release the pedal, wait a few seconds, then depress it again. If the pedal travels nearly to the floor before firm resistance is felt, brake adjustment or repair is necessary. If the pedal feels spongy, there is air in the hydraulic system which must be removed by bleeding.

☐ Check that the brake pedal is secure and in good condition. Check also for signs of fluid leaks on the pedal, floor or carpets, which would indicate failed seals in the brake master cylinder.
☐ Check the servo unit (when applicable) by operating the brake pedal several times, then keeping the pedal depressed and starting the engine. As the engine starts, the pedal will move down slightly. If not, the vacuum hose or the servo itself may be faulty.

Steering wheel and column

☐ Examine the steering wheel for fractures or looseness of the hub, spokes or rim.
☐ Move the steering wheel from side to side and then up and down. Check that the steering wheel is not loose on the column, indicating wear or a loose retaining nut. Continue moving the steering wheel as before, but also turn it slightly from left to right.

☐ Check that the steering wheel is not loose on the column, and that there is no abnormal movement of the steering wheel, indicating wear in the column support bearings or couplings.
☐ Check that the ignition lock (where fitted) engages and disengages correctly.
☐ Steering column adjustment mechanisms (where fitted) must be able to lock the column securely in place with no play evident.

Windscreen, mirrors and sunvisor

☐ The windscreen must be free of cracks or other significant damage within the driver's field of view. (Small stone chips are acceptable.) Rear view mirrors must be secure, intact, and capable of being adjusted.

☐ The driver's sunvisor must be capable of being stored in the "up" position.

Seat belts and seats

Note: *The following checks are applicable to all seat belts, front and rear.*

☐ Examine the webbing of all the belts (including rear belts if fitted) for cuts, serious fraying or deterioration. Fasten and unfasten each belt to check the buckles. If applicable, check the retracting mechanism. Check the security of all seat belt mountings accessible from inside the vehicle, ensuring any height adjustable mountings lock securely in place.

☐ Seat belts with pre-tensioners, once activated, have a "flag" or similar showing on the seat belt stalk. This, in itself, is not a reason for test failure.

☐ The front seats themselves must be securely attached and the backrests must lock in the upright position.

Doors

☐ Both front doors must be able to be opened and closed from outside and inside, and must latch securely when closed.

Bonnet and boot/tailgate

☐ The bonnet and boot/tailgate must latch securely when closed.

2 Checks carried out WITH THE VEHICLE ON THE GROUND

Vehicle identification

☐ Number plates must be in good condition, secure and legible, with letters and numbers correctly spaced – spacing at (A) should be 33 mm and at (B) 11 mm. At the front, digits must be black on a white background and at the rear black on a yellow background. Other background designs (such as honeycomb) are not permitted.

☐ The VIN plate and/or homologation plate must be permanently displayed and legible.

Electrical equipment

☐ Switch on the ignition and check the operation of the horn.

☐ Check the windscreen washers and wipers, examining the wiper blades; renew damaged or perished blades. Also check the operation of the stop-lights.

☐ Check the operation of the sidelights and number plate lights. The lenses and reflectors must be secure, clean and undamaged.

☐ Check the operation and alignment of the headlights. The headlight reflectors must not be tarnished and the lenses must be undamaged.

☐ Switch on the ignition and check the operation of the direction indicators (including the instrument panel tell-tale) and the hazard warning lights. Operation of the sidelights and stop-lights must not affect the indicators - if it does, the cause is usually a bad earth at the rear light cluster. Indicators should flash at a rate of between 60 and 120 times per minute – faster or slower than this could indicate a fault with the flasher unit or a bad earth at one of the light units.

☐ Check the operation of the rear foglight(s), including the warning light on the instrument panel or in the switch.

☐ The warning lights must illuminate in accordance with the manufacturer's design. For most vehicles, the ABS and other warning lights should illuminate when the ignition is switched on, and (if the system is operating properly) extinguish after a few seconds. Refer to the owner's handbook.

Footbrake

☐ Examine the master cylinder, brake pipes and servo unit for leaks, loose mountings, corrosion or other damage. If ABS is fitted, this unit should also be examined for signs of leaks or corrosion.

☐ The fluid reservoir must be secure and the fluid level must be between the upper (**A**) and lower (**B**) markings.

☐ Inspect both front brake flexible hoses for cracks or deterioration of the rubber. Turn the steering from lock to lock, and ensure that the hoses do not contact the wheel, tyre, or any part of the steering or suspension mechanism. With the brake pedal firmly depressed, check the hoses for bulges or leaks under pressure.

Steering and suspension

☐ Have your assistant turn the steering wheel from side to side slightly, up to the point where the steering gear just begins to transmit this movement to the roadwheels. Check for excessive free play between the steering wheel and the steering gear, indicating wear or insecurity of the steering column joints, the column-to-steering gear coupling, or the steering gear itself.

☐ Have your assistant turn the steering wheel more vigorously in each direction, so that the roadwheels just begin to turn. As this is done, examine all the steering joints, linkages, fittings and attachments. Renew any component that shows signs of wear or damage. On vehicles with power steering, check the security and condition of the steering pump, drivebelt and hoses.

☐ Check that the vehicle is standing level, and at approximately the correct ride height.

Shock absorbers

☐ Depress each corner of the vehicle in turn, then release it. The vehicle should rise and then settle in its normal position. If the vehicle continues to rise and fall, the shock absorber is defective. A shock absorber which has seized will also cause the vehicle to fail.

Exhaust system

☐ Start the engine. With your assistant holding a rag over the tailpipe, check the entire system for leaks. Repair or renew leaking sections.

3 Checks carried out **WITH THE VEHICLE RAISED AND THE WHEELS FREE TO TURN**

Jack up the front and rear of the vehicle, and securely support it on axle stands. Position the stands clear of the suspension assemblies. Ensure that the wheels are clear of the ground and that the steering can be turned from lock to lock.

Steering mechanism

☐ Have your assistant turn the steering from lock to lock. Check that the steering turns smoothly, and that no part of the steering mechanism, including a wheel or tyre, fouls any brake hose or pipe or any part of the body structure.
☐ Examine the steering rack rubber gaiters for damage or insecurity of the retaining clips. If power steering is fitted, check for signs of damage or leakage of the fluid hoses, pipes or connections. Also check for excessive stiffness or binding of the steering, a missing split pin or locking device, or severe corrosion of the body structure within 30 cm of any steering component attachment point.

Front and rear suspension and wheel bearings

☐ Starting at the front right-hand side, grasp the roadwheel at the 3 o'clock and 9 o'clock positions and rock gently but firmly. Check for free play or insecurity at the wheel bearings, suspension balljoints, or suspension mount-ings, pivots and attachments.
☐ Now grasp the wheel at the 12 o'clock and 6 o'clock positions and repeat the previous inspection. Spin the wheel, and check for roughness or tightness of the front wheel bearing.

☐ If excess free play is suspected at a component pivot point, this can be confirmed by using a large screwdriver or similar tool and levering between the mounting and the component attachment. This will confirm whether the wear is in the pivot bush, its retaining bolt, or in the mounting itself (the bolt holes can often become elongated).

☐ Carry out all the above checks at the other front wheel, and then at both rear wheels.

Springs and shock absorbers

☐ Examine the suspension struts (when applicable) for serious fluid leakage, corrosion, or damage to the casing. Also check the security of the mounting points.
☐ If coil springs are fitted, check that the spring ends locate in their seats, and that the spring is not corroded, cracked or broken.
☐ If leaf springs are fitted, check that all leaves are intact, that the axle is securely attached to each spring, and that there is no deterioration of the spring eye mountings, bushes, and shackles.

☐ The same general checks apply to vehicles fitted with other suspension types, such as torsion bars, hydraulic displacer units, etc. Ensure that all mountings and attachments are secure, that there are no signs of excessive wear, corrosion or damage, and (on hydraulic types) that there are no fluid leaks or damaged pipes.
☐ Inspect the shock absorbers for signs of serious fluid leakage. Check for wear of the mounting bushes or attachments, or damage to the body of the unit.

Driveshafts
(fwd vehicles only)

☐ Rotate each front wheel in turn and inspect the constant velocity joint gaiters for splits or damage. Also check that each driveshaft is straight and undamaged.

Braking system

☐ If possible without dismantling, check brake pad wear and disc condition. Ensure that the friction lining material has not worn excessively, (A) and that the discs are not fractured, pitted, scored or badly worn (B).

☐ Examine all the rigid brake pipes underneath the vehicle, and the flexible hose(s) at the rear. Look for corrosion, chafing or insecurity of the pipes, and for signs of bulging under pressure, chafing, splits or deterioration of the flexible hoses.
☐ Look for signs of fluid leaks at the brake calipers or on the brake backplates. Repair or renew leaking components.
☐ Slowly spin each wheel, while your assistant depresses and releases the footbrake. Ensure that each brake is operating and does not bind when the pedal is released.

□ Examine the handbrake mechanism, checking for frayed or broken cables, excessive corrosion, or wear or insecurity of the linkage. Check that the mechanism works on each relevant wheel, and releases fully, without binding.

□ It is not possible to test brake efficiency without special equipment, but a road test can be carried out later to check that the vehicle pulls up in a straight line.

Fuel and exhaust systems

□ Inspect the fuel tank (including the filler cap), fuel pipes, hoses and unions. All components must be secure and free from leaks. Locking fuel caps must lock securely and the key must be provided for the MOT test.

□ Examine the exhaust system over its entire length, checking for any damaged, broken or missing mountings, security of the retaining clamps and rust or corrosion.

Wheels and tyres

□ Examine the sidewalls and tread area of each tyre in turn. Check for cuts, tears, lumps, bulges, separation of the tread, and exposure of the ply or cord due to wear or damage. Check that the tyre bead is correctly seated on the wheel rim, that the valve is sound and properly seated, and that the wheel is not distorted or damaged.

□ Check that the tyres are of the correct size for the vehicle, that they are of the same size and type on each axle, and that the pressures are correct.

□ Check the tyre tread depth. The legal minimum at the time of writing is 1.6 mm over the central three-quarters of the tread width. Abnormal tread wear may indicate incorrect front wheel alignment or wear in steering or suspension components.

□ If the spare wheel is fitted externally or in a separate carrier beneath the vehicle, check that mountings are secure and free of excessive corrosion.

Body corrosion

□ Check the condition of the entire vehicle structure for signs of corrosion in load-bearing areas. (These include chassis box sections, side sills, cross-members, pillars, and all suspension, steering, braking system and seat belt mountings and anchorages.) Any corrosion which has seriously reduced the thickness of a load-bearing area (or is within 30 cm of safety-related components such as steering or suspension) is likely to cause the vehicle to fail. In this case professional repairs are likely to be needed.

□ Damage or corrosion which causes sharp or otherwise dangerous edges to be exposed will also cause the vehicle to fail.

Towbars

□ Check the condition of mounting points (both beneath the vehicle and within boot/hatchback areas) for signs of corrosion, ensuring that all fixings are secure and not worn or damaged. There must be no excessive play in detachable tow ball arms or quick-release mechanisms.

4 Checks carried out on **YOUR VEHICLE'S EXHAUST EMISSION SYSTEM**

Petrol models

□ The engine should be warmed up, and running well (ignition system in good order, air filter element clean, etc).

□ Before testing, run the engine at around 2500 rpm for 20 seconds. Let the engine drop to idle, and watch for smoke from the exhaust. If the idle speed is too high, or if dense blue or black smoke emerges for more than 5 seconds, the vehicle will fail. Typically, blue smoke signifies oil burning (engine wear);

black smoke means unburnt fuel (dirty air cleaner element, or other fuel system fault).

□ An exhaust gas analyser for measuring carbon monoxide (CO) and hydrocarbons (HC) is now needed. If one cannot be hired or borrowed, have a local garage perform the check.

CO emissions (mixture)

□ The MOT tester has access to the CO limits for all vehicles. The CO level is measured at idle speed, and at 'fast idle' (2500 to 3000 rpm). The following limits are given as a general guide:

At idle speed – Less than 0.5% CO
At 'fast idle' – Less than 0.3% CO
Lambda reading – 0.97 to 1.03

□ If the CO level is too high, this may point to poor maintenance, a fuel injection system problem, faulty lambda (oxygen) sensor or catalytic converter. Try an injector cleaning treatment, and check the vehicle's ECU for fault codes.

HC emissions

□ The MOT tester has access to HC limits for all vehicles. The HC level is measured at 'fast idle' (2500 to 3000 rpm). The following limits are given as a general guide:

At 'fast idle' – Less then 200 ppm

□ Excessive HC emissions are typically caused by oil being burnt (worn engine), or by a blocked crankcase ventilation system ('breather'). If the engine oil is old and thin, an oil change may help. If the engine is running badly, check the vehicle's ECU for fault codes.

Diesel models

□ The only emission test for diesel engines is measuring exhaust smoke density, using a calibrated smoke meter. The test involves accelerating the engine at least 3 times to its maximum unloaded speed.

Note: *On engines with a timing belt, it is VITAL that the belt is in good condition before the test is carried out.*

□ With the engine warmed up, it is first purged by running at around 2500 rpm for 20 seconds. A governor check is then carried out, by slowly accelerating the engine to its maximum speed. After this, the smoke meter is connected, and the engine is accelerated quickly to maximum speed three times. If the smoke density is less than the limits given below, the vehicle will pass:

Non-turbo vehicles: 2.5m-1
Turbocharged vehicles: 3.0m-1

□ If excess smoke is produced, try fitting a new air cleaner element, or using an injector cleaning treatment. If the engine is running badly, where applicable, check the vehicle's ECU for fault codes. Also check the vehicle's EGR system, where applicable. At high mileages, the injectors may require professional attention.

Engine

- ☐ Engine fails to rotate when attempting to start
- ☐ Engine rotates, but will not start
- ☐ Engine difficult to start when cold
- ☐ Engine difficult to start when hot
- ☐ Starter motor noisy or excessively-rough in engagement
- ☐ Engine starts, but stops immediately
- ☐ Engine idles erratically
- ☐ Engine misfires at idle speed
- ☐ Engine misfires throughout the driving speed range
- ☐ Engine hesitates on acceleration
- ☐ Engine stalls
- ☐ Engine lacks power
- ☐ Engine backfires
- ☐ Oil pressure warning light illuminated with engine running
- ☐ Engine runs-on after switching off
- ☐ Engine noises

Cooling system

- ☐ Overheating
- ☐ Overcooling
- ☐ External coolant leakage
- ☐ Internal coolant leakage
- ☐ Corrosion

Fuel and exhaust systems

- ☐ Excessive fuel consumption
- ☐ Fuel leakage and/or fuel odour
- ☐ Excessive noise or fumes from exhaust system

Clutch

- ☐ Pedal travels to floor – no pressure or very little resistance
- ☐ Clutch fails to disengage (unable to select gears)
- ☐ Clutch slips (engine speed increases, with no increase in vehicle speed)
- ☐ Judder as clutch is engaged
- ☐ Noise when depressing or releasing clutch pedal

Manual transmission

- ☐ Noisy in neutral with engine running
- ☐ Noisy in one particular gear
- ☐ Difficulty engaging gears
- ☐ Jumps out of gear
- ☐ Vibration
- ☐ Lubricant leaks

Driveshafts

- ☐ Vibration when accelerating or decelerating
- ☐ Clicking or knocking noise on turns (at slow speed on full-lock)

Braking system

- ☐ Vehicle pulls to one side under braking
- ☐ Noise (grinding or high-pitched squeal) when brakes applied
- ☐ Excessive brake pedal travel
- ☐ Brake pedal feels spongy when depressed
- ☐ Excessive brake pedal effort required to stop vehicle
- ☐ Judder felt through brake pedal or steering wheel when braking
- ☐ Brakes binding
- ☐ Rear wheels locking under normal braking

Suspension and steering

- ☐ Vehicle pulls to one side
- ☐ Wheel wobble and vibration
- ☐ Excessive pitching and/or rolling around corners, or during braking
- ☐ Wandering or general instability
- ☐ Excessively-stiff steering
- ☐ Excessive play in steering
- ☐ Lack of power assistance
- ☐ Tyre wear excessive

Electrical system

- ☐ Battery will not hold a charge for more than a few days
- ☐ Ignition/no-charge warning light remains illuminated with engine running
- ☐ Ignition/no-charge warning light fails to come on
- ☐ Lights inoperative
- ☐ Instrument readings inaccurate or erratic
- ☐ Horn inoperative, or unsatisfactory in operation
- ☐ Windscreen wipers inoperative, or unsatisfactory in operation
- ☐ Windscreen washers inoperative, or unsatisfactory in operation
- ☐ Electric windows inoperative, or unsatisfactory in operation
- ☐ Central locking system inoperative, or unsatisfactory in operation

Introduction

The vehicle owner who does his or her own maintenance according to the recommended service schedules should not have to use this section of the manual very often. Modern component reliability is such that, provided those items subject to wear or deterioration are inspected or renewed at the specified intervals, sudden failure is comparatively rare. Faults do not usually just happen as a result of sudden failure, but develop over a period of time. Major mechanical failures in particular are usually preceded by characteristic symptoms over hundreds or even thousands of miles. Those components which do occasionally fail without warning are often small and easily carried in the vehicle.

With any fault finding, the first step is to decide where to begin investigations. Sometimes this is obvious, but on other occasions, a little detective work will be necessary. The owner who makes half a dozen haphazard adjustments or replacements may be successful in curing a fault (or its symptoms), but will be none the wiser if the fault recurs, and ultimately may have spent more time and money than was necessary. A calm and logical approach will be found to be more satisfactory in the long run. Always take into account any warning signs or abnormalities that may have been noticed in the period preceding the fault – power loss, high or low gauge readings, unusual smells, etc – and remember that failure of components such as fuses or spark plugs may only be pointers to some underlying fault.

The pages which follow provide an easy-reference guide to the more common problems which may occur during the operation of the vehicle. These problems and their possible causes are grouped under headings denoting various components or systems, such as Engine, Cooling system, etc. The Chapter and/or Section which deals with the problem is also shown in brackets. Whatever the fault, certain basic principles apply. These are as follows:

Verify the fault. This is simply a matter of being sure that you know what the symptoms are before starting work. This is particularly important if you are investigating a fault for someone else, who may not have described it very accurately.

Don't overlook the obvious. For example, if the vehicle won't start, is there fuel in the tank? (Don't take anyone else's word on this particular point, and don't trust the fuel gauge either). If an electrical fault is indicated, look for loose or broken wires before digging out the test gear.

Cure the disease, not the symptom. Substituting a flat battery with a fully-charged one will get you off the hard shoulder, but if the underlying cause is not attended to, the new battery will go the same way. Similarly, changing oil-fouled spark plugs for a new set will get you moving again, but remember that the reason for the fouling (if it wasn't simply an incorrect grade of plug) will have to be established and corrected.

Don't take anything for granted. Particularly, don't forget that a 'new' component may itself be defective (especially if it's been rattling around in the boot for months), and don't leave components out of a fault diagnosis sequence just because they are new or recently-fitted. When you do finally diagnose a difficult fault, you'll probably realise that all the evidence was there from the start.

Consider what work, if any, has recently been carried out. Many faults arise through careless or hurried work. For instance, if any work has been performed under the bonnet, could some of the wiring have been dislodged or incorrectly routed, or a hose trapped? Have all the fasteners been properly tightened? Were new, genuine parts and new gaskets used? There is often a certain amount of detective work to be done in this case, as an apparently-unrelated task can have far-reaching consequences.

Diesel engine fault diagnosis

The majority of starting problems on small diesel engines are electrical in origin. The mechanic who is familiar with petrol engines but less so with diesel may be inclined to view the diesel's injectors and pump in the same light as the spark plugs and distributor, but this is generally a mistake.

When investigating complaints of difficult starting for someone else, make sure that the correct starting procedure is understood and is being followed. Some drivers are unaware of the significance of the preheating warning light – many modern engines are sufficiently forgiving for this not to matter in mild weather, but with the onset of winter, problems begin. Glow plugs in particular are often neglected – just one faulty plug will make cold-weather starting very difficult.

As a rule of thumb, if the engine is difficult to start but runs well when it has finally got going, the problem is electrical (battery, starter motor or preheating system). If poor performance is combined with difficult starting, the problem is likely to be in the fuel system. The low-pressure (supply) side of the fuel system should be checked before suspecting the injectors and high-pressure pump. The most common fuel supply problem is air getting into the system, and any pipe from the fuel tank forwards must be scrutinised if air leakage is suspected.

Engine

Engine fails to rotate when attempting to start

- [ ] Battery terminal connections loose or corroded (see *Weekly checks*)
- [ ] Battery discharged or faulty (Chapter 5A)
- [ ] Broken, loose or disconnected wiring in the starting circuit (Chapter 5A)
- [ ] Defective starter solenoid or ignition switch (Chapter 5A or 10)
- [ ] Defective starter motor (Chapter 5A)
- [ ] Starter pinion or flywheel ring gear teeth loose or broken (Chapter 2A, 2B or 5A)
- [ ] Engine earth strap broken or disconnected (Chapter 12)
- [ ] Engine suffering 'hydraulic lock' (eg, from water ingested after traversing flooded roads, or from a serious internal coolant leak) – consult a Fiat dealer for advice

Engine rotates, but will not start

- [ ] Fuel tank empty
- [ ] Battery discharged (engine rotates slowly) (Chapter 5A)
- [ ] Battery terminal connections loose or corroded (see *Weekly checks*)
- [ ] Ignition components damp or damaged – petrol models (Chapter 1A or 5B)
- [ ] Immobiliser fault, or 'uncoded' ignition key being used (Chapter 12 or *Roadside repairs*)
- [ ] Crankshaft sensor fault (Chapter 4A or 4B)
- [ ] Broken, loose or disconnected wiring in the ignition circuit – petrol models (Chapter 1A or 5B)
- [ ] Worn, faulty or incorrectly-gapped spark plugs – petrol models (Chapter 1A)
- [ ] Preheating system faulty – diesel models (Chapter 5A)
- [ ] Fuel injection system fault (Chapter 4A or 4B)
- [ ] Air in fuel system – diesel models (Chapter 4B)
- [ ] Major mechanical failure (eg, timing belt/chain snapped) (Chapter 2A or 2B)

Engine difficult to start when cold

- [ ] Battery discharged (Chapter 5A)
- [ ] Battery terminal connections loose or corroded (see *Weekly checks*)
- [ ] Worn, faulty or incorrectly-gapped spark plugs – petrol models (Chapter 1A)
- [ ] Other ignition system fault – petrol models (Chapter 1A or 5B)
- [ ] Preheating system faulty – diesel models (Chapter 5A)
- [ ] Fuel injection system fault (Chapter 4A or 4B)
- [ ] Wrong grade of engine oil used (*Weekly checks*, Chapter 1A or 1B)
- [ ] Low cylinder compression (Chapter 2A or 2B)

Engine difficult to start when hot

- [ ] Air filter element dirty or clogged (Chapter 1A or 1B)
- [ ] Fuel injection system fault (Chapter 4A or 4B)
- [ ] Low cylinder compression (Chapter 2A or 2B)

Starter motor noisy or excessively-rough in engagement

- [ ] Starter pinion or flywheel ring gear teeth loose or broken (Chapter 2A, 2B or 5A)
- [ ] Starter motor mounting bolts loose or missing (Chapter 5A)
- [ ] Starter motor internal components worn or damaged (Chapter 5A)

Engine starts, but stops immediately

- [ ] Loose or faulty electrical connections in the ignition circuit – petrol models (Chapter 1A or 5B)
- [ ] Vacuum leak at the throttle body or intake manifold – petrol models (Chapter 4A)
- [ ] Blocked injectors/fuel injection system fault (Chapter 4A or 4B)
- [ ] Air in fuel, possibly due to loose fuel line connection – diesel models (Chapter 4B)

Engine idles erratically

- [ ] Air filter element clogged (Chapter 1A or 1B)
- [ ] Vacuum leak at the throttle body, intake manifold or associated hoses – petrol models (Chapter 4A)
- [ ] Worn, faulty or incorrectly-gapped spark plugs – petrol models (Chapter 1A)
- [ ] Valve clearances incorrect (Chapter 1A)
- [ ] Uneven or low cylinder compression (Chapter 2A or 2B)
- [ ] Camshaft lobes worn (Chapter 2A or 2B)
- [ ] Timing belt/chain incorrectly fitted (Chapter 2A or 2B)
- [ ] Blocked injectors/fuel injection system fault (Chapter 4A or 4B)
- [ ] Air in fuel, possibly due to loose fuel line connection – diesel models (Chapter 4B)

Engine misfires at idle speed

- [ ] Worn, faulty or incorrectly-gapped spark plugs – petrol models (Chapter 1A)
- [ ] Faulty spark plug HT leads – petrol models (Chapter 1A)
- [ ] Vacuum leak at the throttle body, intake manifold or associated hoses – petrol models (Chapter 4A)
- [ ] Blocked injectors/fuel injection system fault (Chapter 4A or 4B)
- [ ] Faulty injector(s) – diesel models (Chapter 4B)
- [ ] Uneven or low cylinder compression (Chapter 2A or 2B)
- [ ] Disconnected, leaking, or perished crankcase ventilation hoses (Chapter 4C)

Engine misfires throughout the driving speed range

- [ ] Fuel filter choked (Chapter 1B)
- [ ] Fuel pump faulty, or delivery pressure low (Chapter 4A or 4B)
- [ ] Fuel tank vent blocked, or fuel pipes restricted (Chapter 4A or 4B)
- [ ] Vacuum leak at the throttle body, intake manifold or associated hoses – petrol models (Chapter 4A)
- [ ] Worn, faulty or incorrectly-gapped spark plugs – petrol models (Chapter 1A)
- [ ] Faulty spark plug HT leads (where fitted) – petrol models (Chapter 1A)
- [ ] Faulty injector(s) – diesel models (Chapter 4B)
- [ ] Faulty ignition coil – petrol models (Chapter 5A)
- [ ] Uneven or low cylinder compression (Chapter 2A or 2B)
- [ ] Blocked injector/fuel injection system fault (Chapter 4A or 4B)
- [ ] Blocked catalytic converter/particulate filter (Chapter 4A or 4B)
- [ ] Engine overheating – petrol models (Chapter 3)
- [ ] Fuel tank level low – diesel models (Chapter 4B)

Engine (continued)

Engine hesitates on acceleration

- [ ] Worn, faulty or incorrectly-gapped spark plugs – petrol models (Chapter 1A)
- [ ] Vacuum leak at the throttle body, intake manifold or associated hoses – petrol models (Chapter 4A)
- [ ] Blocked injectors/fuel injection system fault (Chapter 4A or 4B)
- [ ] Faulty injector(s) – diesel models (Chapter 4B)

Engine stalls

- [ ] Vacuum leak at the throttle body, intake manifold or associated hoses – petrol models (Chapter 4A)
- [ ] Fuel filter choked (Chapter 1B)
- [ ] Fuel pump faulty, or delivery pressure low (Chapter 4A or 4B)
- [ ] Fuel tank vent blocked, or fuel pipes restricted (Chapter 4A or 4B)
- [ ] Blocked injectors/fuel injection system fault (Chapter 4A or 4B)
- [ ] Faulty injector(s) – diesel models (Chapter 4B)

Engine lacks power

- [ ] Air filter element blocked (Chapter 1A or 1B)
- [ ] Fuel filter choked (Chapter 1B)
- [ ] Fuel pipes blocked or restricted (Chapter 4A or 4B)
- [ ] Valve clearances incorrect (Chapter 1A)
- [ ] Worn, faulty or incorrectly-gapped spark plugs – petrol models (Chapter 1A)
- [ ] Engine overheating – petrol models (Chapter 4A)
- [ ] Fuel tank level low – diesel models (Chapter 4B)
- [ ] Accelerator cable problem – petrol models (Chapter 4A)
- [ ] Accelerator position sensor faulty (Chapter 4A or 4B)
- [ ] Vacuum leak at the throttle body, intake manifold or associated hoses – petrol models (Chapter 4A)
- [ ] Blocked injectors/fuel injection system fault (Chapter 4A or 4B)
- [ ] Faulty injector(s) – diesel models (Chapter 4B)
- [ ] Timing belt/chain incorrectly fitted (Chapter 2A or 2B)
- [ ] Fuel pump faulty, or delivery pressure low (Chapter 4A or 4B)
- [ ] Uneven or low cylinder compression (Chapter 2A or 2B)
- [ ] Blocked catalytic converter/particulate filter (Chapter 4A or 4B)
- [ ] Brakes binding (Chapter 1A, 1B or 9)
- [ ] Clutch slipping (Chapter 6)

Engine backfires

- [ ] Timing belt/chain incorrectly fitted (Chapter 2A or 2B)
- [ ] Vacuum leak at the throttle body, intake manifold or associated hoses – petrol models (Chapter 4A)
- [ ] Blocked injectors/fuel injection system fault (Chapter 4A or 4B)
- [ ] Blocked catalytic converter/particulate filter (Chapter 4A or 4B)
- [ ] Spark plug HT leads incorrectly fitted – petrol models (Chapter 1A or 5B)
- [ ] Ignition coil unit faulty – petrol models (Chapter 5B)

Oil pressure warning light illuminated with engine running

- [ ] Low oil level, or incorrect oil grade (see *Weekly checks*)
- [ ] Faulty oil pressure sensor, or wiring damaged (Chapter 5A)
- [ ] Worn engine bearings and/or oil pump (Chapter 2A or 2B)
- [ ] High engine operating temperature (Chapter 3)
- [ ] Oil pump pressure relief valve defective (Chapter 2A or 2B)
- [ ] Oil pump pick-up strainer clogged (Chapter 2A or 2B)

Engine runs-on after switching off

- [ ] Excessive carbon build-up in engine (Chapter 2A or 2B)
- [ ] High engine operating temperature (Chapter 3)
- [ ] Fuel injection system fault (Chapter 4A or 4B)

Engine noises

Pre-ignition (pinking) or knocking during acceleration or under load

- [ ] Ignition timing incorrect/ignition system fault – petrol models (Chapter 1A or 5B)
- [ ] Incorrect grade of spark plug – petrol models (Chapter 1A)
- [ ] Incorrect grade of fuel (Chapter 4)
- [ ] Knock sensor faulty – some petrol models (Chapter 4A)
- [ ] Vacuum leak at the throttle body, intake manifold or associated hoses – petrol models (Chapter 4A)
- [ ] Excessive carbon build-up in engine (Chapter 2A or 2B)
- [ ] Blocked injector/fuel injection system fault (Chapter 4A or 4B)
- [ ] Faulty injector(s) – diesel models (Chapter 4B)

Whistling or wheezing noises

- [ ] Leaking intake manifold or throttle body gasket – petrol models (Chapter 4A)
- [ ] Leaking exhaust manifold gasket or pipe-to-manifold joint (Chapter 4A or 4B)
- [ ] Leaking vacuum hose (Chapter 4A, 4B, 5B or 9)
- [ ] Blowing cylinder head gasket (Chapter 2A or 2B)
- [ ] Partially blocked or leaking crankcase ventilation system (Chapter 4C)

Tapping or rattling noises

- [ ] Valve clearances incorrect (Chapter 1A)
- [ ] Worn valve gear or camshaft (Chapter 2A or 2B)
- [ ] Ancillary component fault (coolant pump, alternator, etc) (Chapter 3, 5A, etc)

Knocking or thumping noises

- [ ] Worn big-end bearings (regular heavy knocking, perhaps less under load) (Chapter 2C)
- [ ] Worn main bearings (rumbling and knocking, perhaps worsening under load) (Chapter 2C)
- [ ] Piston slap – most noticeable when cold, caused by piston/bore wear (Chapter 2C)
- [ ] Ancillary component fault (coolant pump, alternator, etc) (Chapter 3, 5A, etc)
- [ ] Engine mountings worn or defective (Chapter 2A or 2B)
- [ ] Front suspension or steering components worn (Chapter 10)

Cooling system

Overheating

- [ ] Insufficient coolant in system (see *Weekly checks*)
- [ ] Thermostat faulty (Chapter 3)
- [ ] Radiator core blocked, or grille restricted (Chapter 3)
- [ ] Cooling fan faulty, or resistor pack fault on models with twin fans (Chapter 3)
- [ ] Inaccurate coolant temperature sensor (Chapter 3)
- [ ] Airlock in cooling system (Chapter 3)
- [ ] Expansion tank pressure cap faulty (Chapter 3)
- [ ] Engine management system fault (Chapter 4A or 4B)

Overcooling

- [ ] Thermostat faulty (Chapter 3)
- [ ] Inaccurate coolant temperature sensor (Chapter 3)
- [ ] Cooling fan faulty (Chapter 3)
- [ ] Engine management system fault (Chapter 4A or 4B)

External coolant leakage

- [ ] Deteriorated or damaged hoses or hose clips (Chapter 1A or 1B)
- [ ] Radiator core or heater matrix leaking (Chapter 3)
- [ ] Expansion tank pressure cap faulty (Chapter 1A or 1B)
- [ ] Coolant pump internal seal leaking (Chapter 3)
- [ ] Coolant pump gasket leaking (Chapter 3)
- [ ] Boiling due to overheating (Chapter 3)
- [ ] Cylinder block core plug leaking (Chapter 2C)

Internal coolant leakage

- [ ] Leaking cylinder head gasket (Chapter 2A or 2B)
- [ ] Cracked cylinder head or cylinder block (Chapter 2)

Corrosion

- [ ] Infrequent draining and flushing (Chapter 1A or 1B)
- [ ] Incorrect coolant mixture or inappropriate coolant type (see *Weekly checks*)

Fuel and exhaust systems

Excessive fuel consumption

- [ ] Air filter element dirty or clogged (Chapter 1A or 1B)
- [ ] Fuel injection system fault (Chapter 4A or 4B)
- [ ] Engine management system fault (Chapter 4A or 4B)
- [ ] Crankcase ventilation system blocked (Chapter 4C)
- [ ] Tyres under-inflated (see *Weekly checks*)
- [ ] Brakes binding (Chapter 1A, 1B or 9)
- [ ] Fuel leak, causing apparent high consumption (Chapter 1A, 1B, 4A or 4B)

Fuel leakage and/or fuel odour

- [ ] Damaged or corroded fuel tank, pipes or connections (Chapter 4A or 4B)
- [ ] Evaporative emissions system fault – petrol models (Chapter 4C)

Excessive noise or fumes from exhaust system

- [ ] Leaking exhaust system or manifold joints (Chapter 1A, 1B, 4A or 4B)
- [ ] Leaking, corroded or damaged silencers or pipe (Chapter 1A, 1B, 4A or 4B)
- [ ] Broken mountings causing body or suspension contact (Chapter 1A or 1B)

Clutch

Pedal travels to floor – no pressure or very little resistance

- ☐ Air in hydraulic system/faulty master or slave cylinder (Chapter 6)
- ☐ Faulty hydraulic release system (Chapter 6)
- ☐ Clutch pedal return spring detached or broken (Chapter 6)
- ☐ Broken clutch release bearing or fork (Chapter 6)
- ☐ Broken diaphragm spring in clutch pressure plate (Chapter 6)

Clutch fails to disengage (unable to select gears)

- ☐ Air in hydraulic system/faulty master or slave cylinder (Chapter 6)
- ☐ Faulty hydraulic release system (Chapter 6)
- ☐ Clutch disc sticking on transmission input shaft splines (Chapter 6)
- ☐ Clutch disc sticking to flywheel or pressure plate (Chapter 6)
- ☐ Faulty pressure plate assembly (Chapter 6)
- ☐ Clutch release mechanism worn or incorrectly assembled (Chapter 6)

Clutch slips (engine speed increases, with no increase in vehicle speed)

- ☐ Faulty hydraulic release system (Chapter 6)
- ☐ Clutch disc linings excessively worn (Chapter 6)
- ☐ Clutch disc linings contaminated with oil or grease (Chapter 6)
- ☐ Faulty pressure plate or weak diaphragm spring (Chapter 6)

Judder as clutch is engaged

- ☐ Clutch disc linings contaminated with oil or grease (Chapter 6)
- ☐ Clutch disc linings excessively worn (Chapter 6)
- ☐ Faulty or distorted pressure plate or diaphragm spring (Chapter 6).
- ☐ Worn or loose engine or transmission mountings (Chapter 2A, 2B or 2C)
- ☐ Clutch disc hub or transmission input shaft splines worn (Chapter 6)

Noise when depressing or releasing clutch pedal

- ☐ Worn clutch release bearing (Chapter 6)
- ☐ Worn or dry clutch pedal bushes (Chapter 6)
- ☐ Worn or dry clutch master cylinder piston (Chapter 6)
- ☐ Faulty pressure plate assembly (Chapter 6)
- ☐ Pressure plate diaphragm spring broken (Chapter 6)
- ☐ Broken clutch disc cushioning springs (Chapter 6)

Manual transmission

Noisy in neutral with engine running

- ☐ Lack of oil (Chapter 1A or 1B)
- ☐ Input shaft bearings worn (noise apparent with clutch pedal released, but not when depressed) (Chapter 7A)*
- ☐ Clutch release bearing worn (noise apparent with clutch pedal depressed, possibly less when released) (Chapter 6)

Noisy in one particular gear

- ☐ Worn, damaged or chipped gear teeth (Chapter 7A)*

Difficulty engaging gears

- ☐ Clutch fault (Chapter 6)
- ☐ Worn, damaged, or poorly-adjusted gearchange cables (Chapter 7A)
- ☐ Lack of oil (Chapter 1A or 1B)
- ☐ Worn synchroniser units (Chapter 7A)*

Jumps out of gear

- ☐ Worn, damaged, or poorly-adjusted gearchange cables (Chapter 7A)
- ☐ Worn synchroniser units (Chapter 7A)*
- ☐ Worn selector forks (Chapter 7A)*

Vibration

- ☐ Lack of oil (Chapter 1A or 1B)
- ☐ Worn bearings (Chapter 7A)*

Lubricant leaks

- ☐ Leaking driveshaft or selector shaft oil seal (Chapter 7A)
- ☐ Leaking housing joint (Chapter 7A)*
- ☐ Leaking input shaft oil seal (Chapter 7A)*

Although the corrective action necessary to remedy the symptoms described is beyond the scope of the home mechanic, the above information should be helpful in isolating the cause of the condition, so that the owner can communicate clearly with a professional mechanic.

Driveshafts

Vibration when accelerating or decelerating

- [ ] Worn inner constant velocity joint (Chapter 8)
- [ ] Bent or distorted driveshaft (Chapter 8)
- [ ] Worn intermediate bearing (Chapter 8)

Clicking or knocking noise on turns (at slow speed on full-lock)

- [ ] Worn outer constant velocity joint (Chapter 8)
- [ ] Lack of constant velocity joint lubricant, possibly due to damaged gaiter (Chapter 8)
- [ ] Worn intermediate bearing (Chapter 8)

Braking system

Note: *Before assuming that a brake problem exists, make sure that the tyres are in good condition and correctly inflated, that the front wheel alignment is correct, and that the vehicle is not loaded with weight in an unequal manner. Apart from checking the condition of all pipe and hose connections, any faults occurring on the anti-lock braking system should be referred to a Fiat dealer for diagnosis.*

Vehicle pulls to one side under braking

- [ ] Worn, defective, damaged or contaminated brake pads/shoes on one side (Chapter 1A, 1B or 9)
- [ ] Seized or partially-seized brake caliper piston/wheel cylinder (Chapter 1A, 1B or 9)
- [ ] A mixture of brake pad/shoe lining materials fitted between sides (Chapter 1A, 1B or 9)
- [ ] Brake caliper/backplate mounting bolts loose (Chapter 9)
- [ ] Worn or damaged steering or suspension components (Chapter 1A, 1B or 10)

Noise (grinding or high-pitched squeal) when brakes applied

- [ ] Brake pad/shoe friction lining material worn down to metal backing (Chapter 1A, 1B or 9)
- [ ] Excessive corrosion of brake disc/drum (may be apparent after the vehicle has been standing for some time (Chapter 1A, 1B or 9)
- [ ] Foreign object (stone chipping, etc) trapped between brake disc and shield (Chapter 1A, 1B or 9)

Excessive brake pedal travel

- [ ] Faulty master cylinder (Chapter 9)
- [ ] Air in hydraulic system (Chapter 1A, 1B, 6 or 9)
- [ ] Faulty vacuum servo unit (Chapter 9)

Brake pedal feels spongy when depressed

- [ ] Air in hydraulic system (Chapter 1A, 1B, 6 or 9)
- [ ] Deteriorated flexible rubber brake hoses (Chapter 1A, 1B or 9)
- [ ] Master cylinder mounting nuts loose (Chapter 9)
- [ ] Faulty master cylinder (Chapter 9)

Excessive brake pedal effort required to stop vehicle

- [ ] Faulty vacuum servo unit (Chapter 9)
- [ ] Faulty vacuum pump – diesel models (Chapter 9)
- [ ] Disconnected, damaged or insecure brake servo vacuum hose (Chapter 9)
- [ ] Primary or secondary hydraulic circuit failure (Chapter 9)
- [ ] Seized brake caliper/wheel cylinder piston (Chapter 9)
- [ ] Brake pads/shoes incorrectly fitted (Chapter 9)
- [ ] Incorrect grade of brake pads/shoes fitted (Chapter 9)
- [ ] Brake pad/shoe linings contaminated (Chapter 1A, 1B or 9)

Judder felt through brake pedal or steering wheel when braking

Note: *Under heavy braking on models equipped with ABS, vibration may be felt through the brake pedal. This is a normal feature of ABS operation, and does not constitute a fault*

- [ ] Excessive run-out or distortion of discs/drums (Chapter 1A, 1B or 9)
- [ ] Brake pad/shoe linings worn (Chapter 1A, 1B or 9)
- [ ] Brake caliper/backplate mounting bolts loose (Chapter 9)
- [ ] Wear in suspension or steering components or mountings (Chapter 1A, 1B or 10)
- [ ] Front wheels out of balance (see *Weekly checks*)

Brakes binding

- [ ] Seized brake caliper/wheel cylinder piston (Chapter 9)
- [ ] Incorrectly-adjusted handbrake mechanism (Chapter 9)
- [ ] Faulty master cylinder (Chapter 9)

Rear wheels locking under normal braking

- [ ] Rear brake pad/shoe linings contaminated or damaged (Chapter 1 or 9)
- [ ] Rear brake discs/drums warped (Chapter 1A, 1B or 9)

Suspension and steering

Note: *Before diagnosing suspension or steering faults, be sure that the trouble is not due to incorrect tyre pressures, mixtures of tyre types, or binding brakes.*

Vehicle pulls to one side

- [ ] Defective tyre (see *Weekly checks*)
- [ ] Excessive wear in suspension or steering components (Chapter 1A, 1B or 10)
- [ ] Incorrect front wheel alignment (Chapter 10)
- [ ] Accident damage to steering or suspension components (Chapter 1A or 1B)

Wheel wobble and vibration

- [ ] Front wheels out of balance (vibration felt mainly through the steering wheel) (see *Weekly checks*)
- [ ] Rear wheels out of balance (vibration felt throughout the vehicle) (see *Weekly checks*)
- [ ] Roadwheels damaged or distorted (see *Weekly checks*)
- [ ] Faulty or damaged tyre (see *Weekly checks*)
- [ ] Worn steering or suspension joints, bushes or components (Chapter 1A, 1B or 10)
- [ ] Wheel bolts loose (Chapter 1A or 1B)

Excessive pitching and/or rolling around corners, or during braking

- [ ] Defective shock absorbers (Chapter 1A, 1B or 10)
- [ ] Broken or weak spring and/or suspension component (Chapter 1A, 1B or 10)
- [ ] Worn or damaged anti-roll bar or mountings (Chapter 1A, 1B or 10)

Wandering or general instability

- [ ] Incorrect front wheel alignment (Chapter 10)
- [ ] Worn steering or suspension joints, bushes or components (Chapter 1A, 1B or 10)
- [ ] Roadwheels out of balance (see *Weekly checks*)
- [ ] Faulty or damaged tyre (see *Weekly checks*)
- [ ] Wheel bolts loose (Chapter 1A or 1B)
- [ ] Defective shock absorbers (Chapter 1A, 1B or 10)

Excessively-stiff steering

- [ ] Seized steering linkage balljoint or suspension balljoint (Chapter 1A, 1B or 10)
- [ ] Incorrect front wheel alignment (Chapter 10)
- [ ] Steering rack damaged (Chapter 10)
- [ ] Faulty steering column motor (Chapter 10)

Excessive play in steering

- [ ] Worn steering column/intermediate shaft joints (Chapter 10)
- [ ] Worn track rod balljoints (Chapter 1A, 1B or 10)
- [ ] Worn steering rack (Chapter 10)
- [ ] Worn steering or suspension joints, bushes or components (Chapter 1A, 1B or 10)

Lack of power assistance

- [ ] Faulty steering column motor (Chapter 10)

Tyre wear excessive

Tyres worn on inside or outside edges

- [ ] Tyres under-inflated (wear on both edges) (see *Weekly checks*)
- [ ] Incorrect camber or castor angles (wear on one edge only) (Chapter 10)
- [ ] Worn steering or suspension joints, bushes or components (Chapter 1A, 1B or 10)
- [ ] Excessively-hard cornering or braking
- [ ] Accident damage

Tyre treads exhibit feathered edges

- [ ] Incorrect toe-setting (Chapter 10)

Tyres worn in centre of tread

- [ ] Tyres over-inflated (see *Weekly checks*)

Tyres worn on inside and outside edges

- [ ] Tyres under-inflated (see *Weekly checks*)

Tyres worn unevenly

- [ ] Tyres/wheels out of balance (see *Weekly checks*)
- [ ] Excessive wheel or tyre run-out
- [ ] Worn shock absorbers (Chapter 1A, 1B or 10)
- [ ] Faulty tyre (see *Weekly checks*)

Electrical system

Note: *For problems associated with the starting system, refer to the faults listed under 'Engine' earlier in this Section.*

Battery will not hold a charge for more than a few days

- [ ] Battery defective internally (Chapter 5A)
- [ ] Battery terminal connections loose or corroded (see *Weekly checks*)
- [ ] Auxiliary drivebelt worn or incorrectly adjusted (Chapter 1A or 1B)
- [ ] Alternator not charging at correct output (Chapter 5A)
- [ ] Alternator or voltage regulator faulty (Chapter 5A)
- [ ] Short-circuit causing continual battery drain (Chapter 5A or 12)

Ignition/no-charge warning light remains illuminated with engine running

- [ ] Auxiliary drivebelt broken, worn, or incorrectly adjusted (Chapter 1A or 1B)
- [ ] Internal fault in alternator or voltage regulator (Chapter 5A)
- [ ] Broken, disconnected, or loose wiring in charging circuit (Chapter 5A or 12)

Ignition/no-charge warning light fails to come on

- [ ] Warning light bulb blown (Chapter 12)
- [ ] Broken, disconnected, or loose wiring in warning light circuit (Chapter 5A or 12)
- [ ] Alternator faulty (Chapter 5A)

Lights inoperative

- [ ] Bulb blown (Chapter 12)
- [ ] Corrosion of bulb or bulbholder contacts (Chapter 12)
- [ ] Blown fuse (Chapter 12)
- [ ] Faulty relay (Chapter 12)
- [ ] Broken, loose, or disconnected wiring (Chapter 12)
- [ ] Faulty switch (Chapter 12)

Instrument readings inaccurate or erratic

Fuel or temperature gauges give no reading

- [ ] Faulty gauge sender unit (Chapter 3, 4A or 4B)
- [ ] Wiring open-circuit (Chapter 12)
- [ ] Faulty gauge (Chapter 12)

Fuel or temperature gauges give continuous maximum reading

- [ ] Faulty gauge sender unit (Chapter 3, 4A or 4B)
- [ ] Wiring short-circuit (Chapter 12)
- [ ] Faulty gauge (Chapter 12)

Horn inoperative, or unsatisfactory in operation

Horn operates all the time

- [ ] Horn push either earthed or stuck down (Chapter 12)
- [ ] Horn cable-to-horn push earthed (Chapter 12)

Horn fails to operate

- [ ] Blown fuse (Chapter 12)
- [ ] Cable or connections loose, broken or disconnected (Chapter 12)
- [ ] Faulty horn (Chapter 12)

Horn emits intermittent or unsatisfactory sound

- [ ] Cable connections loose (Chapter 12)
- [ ] Horn mountings loose (Chapter 12)
- [ ] Faulty horn (Chapter 12)

Windscreen wipers inoperative, or unsatisfactory in operation

Wipers fail to operate, or operate very slowly

- [ ] Wiper blades stuck to screen, or linkage seized or binding (Chapter 12)
- [ ] Blown fuse (Chapter 12)
- [ ] Battery discharged (Chapter 5A)
- [ ] Cable or connections loose, broken or disconnected (Chapter 12)
- [ ] Faulty relay (Chapter 12)
- [ ] Faulty wiper motor (Chapter 12)

Wiper blades sweep over too large or too small an area of the glass

- [ ] Wiper blades incorrectly fitted, or wrong size used (see *Weekly checks*)
- [ ] Wiper arms incorrectly positioned on spindles (Chapter 12)
- [ ] Excessive wear of wiper linkage (Chapter 12)
- [ ] Wiper motor or linkage mountings loose or insecure (Chapter 12)

Wiper blades fail to clean the glass effectively

- [ ] Wiper blade rubbers dirty, worn or perished (see *Weekly checks*)
- [ ] Wiper blades incorrectly fitted, or wrong size used (see *Weekly checks*)
- [ ] Wiper arm tension springs broken, or arm pivots seized (Chapter 12)
- [ ] Insufficient windscreen washer additive to adequately remove road film (see *Weekly checks*)

Electrical system (continued)

Windscreen washers inoperative, or unsatisfactory in operation

One or more washer jets inoperative

☐ Blocked washer jet
☐ Disconnected, kinked or restricted fluid hose (Chapter 12)
☐ Insufficient fluid in washer reservoir (see *Weekly checks*)

Washer pump fails to operate

☐ Broken or disconnected wiring or connections (Chapter 12)
☐ Blown fuse (Chapter 12)
☐ Faulty washer switch (Chapter 12)
☐ Faulty washer pump (Chapter 12)

Washer pump runs for some time before fluid is emitted from jets

☐ Faulty one-way valve in fluid supply hose (Chapter 12)

Electric windows inoperative, or unsatisfactory in operation

Window glass will only move in one direction

☐ Faulty switch (Chapter 12)

Window glass slow to move

☐ Battery discharged (Chapter 5A)
☐ Regulator seized or damaged, or in need of lubrication (Chapter 11)
☐ Door internal components or trim fouling regulator (Chapter 11)
☐ Faulty motor (Chapter 11)

Window glass fails to move

☐ Blown fuse (Chapter 12)
☐ Faulty relay (Chapter 12)
☐ Broken or disconnected wiring or connections (Chapter 12)
☐ Faulty motor (Chapter 11)

Central locking system inoperative, or unsatisfactory in operation

Complete system failure

☐ Remote handset battery discharged, where applicable
☐ Blown fuse (Chapter 12)
☐ Faulty relay (Chapter 12)
☐ Broken or disconnected wiring or connections (Chapter 12)
☐ Faulty motor (Chapter 11)

Latch locks but will not unlock, or unlocks but will not lock

☐ Remote handset battery discharged, where applicable
☐ Faulty master switch (Chapter 12)
☐ Broken or disconnected latch operating rods or levers (Chapter 11)
☐ Faulty relay (Chapter 12)
☐ Faulty motor (Chapter 11)

One solenoid/motor fails to operate

☐ Broken or disconnected wiring or connections (Chapter 12)
☐ Faulty operating assembly (Chapter 11)
☐ Broken, binding or disconnected latch operating rods or levers (Chapter 11)
☐ Fault in door latch (Chapter 11)

A

ABS (Anti-lock brake system) A system, usually electronically controlled, that senses incipient wheel lockup during braking and relieves hydraulic pressure at wheels that are about to skid.

Air bag An inflatable bag hidden in the steering wheel (driver's side) or the dash or glovebox (passenger side). In a head-on collision, the bags inflate, preventing the driver and front passenger from being thrown forward into the steering wheel or windscreen.

Air cleaner A metal or plastic housing, containing a filter element, which removes dust and dirt from the air being drawn into the engine.

Air filter element The actual filter in an air cleaner system, usually manufactured from pleated paper and requiring renewal at regular intervals.

Air filter

Allen key A hexagonal wrench which fits into a recessed hexagonal hole.

Alligator clip A long-nosed spring-loaded metal clip with meshing teeth. Used to make temporary electrical connections.

Alternator A component in the electrical system which converts mechanical energy from a drivebelt into electrical energy to charge the battery and to operate the starting system, ignition system and electrical accessories.

Ampere (amp) A unit of measurement for the flow of electric current. One amp is the amount of current produced by one volt acting through a resistance of one ohm.

Anaerobic sealer A substance used to prevent bolts and screws from loosening. Anaerobic means that it does not require oxygen for activation. The Loctite brand is widely used.

Antifreeze A substance (usually ethylene glycol) mixed with water, and added to a vehicle's cooling system, to prevent freezing of the coolant in winter. Antifreeze also contains chemicals to inhibit corrosion and the formation of rust and other deposits that would tend to clog the radiator and coolant passages and reduce cooling efficiency.

Anti-seize compound A coating that reduces the risk of seizing on fasteners that are subjected to high temperatures, such as exhaust manifold bolts and nuts.

Asbestos A natural fibrous mineral with great heat resistance, commonly used in the composition of brake friction materials.

Asbestos is a health hazard and the dust created by brake systems should never be inhaled or ingested.

Axle A shaft on which a wheel revolves, or which revolves with a wheel. Also, a solid beam that connects the two wheels at one end of the vehicle. An axle which also transmits power to the wheels is known as a live axle.

Axleshaft A single rotating shaft, on either side of the differential, which delivers power from the final drive assembly to the drive wheels. Also called a driveshaft or a halfshaft.

B

Ball bearing An anti-friction bearing consisting of a hardened inner and outer race with hardened steel balls between two races.

Bearing The curved surface on a shaft or in a bore, or the part assembled into either, that permits relative motion between them with minimum wear and friction.

Bearing

Big-end bearing The bearing in the end of the connecting rod that's attached to the crankshaft.

Bleed nipple A valve on a brake wheel cylinder, caliper or other hydraulic component that is opened to purge the hydraulic system of air. Also called a bleed screw.

Brake bleeding Procedure for removing air from lines of a hydraulic brake system.

Brake bleeding

Brake disc The component of a disc brake that rotates with the wheels.

Brake drum The component of a drum brake that rotates with the wheels.

Brake linings The friction material which contacts the brake disc or drum to retard the vehicle's speed. The linings are bonded or riveted to the brake pads or shoes.

Brake pads The replaceable friction pads that pinch the brake disc when the brakes are applied. Brake pads consist of a friction material bonded or riveted to a rigid backing plate.

Brake shoe The crescent-shaped carrier to which the brake linings are mounted and which forces the lining against the rotating drum during braking.

Braking systems For more information on braking systems, consult the *Haynes Automotive Brake Manual*.

Breaker bar A long socket wrench handle providing greater leverage.

Bulkhead The insulated partition between the engine and the passenger compartment.

C

Caliper The non-rotating part of a disc-brake assembly that straddles the disc and carries the brake pads. The caliper also contains the hydraulic components that cause the pads to pinch the disc when the brakes are applied. A caliper is also a measuring tool that can be set to measure inside or outside dimensions of an object.

Camshaft A rotating shaft on which a series of cam lobes operate the valve mechanisms. The camshaft may be driven by gears, by sprockets and chain or by sprockets and a belt.

Canister A container in an evaporative emission control system; contains activated charcoal granules to trap vapours from the fuel system.

Canister

Carburettor A device which mixes fuel with air in the proper proportions to provide a desired power output from a spark ignition internal combustion engine.

Castellated Resembling the parapets along the top of a castle wall. For example, a castellated balljoint stud nut.

Castor In wheel alignment, the backward or forward tilt of the steering axis. Castor is positive when the steering axis is inclined rearward at the top.

Catalytic converter A silencer-like device in the exhaust system which converts certain pollutants in the exhaust gases into less harmful substances.

Catalytic converter

Circlip A ring-shaped clip used to prevent endwise movement of cylindrical parts and shafts. An internal circlip is installed in a groove in a housing; an external circlip fits into a groove on the outside of a cylindrical piece such as a shaft.

Clearance The amount of space between two parts. For example, between a piston and a cylinder, between a bearing and a journal, etc.

Coil spring A spiral of elastic steel found in various sizes throughout a vehicle, for example as a springing medium in the suspension and in the valve train.

Compression Reduction in volume, and increase in pressure and temperature, of a gas, caused by squeezing it into a smaller space.

Compression ratio The relationship between cylinder volume when the piston is at top dead centre and cylinder volume when the piston is at bottom dead centre.

Constant velocity (CV) joint A type of universal joint that cancels out vibrations caused by driving power being transmitted through an angle.

Core plug A disc or cup-shaped metal device inserted in a hole in a casting through which core was removed when the casting was formed. Also known as a freeze plug or expansion plug.

Crankcase The lower part of the engine block in which the crankshaft rotates.

Crankshaft The main rotating member, or shaft, running the length of the crankcase, with offset "throws" to which the connecting rods are attached.

Crankshaft assembly

Crocodile clip See Alligator clip

D

Diagnostic code Code numbers obtained by accessing the diagnostic mode of an engine management computer. This code can be used to determine the area in the system where a malfunction may be located.

Disc brake A brake design incorporating a rotating disc onto which brake pads are squeezed. The resulting friction converts the energy of a moving vehicle into heat.

Double-overhead cam (DOHC) An engine that uses two overhead camshafts, usually one for the intake valves and one for the exhaust valves.

Drivebelt(s) The belt(s) used to drive accessories such as the alternator, water pump, power steering pump, air conditioning compressor, etc. off the crankshaft pulley.

Accessory drivebelts

Driveshaft Any shaft used to transmit motion. Commonly used when referring to the axleshafts on a front wheel drive vehicle.

Drum brake A type of brake using a drum-shaped metal cylinder attached to the inner surface of the wheel. When the brake pedal is pressed, curved brake shoes with friction linings press against the inside of the drum to slow or stop the vehicle.

E

EGR valve A valve used to introduce exhaust gases into the intake air stream.

Electronic control unit (ECU) A computer which controls (for instance) ignition and fuel injection systems, or an anti-lock braking system. For more information refer to the *Haynes Automotive Electrical and Electronic Systems Manual*.

Electronic Fuel Injection (EFI) A computer controlled fuel system that distributes fuel through an injector located in each intake port of the engine.

Emergency brake A braking system, independent of the main hydraulic system, that can be used to slow or stop the vehicle if the primary brakes fail, or to hold the vehicle stationary even though the brake pedal isn't depressed. It usually consists of a hand lever that actuates either front or rear brakes mechanically through a series of cables and linkages. Also known as a handbrake or parking brake.

Endfloat The amount of lengthwise movement between two parts. As applied to a crankshaft, the distance that the crankshaft can move forward and back in the cylinder block.

Engine management system (EMS) A computer controlled system which manages the fuel injection and the ignition systems in an integrated fashion.

Exhaust manifold A part with several passages through which exhaust gases leave the engine combustion chambers and enter the exhaust pipe.

F

Fan clutch A viscous (fluid) drive coupling device which permits variable engine fan speeds in relation to engine speeds.

Feeler blade A thin strip or blade of hardened steel, ground to an exact thickness, used to check or measure clearances between parts.

Feeler blade

Firing order The order in which the engine cylinders fire, or deliver their power strokes, beginning with the number one cylinder.

Flywheel A heavy spinning wheel in which energy is absorbed and stored by means of momentum. On cars, the flywheel is attached to the crankshaft to smooth out firing impulses.

Free play The amount of travel before any action takes place. The "looseness" in a linkage, or an assembly of parts, between the initial application of force and actual movement. For example, the distance the brake pedal moves before the pistons in the master cylinder are actuated.

Fuse An electrical device which protects a circuit against accidental overload. The typical fuse contains a soft piece of metal which is calibrated to melt at a predetermined current flow (expressed as amps) and break the circuit.

Fusible link A circuit protection device consisting of a conductor surrounded by heat-resistant insulation. The conductor is smaller than the wire it protects, so it acts as the weakest link in the circuit. Unlike a blown fuse, a failed fusible link must frequently be cut from the wire for replacement.

G

Gap The distance the spark must travel in jumping from the centre electrode to the side electrode in a spark plug. Also refers to the spacing between the points in a contact breaker assembly in a conventional points-type ignition, or to the distance between the reluctor or rotor and the pickup coil in an electronic ignition.

Adjusting spark plug gap

Gasket Any thin, soft material - usually cork, cardboard, asbestos or soft metal - installed between two metal surfaces to ensure a good seal. For instance, the cylinder head gasket seals the joint between the block and the cylinder head.

Gasket

Gauge An instrument panel display used to monitor engine conditions. A gauge with a movable pointer on a dial or a fixed scale is an analogue gauge. A gauge with a numerical readout is called a digital gauge.

H

Halfshaft A rotating shaft that transmits power from the final drive unit to a drive wheel, usually when referring to a live rear axle.

Harmonic balancer A device designed to reduce torsion or twisting vibration in the crankshaft. May be incorporated in the crankshaft pulley. Also known as a vibration damper.

Hone An abrasive tool for correcting small irregularities or differences in diameter in an engine cylinder, brake cylinder, etc.

Hydraulic tappet A tappet that utilises hydraulic pressure from the engine's lubrication system to maintain zero clearance (constant contact with both camshaft and valve stem). Automatically adjusts to variation in valve stem length. Hydraulic tappets also reduce valve noise.

I

Ignition timing The moment at which the spark plug fires, usually expressed in the number of crankshaft degrees before the piston reaches the top of its stroke.

Inlet manifold A tube or housing with passages through which flows the air-fuel mixture (carburettor vehicles and vehicles with throttle body injection) or air only (port fuel-injected vehicles) to the port openings in the cylinder head.

J

Jump start Starting the engine of a vehicle with a discharged or weak battery by attaching jump leads from the weak battery to a charged or helper battery.

L

Load Sensing Proportioning Valve (LSPV) A brake hydraulic system control valve that works like a proportioning valve, but also takes into consideration the amount of weight carried by the rear axle.

Locknut A nut used to lock an adjustment nut, or other threaded component, in place. For example, a locknut is employed to keep the adjusting nut on the rocker arm in position.

Lockwasher A form of washer designed to prevent an attaching nut from working loose.

M

MacPherson strut A type of front suspension system devised by Earle MacPherson at Ford of England. In its original form, a simple lateral link with the anti-roll bar creates the lower control arm. A long strut - an integral coil spring and shock absorber - is mounted between the body and the steering knuckle. Many modern so-called MacPherson strut systems use a conventional lower A-arm and don't rely on the anti-roll bar for location.

Multimeter An electrical test instrument with the capability to measure voltage, current and resistance.

N

NOx Oxides of Nitrogen. A common toxic pollutant emitted by petrol and diesel engines at higher temperatures.

O

Ohm The unit of electrical resistance. One volt applied to a resistance of one ohm will produce a current of one amp.

Ohmmeter An instrument for measuring electrical resistance.

O-ring A type of sealing ring made of a special rubber-like material; in use, the O-ring is compressed into a groove to provide the sealing action.

Overhead cam (ohc) engine An engine with the camshaft(s) located on top of the cylinder head(s).

Overhead valve (ohv) engine An engine with the valves located in the cylinder head, but with the camshaft located in the engine block.

Oxygen sensor A device installed in the engine exhaust manifold, which senses the oxygen content in the exhaust and converts this information into an electric current. Also called a Lambda sensor.

P

Phillips screw A type of screw head having a cross instead of a slot for a corresponding type of screwdriver.

Plastigage A thin strip of plastic thread, available in different sizes, used for measuring clearances. For example, a strip of Plastigage is laid across a bearing journal. The parts are assembled and dismantled; the width of the crushed strip indicates the clearance between journal and bearing.

Plastigage

Propeller shaft The long hollow tube with universal joints at both ends that carries power from the transmission to the differential on front-engined rear wheel drive vehicles.

Proportioning valve A hydraulic control valve which limits the amount of pressure to the rear brakes during panic stops to prevent wheel lock-up.

R

Rack-and-pinion steering A steering system with a pinion gear on the end of the steering shaft that mates with a rack (think of a geared wheel opened up and laid flat). When the steering wheel is turned, the pinion turns, moving the rack to the left or right. This movement is transmitted through the track rods to the steering arms at the wheels.

Radiator A liquid-to-air heat transfer device designed to reduce the temperature of the coolant in an internal combustion engine cooling system.

Refrigerant Any substance used as a heat transfer agent in an air-conditioning system. R-12 has been the principle refrigerant for many years; recently, however, manufacturers have begun using R-134a, a non-CFC substance that is considered less harmful to the ozone in the upper atmosphere.

Rocker arm A lever arm that rocks on a shaft or pivots on a stud. In an overhead valve engine, the rocker arm converts the upward movement of the pushrod into a downward movement to open a valve.

Rotor In a distributor, the rotating device inside the cap that connects the centre electrode and the outer terminals as it turns, distributing the high voltage from the coil secondary winding to the proper spark plug. Also, that part of an alternator which rotates inside the stator. Also, the rotating assembly of a turbocharger, including the compressor wheel, shaft and turbine wheel.

Runout The amount of wobble (in-and-out movement) of a gear or wheel as it's rotated. The amount a shaft rotates "out-of-true." The out-of-round condition of a rotating part.

S

Sealant A liquid or paste used to prevent leakage at a joint. Sometimes used in conjunction with a gasket.

Sealed beam lamp An older headlight design which integrates the reflector, lens and filaments into a hermetically-sealed one-piece unit. When a filament burns out or the lens cracks, the entire unit is simply replaced.

Serpentine drivebelt A single, long, wide accessory drivebelt that's used on some newer vehicles to drive all the accessories, instead of a series of smaller, shorter belts. Serpentine drivebelts are usually tensioned by an automatic tensioner.

Serpentine drivebelt

Shim Thin spacer, commonly used to adjust the clearance or relative positions between two parts. For example, shims inserted into or under bucket tappets control valve clearances. Clearance is adjusted by changing the thickness of the shim.

Slide hammer A special puller that screws into or hooks onto a component such as a shaft or bearing; a heavy sliding handle on the shaft bottoms against the end of the shaft to knock the component free.

Sprocket A tooth or projection on the periphery of a wheel, shaped to engage with a chain or drivebelt. Commonly used to refer to the sprocket wheel itself.

Starter inhibitor switch On vehicles with an automatic transmission, a switch that prevents starting if the vehicle is not in Neutral or Park.

Strut See MacPherson strut.

T

Tappet A cylindrical component which transmits motion from the cam to the valve stem, either directly or via a pushrod and rocker arm. Also called a cam follower.

Thermostat A heat-controlled valve that regulates the flow of coolant between the cylinder block and the radiator, so maintaining optimum engine operating temperature. A thermostat is also used in some air cleaners in which the temperature is regulated.

Thrust bearing The bearing in the clutch assembly that is moved in to the release levers by clutch pedal action to disengage the clutch. Also referred to as a release bearing.

Timing belt A toothed belt which drives the camshaft. Serious engine damage may result if it breaks in service.

Timing chain A chain which drives the camshaft.

Toe-in The amount the front wheels are closer together at the front than at the rear. On rear wheel drive vehicles, a slight amount of toe-in is usually specified to keep the front wheels running parallel on the road by offsetting other forces that tend to spread the wheels apart.

Toe-out The amount the front wheels are closer together at the rear than at the front. On front wheel drive vehicles, a slight amount of toe-out is usually specified.

Tools For full information on choosing and using tools, refer to the *Haynes Automotive Tools Manual*.

Tracer A stripe of a second colour applied to a wire insulator to distinguish that wire from another one with the same colour insulator.

Tune-up A process of accurate and careful adjustments and parts replacement to obtain the best possible engine performance.

Turbocharger A centrifugal device, driven by exhaust gases, that pressurises the intake air. Normally used to increase the power output from a given engine displacement, but can also be used primarily to reduce exhaust emissions (as on VW's "Umwelt" Diesel engine).

U

Universal joint or U-joint A double-pivoted connection for transmitting power from a driving to a driven shaft through an angle. A U-joint consists of two Y-shaped yokes and a cross-shaped member called the spider.

V

Valve A device through which the flow of liquid, gas, vacuum, or loose material in bulk may be started, stopped, or regulated by a movable part that opens, shuts, or partially obstructs one or more ports or passageways. A valve is also the movable part of such a device.

Valve clearance The clearance between the valve tip (the end of the valve stem) and the rocker arm or tappet. The valve clearance is measured when the valve is closed.

Vernier caliper A precision measuring instrument that measures inside and outside dimensions. Not quite as accurate as a micrometer, but more convenient.

Viscosity The thickness of a liquid or its resistance to flow.

Volt A unit for expressing electrical "pressure" in a circuit. One volt that will produce a current of one ampere through a resistance of one ohm.

W

Welding Various processes used to join metal items by heating the areas to be joined to a molten state and fusing them together. For more information refer to the *Haynes Automotive Welding Manual*.

Wiring diagram A drawing portraying the components and wires in a vehicle's electrical system, using standardised symbols. For more information refer to the *Haynes Automotive Electrical and Electronic Systems Manual*.

Note: *References throughout this index are in the form* **"Chapter number"** • **"Page number".** *So, for example, 2C•15 refers to page 15 of Chapter 2C.*

Note: *References throughout this index are in the form* "**Chapter number**" • "**Page number**". *So, for example, 2C•15 refers to page 15 of Chapter 2C.*

Note: *References throughout this index are in the form "**Chapter number**" • "**Page number**". So, for example, 2C•15 refers to page 15 of Chapter 2C.*

Preserving Our Motoring Heritage

> < The Model J Duesenberg Derham Tourster. Only eight of these magnificent cars were ever built – this is the only example to be found outside the United States of America

Almost every car you've ever loved, loathed or desired is gathered under one roof at the Haynes Motor Museum. Over 300 immaculately presented cars and motorbikes represent every aspect of our motoring heritage, from elegant reminders of bygone days, such as the superb Model J Duesenberg to curiosities like the bug-eyed BMW Isetta. There are also many old friends and flames. Perhaps you remember the 1959 Ford Popular that you did your courting in? The magnificent 'Red Collection' is a spectacle of classic sports cars including AC, Alfa Romeo, Austin Healey, Ferrari, Lamborghini, Maserati, MG, Riley, Porsche and Triumph.

A Perfect Day Out

Each and every vehicle at the Haynes Motor Museum has played its part in the history and culture of Motoring. Today, they make a wonderful spectacle and a great day out for all the family. Bring the kids, bring Mum and Dad, but above all bring your camera to capture those golden memories for ever. You will also find an impressive array of motoring memorabilia, a comfortable 70 seat video cinema and one of the most extensive transport book shops in Britain. The Pit Stop Cafe serves everything from a cup of tea to wholesome, home-made meals or, if you prefer, you can enjoy the large picnic area nestled in the beautiful rural surroundings of Somerset.

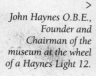

> John Haynes O.B.E., Founder and Chairman of the museum at the wheel of a Haynes Light 12.

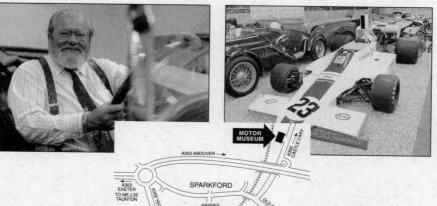

> < Graham Hill's Lola Cosworth Formula 1 car next to a 1934 Riley Sports.

The Museum is situated on the A359 Yeovil to Frome road at Sparkford, just off the A303 in Somerset. It is about 40 miles south of Bristol, and 25 minutes drive from the M5 intersection at Taunton.
Open 9.30am - 5.30pm (10.00am - 4.00pm Winter) 7 days a week, *except Christmas Day, Boxing Day and New Years Day*
Special rates available for schools, coach parties and outings Charitable Trust No. 292048